CASE CLOSED™

VOLUME 58

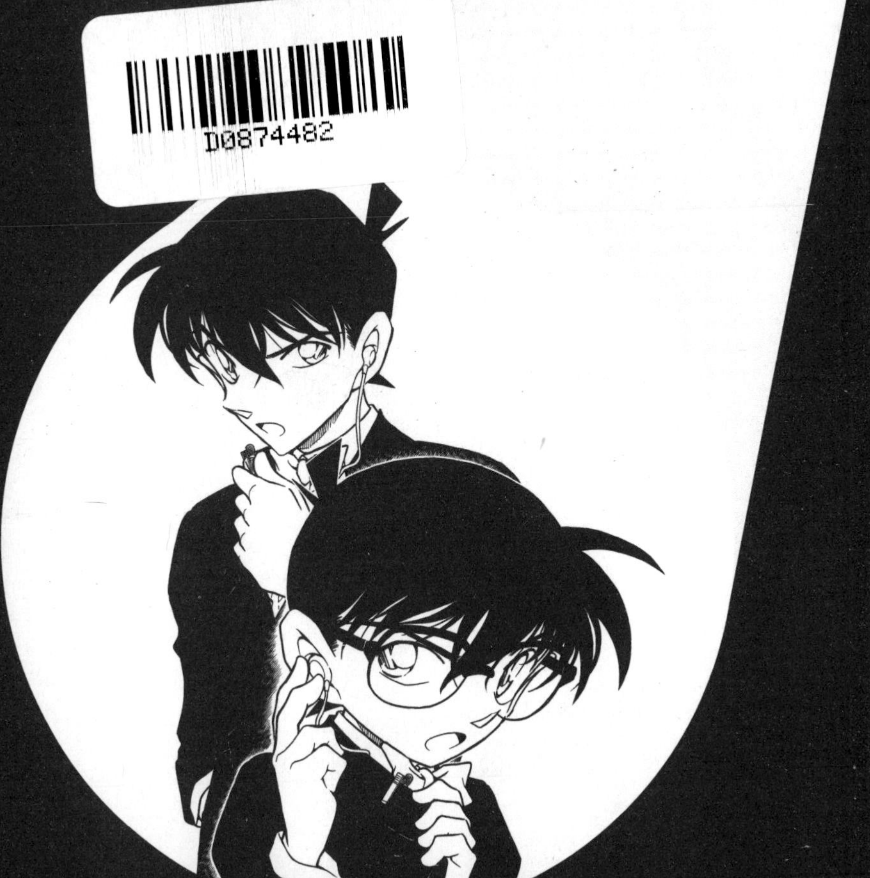

Gosho Aoyama

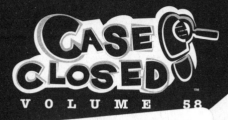

Case Briefing:

Subject:
Occupation:
Special Skills:
Equipment:

Jimmy Kudo, a.k.a. Conan Edogawa
High School Student/Detective
Analytical thinking and deductive reasoning, Soccer
Bow Tie Voice Transmitter, Super Sneakers,
Homing Glasses, Stretchy Suspenders

The subject is hot on the trail of a pair of suspicious men in black when he is attacked from behind and administered a strange substance which physically transforms him into a first grader. When the subject confides in the eccentric inventor Dr. Agasa, they decide to keep the subject's true identity a secret for the safety of everyone around him. Assuming the new identity of first-grader Conan Edogawa, the subject continues to assist the police force on their most baffling cases. The only problem is that most crime-solving professionals won't take a little kid's advice!

Table of Contents

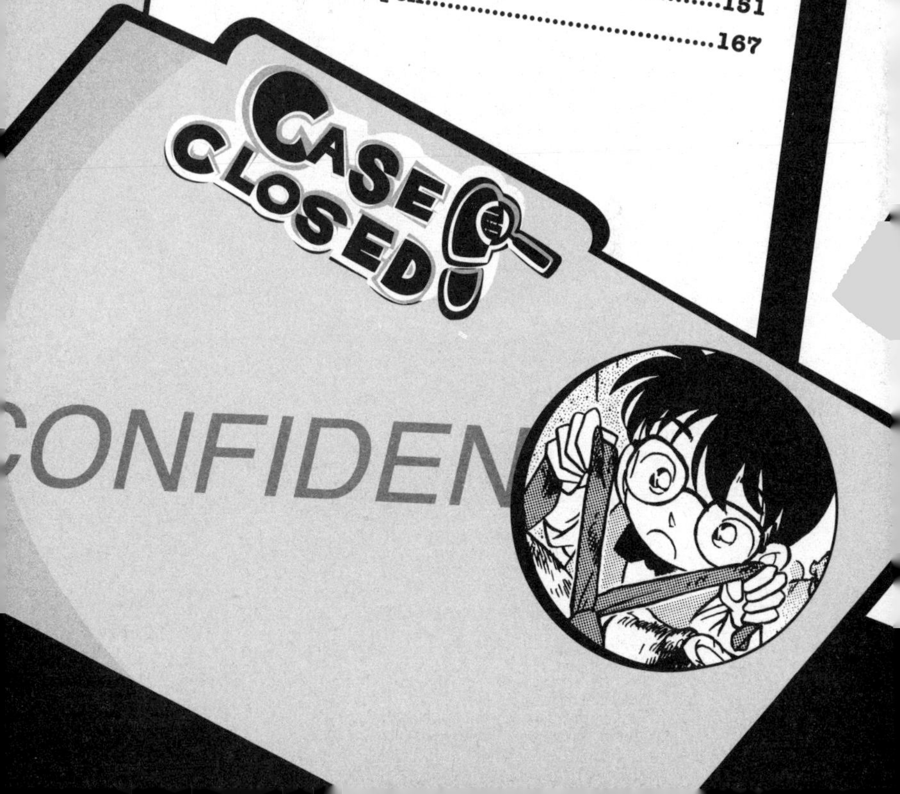

CASE CLOSED
CONFIDEN

CASE CLOSED

Volume 58
Shonen Sunday Edition

Story and Art by GOSHO AOYAMA

MEITANTEI CONAN Vol. 58
by Gosho AOYAMA
© 1994 Gosho AOYAMA
All rights reserved.
Original Japanese edition published by SHOGAKUKAN.
English translation rights in the United States of America, Canada,
the United Kingdom and Ireland arranged with SHOGAKUKAN.

Translation
Tetsuichiro Miyaki

Touch-up & Lettering
Freeman Wong

Cover & Graphic Design
Andrea Rice

Editor
Shaenon K. Garrity

Printed in the U.S.A.

Published by VIZ Media, LLC
P.O. Box 77010
San Francisco, CA 94107

10 9 8 7 6 5 4 3 2 1
First printing, April 2016

FILE 1: PURSUIT AND...

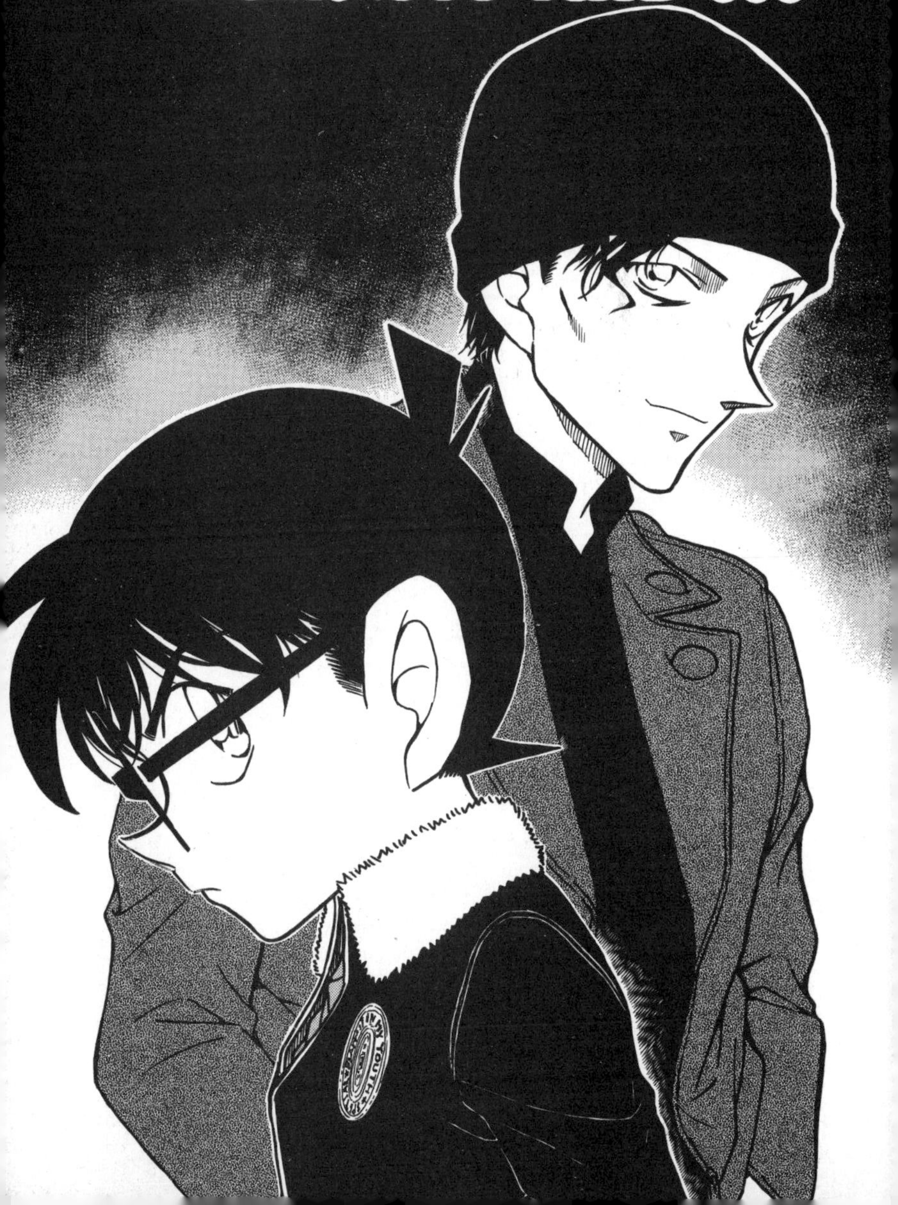

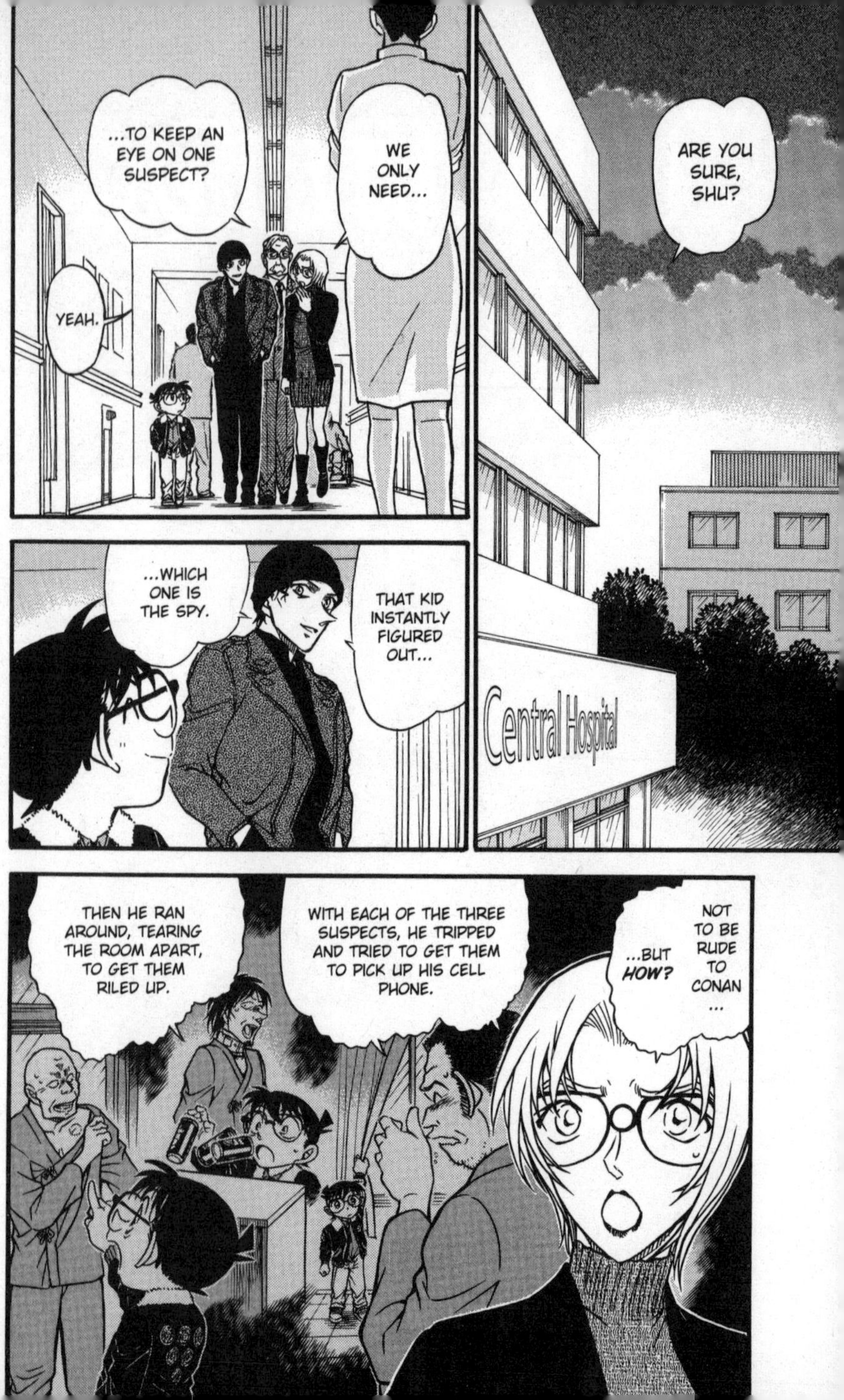
ARE YOU SURE, SHU?
Central Hospital
WE ONLY NEED...
...TO KEEP AN EYE ON ONE SUSPECT?
YEAH.
THAT KID INSTANTLY FIGURED OUT...
...WHICH ONE IS THE SPY.
NOT TO BE RUDE TO CONAN ...
...BUT *HOW?*
WITH EACH OF THE THREE SUSPECTS, HE TRIPPED AND TRIED TO GET THEM TO PICK UP HIS CELL PHONE.
THEN HE RAN AROUND, TEARING THE ROOM APART, TO GET THEM RILED UP.

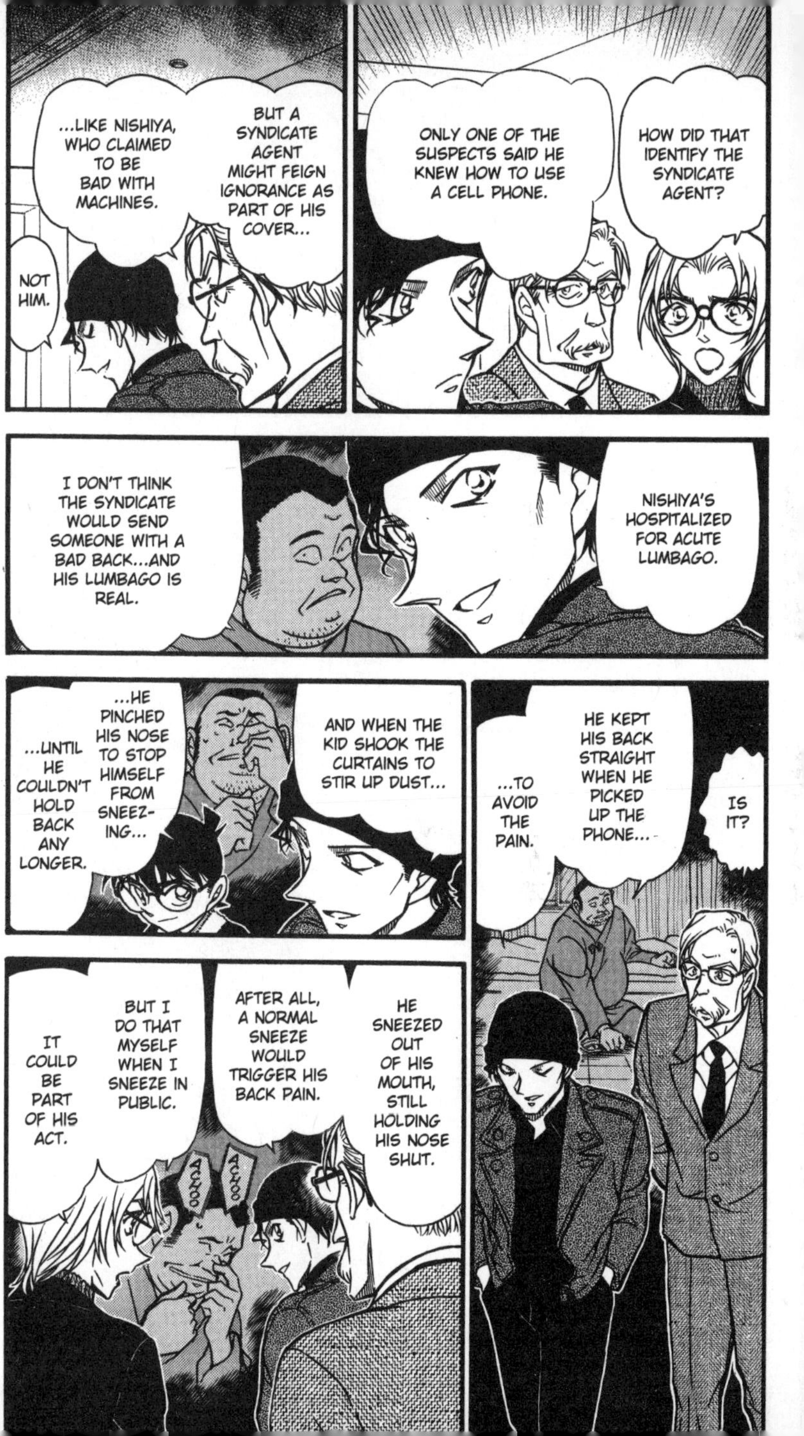
HOW DID THAT IDENTIFY THE SYNDICATE AGENT?
ONLY ONE OF THE SUSPECTS SAID HE KNEW HOW TO USE A CELL PHONE.
BUT A SYNDICATE AGENT MIGHT FEIGN IGNORANCE AS PART OF HIS COVER...
...LIKE NISHIYA, WHO CLAIMED TO BE BAD WITH MACHINES.
NOT HIM.
NISHIYA'S HOSPITALIZED FOR ACUTE LUMBAGO.
I DON'T THINK THE SYNDICATE WOULD SEND SOMEONE WITH A BAD BACK...AND HIS LUMBAGO IS REAL.
IS IT?
HE KEPT HIS BACK STRAIGHT WHEN HE PICKED UP THE PHONE...
...TO AVOID THE PAIN.
AND WHEN THE KID SHOOK THE CURTAINS TO STIR UP DUST...
...HE PINCHED HIS NOSE TO STOP HIMSELF FROM SNEEZ-ING...
...UNTIL HE COULDN'T HOLD BACK ANY LONGER.
HE SNEEZED OUT OF HIS MOUTH, STILL HOLDING HIS NOSE SHUT.
ACHOO
ACHOO
AFTER ALL, A NORMAL SNEEZE WOULD TRIGGER HIS BACK PAIN.
BUT I DO THAT MYSELF WHEN I SNEEZE IN PUBLIC.
IT COULD BE PART OF HIS ACT.

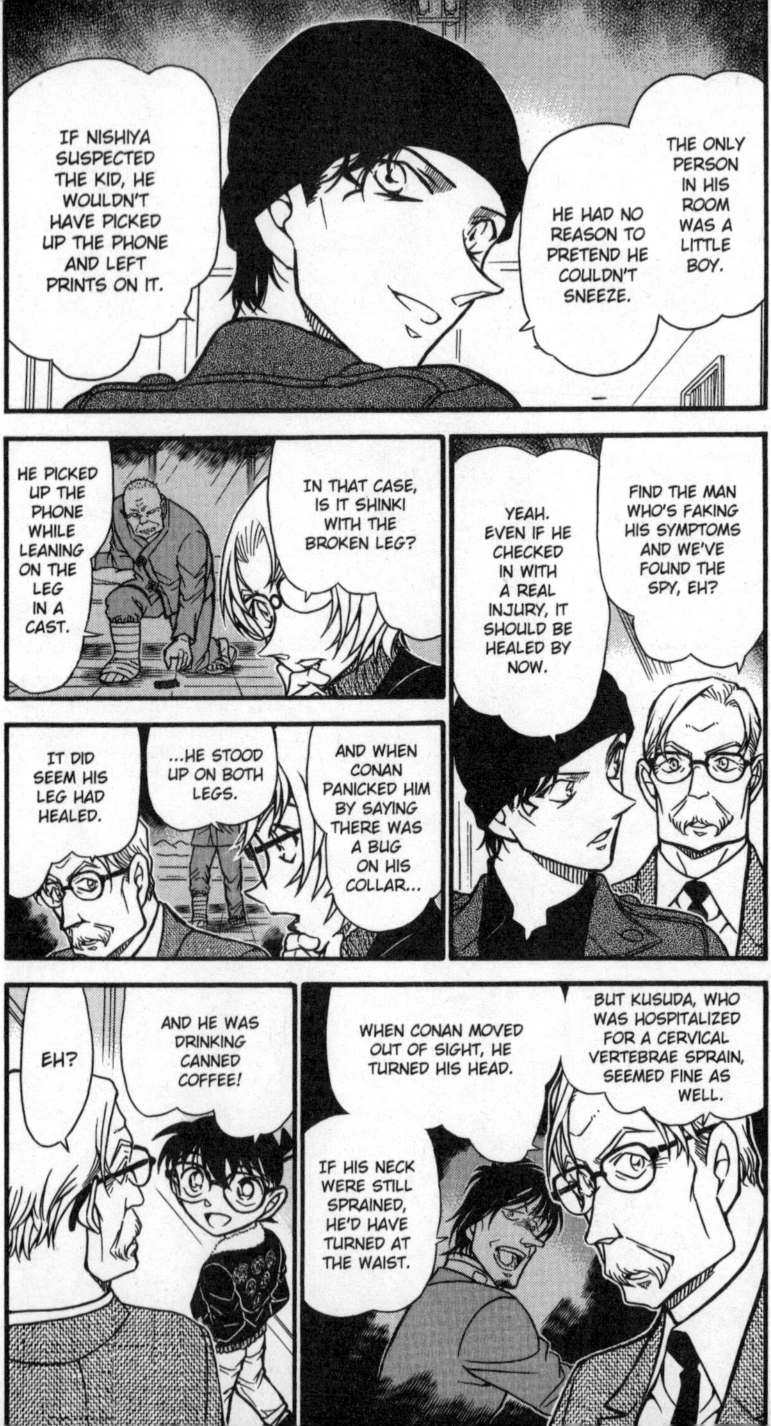
THE ONLY PERSON IN HIS ROOM WAS A LITTLE BOY.
HE HAD NO REASON TO PRETEND HE COULDN'T SNEEZE.
IF NISHIYA SUSPECTED THE KID, HE WOULDN'T HAVE PICKED UP THE PHONE AND LEFT PRINTS ON IT.
FIND THE MAN WHO'S FAKING HIS SYMPTOMS AND WE'VE FOUND THE SPY, EH?
YEAH. EVEN IF HE CHECKED IN WITH A REAL INJURY, IT SHOULD BE HEALED BY NOW.
IN THAT CASE, IS IT SHINKI WITH THE BROKEN LEG?
HE PICKED UP THE PHONE WHILE LEANING ON THE LEG IN A CAST.
AND WHEN CONAN PANICKED HIM BY SAYING THERE WAS A BUG ON HIS COLLAR...
...HE STOOD UP ON BOTH LEGS.
IT DID SEEM HIS LEG HAD HEALED.
BUT KUSUDA, WHO WAS HOSPITALIZED FOR A CERVICAL VERTEBRAE SPRAIN, SEEMED FINE AS WELL.
WHEN CONAN MOVED OUT OF SIGHT, HE TURNED HIS HEAD.
IF HIS NECK WERE STILL SPRAINED, HE'D HAVE TURNED AT THE WAIST.
AND HE WAS DRINKING CANNED COFFEE!
EH?

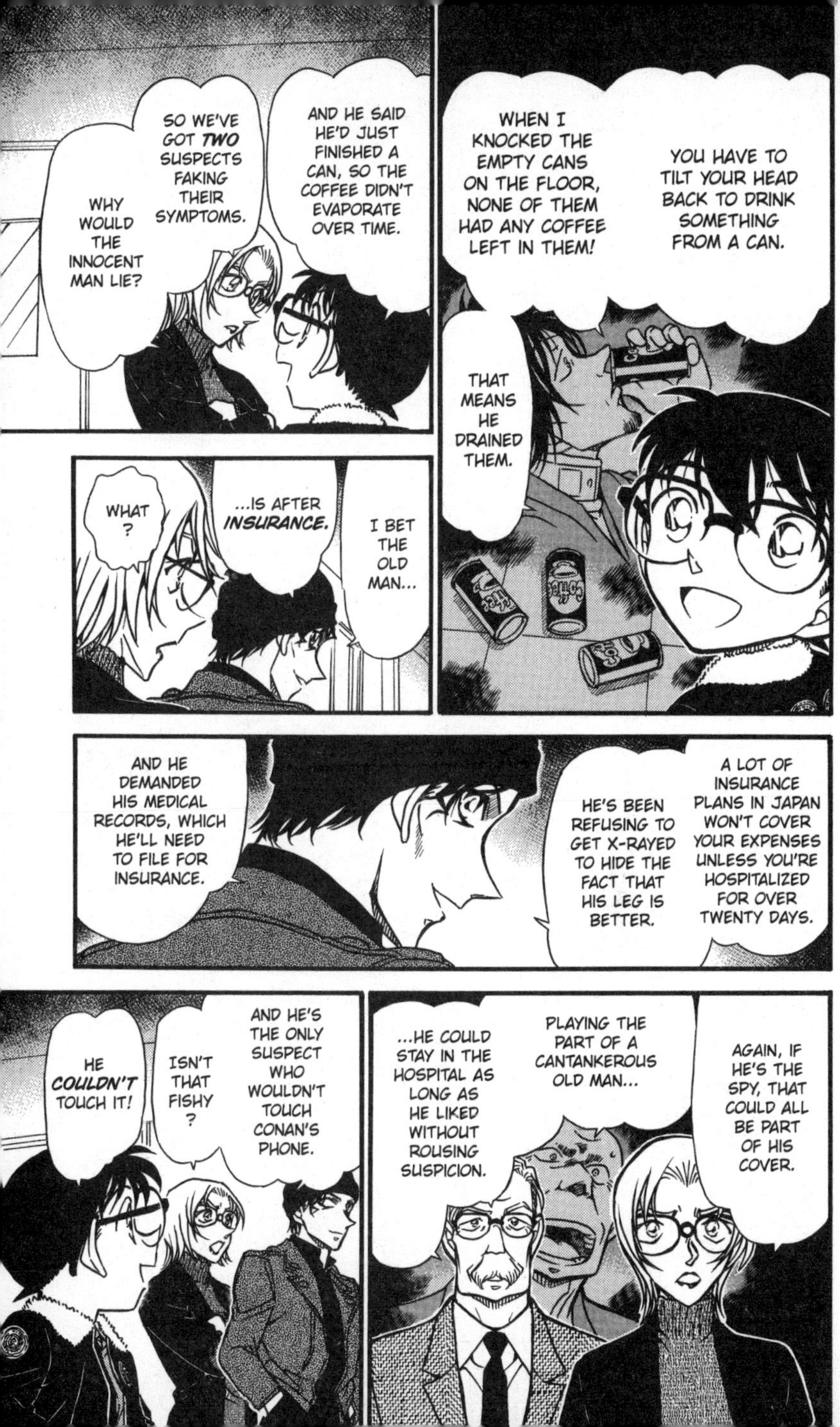
YOU HAVE TO TILT YOUR HEAD BACK TO DRINK SOMETHING FROM A CAN.
WHEN I KNOCKED THE EMPTY CANS ON THE FLOOR, NONE OF THEM HAD ANY COFFEE LEFT IN THEM!
THAT MEANS HE DRAINED THEM.
AND HE SAID HE'D JUST FINISHED A CAN, SO THE COFFEE DIDN'T EVAPORATE OVER TIME.
SO WE'VE GOT ***TWO*** SUSPECTS FAKING THEIR SYMPTOMS.
WHY WOULD THE INNOCENT MAN LIE?
I BET THE OLD MAN...
...IS AFTER ***INSURANCE.***
WHAT?
A LOT OF INSURANCE PLANS IN JAPAN WON'T COVER YOUR EXPENSES UNLESS YOU'RE HOSPITALIZED FOR OVER TWENTY DAYS.
HE'S BEEN REFUSING TO GET X-RAYED TO HIDE THE FACT THAT HIS LEG IS BETTER.
AND HE DEMANDED HIS MEDICAL RECORDS, WHICH HE'LL NEED TO FILE FOR INSURANCE.
AGAIN, IF HE'S THE SPY, THAT COULD ALL BE PART OF HIS COVER.
PLAYING THE PART OF A CANTANKEROUS OLD MAN...
...HE COULD STAY IN THE HOSPITAL AS LONG AS HE LIKED WITHOUT ROUSING SUSPICION.
AND HE'S THE ONLY SUSPECT WHO WOULDN'T TOUCH CONAN'S PHONE.
ISN'T THAT FISHY?
HE ***COULDN'T*** TOUCH IT!

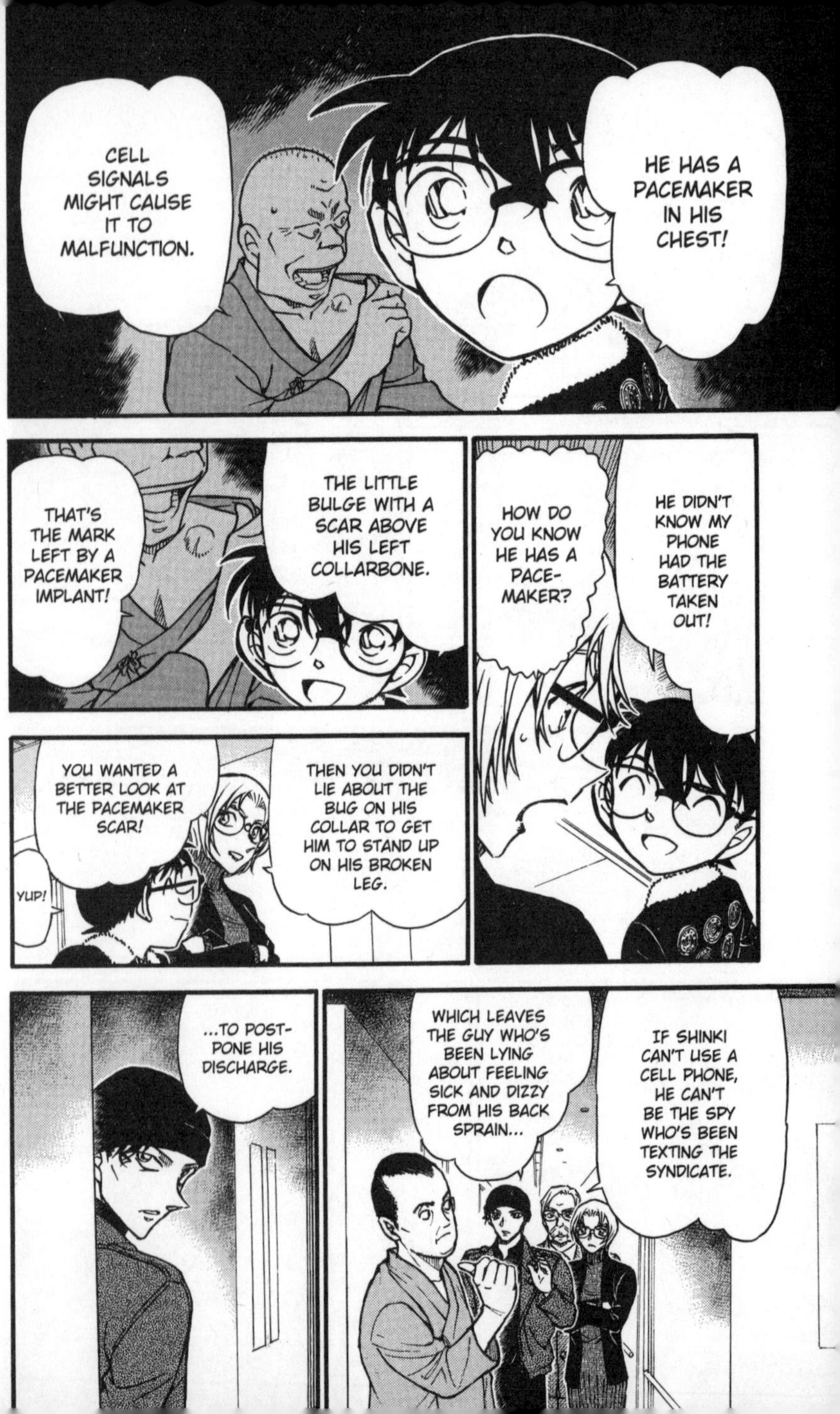
HE HAS A PACEMAKER IN HIS CHEST!
CELL SIGNALS MIGHT CAUSE IT TO MALFUNCTION.
HE DIDN'T KNOW MY PHONE HAD THE BATTERY TAKEN OUT!
HOW DO YOU KNOW HE HAS A PACE-MAKER?
THE LITTLE BULGE WITH A SCAR ABOVE HIS LEFT COLLARBONE.
THAT'S THE MARK LEFT BY A PACEMAKER IMPLANT!
THEN YOU DIDN'T LIE ABOUT THE BUG ON HIS COLLAR TO GET HIM TO STAND UP ON HIS BROKEN LEG.
YOU WANTED A BETTER LOOK AT THE PACEMAKER SCAR!
YUP!
IF SHINKI CAN'T USE A CELL PHONE, HE CAN'T BE THE SPY WHO'S BEEN TEXTING THE SYNDICATE.
WHICH LEAVES THE GUY WHO'S BEEN LYING ABOUT FEELING SICK AND DIZZY FROM HIS BACK SPRAIN...
...TO POST-PONE HIS DISCHARGE.

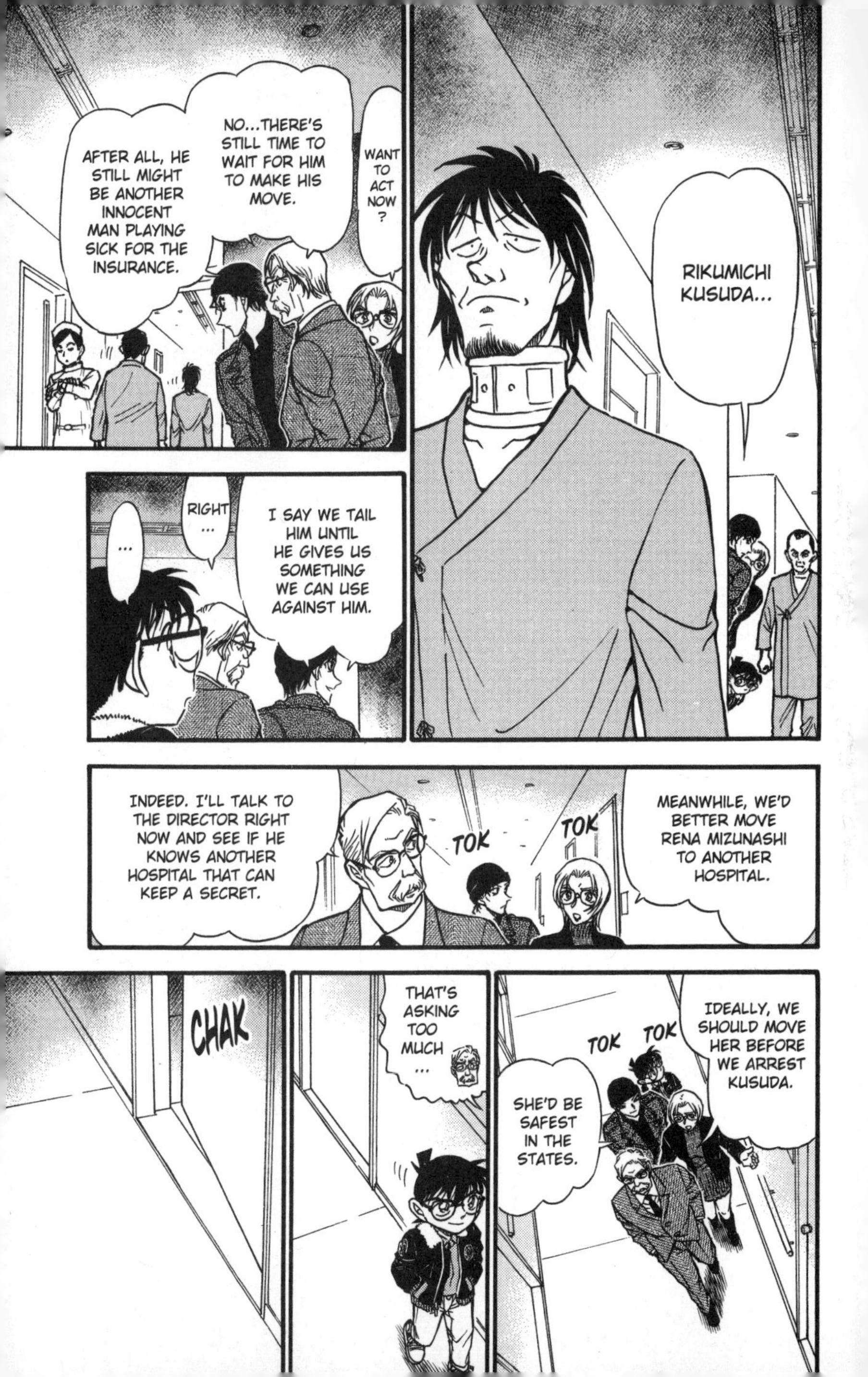
RIKUMICHI KUSUDA...
WANT TO ACT NOW?
NO...THERE'S STILL TIME TO WAIT FOR HIM TO MAKE HIS MOVE.
AFTER ALL, HE STILL MIGHT BE ANOTHER INNOCENT MAN PLAYING SICK FOR THE INSURANCE.
I SAY WE TAIL HIM UNTIL HE GIVES US SOMETHING WE CAN USE AGAINST HIM.
RIGHT...
...
MEANWHILE, WE'D BETTER MOVE RENA MIZUNASHI TO ANOTHER HOSPITAL.
TOK
TOK
INDEED. I'LL TALK TO THE DIRECTOR RIGHT NOW AND SEE IF HE KNOWS ANOTHER HOSPITAL THAT CAN KEEP A SECRET.
IDEALLY, WE SHOULD MOVE HER BEFORE WE ARREST KUSUDA.
TOK
TOK
SHE'D BE SAFEST IN THE STATES.
THAT'S ASKING TOO MUCH...
CHAK

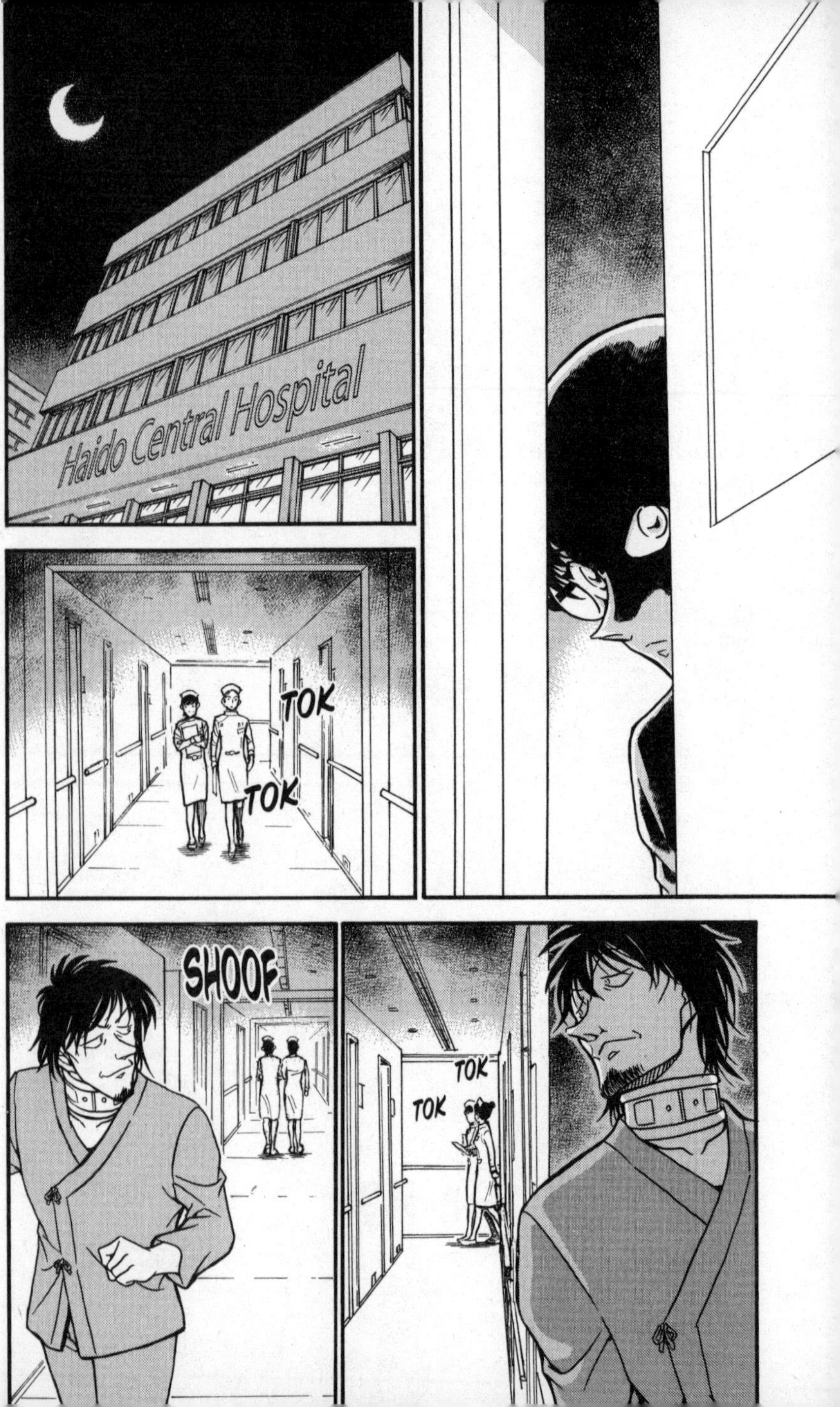
Haido Central Hospital
TOK
TOK
TOK
TOK
SHOOF

Nurse Station

MR. NEGISHI'S CALLING FOR A NURSE AGAIN.

BZZ BZZ

HUH ?

KLIK

Nurse Station

MAYBE THE BUTTON'S BROKEN ...

TOK

TOK

NOPE

NOT IN THIS WING EITHER...

MIZU-NASHI ...

PCH

PCH

806A	Katsuru	NOPE 5
3	Shigeoka Si	08
3	Masaaki Asa	406A
3	Shigeru Ki	40
3	Shigeo Takaiwa	407
308B	Yoshitaka Kogure	4
401A	Fu	5
401B	Sawa	5
402A		5
402B	Akane Shigeoka	5
403A	Natsumi Shijo	505
403B		506

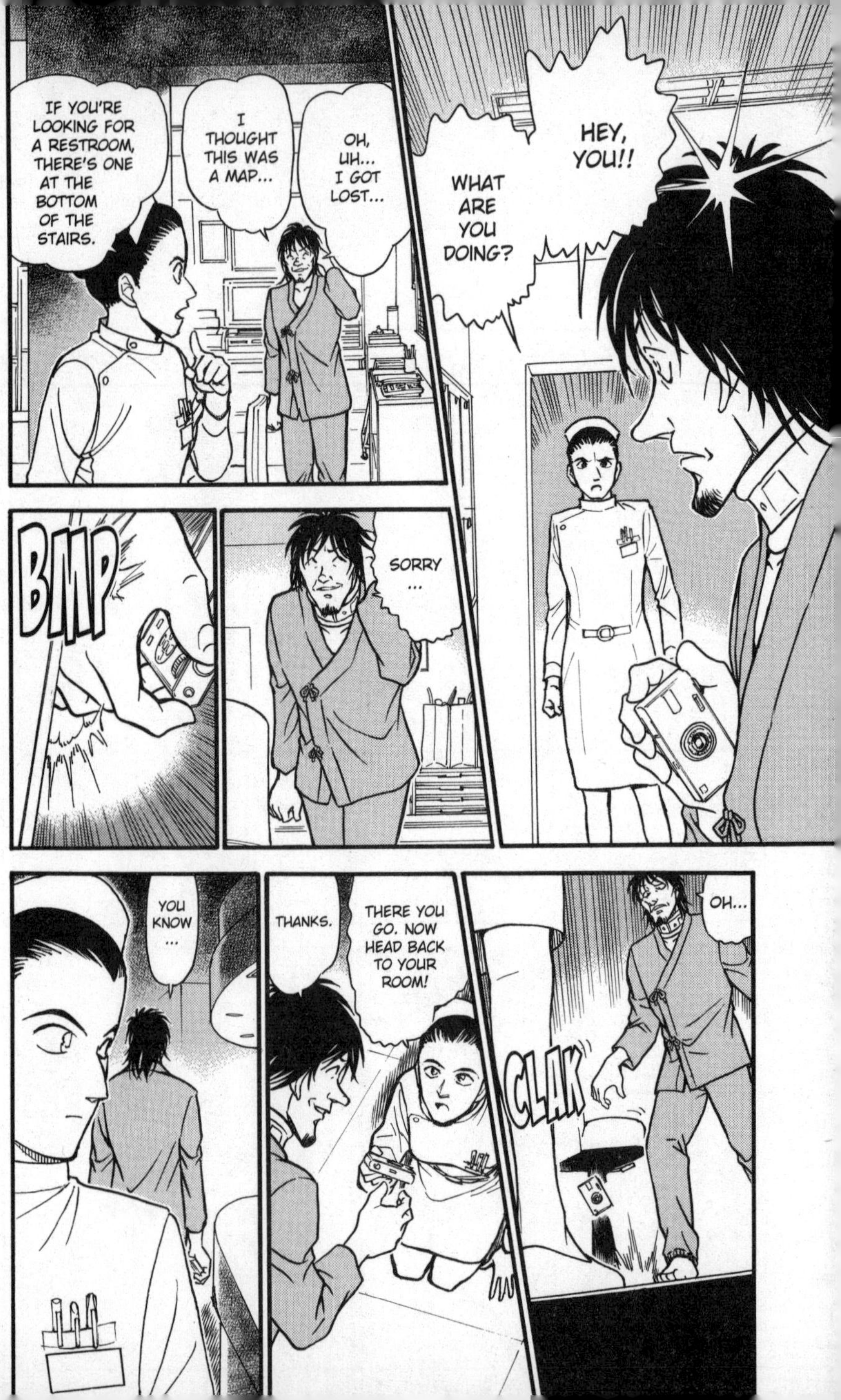
HEY, YOU!!
WHAT ARE YOU DOING?
OH, UH... I GOT LOST...
I THOUGHT THIS WAS A MAP...
IF YOU'RE LOOKING FOR A RESTROOM, THERE'S ONE AT THE BOTTOM OF THE STAIRS.
SORRY ...
BMP
OH...
CLAK
THERE YOU GO. NOW HEAD BACK TO YOUR ROOM!
THANKS.
YOU KNOW ...

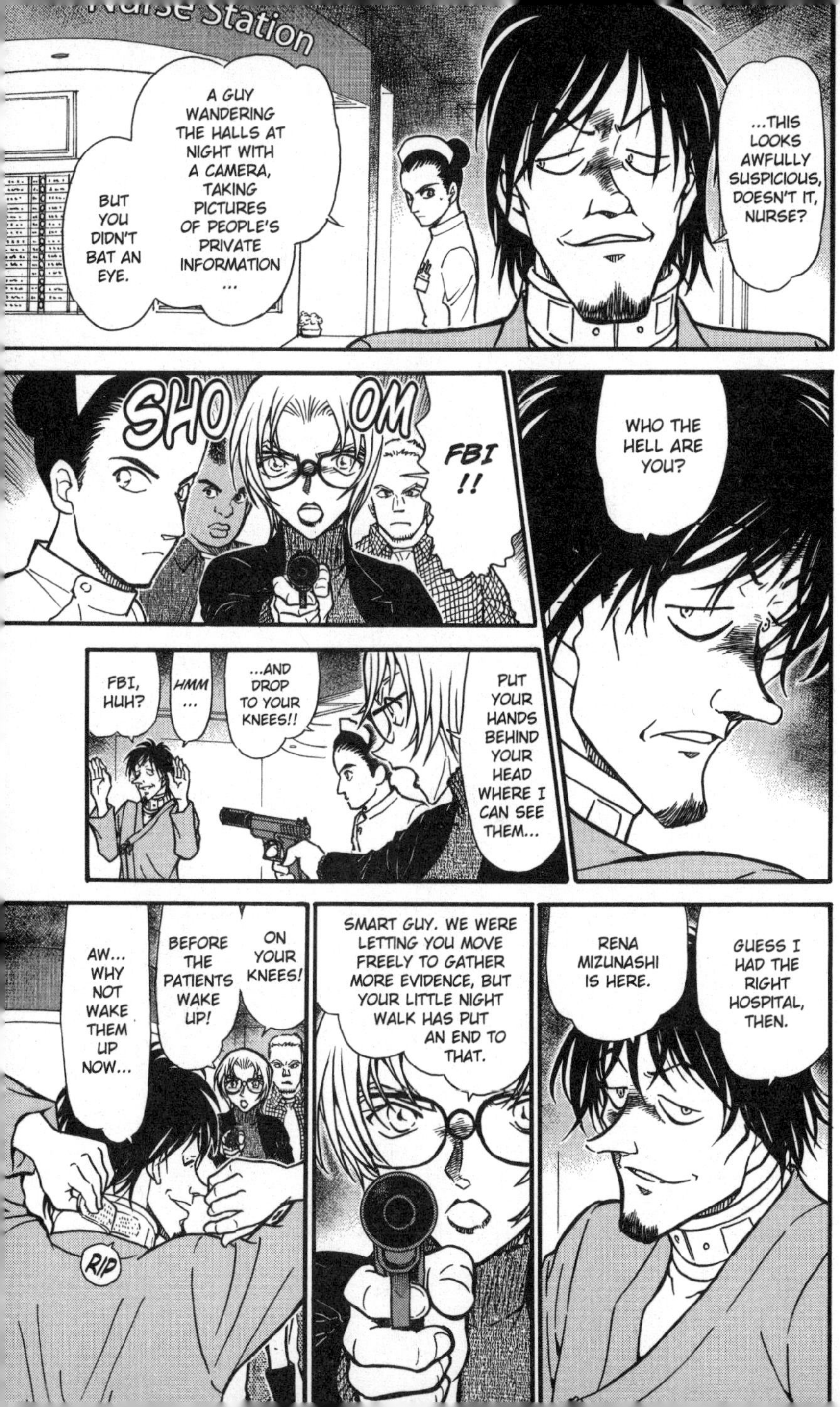
Nurse Station
...THIS LOOKS AWFULLY SUSPICIOUS, DOESN'T IT, NURSE?
A GUY WANDERING THE HALLS AT NIGHT WITH A CAMERA, TAKING PICTURES OF PEOPLE'S PRIVATE INFORMATION ...
BUT YOU DIDN'T BAT AN EYE.
WHO THE HELL ARE YOU?
SHOOM
FBI !!
PUT YOUR HANDS BEHIND YOUR HEAD WHERE I CAN SEE THEM...
...AND DROP TO YOUR KNEES!!
HMM...
FBI, HUH?
GUESS I HAD THE RIGHT HOSPITAL, THEN.
RENA MIZUNASHI IS HERE.
SMART GUY. WE WERE LETTING YOU MOVE FREELY TO GATHER MORE EVIDENCE, BUT YOUR LITTLE NIGHT WALK HAS PUT AN END TO THAT.
ON YOUR KNEES!
BEFORE THE PATIENTS WAKE UP!
AW... WHY NOT WAKE THEM UP NOW...
RIP

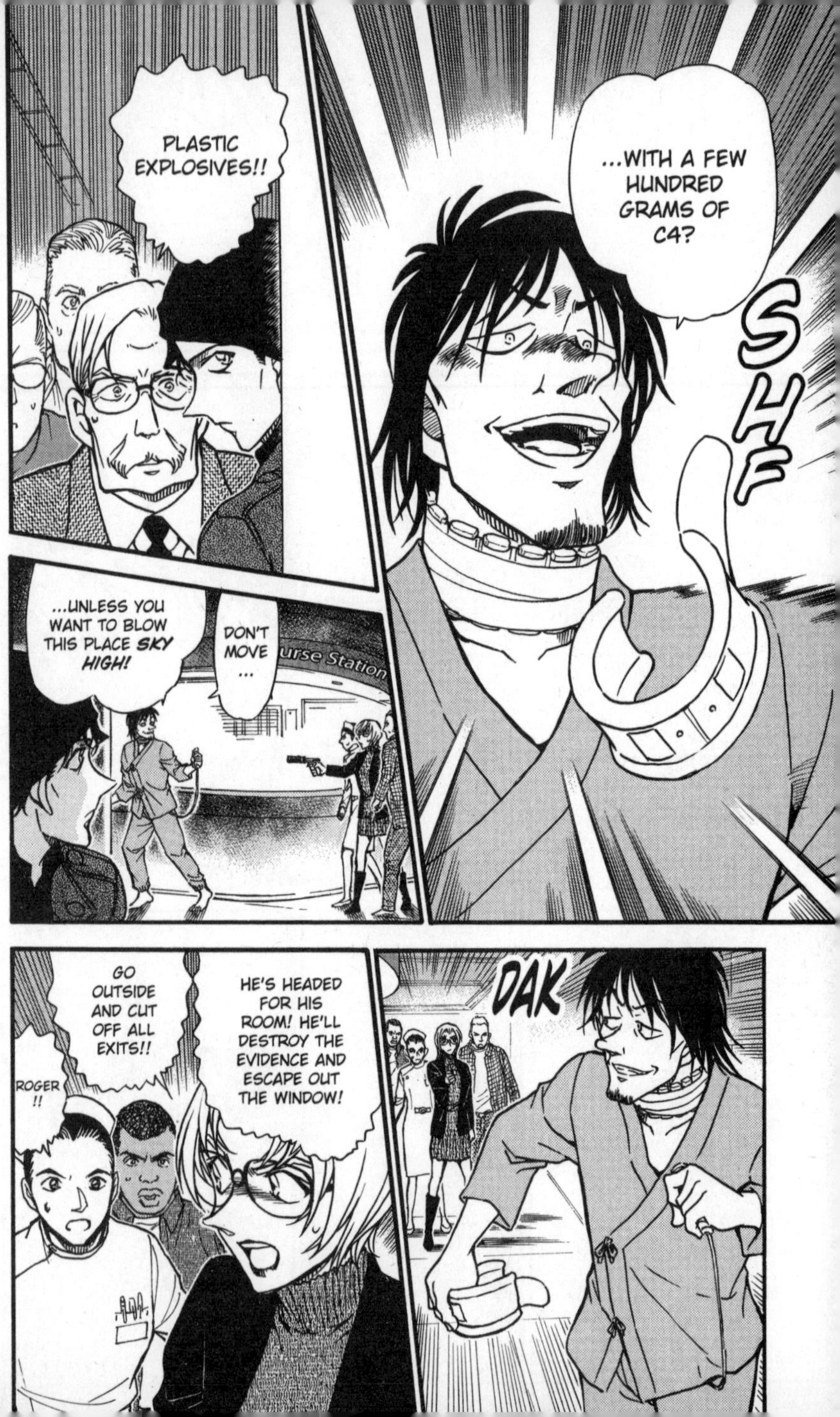
...WITH A FEW HUNDRED GRAMS OF C4?
SHF
PLASTIC EXPLOSIVES!!
DON'T MOVE ...
...UNLESS YOU WANT TO BLOW THIS PLACE **SKY HIGH!**
urse Station
DAK
HE'S HEADED FOR HIS ROOM! HE'LL DESTROY THE EVIDENCE AND ESCAPE OUT THE WINDOW!
GO OUTSIDE AND CUT OFF ALL EXITS!!
ROGER !!

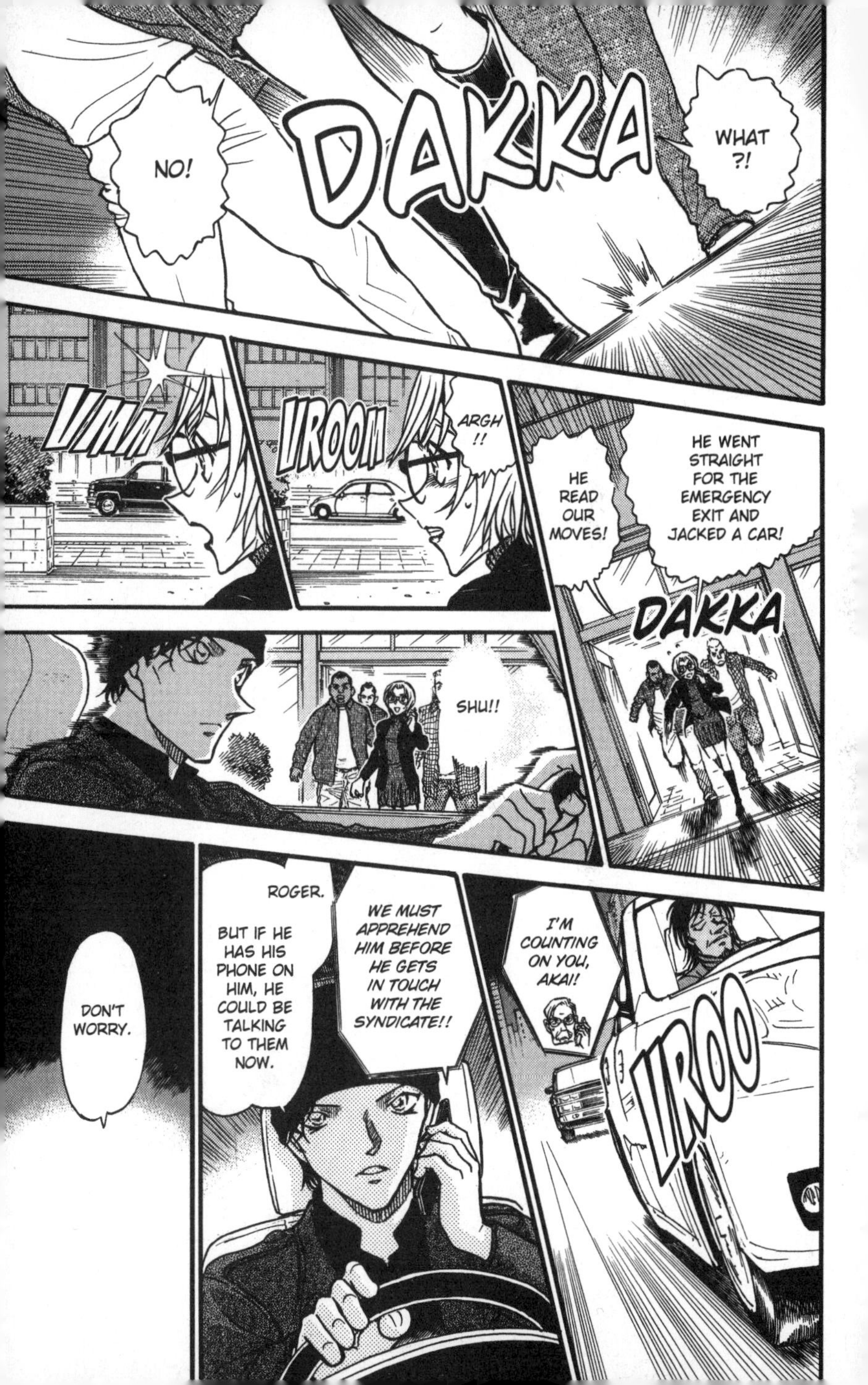
WHAT ?!
DAKKA
NO!
HE WENT STRAIGHT FOR THE EMERGENCY EXIT AND JACKED A CAR!
HE READ OUR MOVES!
DAKKA
ARGH !!
VROOM
VMMM
SHU!!
I'M COUNTING ON YOU, AKAI!
VROO
WE MUST APPREHEND HIM BEFORE HE GETS IN TOUCH WITH THE SYNDICATE!!
ROGER.
BUT IF HE HAS HIS PHONE ON HIM, HE COULD BE TALKING TO THEM NOW.
DON'T WORRY.

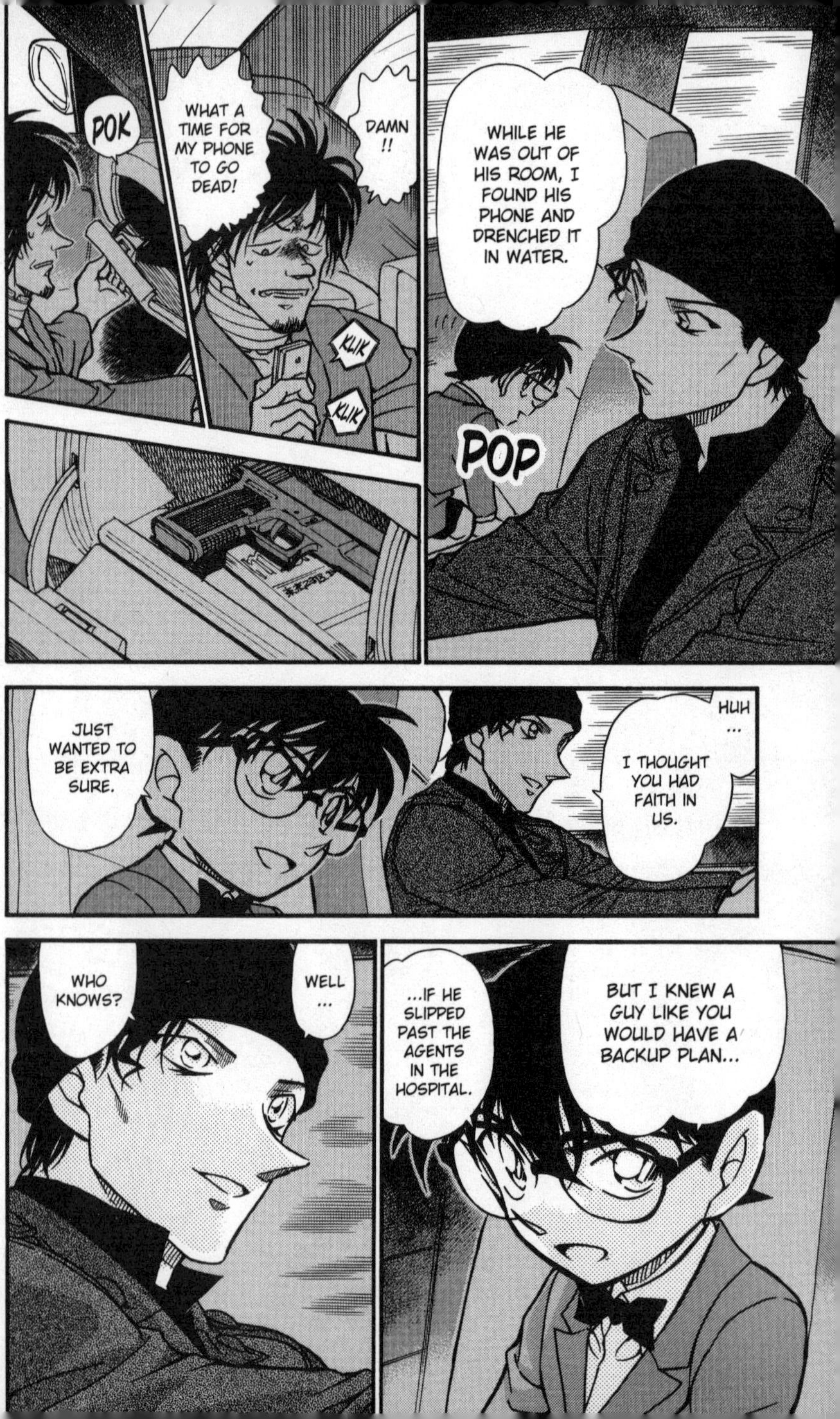
WHILE HE WAS OUT OF HIS ROOM, I FOUND HIS PHONE AND DRENCHED IT IN WATER.
POP
DAMN !!
WHAT A TIME FOR MY PHONE TO GO DEAD!
KLIK
KLIK
POK
HUH ...
I THOUGHT YOU HAD FAITH IN US.
JUST WANTED TO BE EXTRA SURE.
BUT I KNEW A GUY LIKE YOU WOULD HAVE A BACKUP PLAN...
...IF HE SLIPPED PAST THE AGENTS IN THE HOSPITAL.
WELL ...
WHO KNOWS?

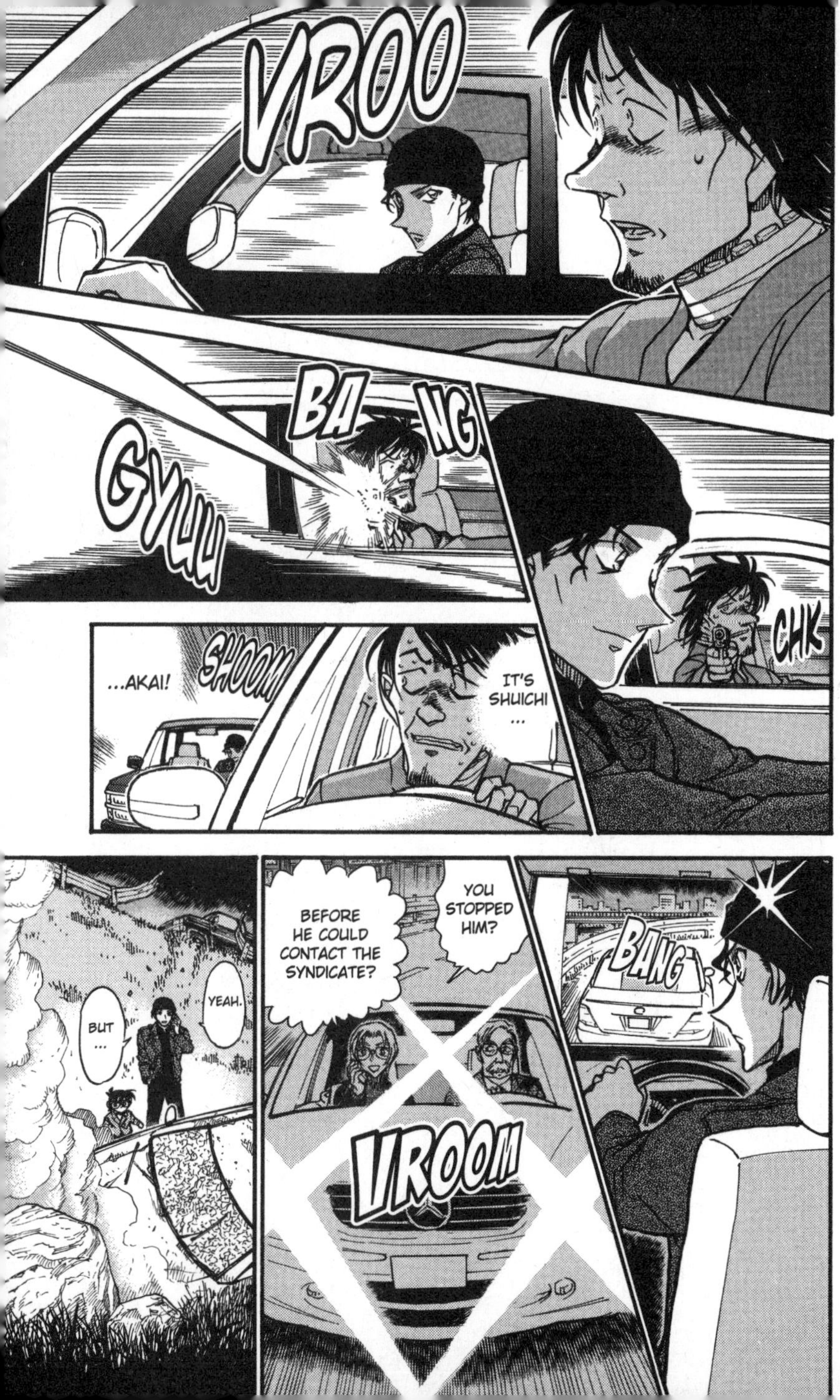
VROO
CHK
BA NG
GYUU
SHOOM
IT'S SHUICHI ...
...AKAI!
BANG
YOU STOPPED HIM?
BEFORE HE COULD CONTACT THE SYNDICATE?
VROOM
YEAH.
BUT ...

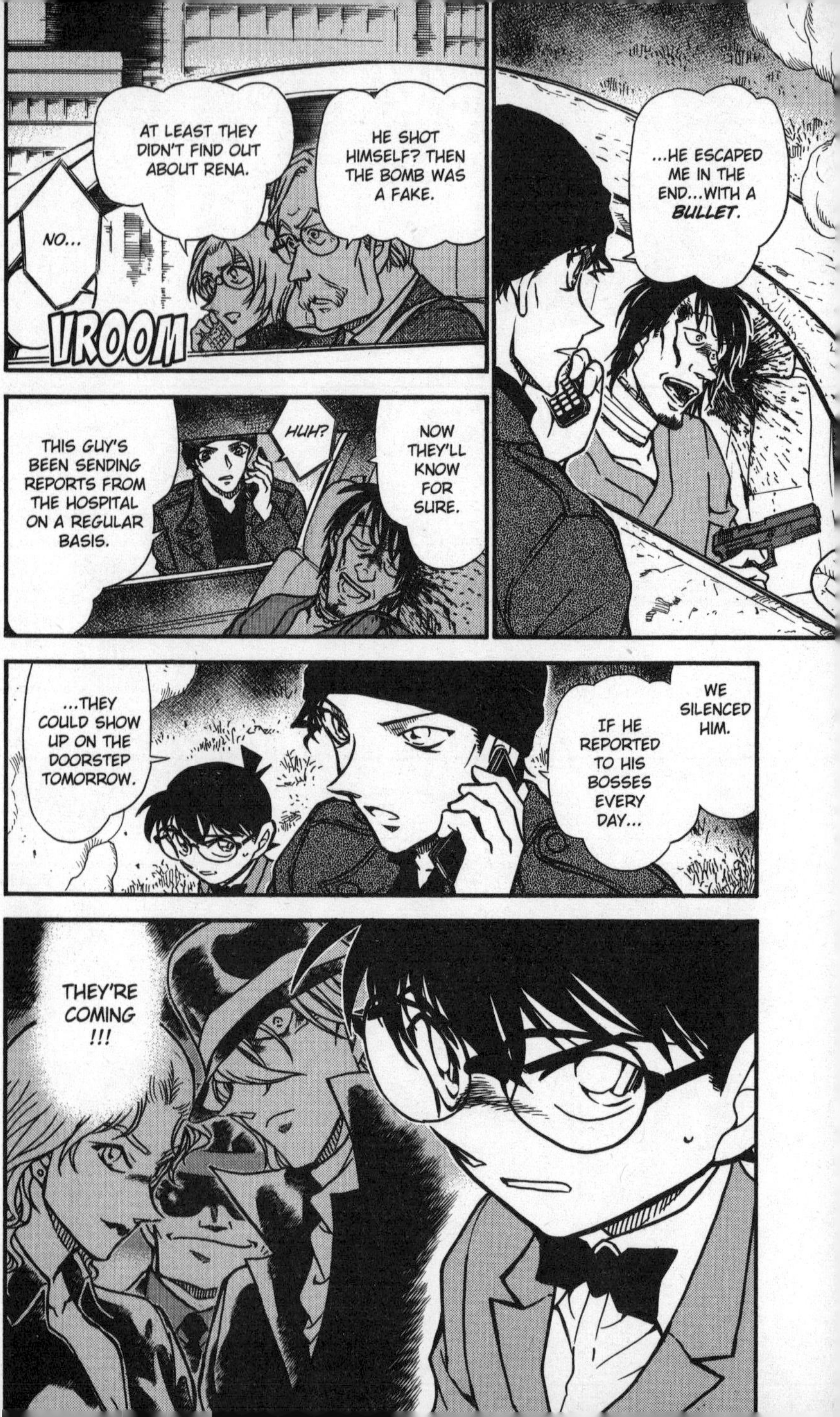
...HE ESCAPED ME IN THE END...WITH A BULLET.
HE SHOT HIMSELF? THEN THE BOMB WAS A FAKE.
AT LEAST THEY DIDN'T FIND OUT ABOUT RENA.
NO...
VROOM
NOW THEY'LL KNOW FOR SURE.
HUH?
THIS GUY'S BEEN SENDING REPORTS FROM THE HOSPITAL ON A REGULAR BASIS.
WE SILENCED HIM.
IF HE REPORTED TO HIS BOSSES EVERY DAY...
...THEY COULD SHOW UP ON THE DOORSTEP TOMORROW.
THEY'RE COMING!!!

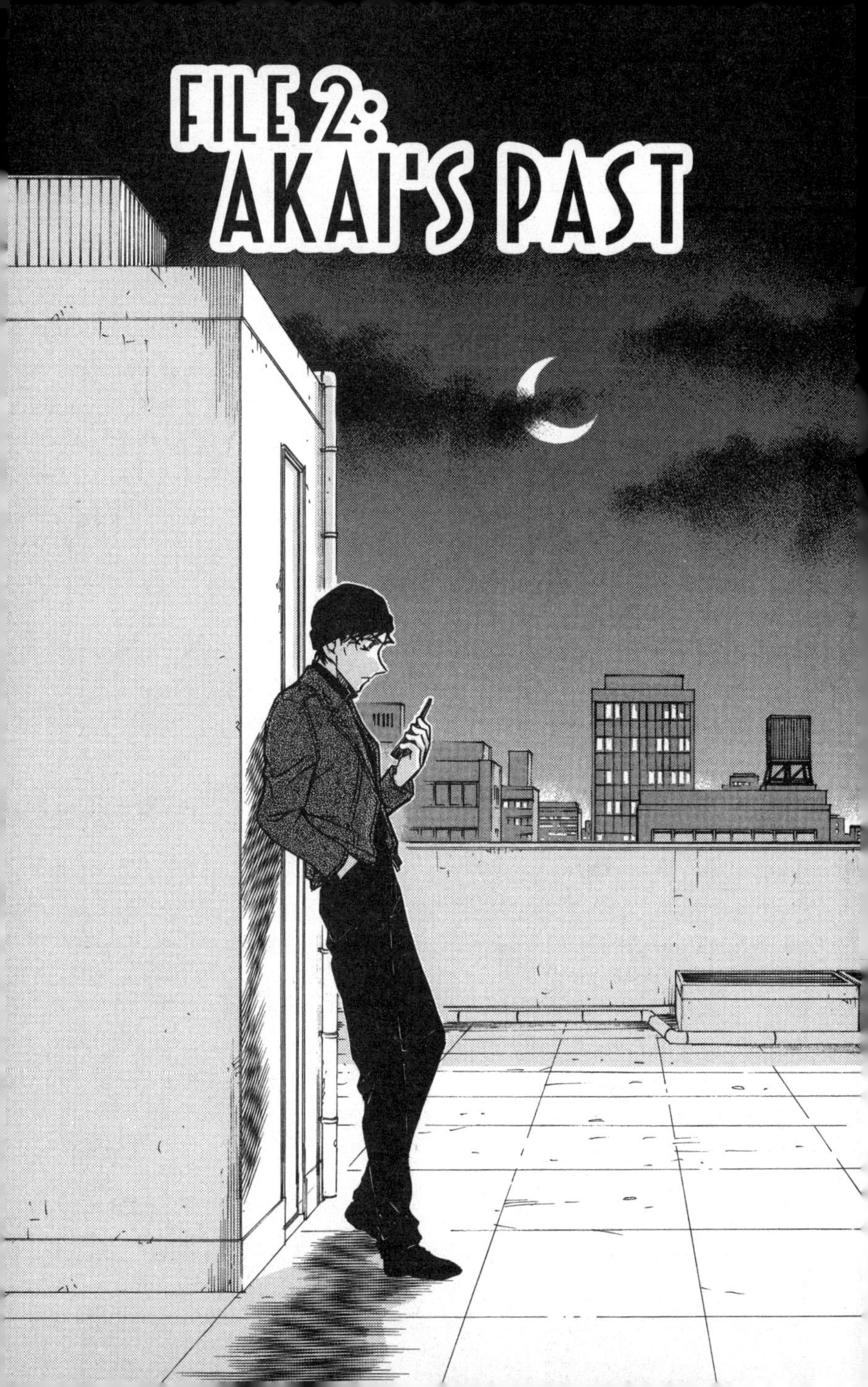
FILE 2:
AKAI'S PAST

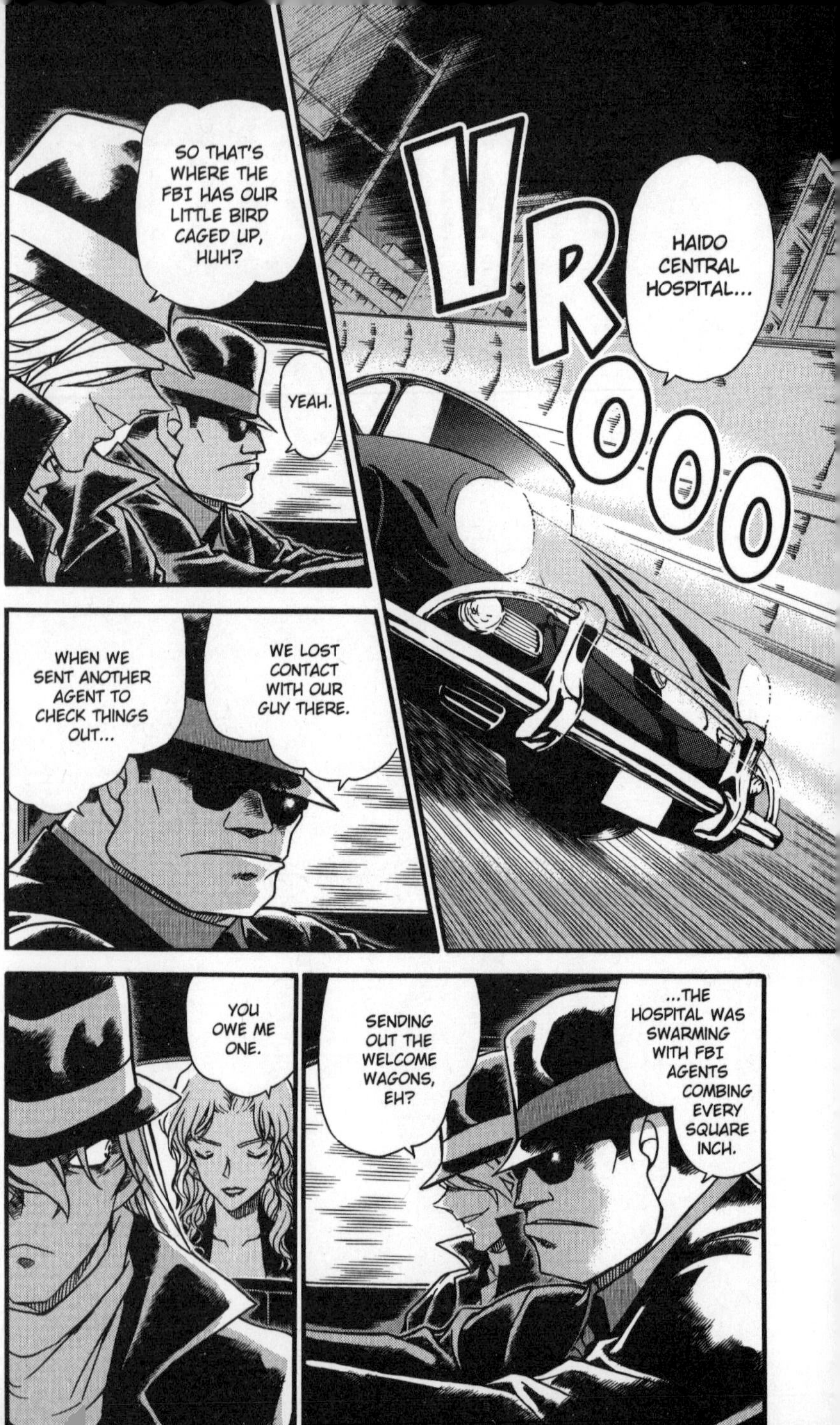

HAIDO CENTRAL HOSPITAL...
VROOO
SO THAT'S WHERE THE FBI HAS OUR LITTLE BIRD CAGED UP, HUH?
YEAH.
WE LOST CONTACT WITH OUR GUY THERE.
WHEN WE SENT ANOTHER AGENT TO CHECK THINGS OUT...
...THE HOSPITAL WAS SWARMING WITH FBI AGENTS COMBING EVERY SQUARE INCH.
SENDING OUT THE WELCOME WAGONS, EH?
YOU OWE ME ONE.

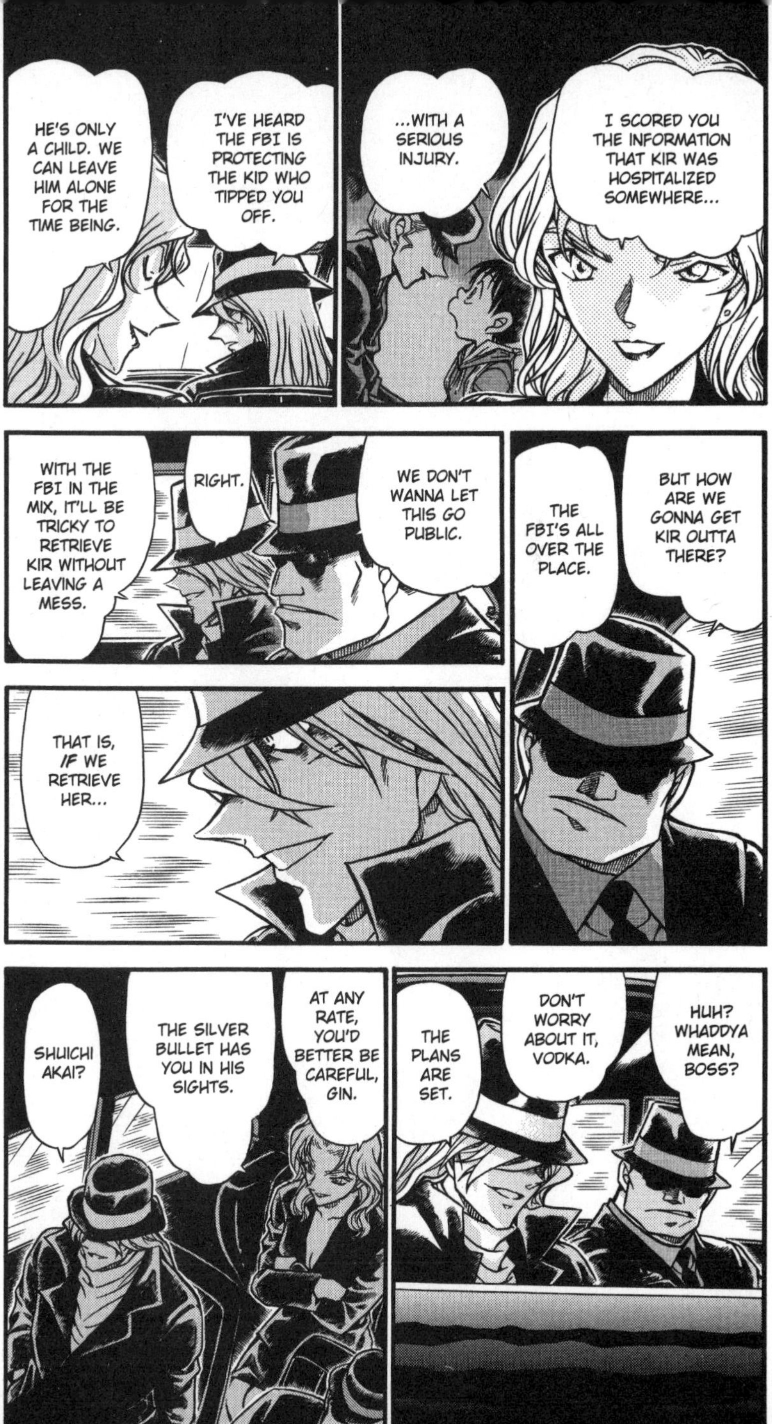
I SCORED YOU THE INFORMATION THAT KIR WAS HOSPITALIZED SOMEWHERE...
...WITH A SERIOUS INJURY.
I'VE HEARD THE FBI IS PROTECTING THE KID WHO TIPPED YOU OFF.
HE'S ONLY A CHILD. WE CAN LEAVE HIM ALONE FOR THE TIME BEING.
BUT HOW ARE WE GONNA GET KIR OUTTA THERE?
THE FBI'S ALL OVER THE PLACE.
WE DON'T WANNA LET THIS GO PUBLIC.
RIGHT.
WITH THE FBI IN THE MIX, IT'LL BE TRICKY TO RETRIEVE KIR WITHOUT LEAVING A MESS.
THAT IS, *IF* WE RETRIEVE HER...
HUH? WHADDYA MEAN, BOSS?
DON'T WORRY ABOUT IT, VODKA.
THE PLANS ARE SET.
AT ANY RATE, YOU'D BETTER BE CAREFUL, GIN.
THE SILVER BULLET HAS YOU IN HIS SIGHTS.
SHUICHI AKAI?

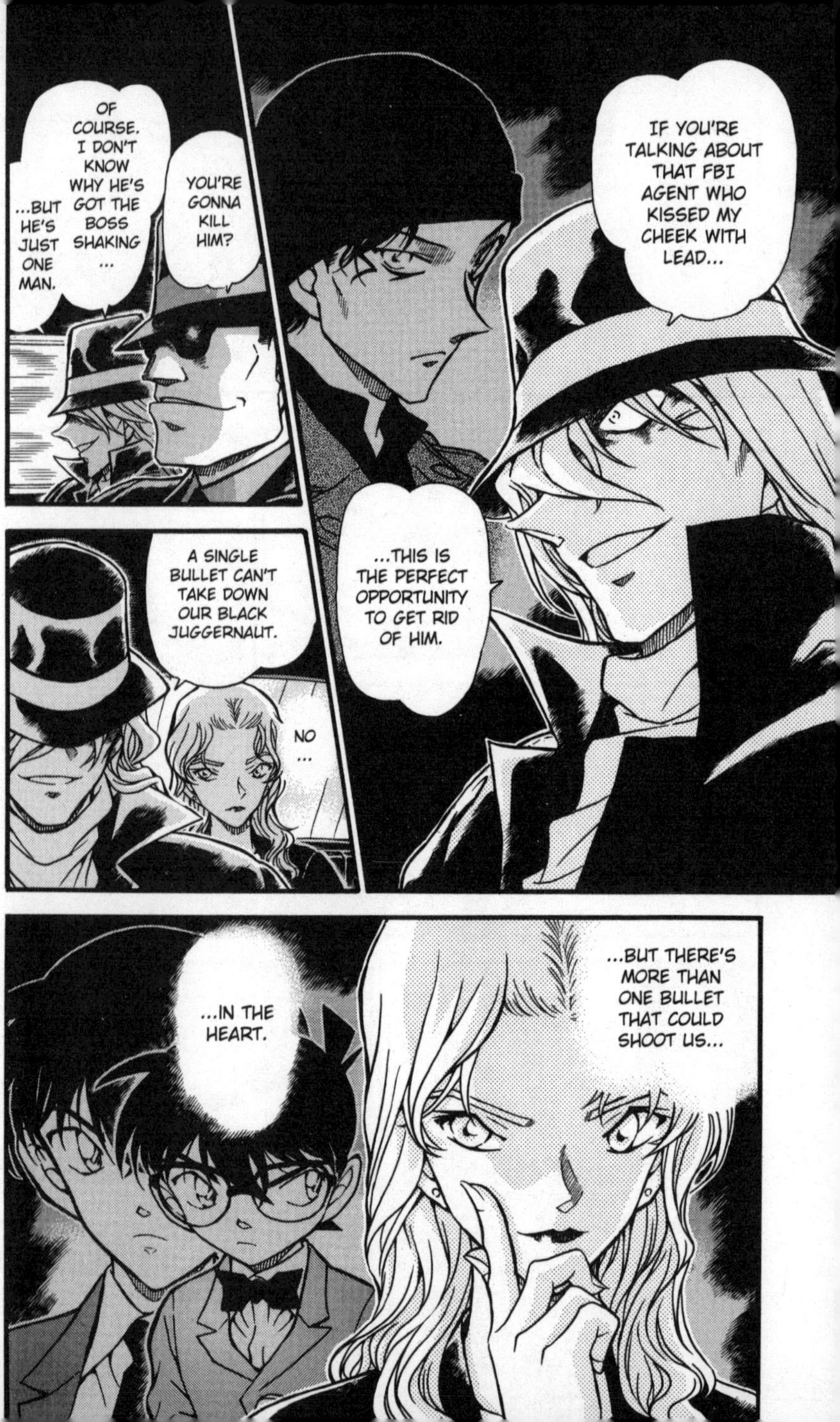
IF YOU'RE TALKING ABOUT THAT FBI AGENT WHO KISSED MY CHEEK WITH LEAD...
...THIS IS THE PERFECT OPPORTUNITY TO GET RID OF HIM.
YOU'RE GONNA KILL HIM?
OF COURSE. I DON'T KNOW WHY HE'S GOT THE BOSS SHAKING ...
...BUT HE'S JUST ONE MAN.
A SINGLE BULLET CAN'T TAKE DOWN OUR BLACK JUGGERNAUT.
NO ...
...BUT THERE'S MORE THAN ONE BULLET THAT COULD SHOOT US...
...IN THE HEART.

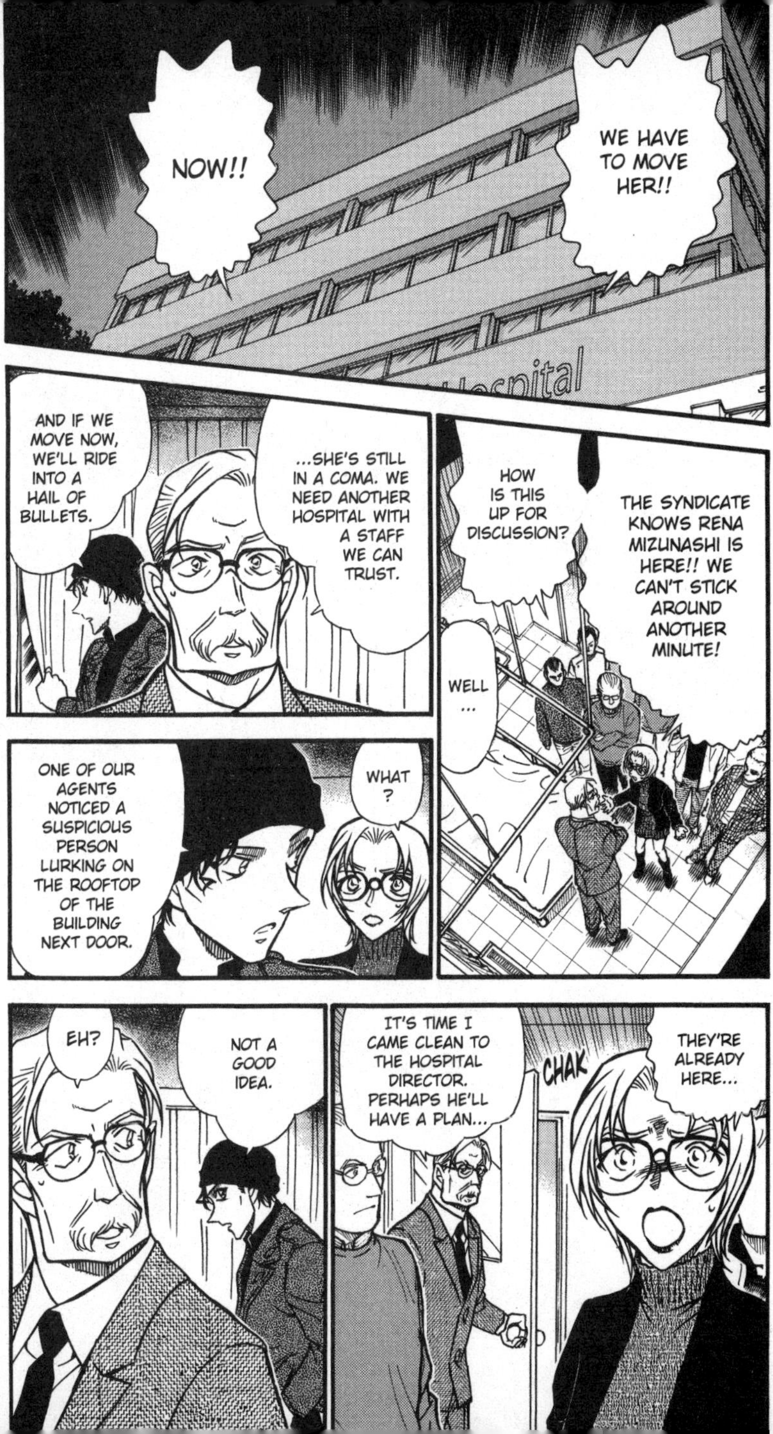
WE HAVE TO MOVE HER!!
NOW!!
THE SYNDICATE KNOWS RENA MIZUNASHI IS HERE!! WE CAN'T STICK AROUND ANOTHER MINUTE!
HOW IS THIS UP FOR DISCUSSION?
WELL...
...SHE'S STILL IN A COMA. WE NEED ANOTHER HOSPITAL WITH A STAFF WE CAN TRUST.
AND IF WE MOVE NOW, WE'LL RIDE INTO A HAIL OF BULLETS.
WHAT?
ONE OF OUR AGENTS NOTICED A SUSPICIOUS PERSON LURKING ON THE ROOFTOP OF THE BUILDING NEXT DOOR.
THEY'RE ALREADY HERE...
CHAK
IT'S TIME I CAME CLEAN TO THE HOSPITAL DIRECTOR. PERHAPS HE'LL HAVE A PLAN...
NOT A GOOD IDEA.
EH?

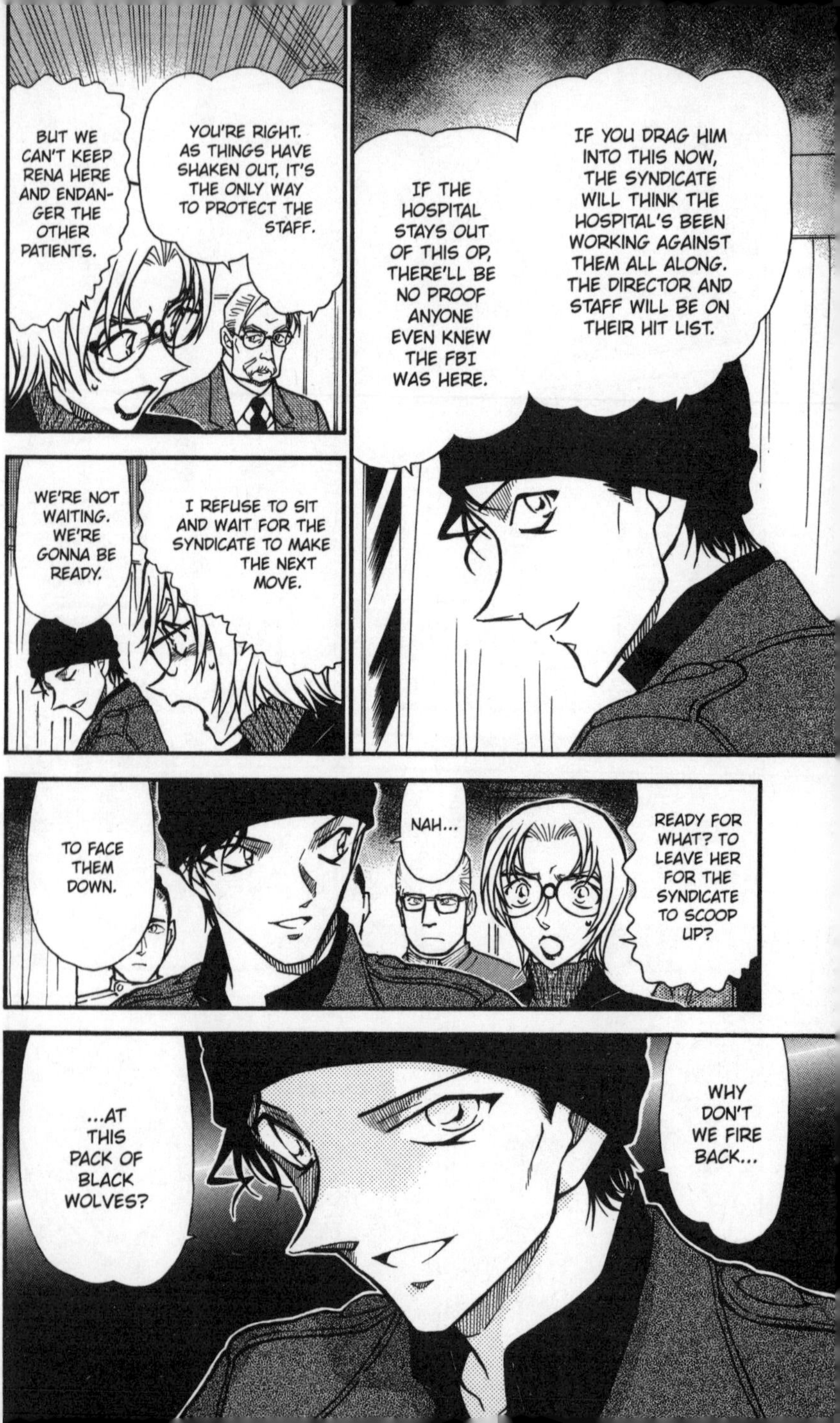
IF YOU DRAG HIM INTO THIS NOW, THE SYNDICATE WILL THINK THE HOSPITAL'S BEEN WORKING AGAINST THEM ALL ALONG. THE DIRECTOR AND STAFF WILL BE ON THEIR HIT LIST.
IF THE HOSPITAL STAYS OUT OF THIS OP, THERE'LL BE NO PROOF ANYONE EVEN KNEW THE FBI WAS HERE.
YOU'RE RIGHT. AS THINGS HAVE SHAKEN OUT, IT'S THE ONLY WAY TO PROTECT THE STAFF.
BUT WE CAN'T KEEP RENA HERE AND ENDANGER THE OTHER PATIENTS.
I REFUSE TO SIT AND WAIT FOR THE SYNDICATE TO MAKE THE NEXT MOVE.
WE'RE NOT WAITING. WE'RE GONNA BE READY.
READY FOR WHAT? TO LEAVE HER FOR THE SYNDICATE TO SCOOP UP?
NAH...
TO FACE THEM DOWN.
WHY DON'T WE FIRE BACK...
...AT THIS PACK OF BLACK WOLVES?

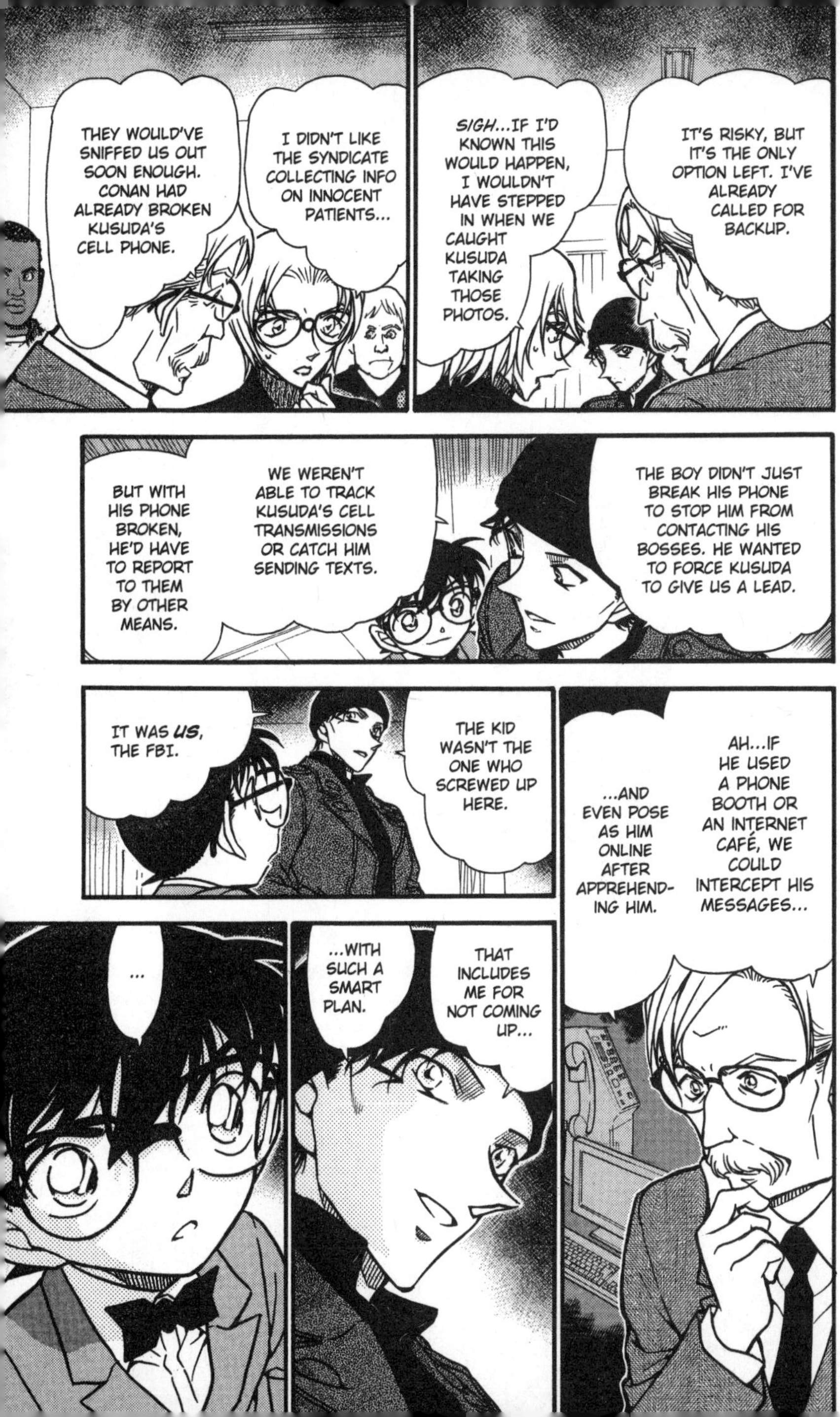
IT'S RISKY, BUT IT'S THE ONLY OPTION LEFT. I'VE ALREADY CALLED FOR BACKUP.
SIGH...IF I'D KNOWN THIS WOULD HAPPEN, I WOULDN'T HAVE STEPPED IN WHEN WE CAUGHT KUSUDA TAKING THOSE PHOTOS.
I DIDN'T LIKE THE SYNDICATE COLLECTING INFO ON INNOCENT PATIENTS...
THEY WOULD'VE SNIFFED US OUT SOON ENOUGH. CONAN HAD ALREADY BROKEN KUSUDA'S CELL PHONE.
THE BOY DIDN'T JUST BREAK HIS PHONE TO STOP HIM FROM CONTACTING HIS BOSSES. HE WANTED TO FORCE KUSUDA TO GIVE US A LEAD.
WE WEREN'T ABLE TO TRACK KUSUDA'S CELL TRANSMISSIONS OR CATCH HIM SENDING TEXTS.
BUT WITH HIS PHONE BROKEN, HE'D HAVE TO REPORT TO THEM BY OTHER MEANS.
AH...IF HE USED A PHONE BOOTH OR AN INTERNET CAFÉ, WE COULD INTERCEPT HIS MESSAGES...
...AND EVEN POSE AS HIM ONLINE AFTER APPREHEND-ING HIM.
THE KID WASN'T THE ONE WHO SCREWED UP HERE.
IT WAS *US*, THE FBI.
THAT INCLUDES ME FOR NOT COMING UP...
...WITH SUCH A SMART PLAN.
...

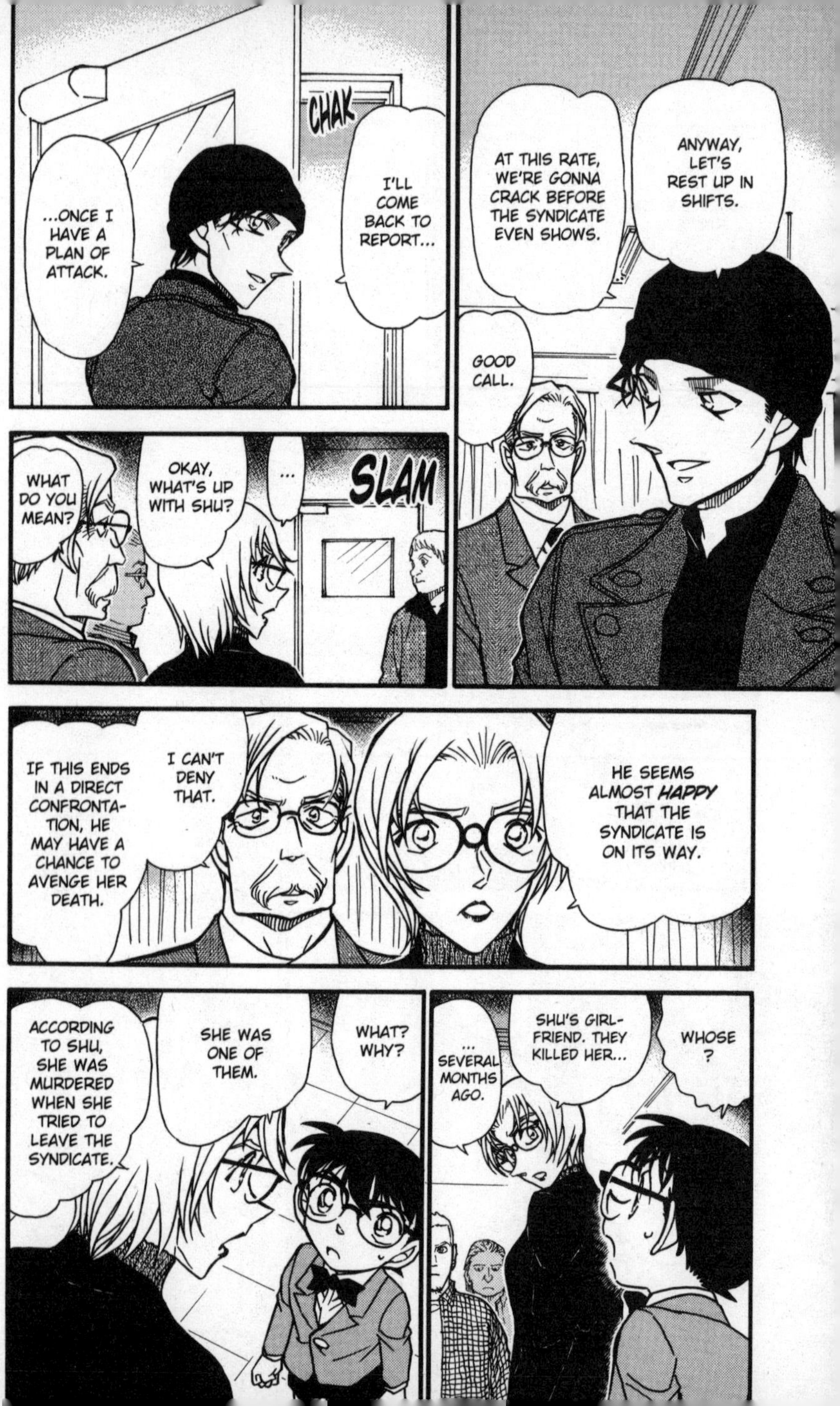
ANYWAY, LET'S REST UP IN SHIFTS.
AT THIS RATE, WE'RE GONNA CRACK BEFORE THE SYNDICATE EVEN SHOWS.
GOOD CALL.
CHAK
I'LL COME BACK TO REPORT...
...ONCE I HAVE A PLAN OF ATTACK.
SLAM
...
OKAY, WHAT'S UP WITH SHU?
WHAT DO YOU MEAN?
HE SEEMS ALMOST *HAPPY* THAT THE SYNDICATE IS ON ITS WAY.
I CAN'T DENY THAT.
IF THIS ENDS IN A DIRECT CONFRONTA-TION, HE MAY HAVE A CHANCE TO AVENGE HER DEATH.
WHOSE?
SHU'S GIRL-FRIEND. THEY KILLED HER...
...SEVERAL MONTHS AGO.
WHAT? WHY?
SHE WAS ONE OF THEM.
ACCORDING TO SHU, SHE WAS MURDERED WHEN SHE TRIED TO LEAVE THE SYNDICATE.

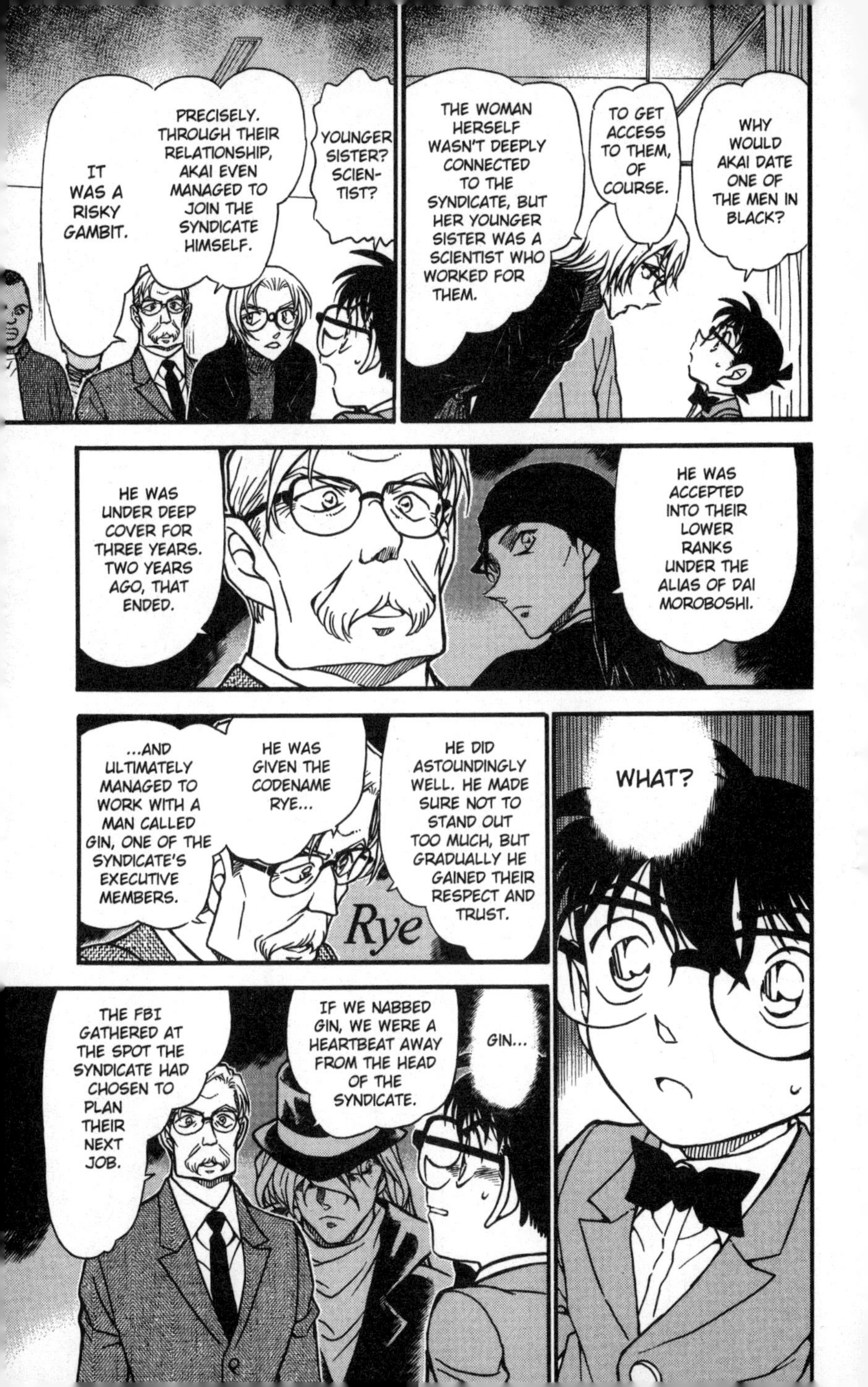
WHY WOULD AKAI DATE ONE OF THE MEN IN BLACK?
TO GET ACCESS TO THEM, OF COURSE.
THE WOMAN HERSELF WASN'T DEEPLY CONNECTED TO THE SYNDICATE, BUT HER YOUNGER SISTER WAS A SCIENTIST WHO WORKED FOR THEM.
YOUNGER SISTER? SCIEN-TIST?
PRECISELY. THROUGH THEIR RELATIONSHIP, AKAI EVEN MANAGED TO JOIN THE SYNDICATE HIMSELF.
IT WAS A RISKY GAMBIT.
HE WAS ACCEPTED INTO THEIR LOWER RANKS UNDER THE ALIAS OF DAI MOROBOSHI.
HE WAS UNDER DEEP COVER FOR THREE YEARS. TWO YEARS AGO, THAT ENDED.
WHAT?
HE DID ASTOUNDINGLY WELL. HE MADE SURE NOT TO STAND OUT TOO MUCH, BUT GRADUALLY HE GAINED THEIR RESPECT AND TRUST.
HE WAS GIVEN THE CODENAME RYE...
Rye
...AND ULTIMATELY MANAGED TO WORK WITH A MAN CALLED GIN, ONE OF THE SYNDICATE'S EXECUTIVE MEMBERS.
GIN...
IF WE NABBED GIN, WE WERE A HEARTBEAT AWAY FROM THE HEAD OF THE SYNDICATE.
THE FBI GATHERED AT THE SPOT THE SYNDICATE HAD CHOSEN TO PLAN THEIR NEXT JOB.

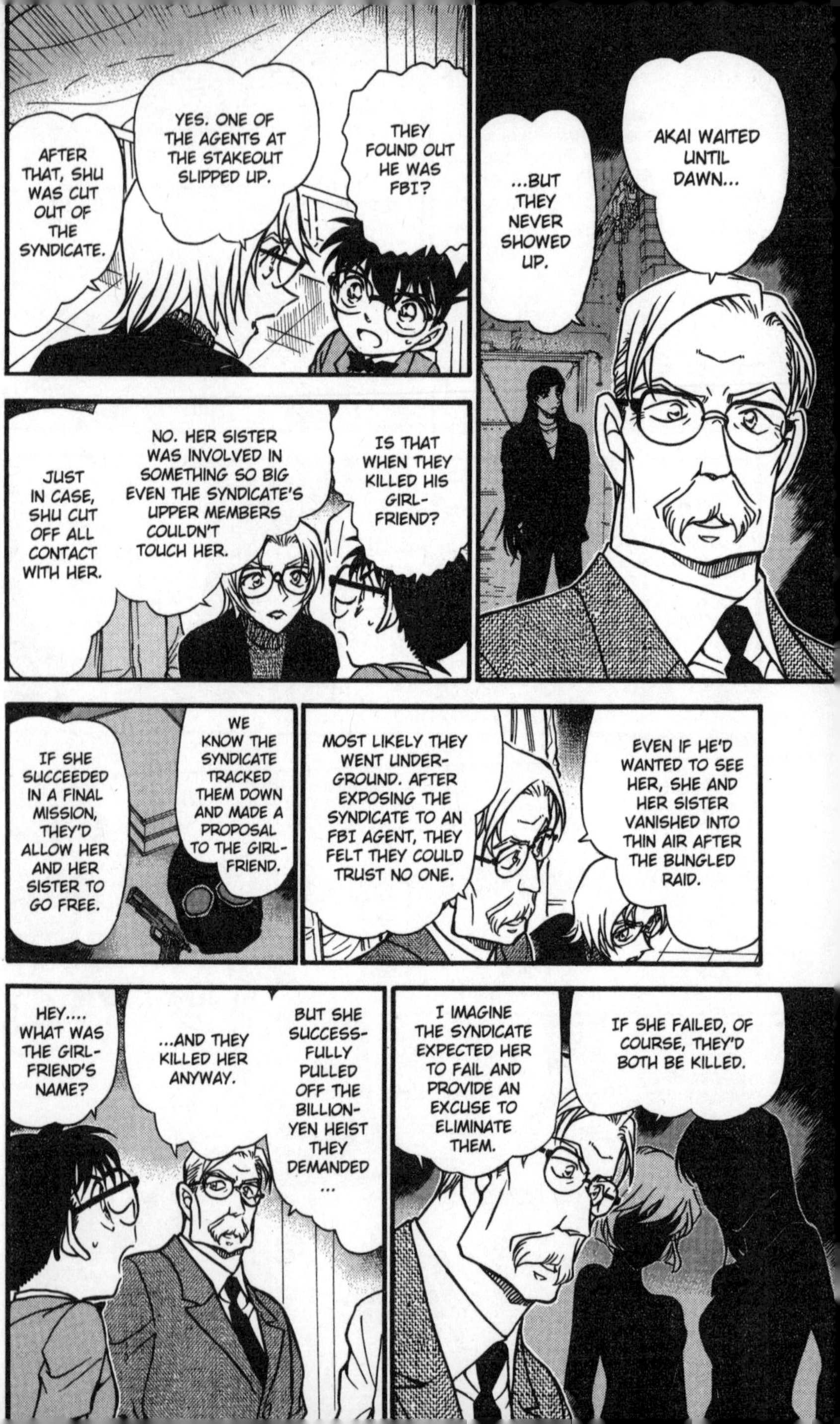
AKAI WAITED UNTIL DAWN...
...BUT THEY NEVER SHOWED UP.
THEY FOUND OUT HE WAS FBI?
YES. ONE OF THE AGENTS AT THE STAKEOUT SLIPPED UP.
AFTER THAT, SHU WAS CUT OUT OF THE SYNDICATE.
IS THAT WHEN THEY KILLED HIS GIRL-FRIEND?
NO. HER SISTER WAS INVOLVED IN SOMETHING SO BIG EVEN THE SYNDICATE'S UPPER MEMBERS COULDN'T TOUCH HER.
JUST IN CASE, SHU CUT OFF ALL CONTACT WITH HER.
EVEN IF HE'D WANTED TO SEE HER, SHE AND HER SISTER VANISHED INTO THIN AIR AFTER THE BUNGLED RAID.
MOST LIKELY THEY WENT UNDER-GROUND. AFTER EXPOSING THE SYNDICATE TO AN FBI AGENT, THEY FELT THEY COULD TRUST NO ONE.
WE KNOW THE SYNDICATE TRACKED THEM DOWN AND MADE A PROPOSAL TO THE GIRL-FRIEND.
IF SHE SUCCEEDED IN A FINAL MISSION, THEY'D ALLOW HER AND HER SISTER TO GO FREE.
IF SHE FAILED, OF COURSE, THEY'D BOTH BE KILLED.
I IMAGINE THE SYNDICATE EXPECTED HER TO FAIL AND PROVIDE AN EXCUSE TO ELIMINATE THEM.
BUT SHE SUCCESS-FULLY PULLED OFF THE BILLION-YEN HEIST THEY DEMANDED ...
...AND THEY KILLED HER ANYWAY.
HEY.... WHAT WAS THE GIRL-FRIEND'S NAME?

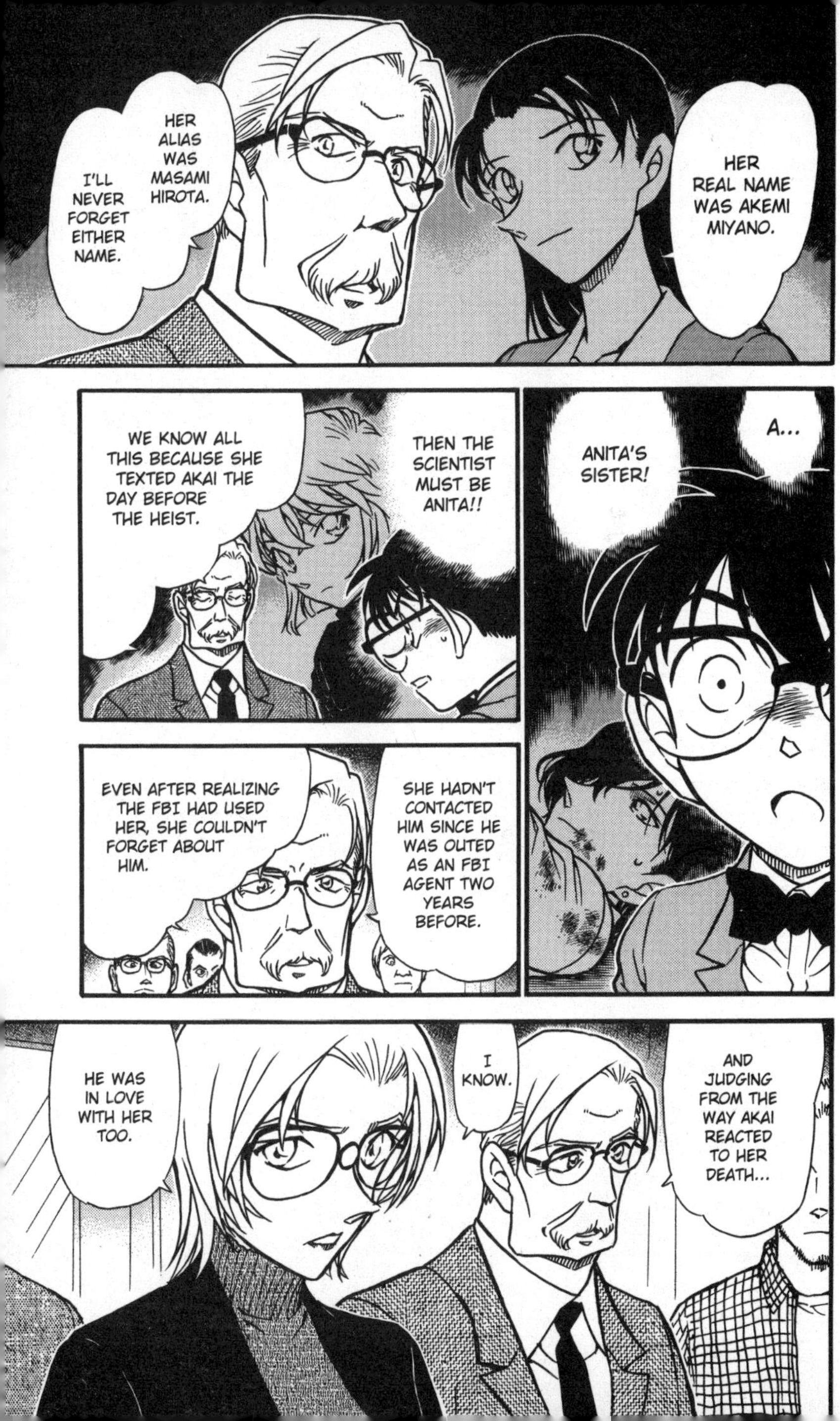
HER REAL NAME WAS AKEMI MIYANO.
HER ALIAS WAS MASAMI HIROTA.
I'LL NEVER FORGET EITHER NAME.
A...
ANITA'S SISTER!
THEN THE SCIENTIST MUST BE ANITA!!
WE KNOW ALL THIS BECAUSE SHE TEXTED AKAI THE DAY BEFORE THE HEIST.
SHE HADN'T CONTACTED HIM SINCE HE WAS OUTED AS AN FBI AGENT TWO YEARS BEFORE.
EVEN AFTER REALIZING THE FBI HAD USED HER, SHE COULDN'T FORGET ABOUT HIM.
AND JUDGING FROM THE WAY AKAI REACTED TO HER DEATH...
I KNOW.
HE WAS IN LOVE WITH HER TOO.

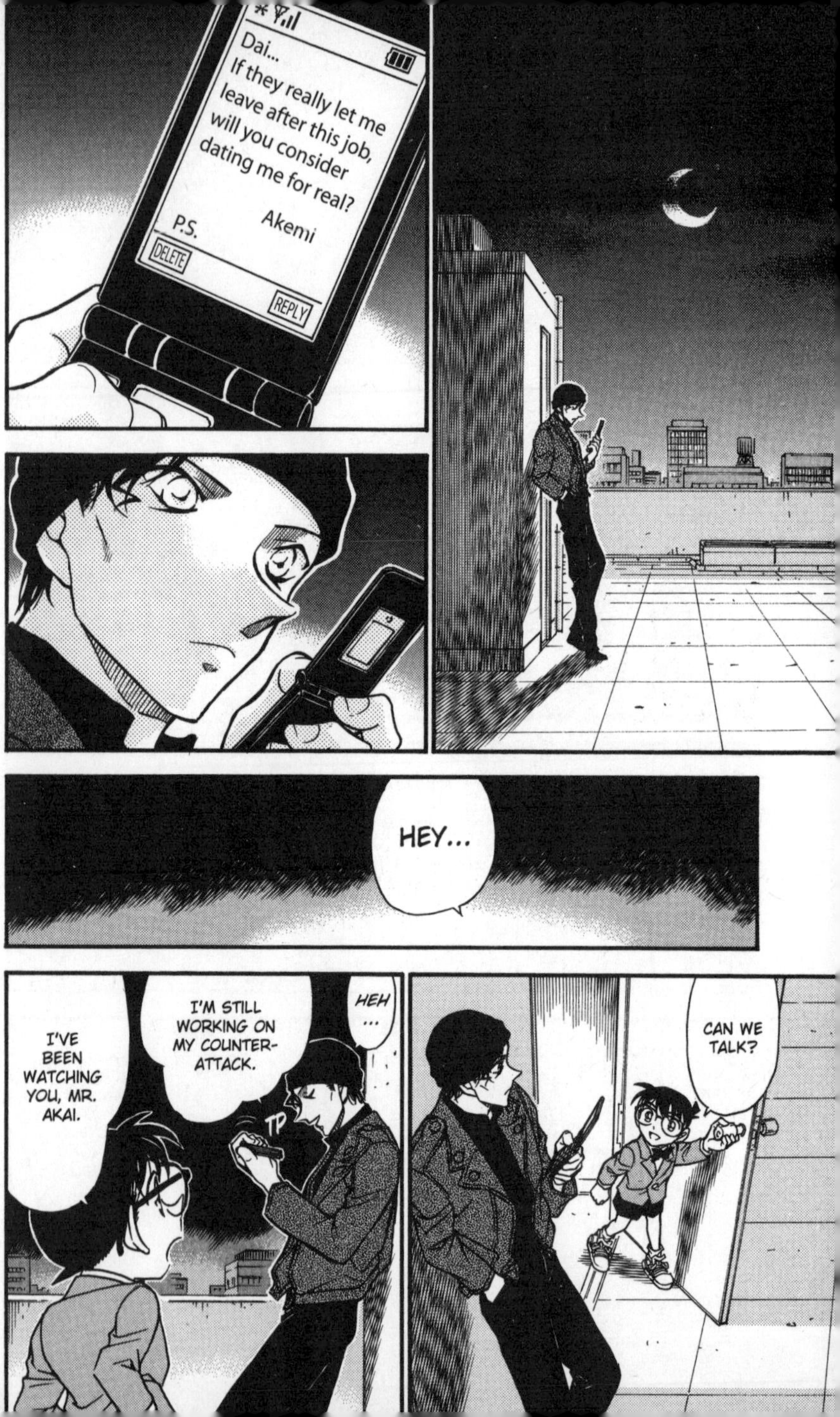
Dai... If they really let me leave after this job, will you consider dating me for real? Akemi
P.S.
DELETE
REPLY
HEY...
CAN WE TALK?
HEH ...
I'M STILL WORKING ON MY COUNTER-ATTACK.
TP
I'VE BEEN WATCHING YOU, MR. AKAI.

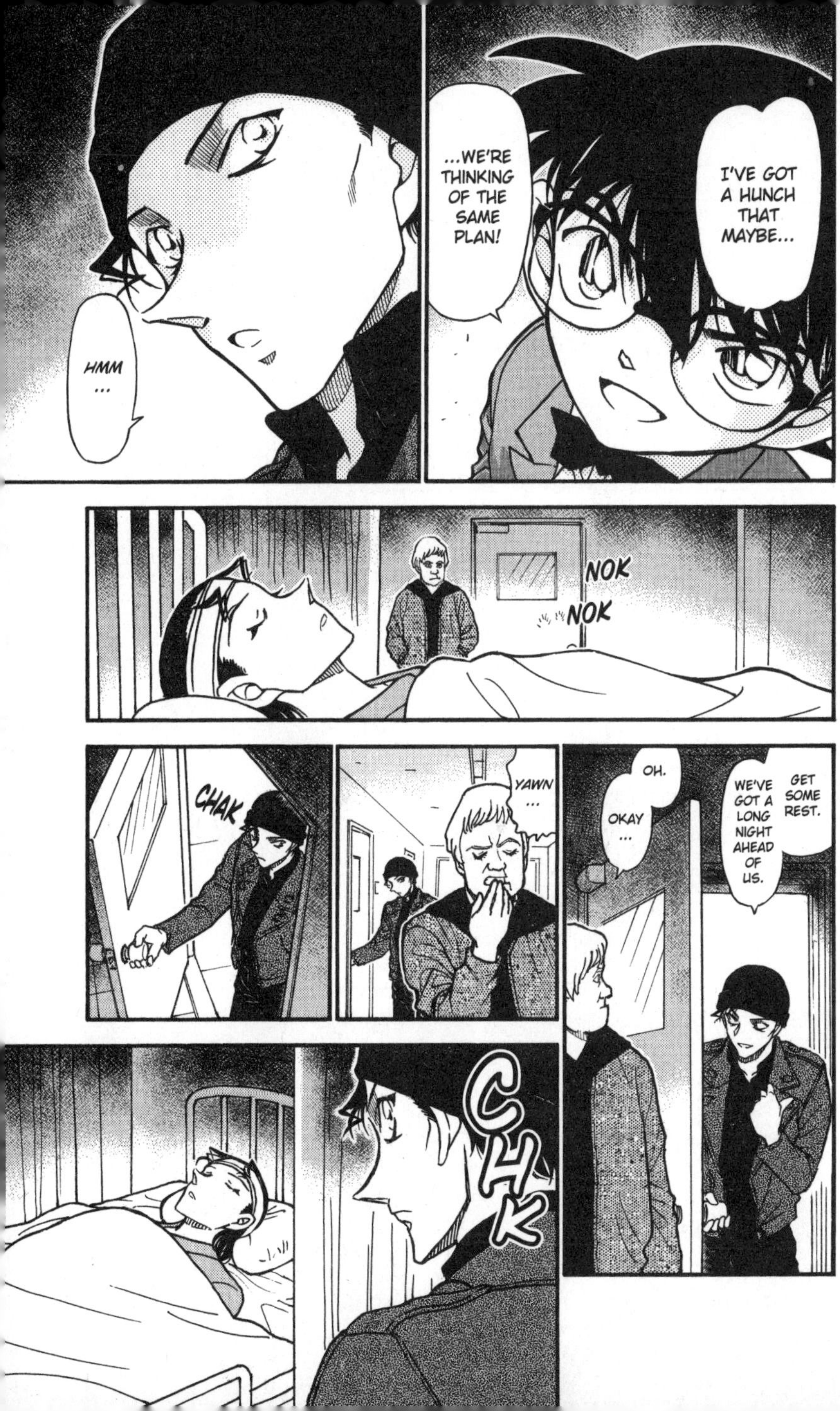
I'VE GOT A HUNCH THAT MAYBE...
...WE'RE THINKING OF THE SAME PLAN!
HMM ...
NOK NOK
GET SOME REST.
WE'VE GOT A LONG NIGHT AHEAD OF US.
OH.
OKAY ...
YAWN ...
CHAK
CHK

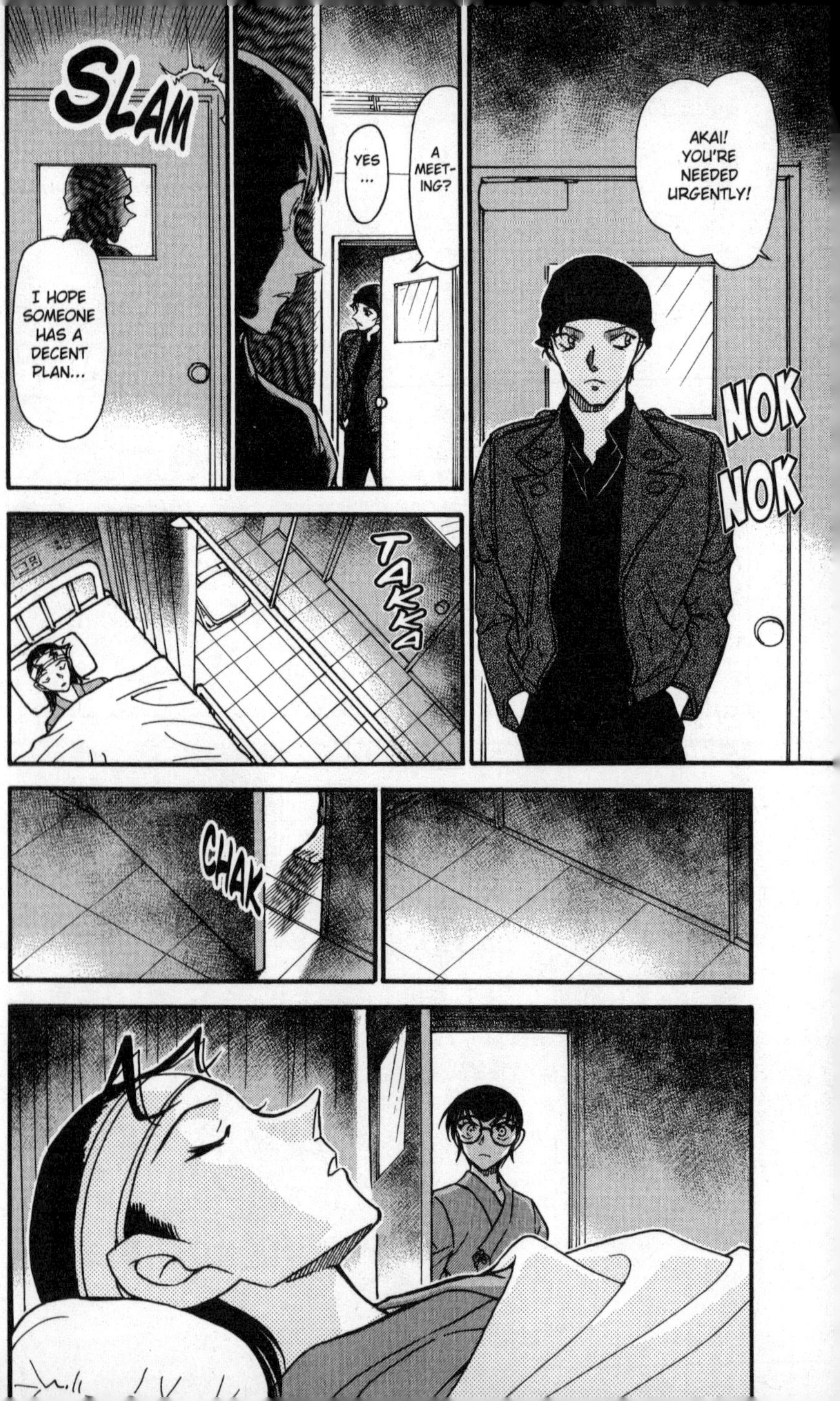
AKAI! YOU'RE NEEDED URGENTLY!
NOK NOK
A MEET-ING?
YES...
SLAM
I HOPE SOMEONE HAS A DECENT PLAN...
TAKKA
CHAK

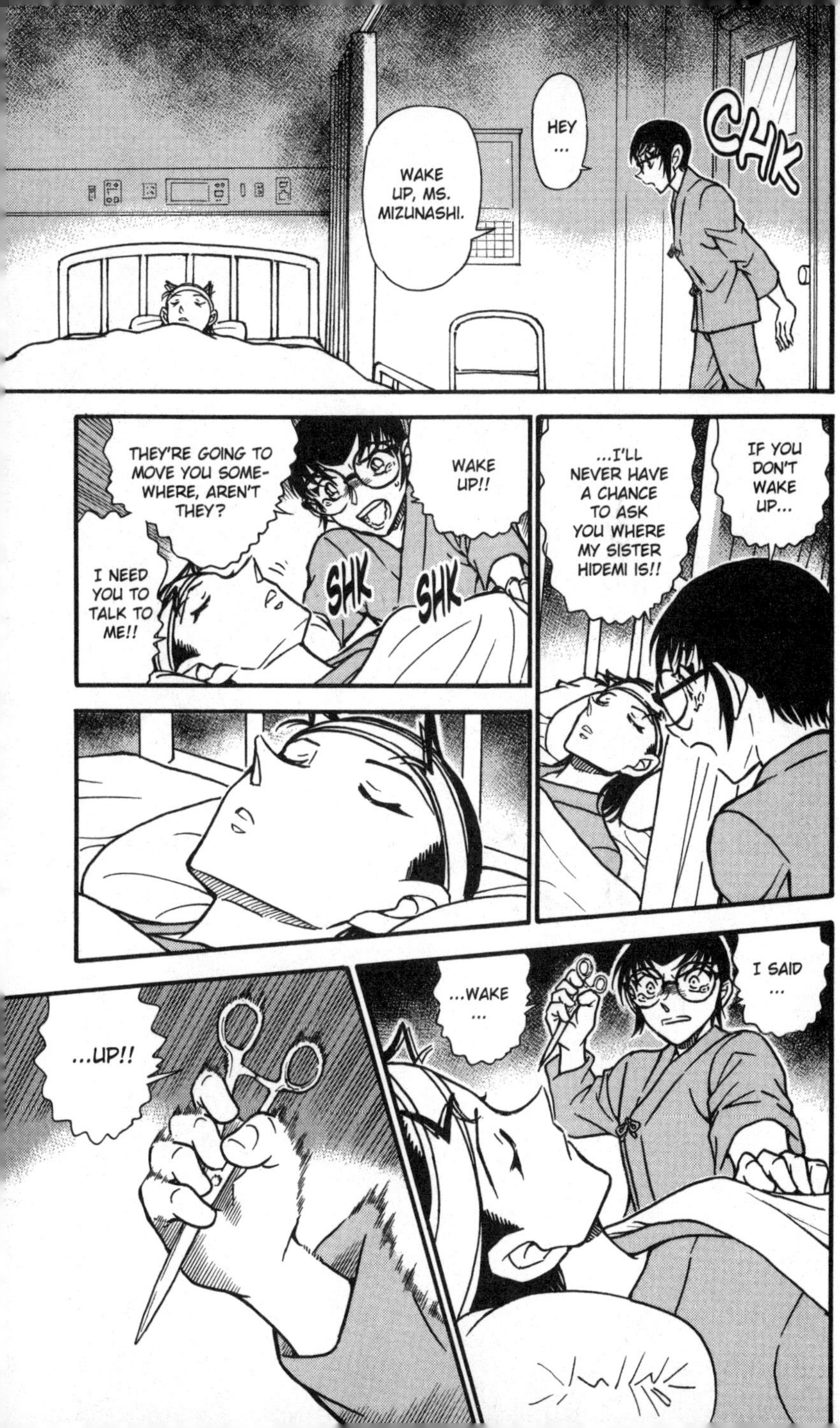
CHK
HEY...
WAKE UP, MS. MIZUNASHI.
IF YOU DON'T WAKE UP...
...I'LL NEVER HAVE A CHANCE TO ASK YOU WHERE MY SISTER HIDEMI IS!!
WAKE UP!!
SHK
SHK
THEY'RE GOING TO MOVE YOU SOMEWHERE, AREN'T THEY?
I NEED YOU TO TALK TO ME!!
I SAID...
...WAKE...
...UP!!

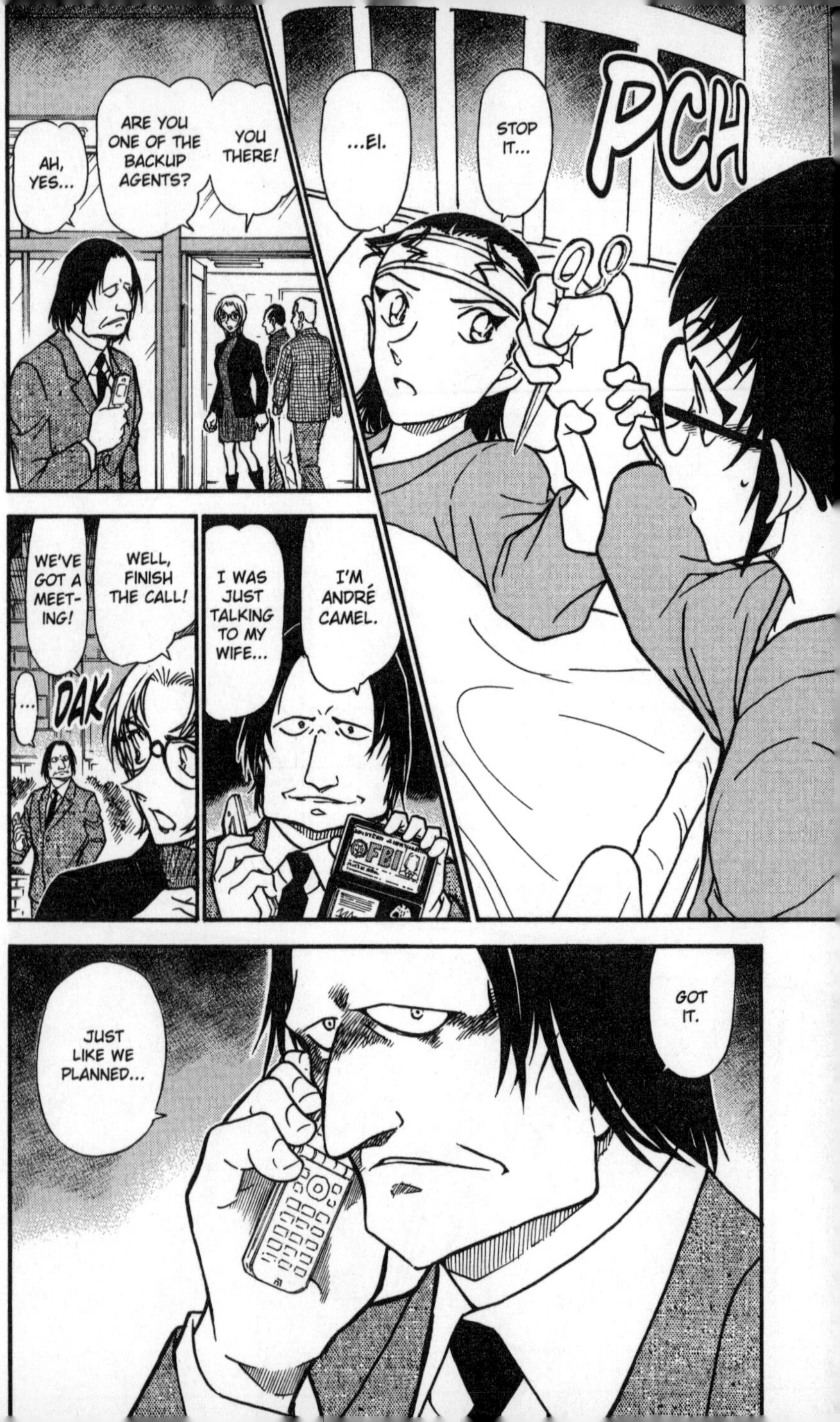
PCH
STOP IT...
...EI.
YOU THERE!
ARE YOU ONE OF THE BACKUP AGENTS?
AH, YES...
I'M ANDRÉ CAMEL.
I WAS JUST TALKING TO MY WIFE...
WELL, FINISH THE CALL!
WE'VE GOT A MEETING!
DAK
...
GOT IT.
JUST LIKE WE PLANNED...

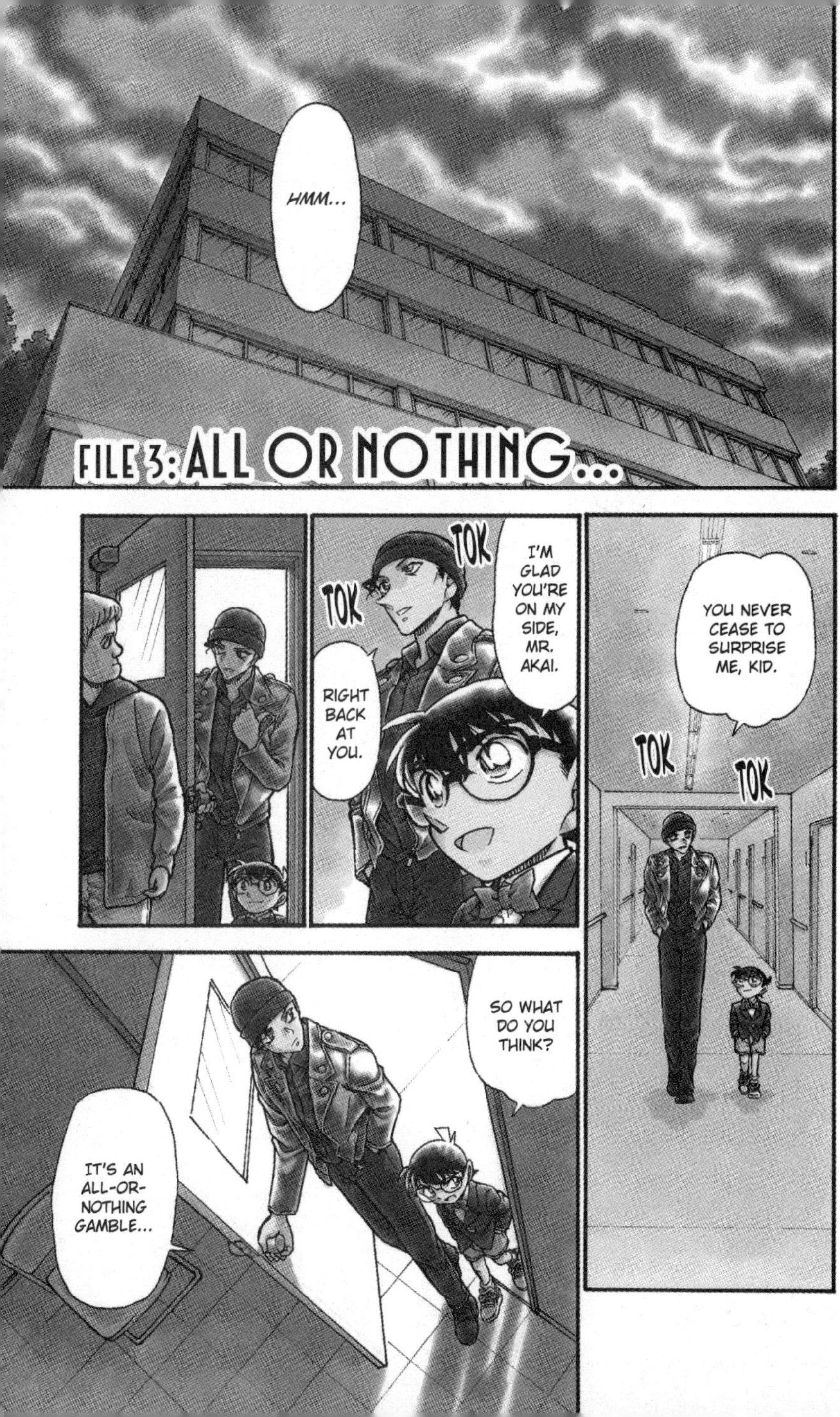
HMM...
FILE 3: ALL OR NOTHING...
YOU NEVER CEASE TO SURPRISE ME, KID.
TOK
TOK
TOK
I'M GLAD YOU'RE ON MY SIDE, MR. AKAI.
TOK
RIGHT BACK AT YOU.
SO WHAT DO YOU THINK?
IT'S AN ALL-OR-NOTHING GAMBLE...

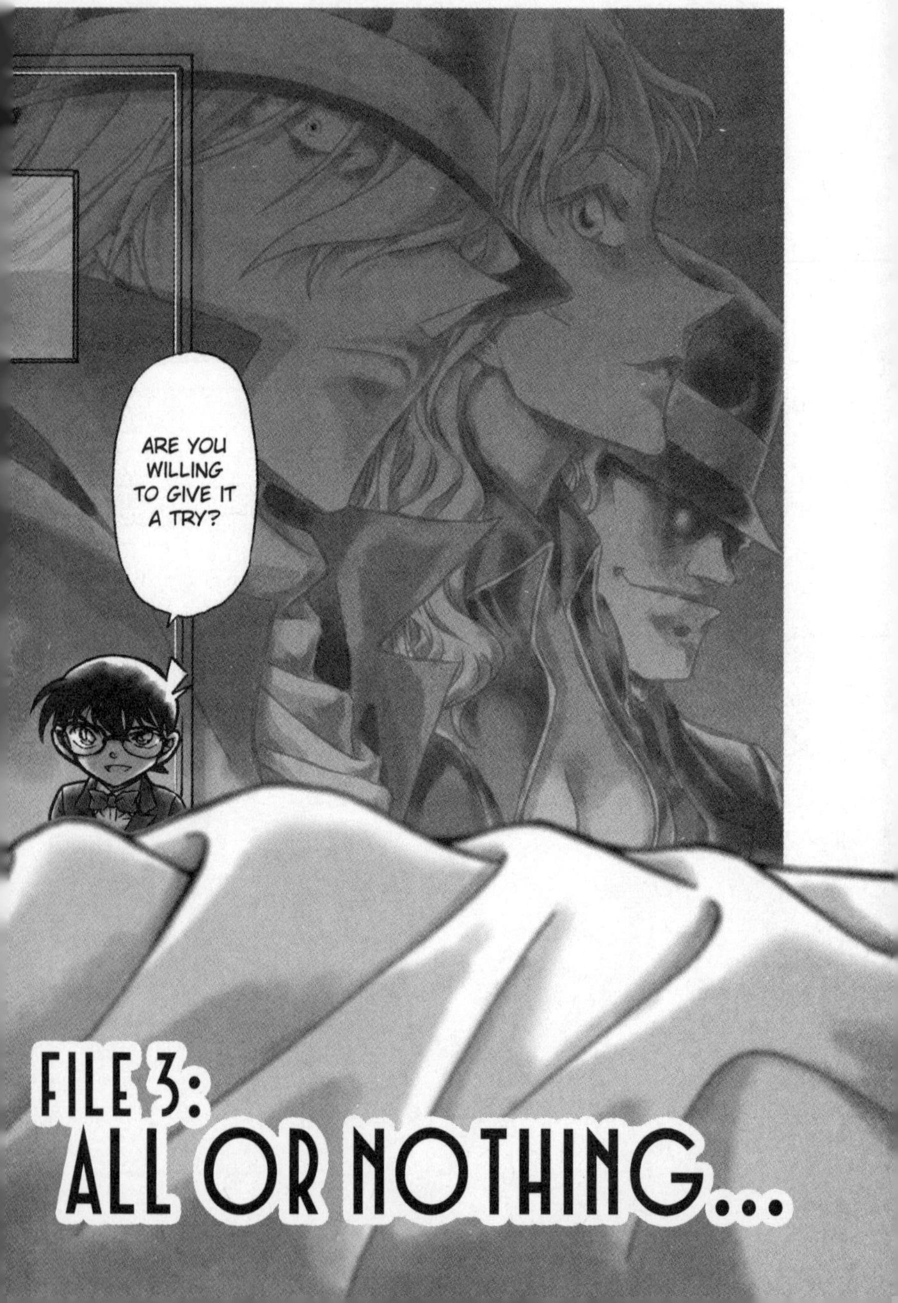
ARE YOU WILLING TO GIVE IT A TRY?
FILE 3:
ALL OR NOTHING...

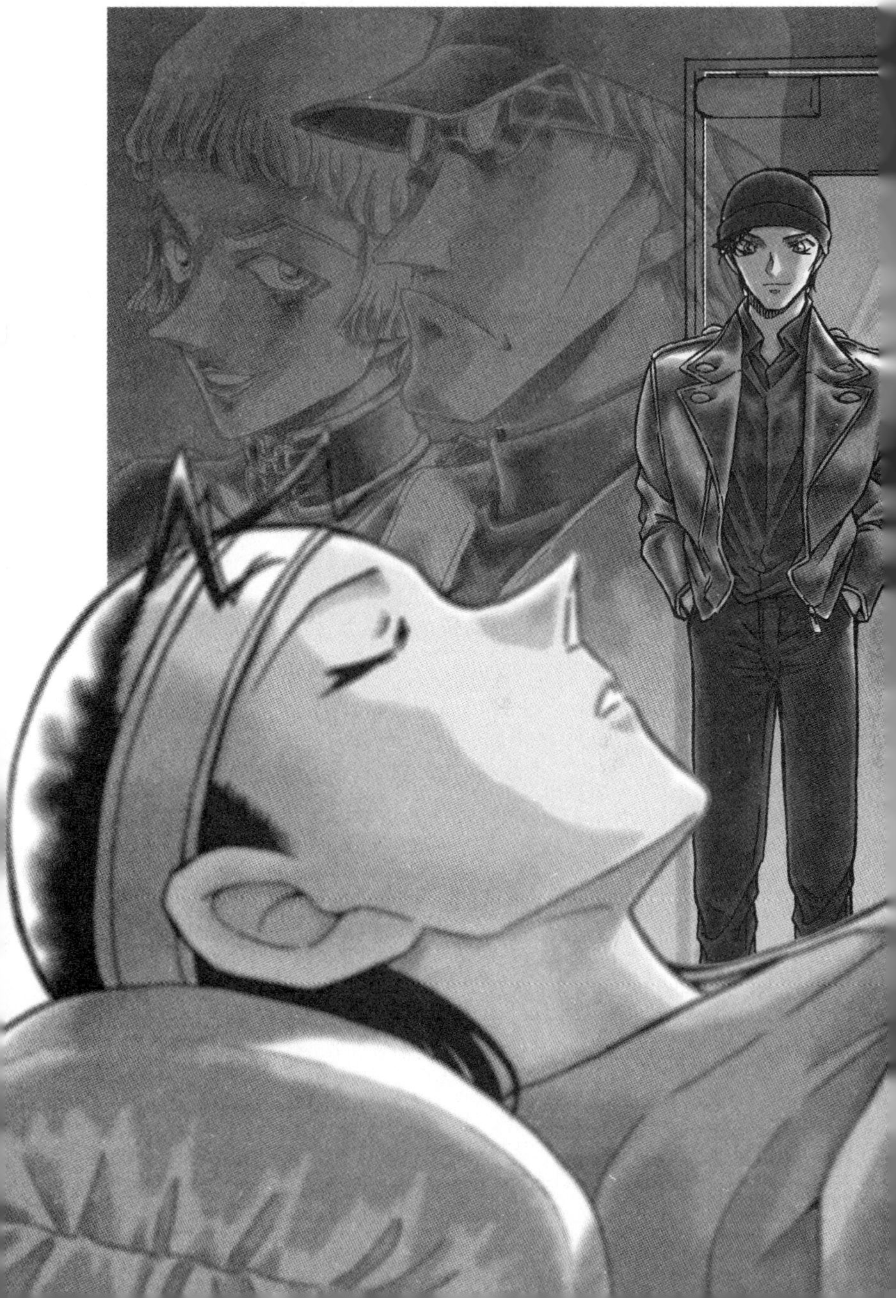

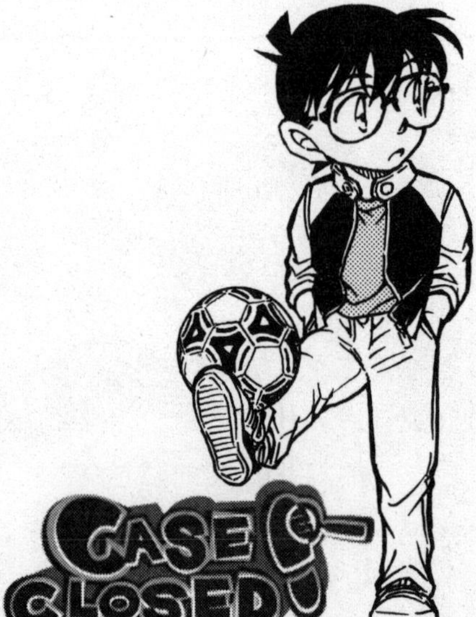
CASE CLOSED

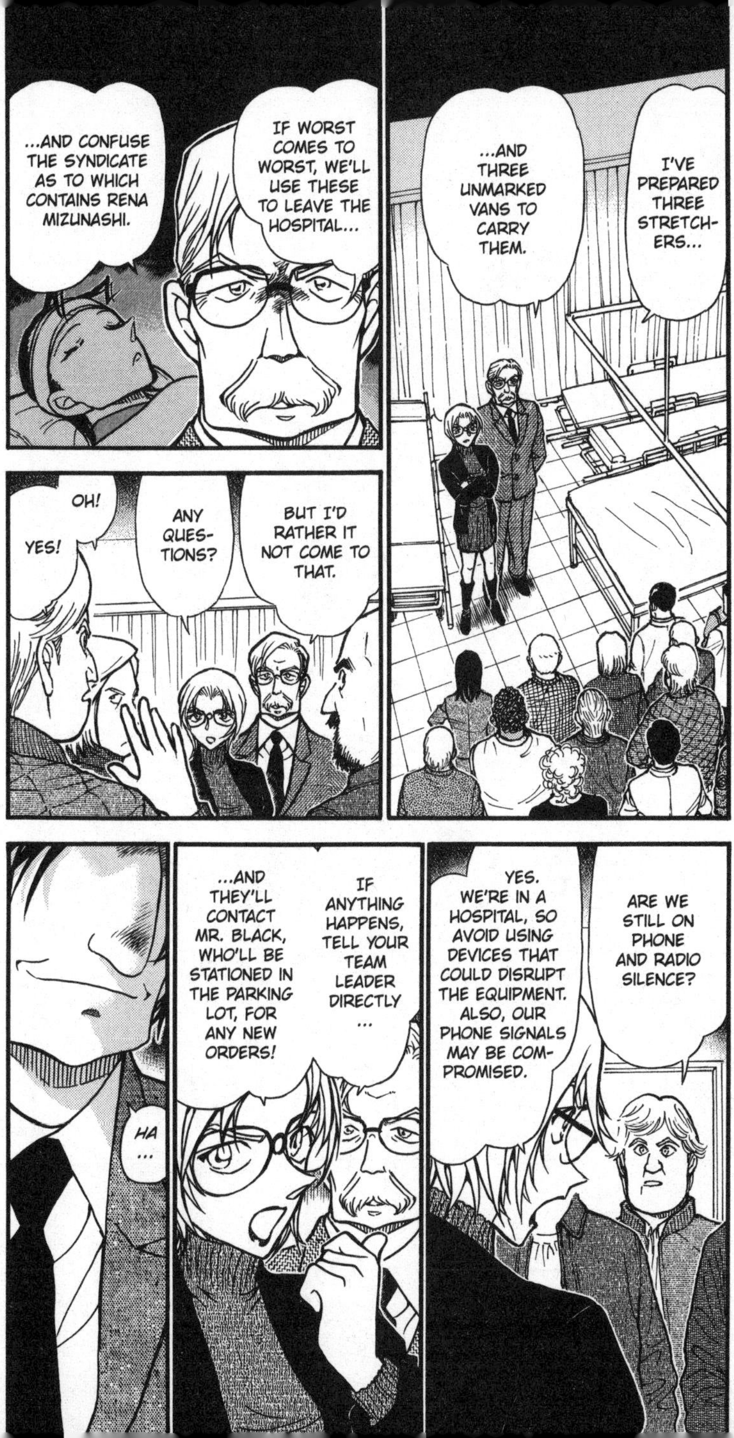
I'VE PREPARED THREE STRETCHERS...
...AND THREE UNMARKED VANS TO CARRY THEM.
IF WORST COMES TO WORST, WE'LL USE THESE TO LEAVE THE HOSPITAL...
...AND CONFUSE THE SYNDICATE AS TO WHICH CONTAINS RENA MIZUNASHI.
BUT I'D RATHER IT NOT COME TO THAT.
ANY QUESTIONS?
OH!
YES!
ARE WE STILL ON PHONE AND RADIO SILENCE?
YES. WE'RE IN A HOSPITAL, SO AVOID USING DEVICES THAT COULD DISRUPT THE EQUIPMENT. ALSO, OUR PHONE SIGNALS MAY BE COMPROMISED.
IF ANYTHING HAPPENS, TELL YOUR TEAM LEADER DIRECTLY...
...AND THEY'LL CONTACT MR. BLACK, WHO'LL BE STATIONED IN THE PARKING LOT, FOR ANY NEW ORDERS!
HA...

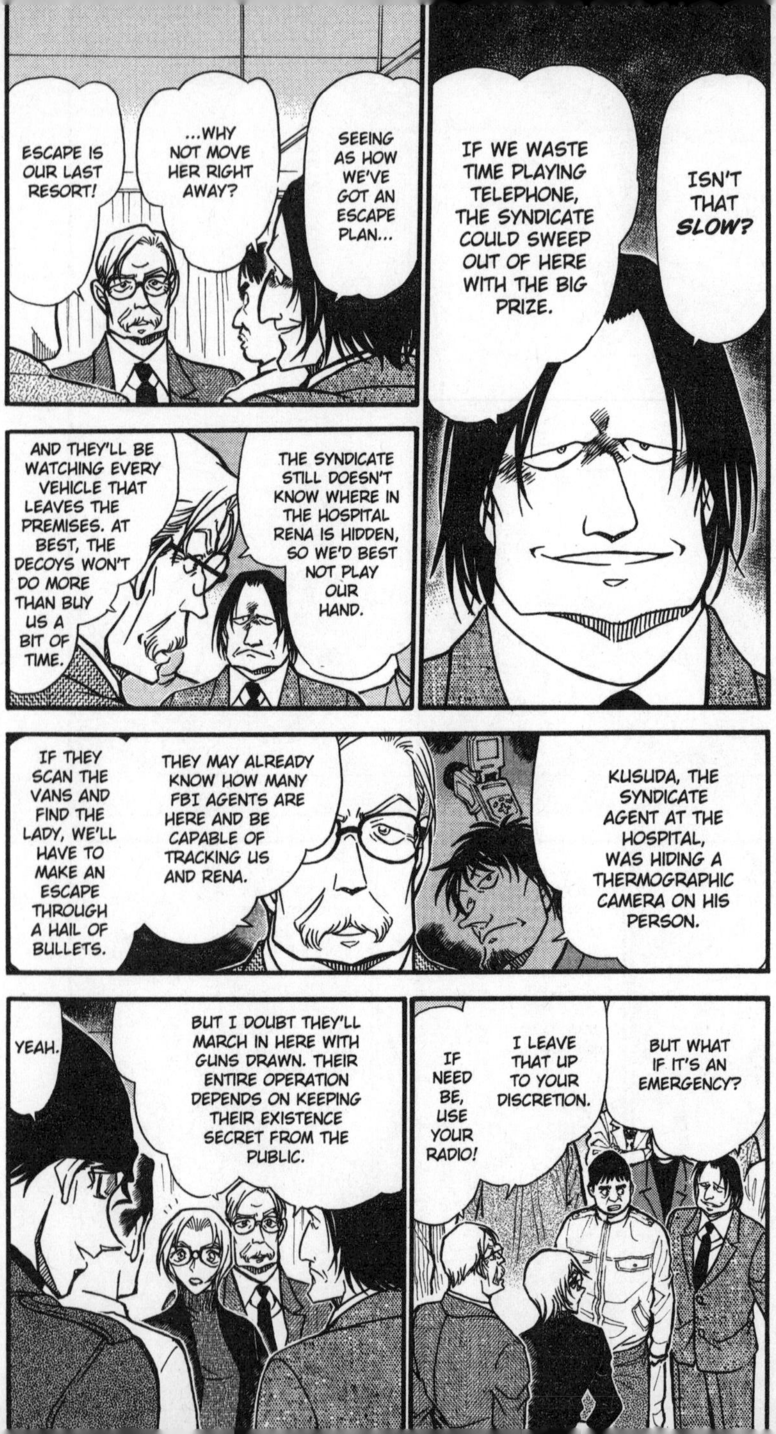
ISN'T THAT *SLOW?*
IF WE WASTE TIME PLAYING TELEPHONE, THE SYNDICATE COULD SWEEP OUT OF HERE WITH THE BIG PRIZE.
SEEING AS HOW WE'VE GOT AN ESCAPE PLAN...
...WHY NOT MOVE HER RIGHT AWAY?
ESCAPE IS OUR LAST RESORT!
THE SYNDICATE STILL DOESN'T KNOW WHERE IN THE HOSPITAL RENA IS HIDDEN, SO WE'D BEST NOT PLAY OUR HAND.
AND THEY'LL BE WATCHING EVERY VEHICLE THAT LEAVES THE PREMISES. AT BEST, THE DECOYS WON'T DO MORE THAN BUY US A BIT OF TIME.
KUSUDA, THE SYNDICATE AGENT AT THE HOSPITAL, WAS HIDING A THERMOGRAPHIC CAMERA ON HIS PERSON.
THEY MAY ALREADY KNOW HOW MANY FBI AGENTS ARE HERE AND BE CAPABLE OF TRACKING US AND RENA.
IF THEY SCAN THE VANS AND FIND THE LADY, WE'LL HAVE TO MAKE AN ESCAPE THROUGH A HAIL OF BULLETS.
BUT WHAT IF IT'S AN EMERGENCY?
I LEAVE THAT UP TO YOUR DISCRETION.
IF NEED BE, USE YOUR RADIO!
BUT I DOUBT THEY'LL MARCH IN HERE WITH GUNS DRAWN. THEIR ENTIRE OPERATION DEPENDS ON KEEPING THEIR EXISTENCE SECRET FROM THE PUBLIC.
YEAH.

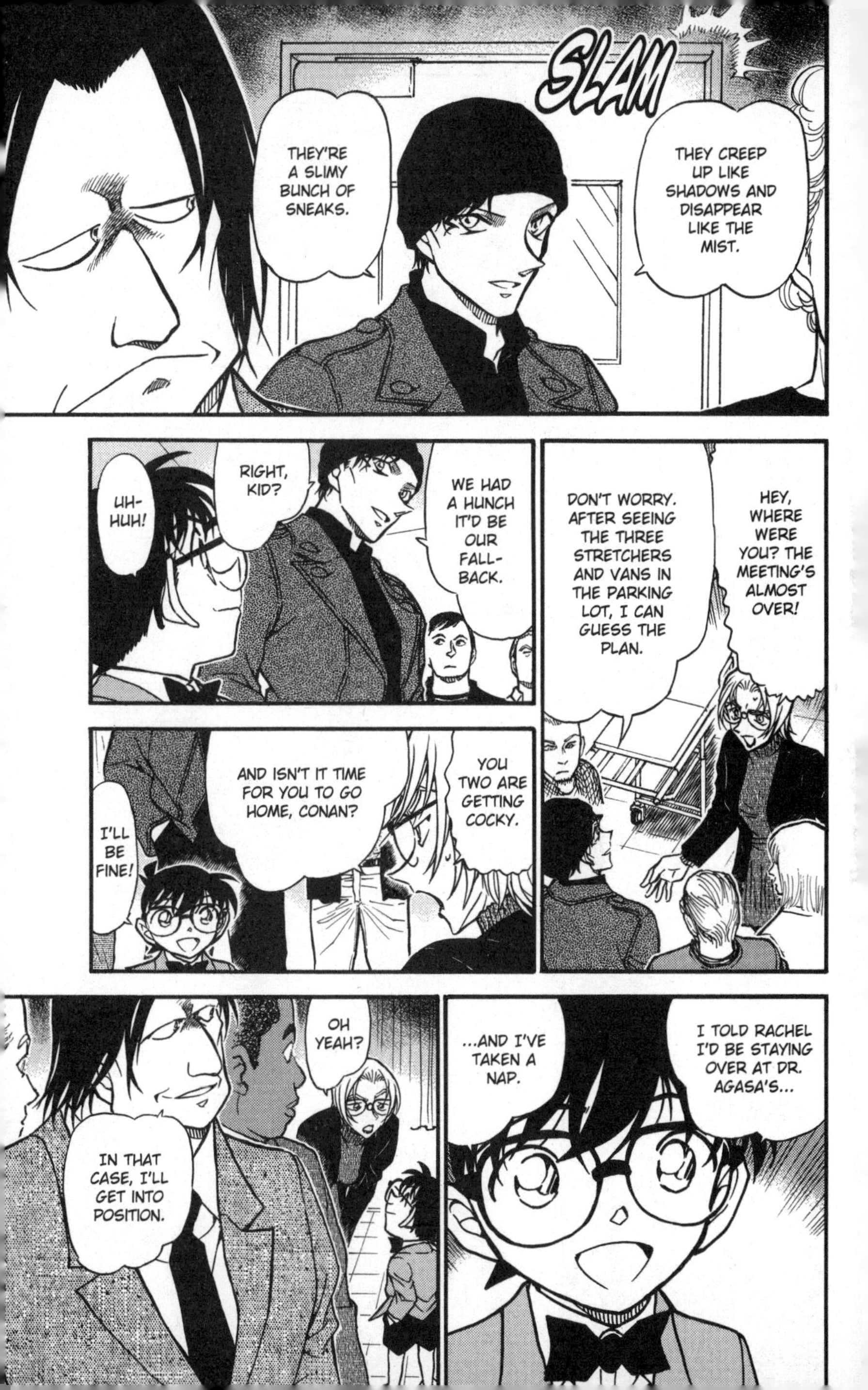
SLAM
THEY CREEP UP LIKE SHADOWS AND DISAPPEAR LIKE THE MIST.
THEY'RE A SLIMY BUNCH OF SNEAKS.
HEY, WHERE WERE YOU? THE MEETING'S ALMOST OVER!
DON'T WORRY. AFTER SEEING THE THREE STRETCHERS AND VANS IN THE PARKING LOT, I CAN GUESS THE PLAN.
WE HAD A HUNCH IT'D BE OUR FALL-BACK.
RIGHT, KID?
UH-HUH!
YOU TWO ARE GETTING COCKY.
AND ISN'T IT TIME FOR YOU TO GO HOME, CONAN?
I'LL BE FINE!
I TOLD RACHEL I'D BE STAYING OVER AT DR. AGASA'S...
...AND I'VE TAKEN A NAP.
OH YEAH?
IN THAT CASE, I'LL GET INTO POSITION.

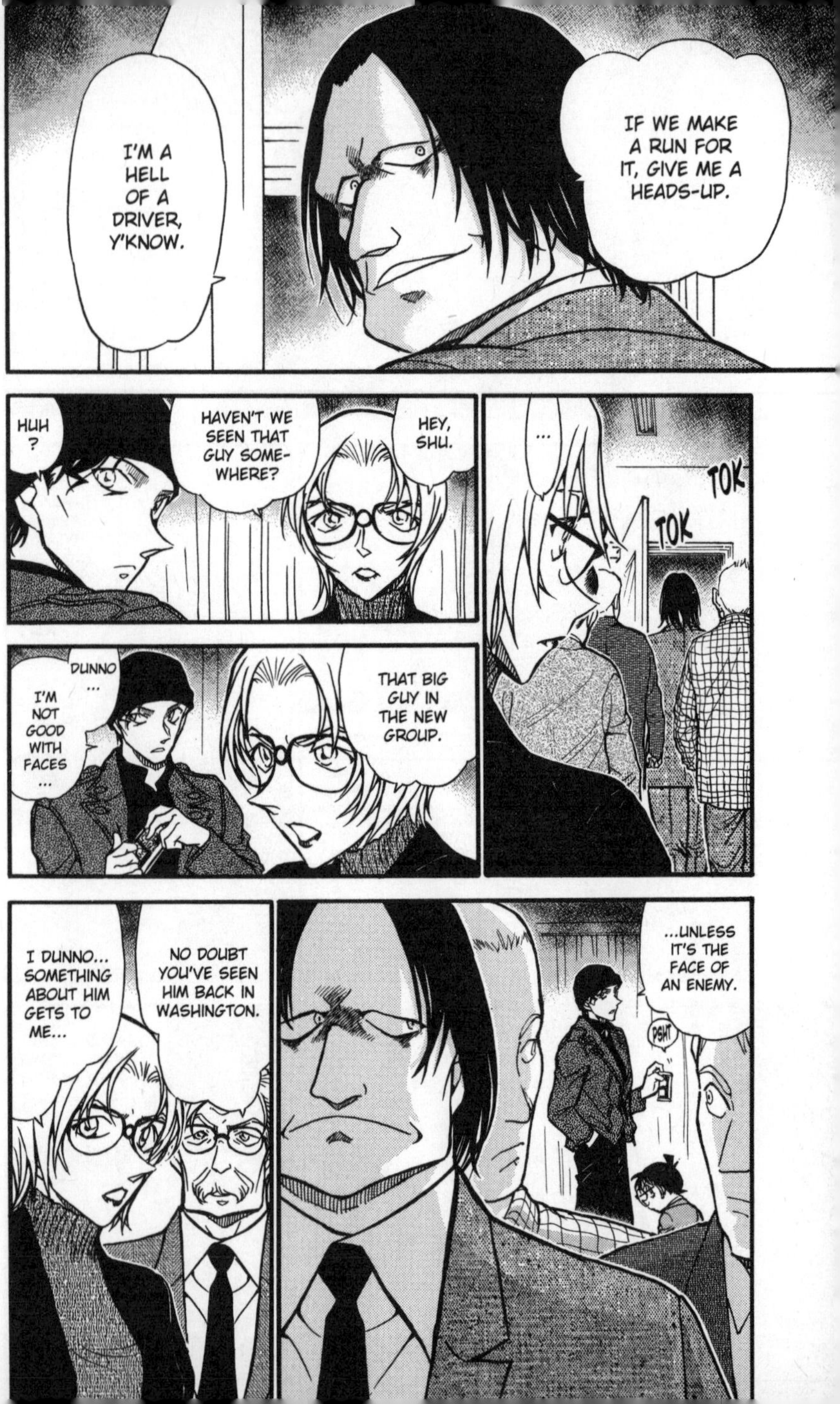
IF WE MAKE A RUN FOR IT, GIVE ME A HEADS-UP.
I'M A HELL OF A DRIVER, Y'KNOW.
...
TOK
TOK
HEY, SHU.
HAVEN'T WE SEEN THAT GUY SOME-WHERE?
HUH?
THAT BIG GUY IN THE NEW GROUP.
DUNNO...
I'M NOT GOOD WITH FACES...
...UNLESS IT'S THE FACE OF AN ENEMY.
PSHT
NO DOUBT YOU'VE SEEN HIM BACK IN WASHINGTON.
I DUNNO... SOMETHING ABOUT HIM GETS TO ME...

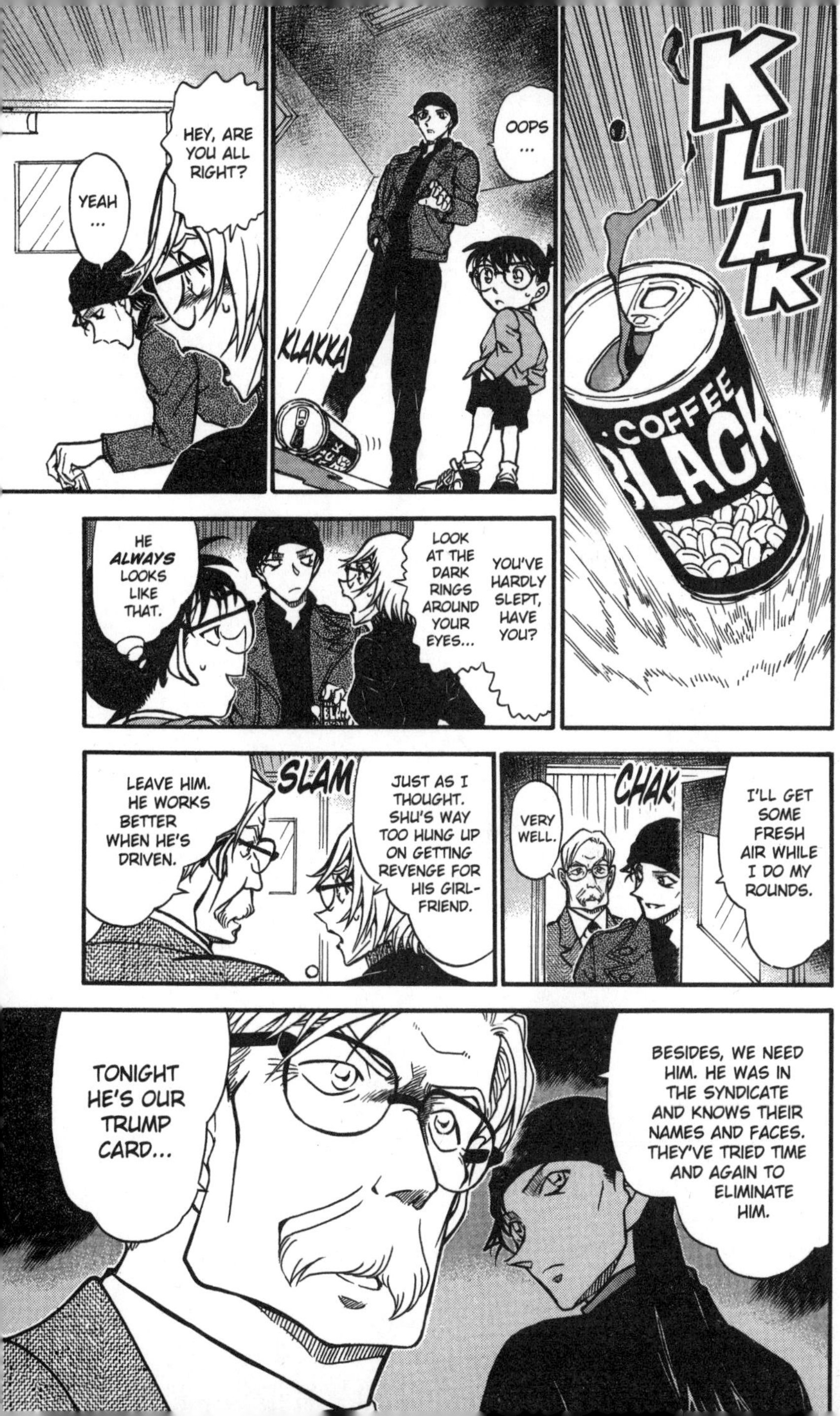
KLAK
COFFEE BLACK
OOPS ...
KLAKKA
HEY, ARE YOU ALL RIGHT?
YEAH ...
YOU'VE HARDLY SLEPT, HAVE YOU?
LOOK AT THE DARK RINGS AROUND YOUR EYES...
HE ALWAYS LOOKS LIKE THAT.
CHAK
I'LL GET SOME FRESH AIR WHILE I DO MY ROUNDS.
VERY WELL.
SLAM
JUST AS I THOUGHT. SHU'S WAY TOO HUNG UP ON GETTING REVENGE FOR HIS GIRL-FRIEND.
LEAVE HIM. HE WORKS BETTER WHEN HE'S DRIVEN.
BESIDES, WE NEED HIM. HE WAS IN THE SYNDICATE AND KNOWS THEIR NAMES AND FACES. THEY'VE TRIED TIME AND AGAIN TO ELIMINATE HIM.
TONIGHT HE'S OUR TRUMP CARD...

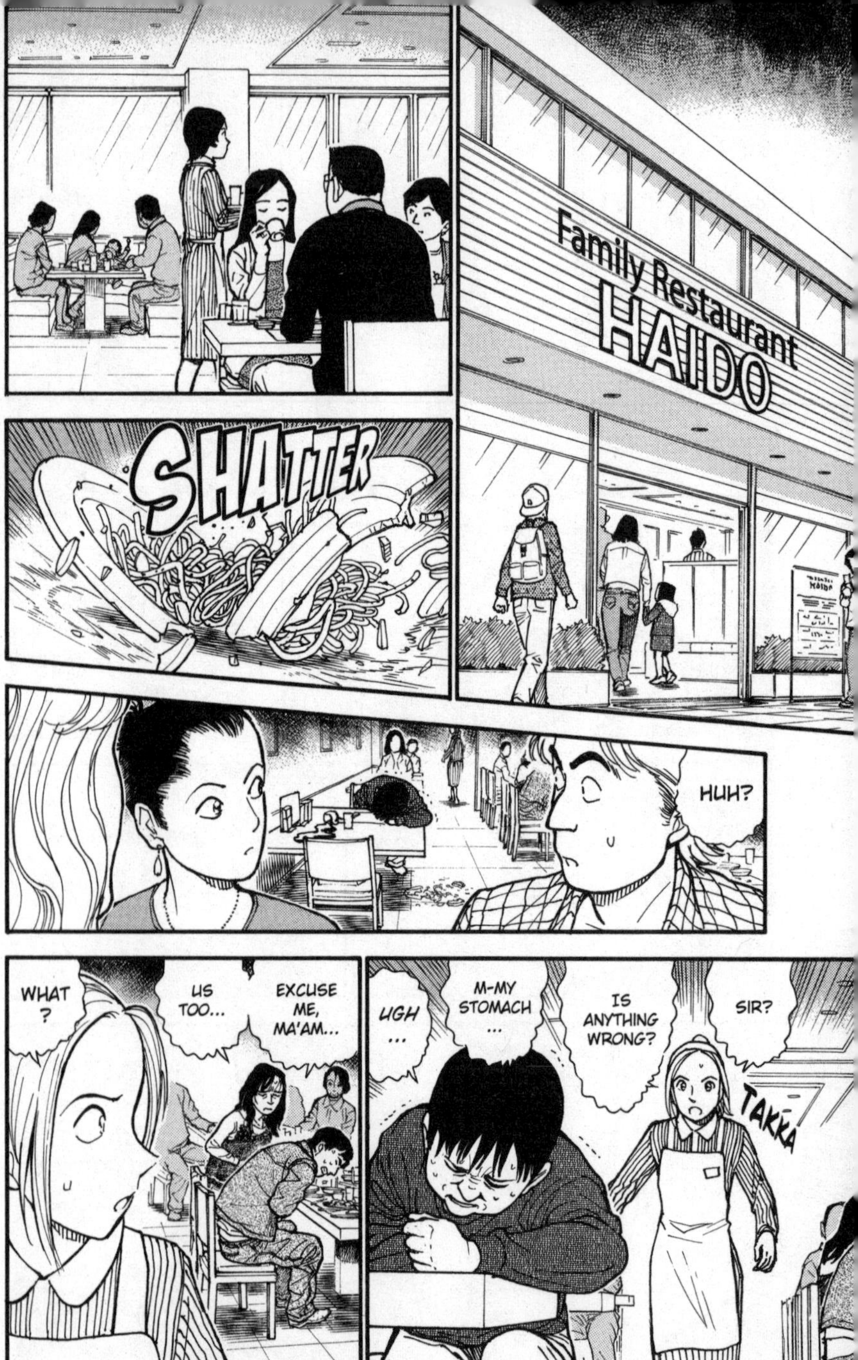
Family Restaurant
HAIDO
SHATTER
HUH?
SIR?
IS ANYTHING WRONG?
TAKKA
M-MY STOMACH...
UGH...
EXCUSE ME, MA'AM...
US TOO...
WHAT?

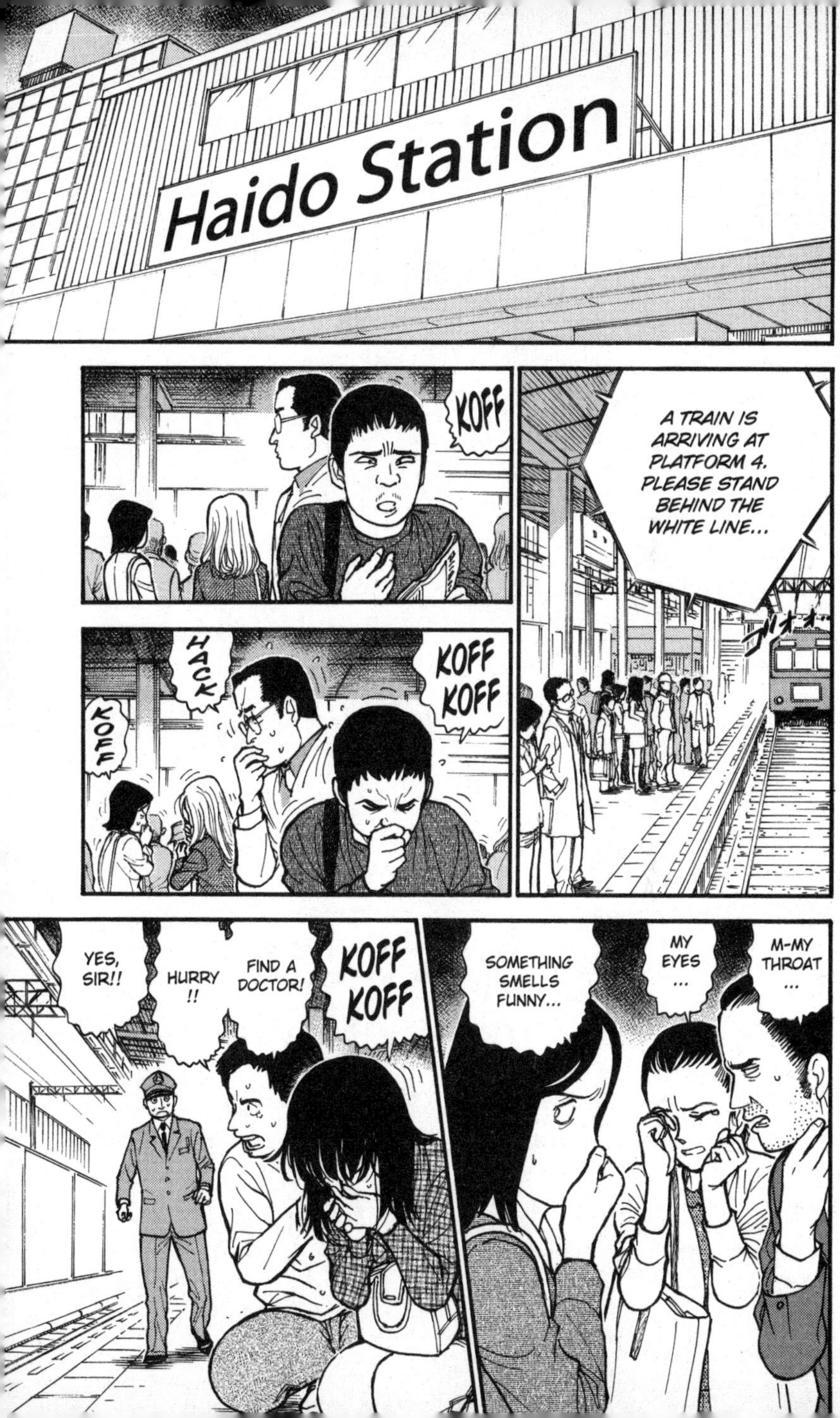
Haido Station
A TRAIN IS ARRIVING AT PLATFORM 4. PLEASE STAND BEHIND THE WHITE LINE...
KOFF
KOFF KOFF
HACK
KOFF
M-MY THROAT...
MY EYES...
SOMETHING SMELLS FUNNY...
KOFF KOFF
FIND A DOCTOR!
HURRY!!
YES, SIR!!

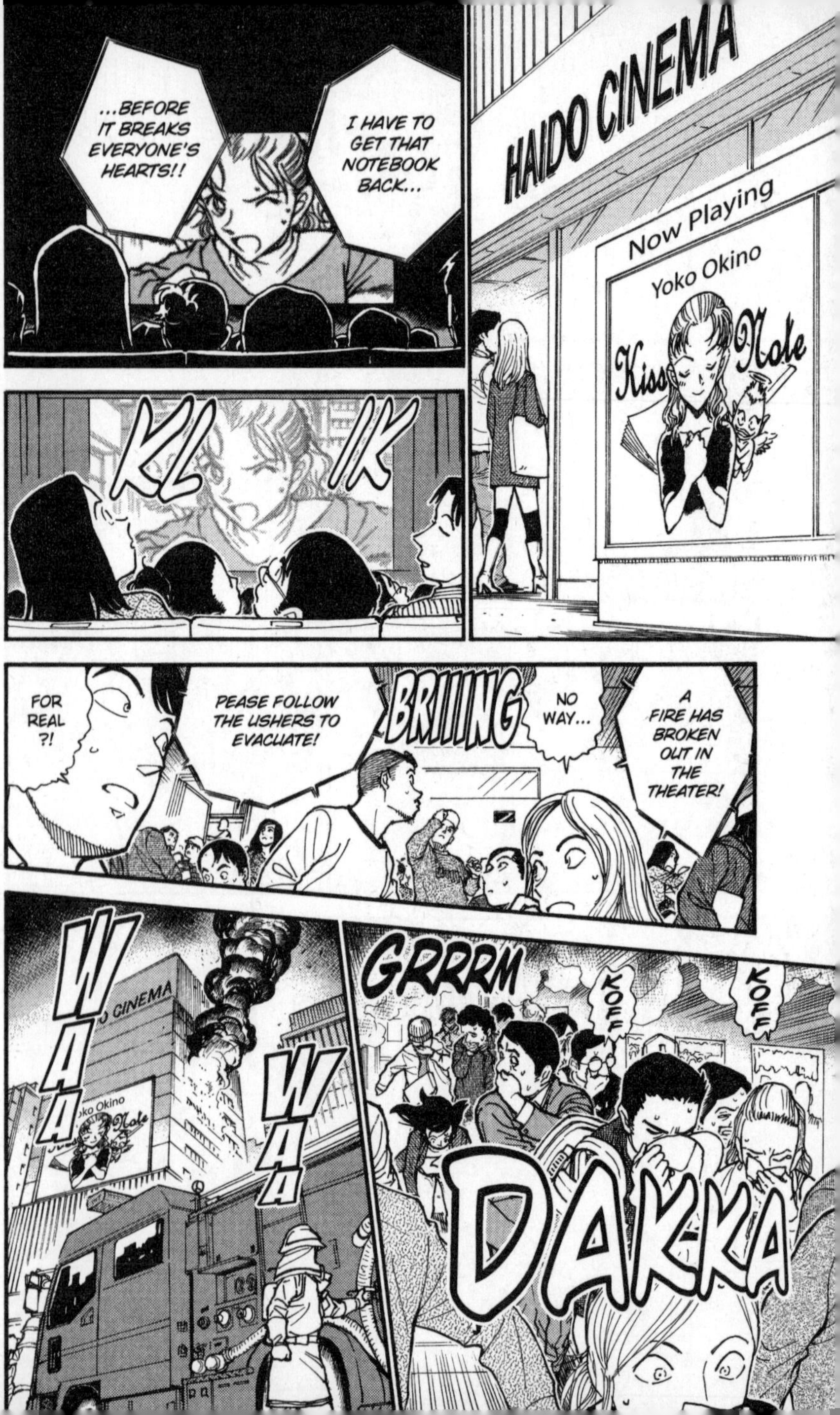
HAIDO CINEMA
Now Playing
Yoko Okino
Kiss Note
I HAVE TO GET THAT NOTEBOOK BACK...
...BEFORE IT BREAKS EVERYONE'S HEARTS!!
KL IK
A FIRE HAS BROKEN OUT IN THE THEATER!
NO WAY...
BRIIING
PEASE FOLLOW THE USHERS TO EVACUATE!
FOR REAL ?!
KOFF
KOFF
GRRRM
DAKKA
WAAA
WAA

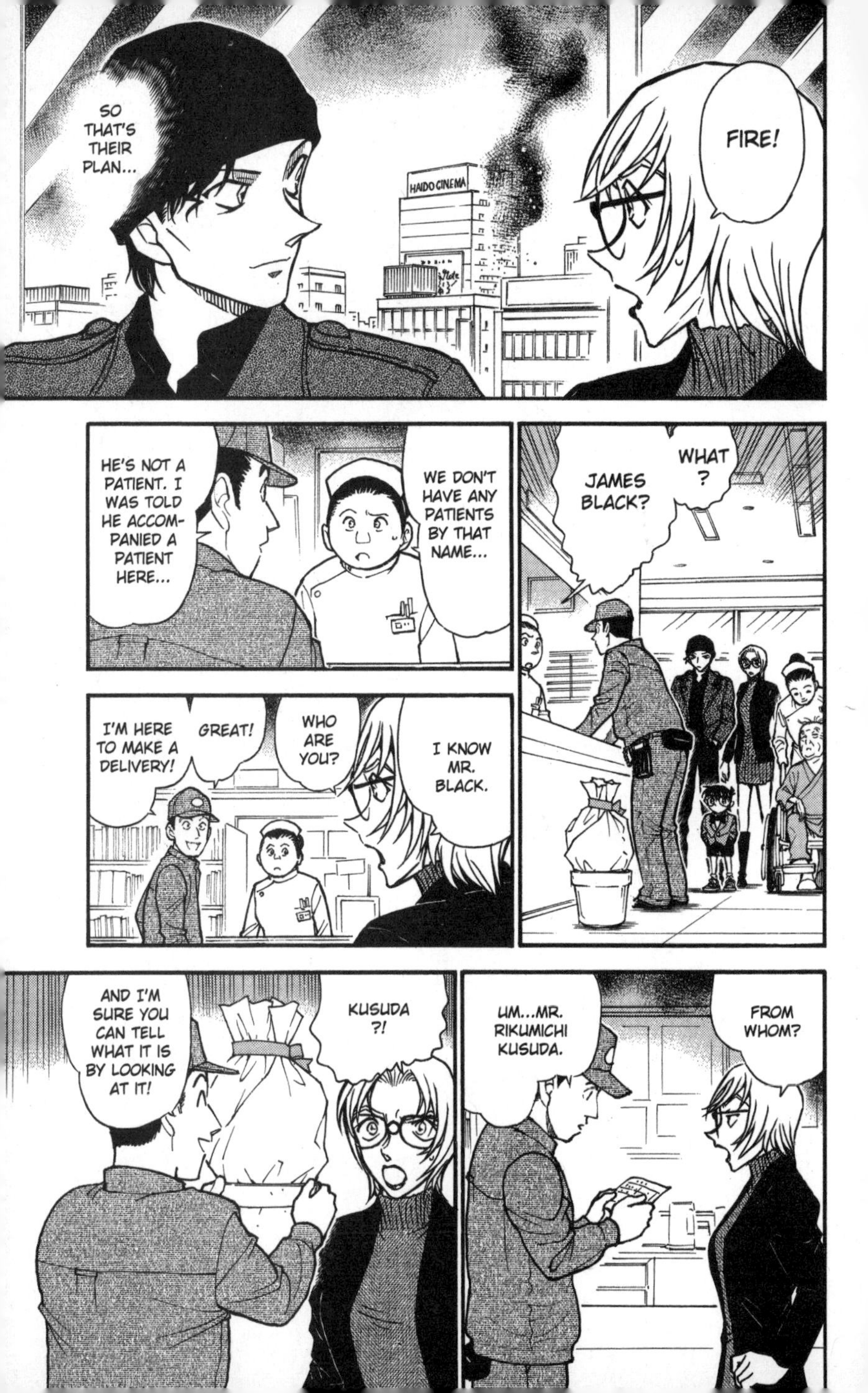
FIRE!
HAIDO CINEMA
SO THAT'S THEIR PLAN...
WHAT?
JAMES BLACK?
WE DON'T HAVE ANY PATIENTS BY THAT NAME...
HE'S NOT A PATIENT. I WAS TOLD HE ACCOMPANIED A PATIENT HERE...
I KNOW MR. BLACK.
WHO ARE YOU?
GREAT!
I'M HERE TO MAKE A DELIVERY!
FROM WHOM?
UM...MR. RIKUMICHI KUSUDA.
KUSUDA?!
AND I'M SURE YOU CAN TELL WHAT IT IS BY LOOKING AT IT!

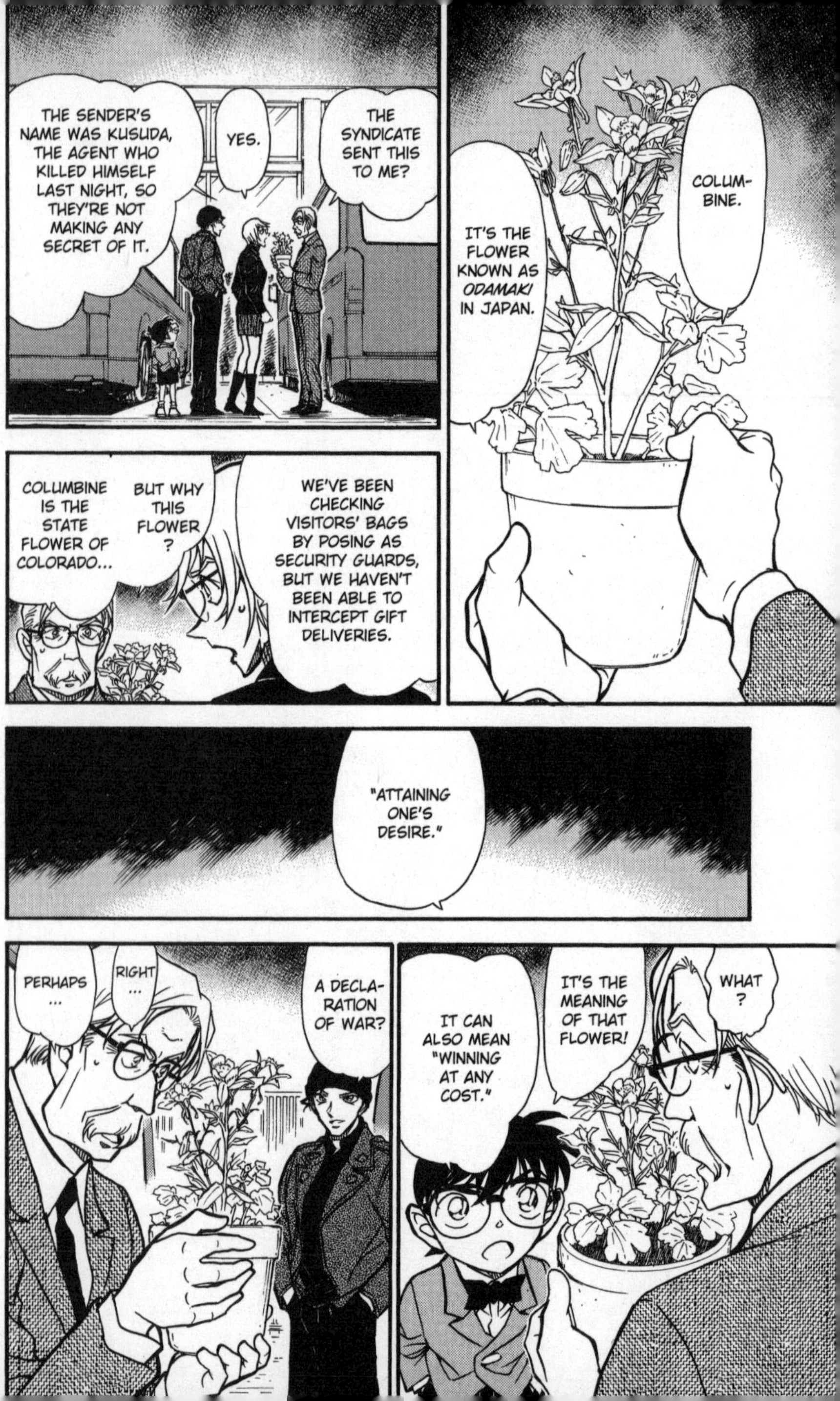
COLUMBINE.
IT'S THE FLOWER KNOWN AS *ODAMAKI* IN JAPAN.
THE SYNDICATE SENT THIS TO ME?
YES.
THE SENDER'S NAME WAS KUSUDA, THE AGENT WHO KILLED HIMSELF LAST NIGHT, SO THEY'RE NOT MAKING ANY SECRET OF IT.
WE'VE BEEN CHECKING VISITORS' BAGS BY POSING AS SECURITY GUARDS, BUT WE HAVEN'T BEEN ABLE TO INTERCEPT GIFT DELIVERIES.
BUT WHY THIS FLOWER?
COLUMBINE IS THE STATE FLOWER OF COLORADO...
"ATTAINING ONE'S DESIRE."
WHAT?
IT'S THE MEANING OF THAT FLOWER!
IT CAN ALSO MEAN "WINNING AT ANY COST."
A DECLARATION OF WAR?
RIGHT...
PERHAPS...

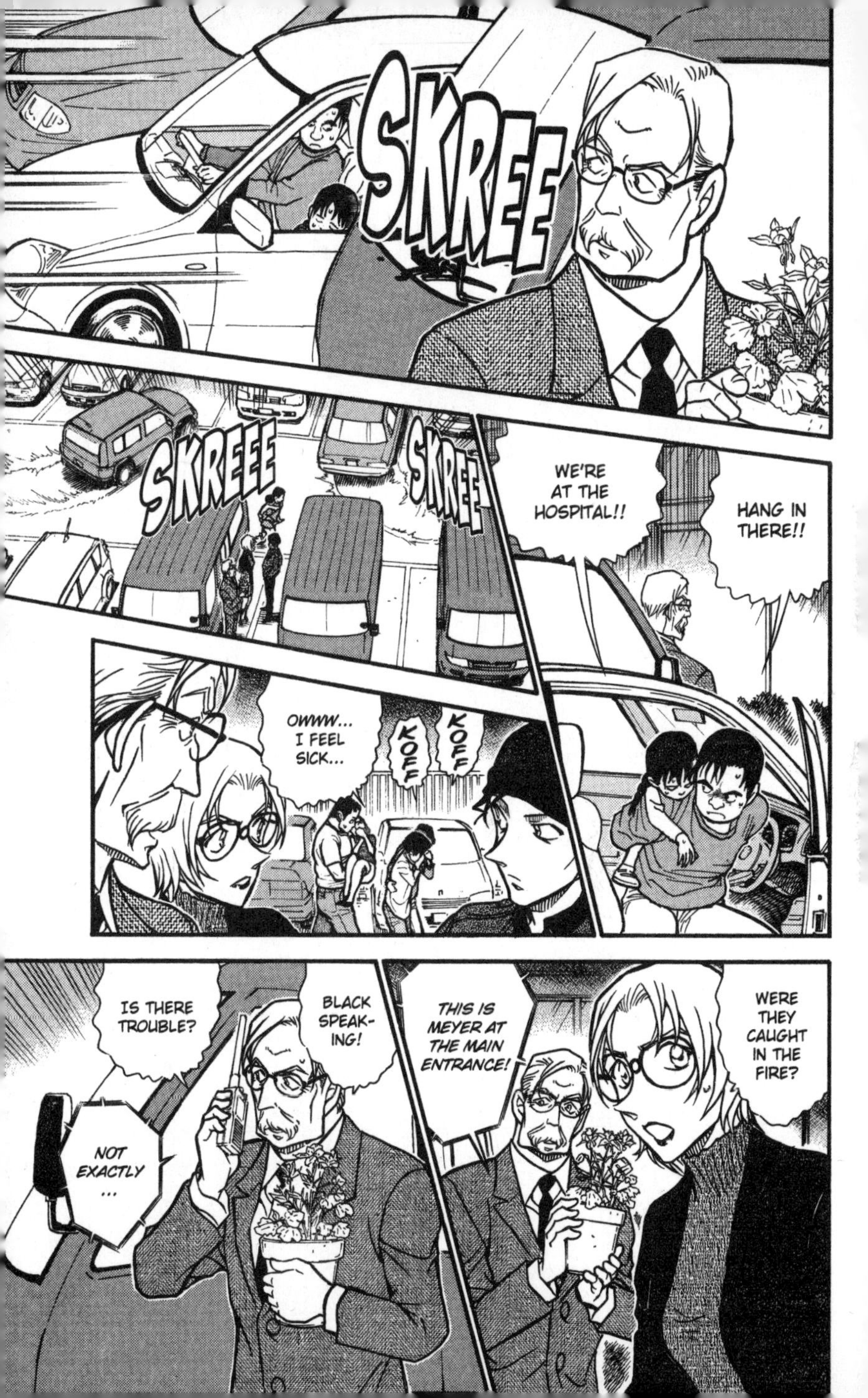
SKREE
HANG IN THERE!!
WE'RE AT THE HOSPITAL!!
SKREE
SKREEE
KOFF
KOFF
OWWW... I FEEL SICK...
WERE THEY CAUGHT IN THE FIRE?
THIS IS MEYER AT THE MAIN ENTRANCE!
BLACK SPEAK-ING!
IS THERE TROUBLE?
NOT EXACTLY ...

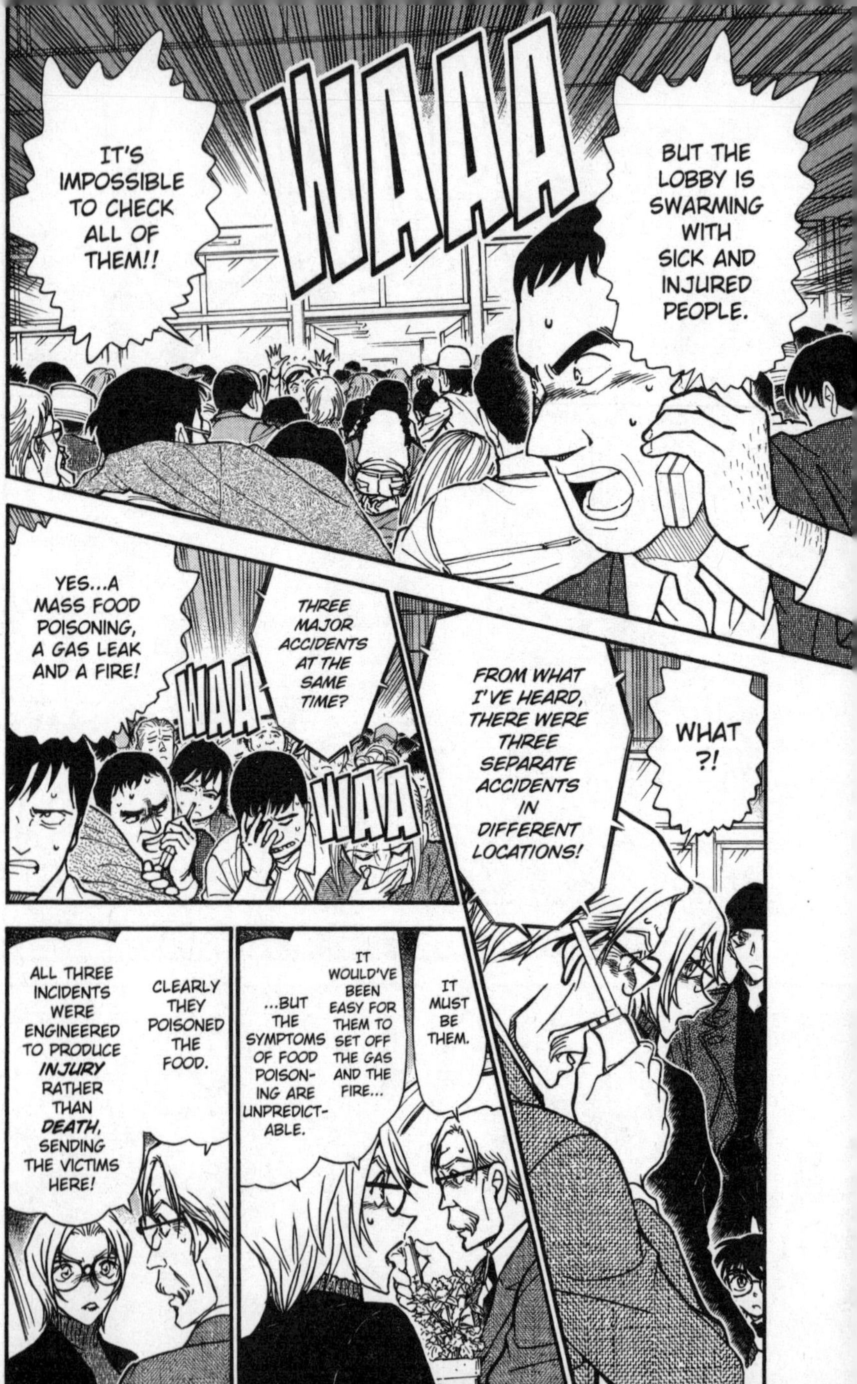
BUT THE LOBBY IS SWARMING WITH SICK AND INJURED PEOPLE.
WAAA
IT'S IMPOSSIBLE TO CHECK ALL OF THEM!!
WHAT ?!
FROM WHAT I'VE HEARD, THERE WERE THREE SEPARATE ACCIDENTS IN DIFFERENT LOCATIONS!
THREE MAJOR ACCIDENTS AT THE SAME TIME?
YES...A MASS FOOD POISONING, A GAS LEAK AND A FIRE!
WAA
WAA
IT MUST BE THEM.
IT WOULD'VE BEEN EASY FOR THEM TO SET OFF THE GAS AND THE FIRE...
...BUT THE SYMPTOMS OF FOOD POISON-ING ARE UNPREDICT-ABLE.
CLEARLY THEY POISONED THE FOOD.
ALL THREE INCIDENTS WERE ENGINEERED TO PRODUCE *INJURY* RATHER THAN *DEATH*, SENDING THE VICTIMS HERE!

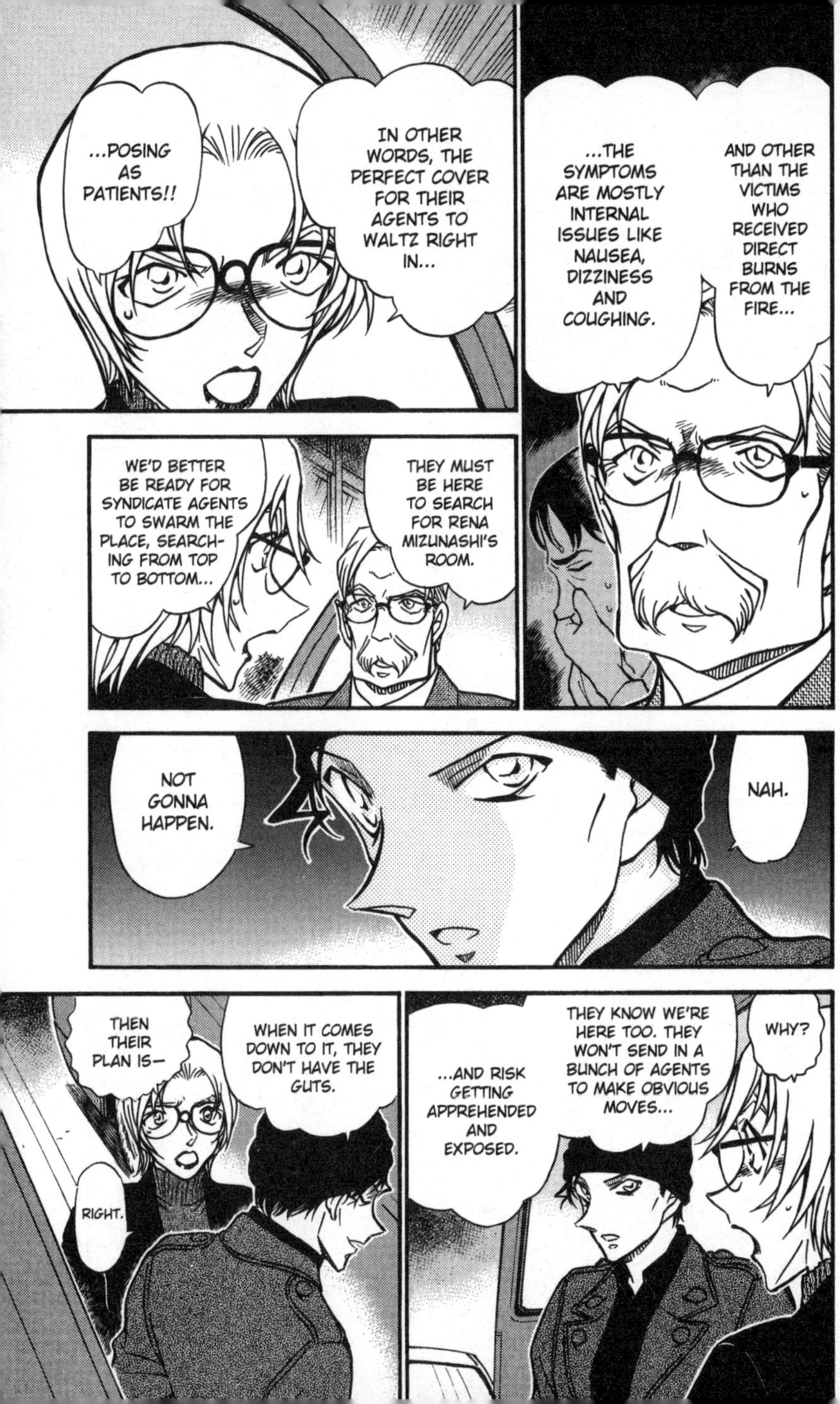
AND OTHER THAN THE VICTIMS WHO RECEIVED DIRECT BURNS FROM THE FIRE...
...THE SYMPTOMS ARE MOSTLY INTERNAL ISSUES LIKE NAUSEA, DIZZINESS AND COUGHING.
IN OTHER WORDS, THE PERFECT COVER FOR THEIR AGENTS TO WALTZ RIGHT IN...
...POSING AS PATIENTS!!
THEY MUST BE HERE TO SEARCH FOR RENA MIZUNASHI'S ROOM.
WE'D BETTER BE READY FOR SYNDICATE AGENTS TO SWARM THE PLACE, SEARCHING FROM TOP TO BOTTOM...
NAH.
NOT GONNA HAPPEN.
WHY?
THEY KNOW WE'RE HERE TOO. THEY WON'T SEND IN A BUNCH OF AGENTS TO MAKE OBVIOUS MOVES...
...AND RISK GETTING APPREHENDED AND EXPOSED.
WHEN IT COMES DOWN TO IT, THEY DON'T HAVE THE GUTS.
THEN THEIR PLAN IS—
RIGHT.

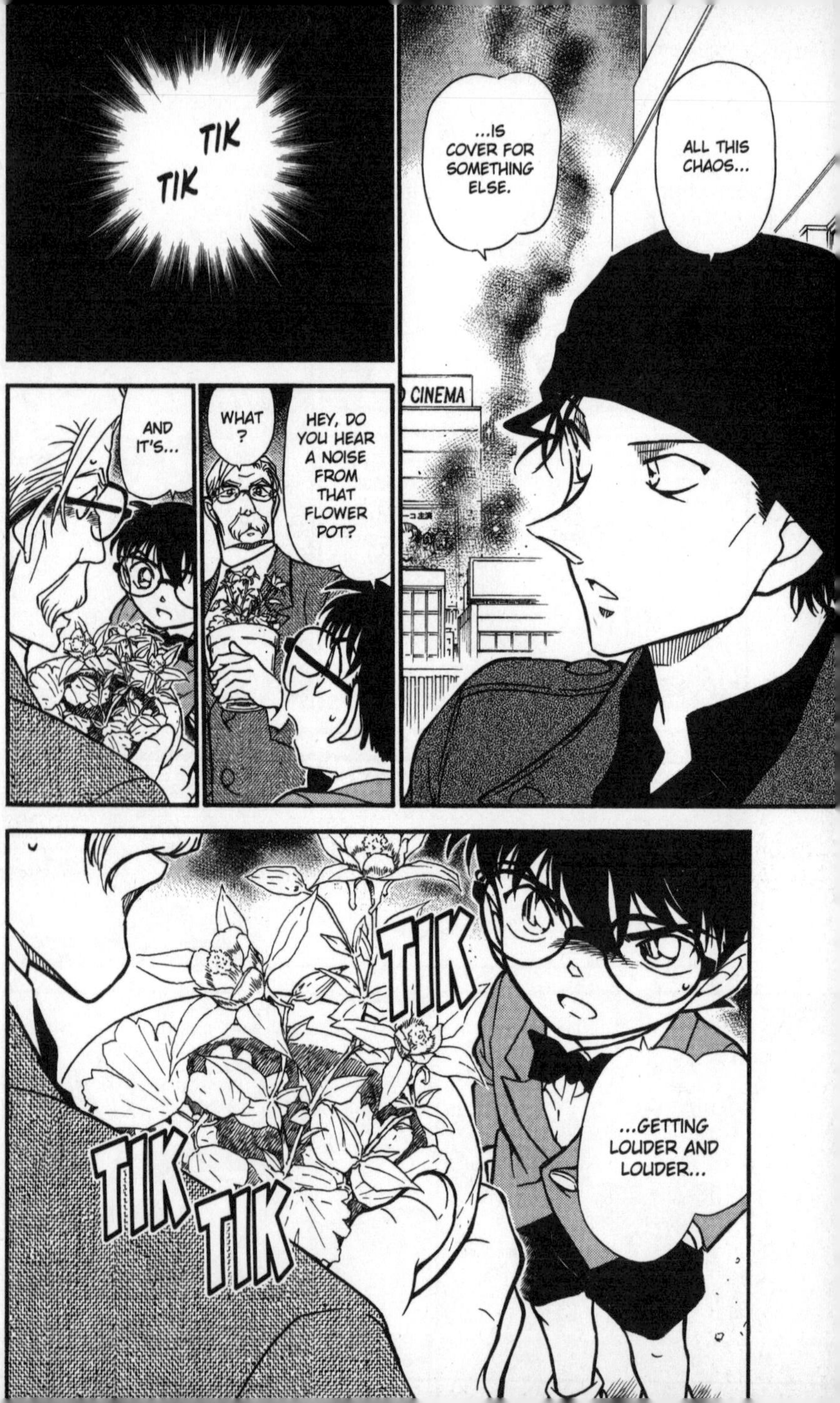

ALL THIS CHAOS...
...IS COVER FOR SOMETHING ELSE.
CINEMA
TIK
TIK
HEY, DO YOU HEAR A NOISE FROM THAT FLOWER POT?
WHAT?
AND IT'S...
TIK
...GETTING LOUDER AND LOUDER...
TIK
TIK

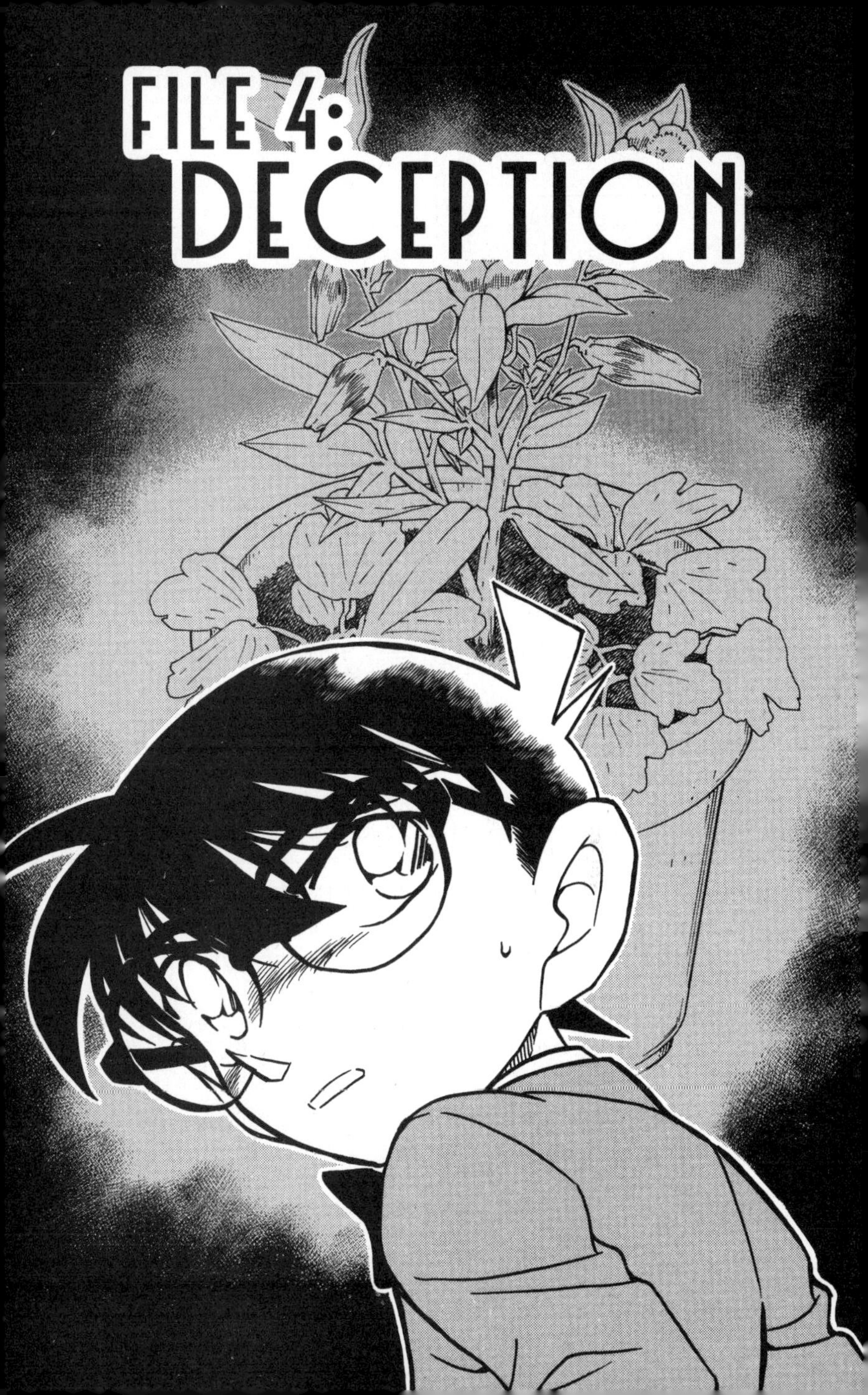
FILE 4:
DECEPTION

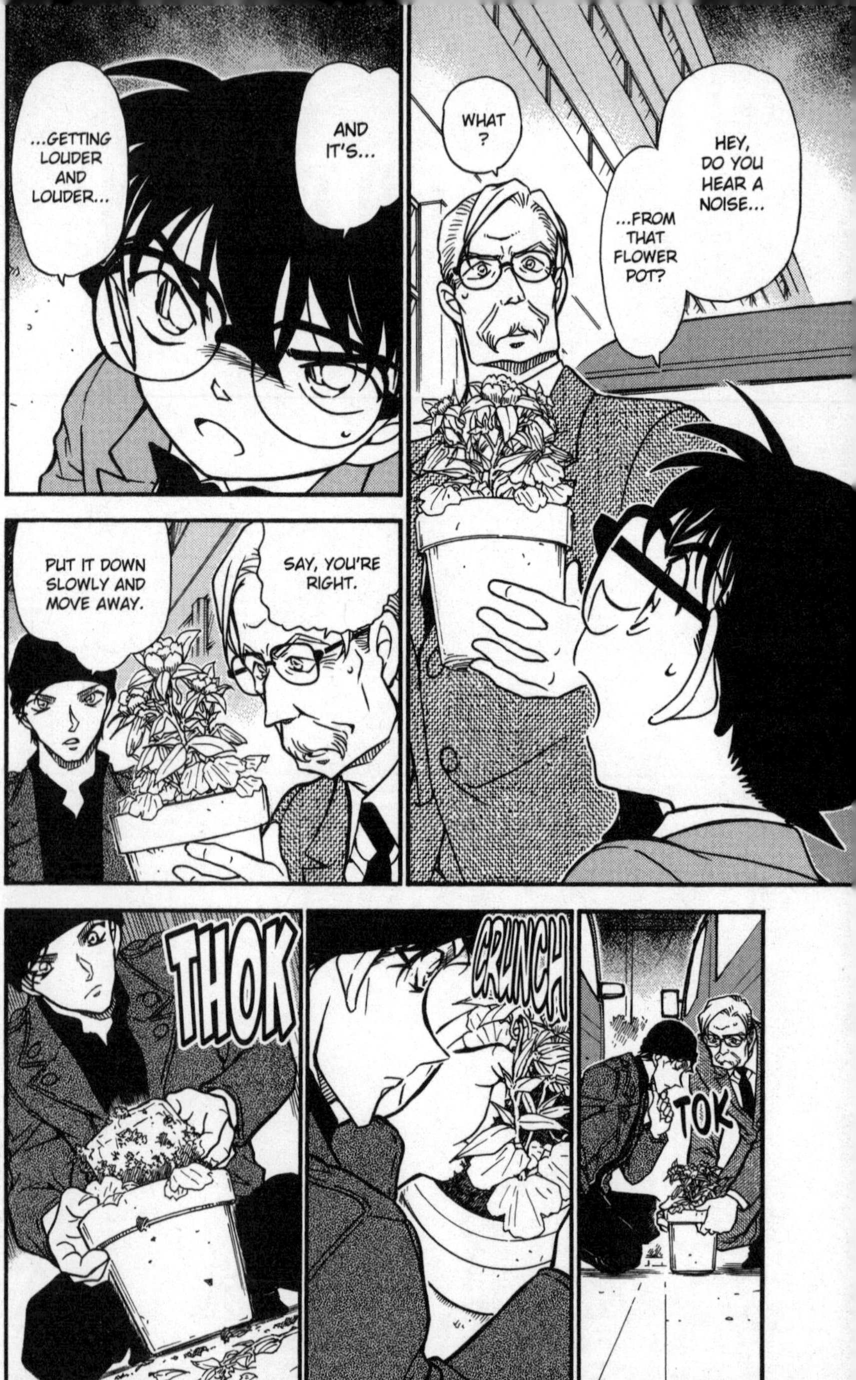
HEY, DO YOU HEAR A NOISE...
...FROM THAT FLOWER POT?
WHAT?
AND IT'S...
...GETTING LOUDER AND LOUDER...
SAY, YOU'RE RIGHT.
PUT IT DOWN SLOWLY AND MOVE AWAY.
TOK
CRUNCH
THOK

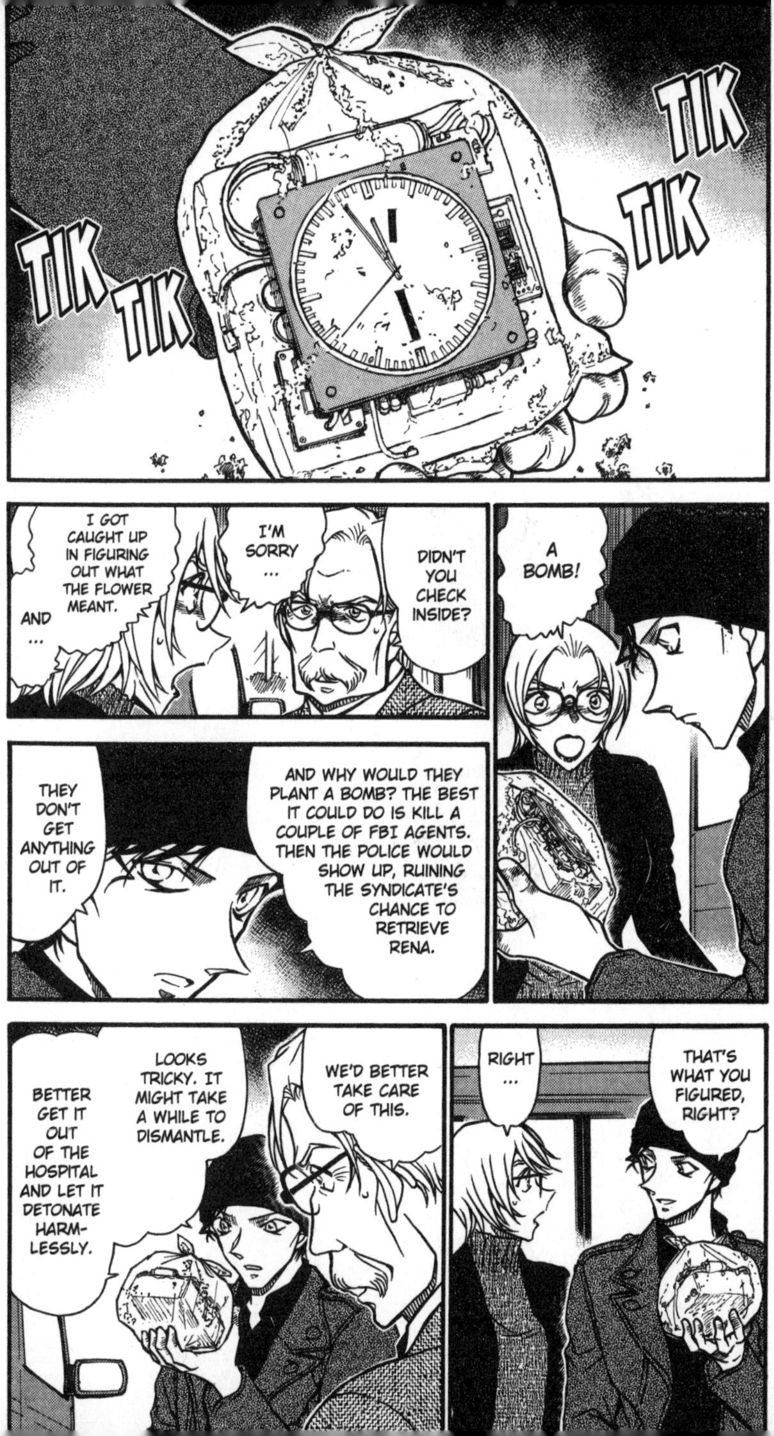
TIK
TIK
TIK
TIK
A BOMB!
DIDN'T YOU CHECK INSIDE?
I'M SORRY ...
I GOT CAUGHT UP IN FIGURING OUT WHAT THE FLOWER MEANT.
AND ...
AND WHY WOULD THEY PLANT A BOMB? THE BEST IT COULD DO IS KILL A COUPLE OF FBI AGENTS. THEN THE POLICE WOULD SHOW UP, RUINING THE SYNDICATE'S CHANCE TO RETRIEVE RENA.
THEY DON'T GET ANYTHING OUT OF IT.
THAT'S WHAT YOU FIGURED, RIGHT?
RIGHT ...
WE'D BETTER TAKE CARE OF THIS.
LOOKS TRICKY. IT MIGHT TAKE A WHILE TO DISMANTLE.
BETTER GET IT OUT OF THE HOSPITAL AND LET IT DETONATE HARMLESSLY.

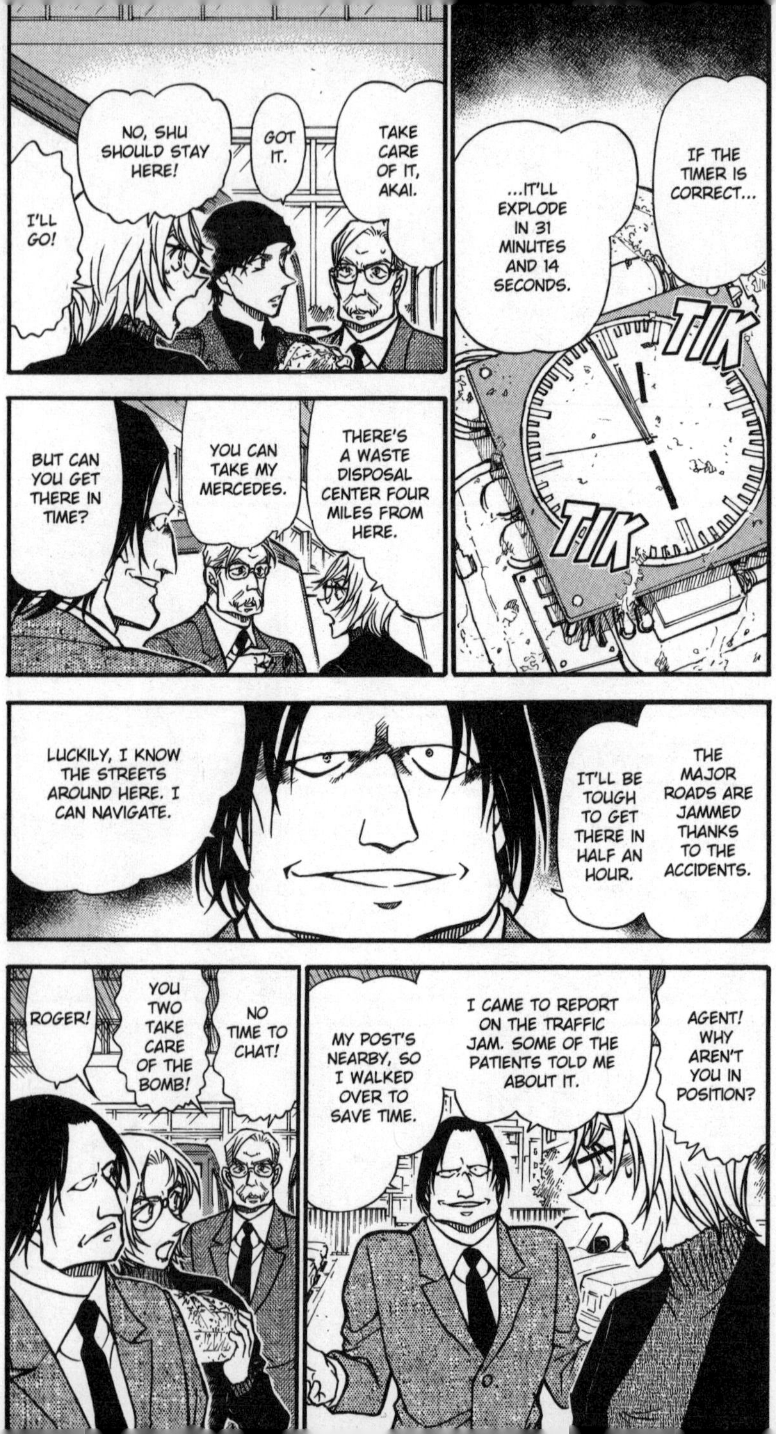
IF THE TIMER IS CORRECT...
...IT'LL EXPLODE IN 31 MINUTES AND 14 SECONDS.
TIK
TIK
TAKE CARE OF IT, AKAI.
GOT IT.
NO, SHU SHOULD STAY HERE!
I'LL GO!
THERE'S A WASTE DISPOSAL CENTER FOUR MILES FROM HERE.
YOU CAN TAKE MY MERCEDES.
BUT CAN YOU GET THERE IN TIME?
THE MAJOR ROADS ARE JAMMED THANKS TO THE ACCIDENTS.
IT'LL BE TOUGH TO GET THERE IN HALF AN HOUR.
LUCKILY, I KNOW THE STREETS AROUND HERE. I CAN NAVIGATE.
AGENT! WHY AREN'T YOU IN POSITION?
I CAME TO REPORT ON THE TRAFFIC JAM. SOME OF THE PATIENTS TOLD ME ABOUT IT.
MY POST'S NEARBY, SO I WALKED OVER TO SAVE TIME.
NO TIME TO CHAT!
YOU TWO TAKE CARE OF THE BOMB!
ROGER!

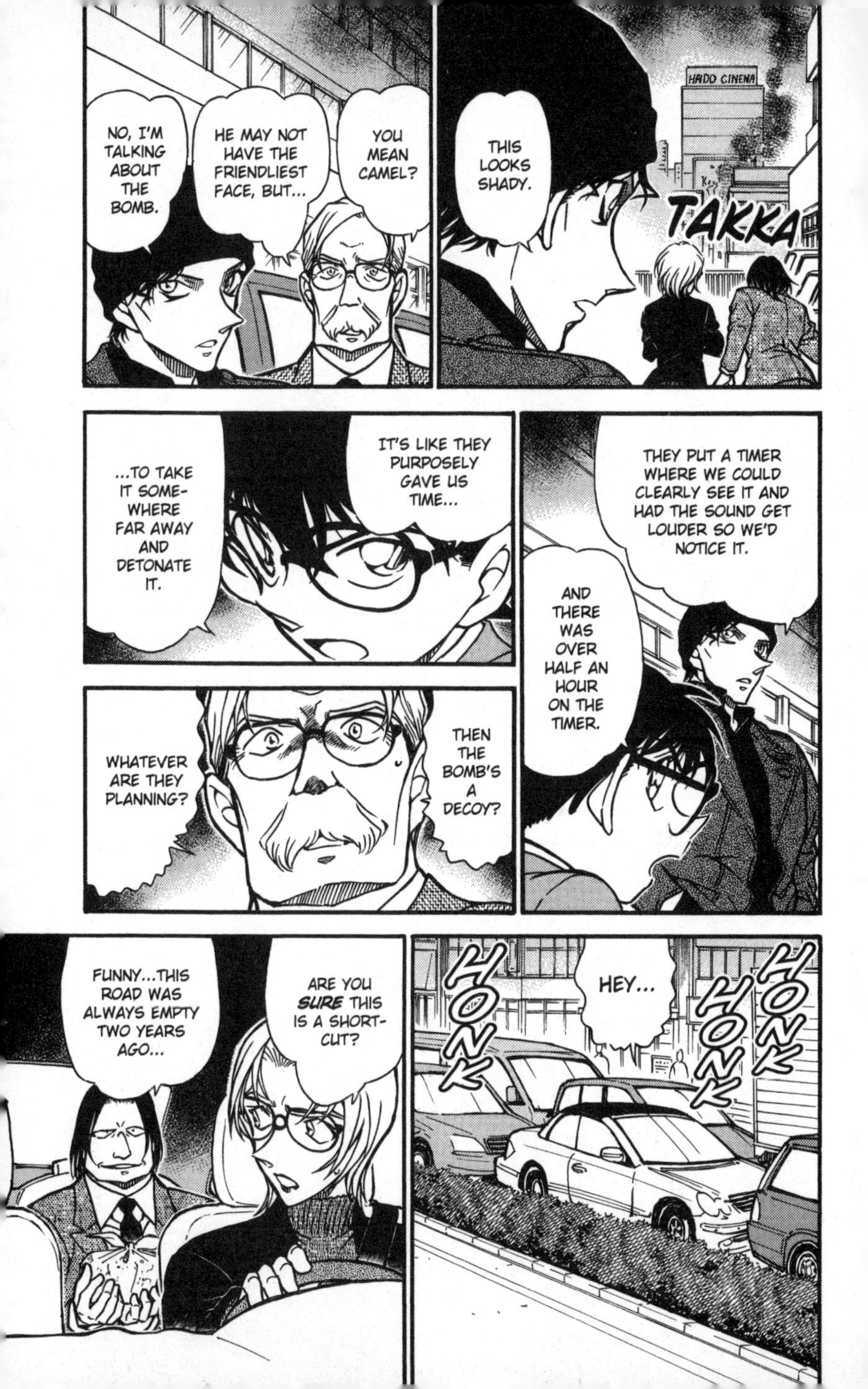
HAIDO CINEMA
THIS LOOKS SHADY.
TAKKA
YOU MEAN CAMEL?
HE MAY NOT HAVE THE FRIENDLIEST FACE, BUT...
NO, I'M TALKING ABOUT THE BOMB.
THEY PUT A TIMER WHERE WE COULD CLEARLY SEE IT AND HAD THE SOUND GET LOUDER SO WE'D NOTICE IT.
AND THERE WAS OVER HALF AN HOUR ON THE TIMER.
IT'S LIKE THEY PURPOSELY GAVE US TIME...
...TO TAKE IT SOMEWHERE FAR AWAY AND DETONATE IT.
THEN THE BOMB'S A DECOY?
WHATEVER ARE THEY PLANNING?
HONK HONK
HEY...
HONK
ARE YOU *SURE* THIS IS A SHORT-CUT?
FUNNY...THIS ROAD WAS ALWAYS EMPTY TWO YEARS AGO...

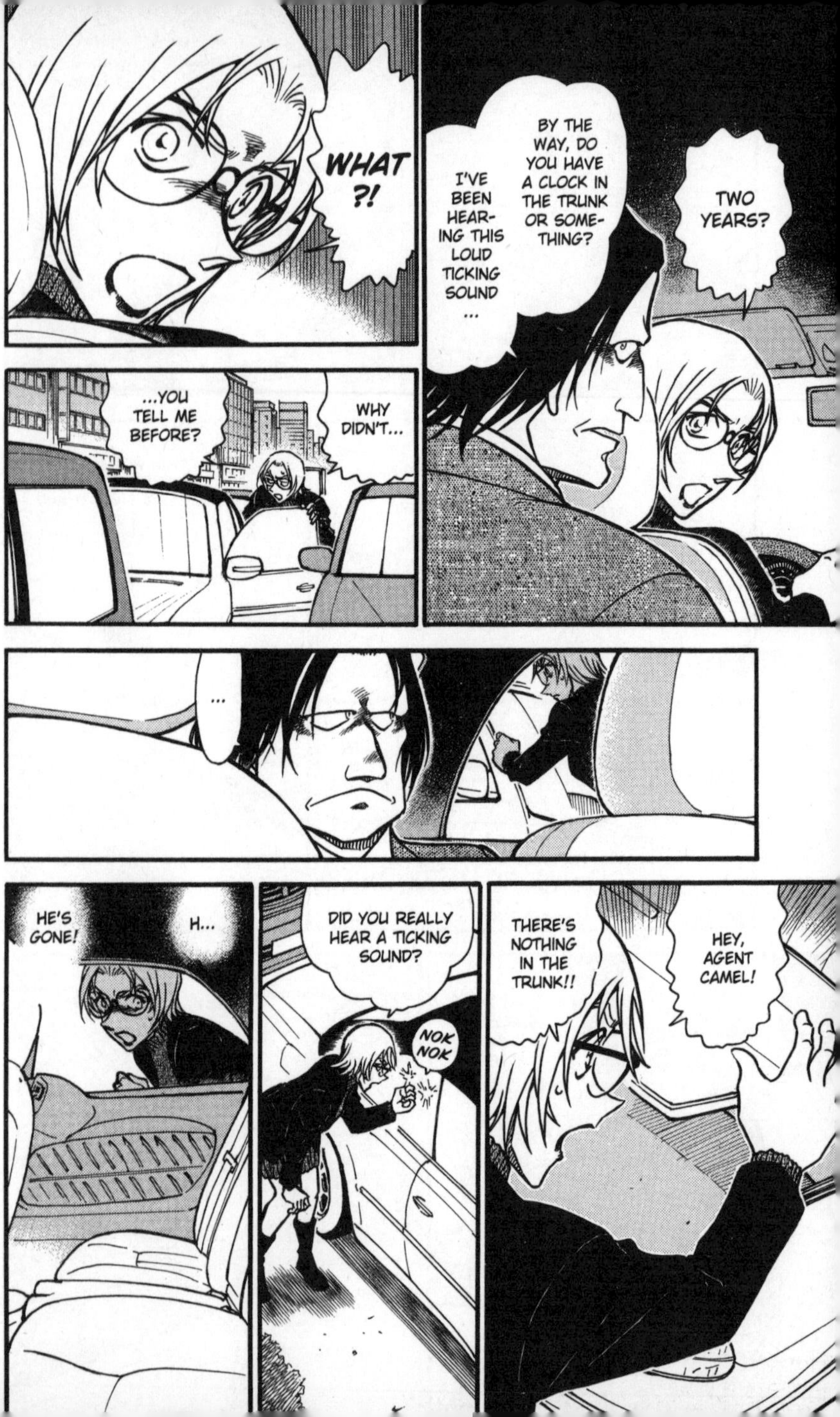
TWO YEARS?
BY THE WAY, DO YOU HAVE A CLOCK IN THE TRUNK OR SOMETHING?
I'VE BEEN HEARING THIS LOUD TICKING SOUND ...
WHAT ?!
WHY DIDN'T...
...YOU TELL ME BEFORE?
...
HEY, AGENT CAMEL!
THERE'S NOTHING IN THE TRUNK!!
DID YOU REALLY HEAR A TICKING SOUND?
NOK NOK
H...
HE'S GONE!

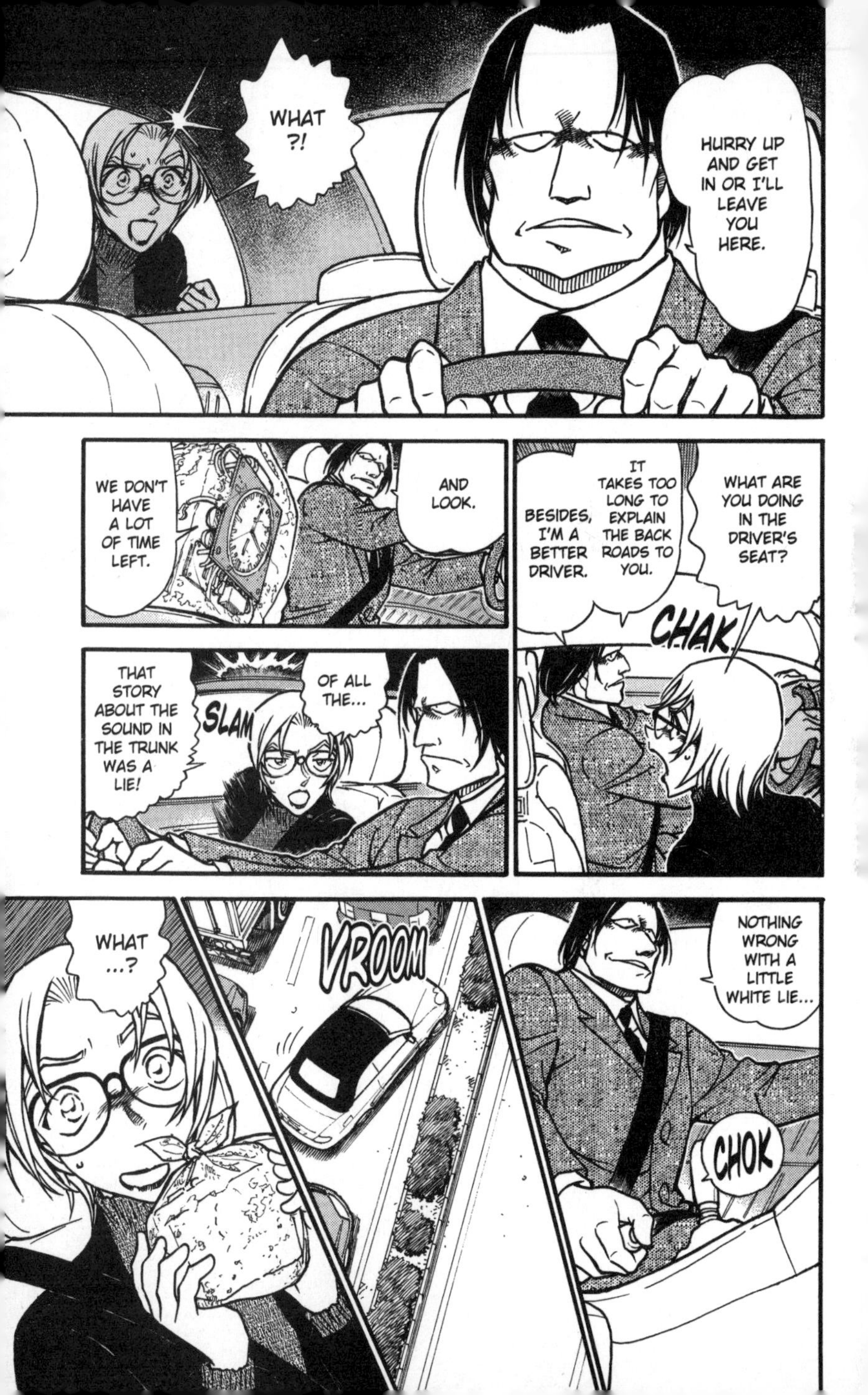
HURRY UP AND GET IN OR I'LL LEAVE YOU HERE.
WHAT ?!
WHAT ARE YOU DOING IN THE DRIVER'S SEAT?
IT TAKES TOO LONG TO EXPLAIN THE BACK ROADS TO YOU.
BESIDES, I'M A BETTER DRIVER.
CHAK
AND LOOK.
WE DON'T HAVE A LOT OF TIME LEFT.
OF ALL THE...
SLAM
THAT STORY ABOUT THE SOUND IN THE TRUNK WAS A LIE!
NOTHING WRONG WITH A LITTLE WHITE LIE...
CHOK
VROOM
WHAT ...?

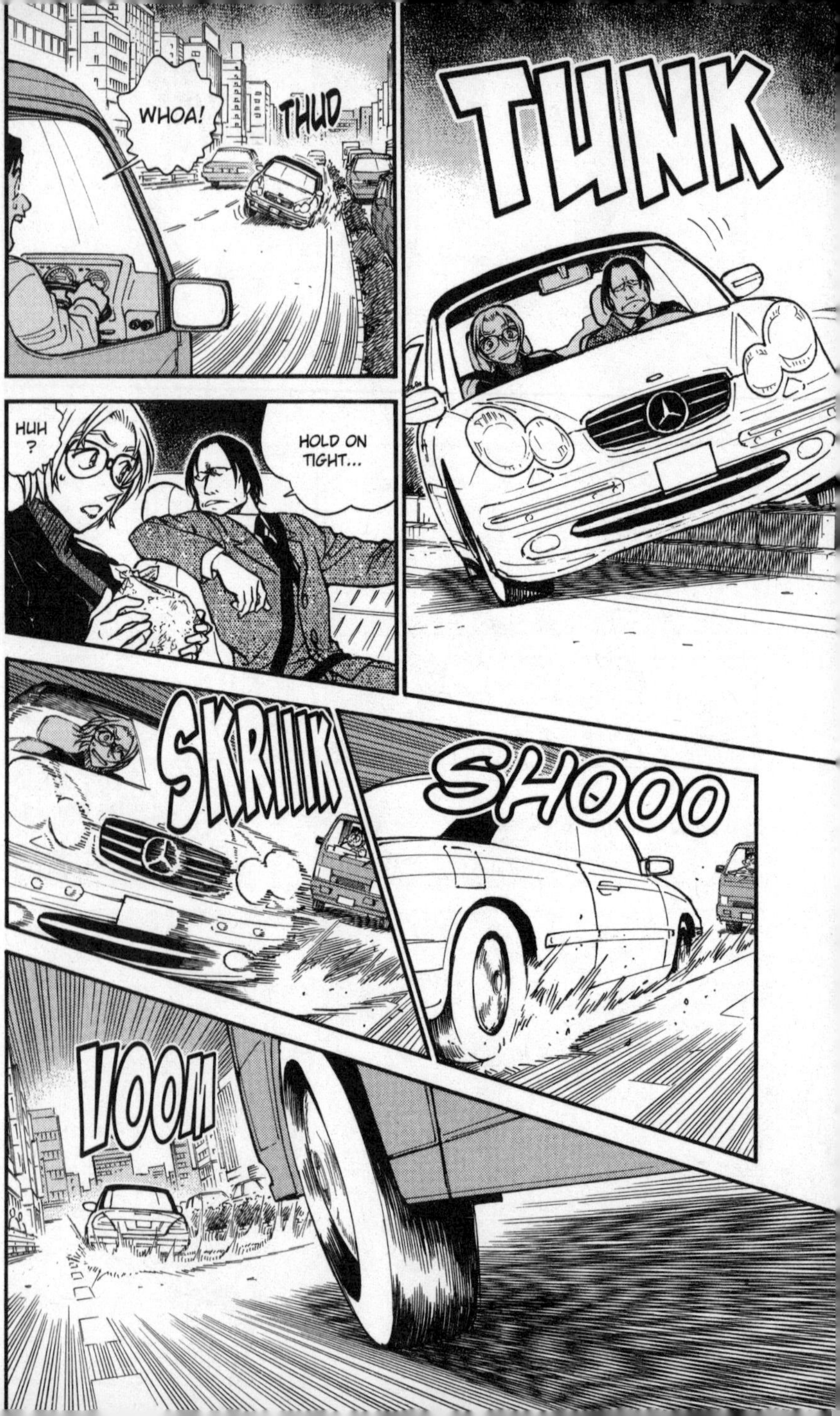
TUNK
WHOA!
THUD
HUH ?
HOLD ON TIGHT...
SHOOO
SKRIIIK
VOOM

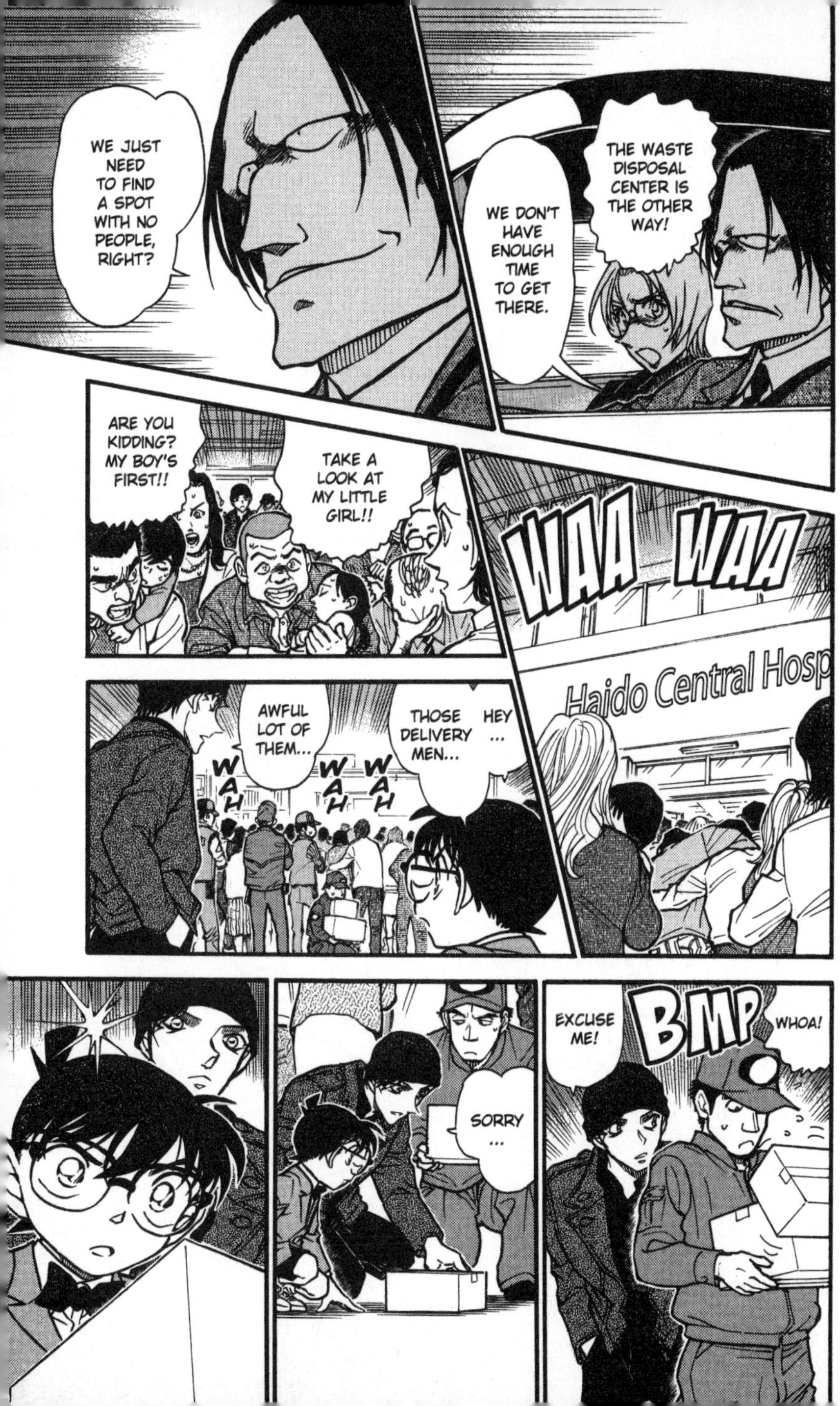

THE WASTE DISPOSAL CENTER IS THE OTHER WAY!
WE DON'T HAVE ENOUGH TIME TO GET THERE.
WE JUST NEED TO FIND A SPOT WITH NO PEOPLE, RIGHT?
WAA WAA
Haido Central Hosp
TAKE A LOOK AT MY LITTLE GIRL!!
ARE YOU KIDDING? MY BOY'S FIRST!!
HEY ...
THOSE DELIVERY MEN...
AWFUL LOT OF THEM...
WAH
WAH
WAH
WHOA!
BMP
EXCUSE ME!
SORRY ...

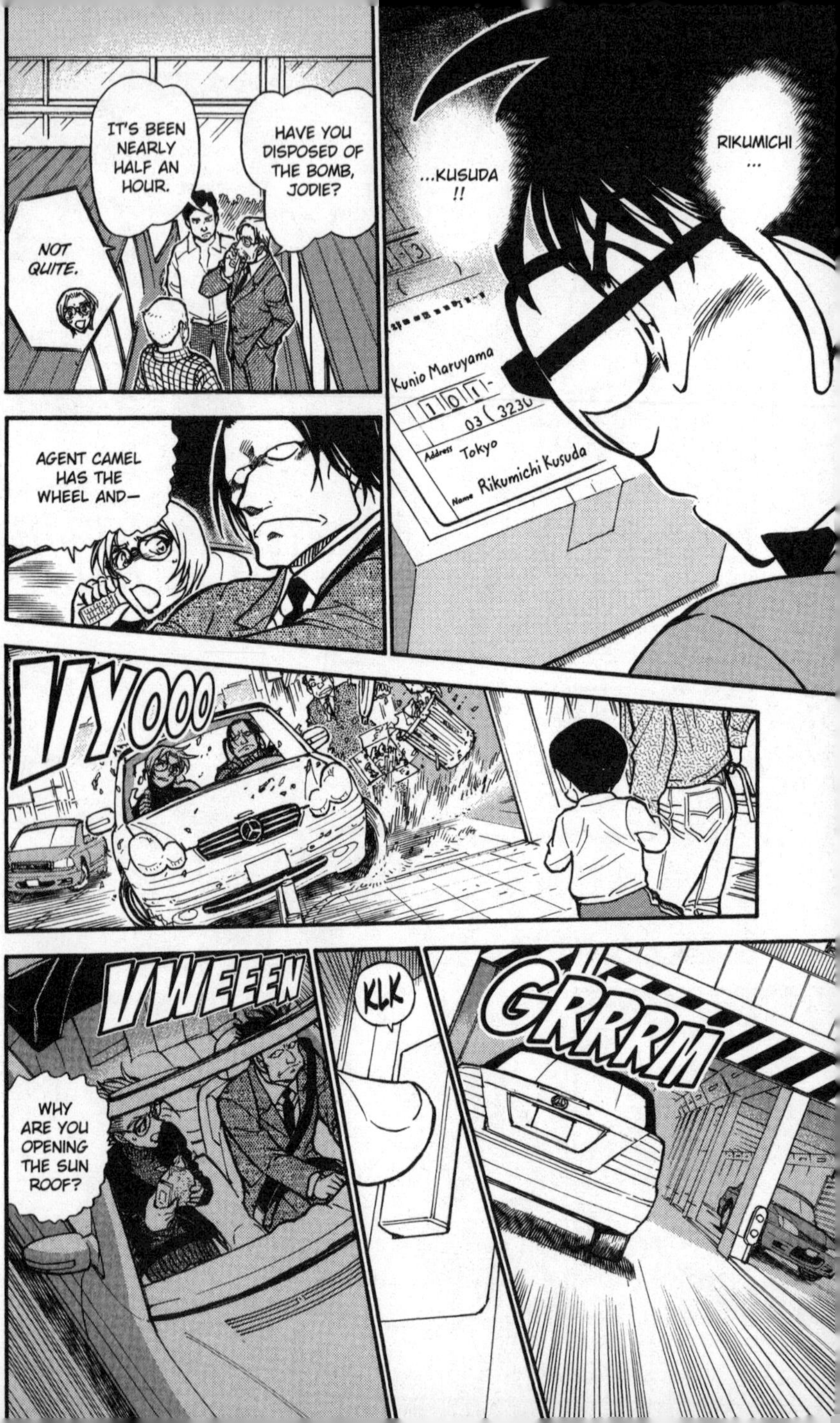
RIKUMICHI ...
...KUSUDA !!
Kunio Maruyama
101-
03 (3230
Address Tokyo
Name Rikumichi Kusuda
HAVE YOU DISPOSED OF THE BOMB, JODIE?
IT'S BEEN NEARLY HALF AN HOUR.
NOT QUITE.
AGENT CAMEL HAS THE WHEEL AND—
VYOOO
GRRRM
KLK
VWEEEN
WHY ARE YOU OPENING THE SUN ROOF?

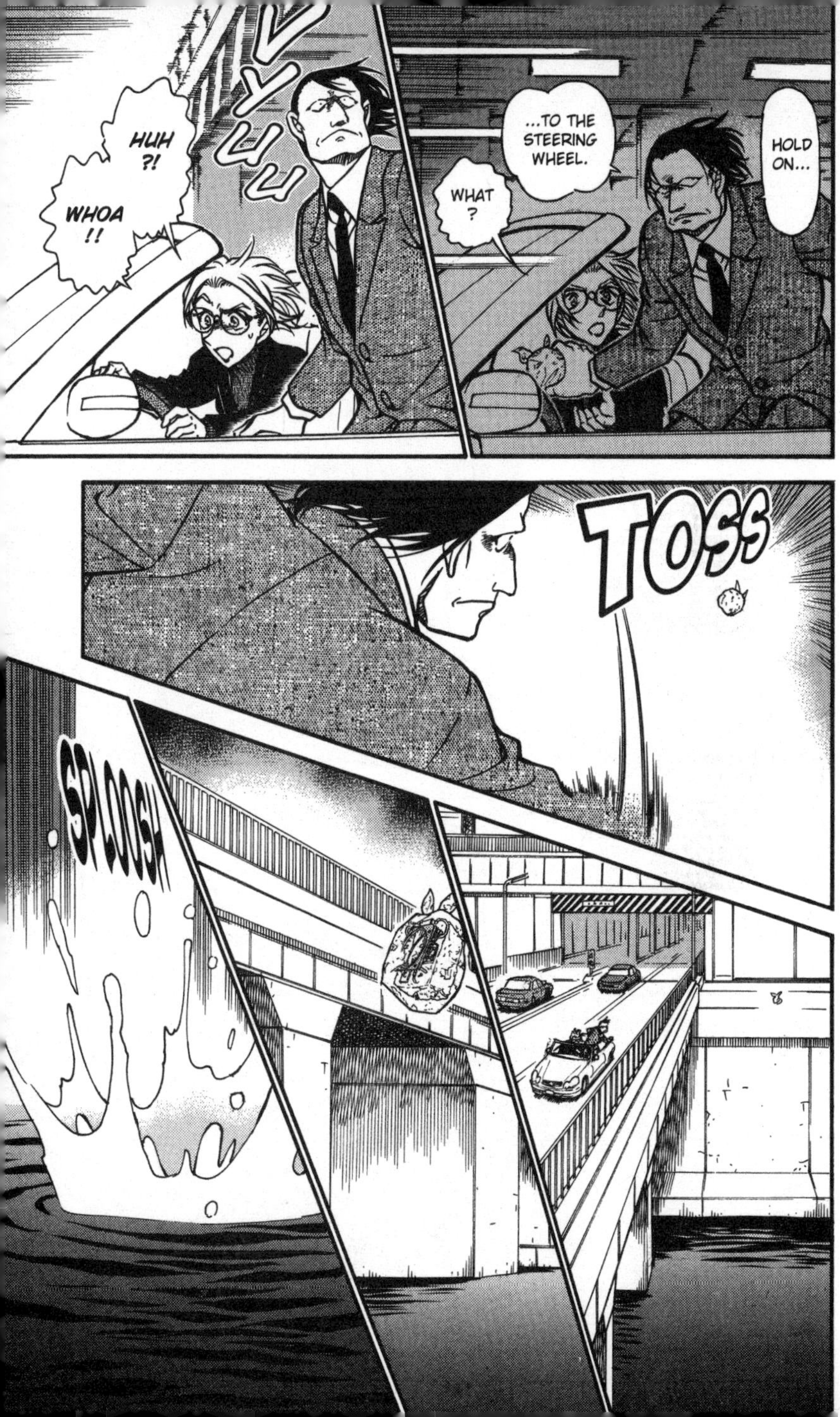
HOLD ON...
...TO THE STEERING WHEEL.
WHAT ?
VYUUU
HUH ?!
WHOA !!
TOSS
SPLOOSH

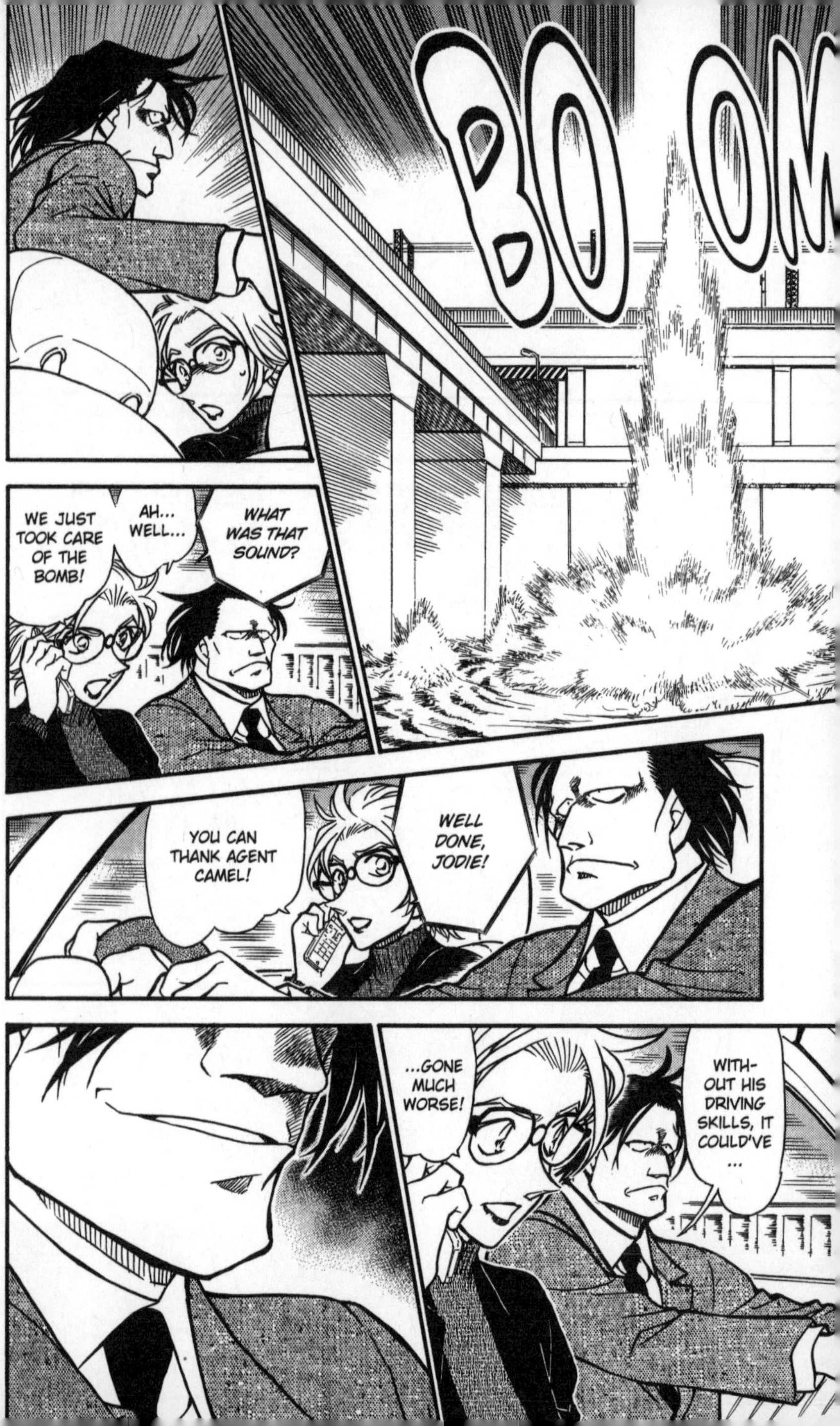
BOOM
WHAT WAS THAT SOUND?
AH... WELL...
WE JUST TOOK CARE OF THE BOMB!
WELL DONE, JODIE!
YOU CAN THANK AGENT CAMEL!
WITH-OUT HIS DRIVING SKILLS, IT COULD'VE ...
...GONE MUCH WORSE!

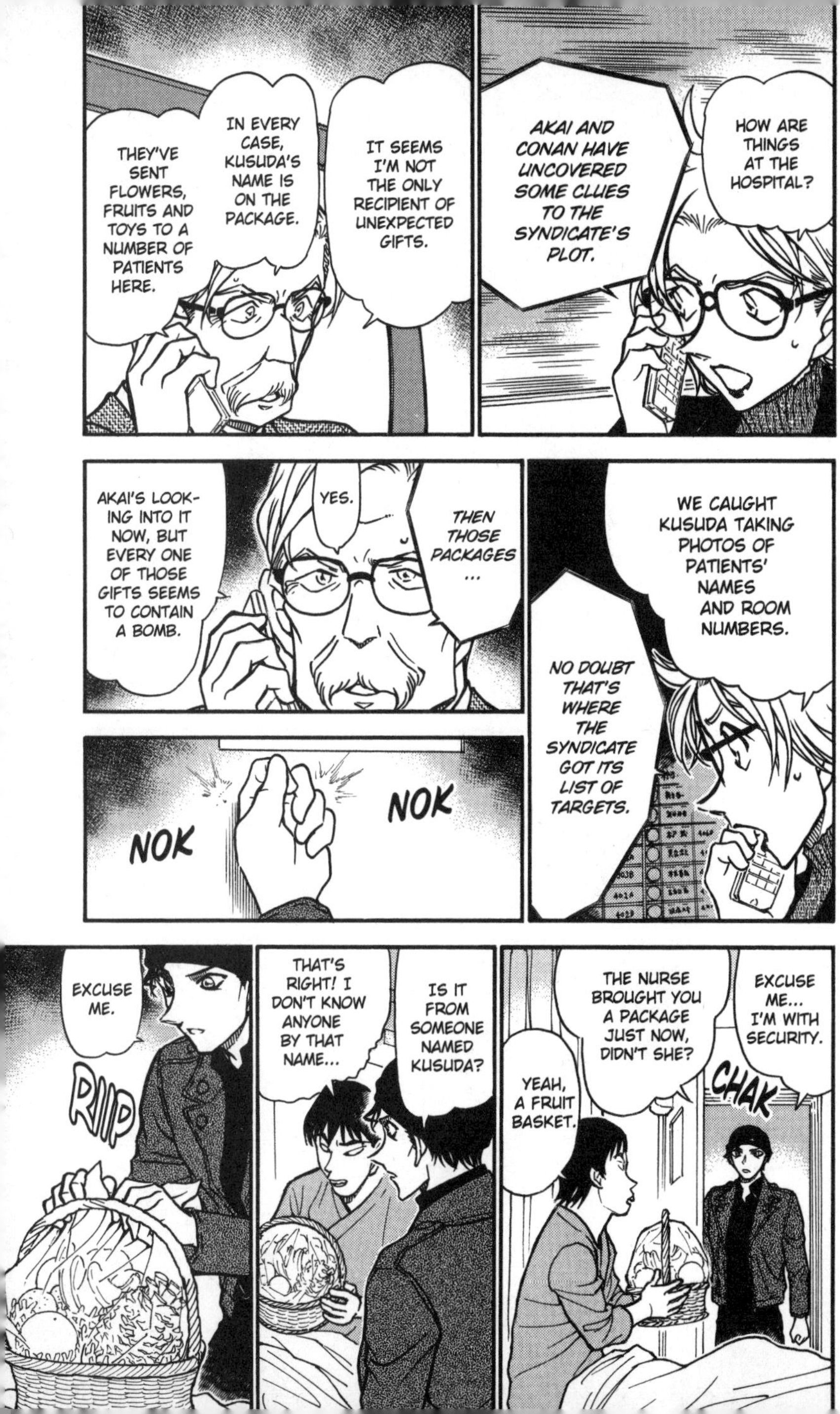
HOW ARE THINGS AT THE HOSPITAL?
AKAI AND CONAN HAVE UNCOVERED SOME CLUES TO THE SYNDICATE'S PLOT.
IT SEEMS I'M NOT THE ONLY RECIPIENT OF UNEXPECTED GIFTS.
IN EVERY CASE, KUSUDA'S NAME IS ON THE PACKAGE.
THEY'VE SENT FLOWERS, FRUITS AND TOYS TO A NUMBER OF PATIENTS HERE.
WE CAUGHT KUSUDA TAKING PHOTOS OF PATIENTS' NAMES AND ROOM NUMBERS.
NO DOUBT THAT'S WHERE THE SYNDICATE GOT ITS LIST OF TARGETS.
THEN THOSE PACKAGES...
YES.
AKAI'S LOOKING INTO IT NOW, BUT EVERY ONE OF THOSE GIFTS SEEMS TO CONTAIN A BOMB.
NOK
NOK
CHAK
EXCUSE ME... I'M WITH SECURITY.
THE NURSE BROUGHT YOU A PACKAGE JUST NOW, DIDN'T SHE?
YEAH, A FRUIT BASKET.
IS IT FROM SOMEONE NAMED KUSUDA?
THAT'S RIGHT! I DON'T KNOW ANYONE BY THAT NAME...
EXCUSE ME.
RIIP

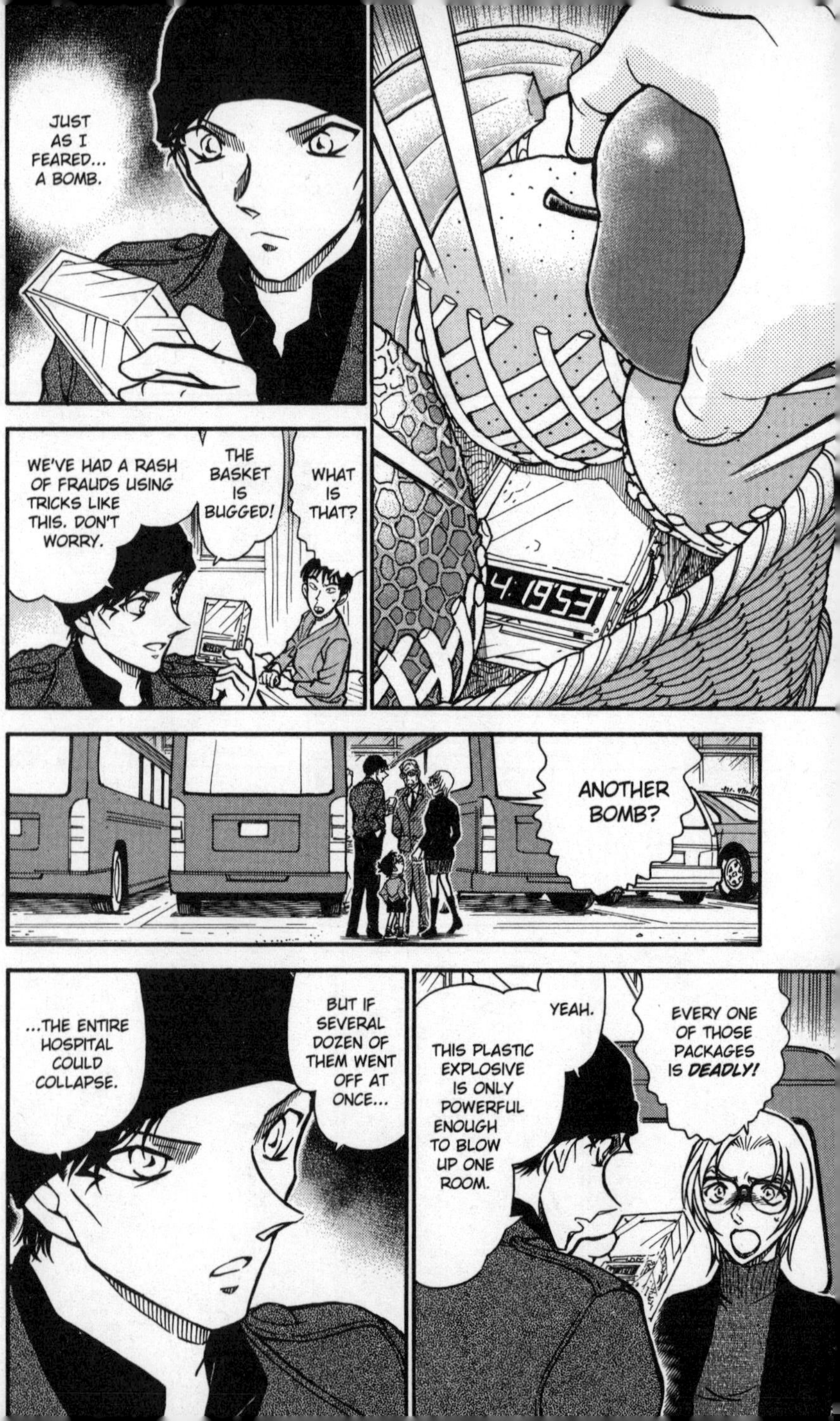
JUST AS I FEARED... A BOMB.
WHAT IS THAT?
THE BASKET IS BUGGED!
WE'VE HAD A RASH OF FRAUDS USING TRICKS LIKE THIS. DON'T WORRY.
ANOTHER BOMB?
EVERY ONE OF THOSE PACKAGES IS ***DEADLY!***
YEAH.
THIS PLASTIC EXPLOSIVE IS ONLY POWERFUL ENOUGH TO BLOW UP ONE ROOM.
BUT IF SEVERAL DOZEN OF THEM WENT OFF AT ONCE...
...THE ENTIRE HOSPITAL COULD COLLAPSE.

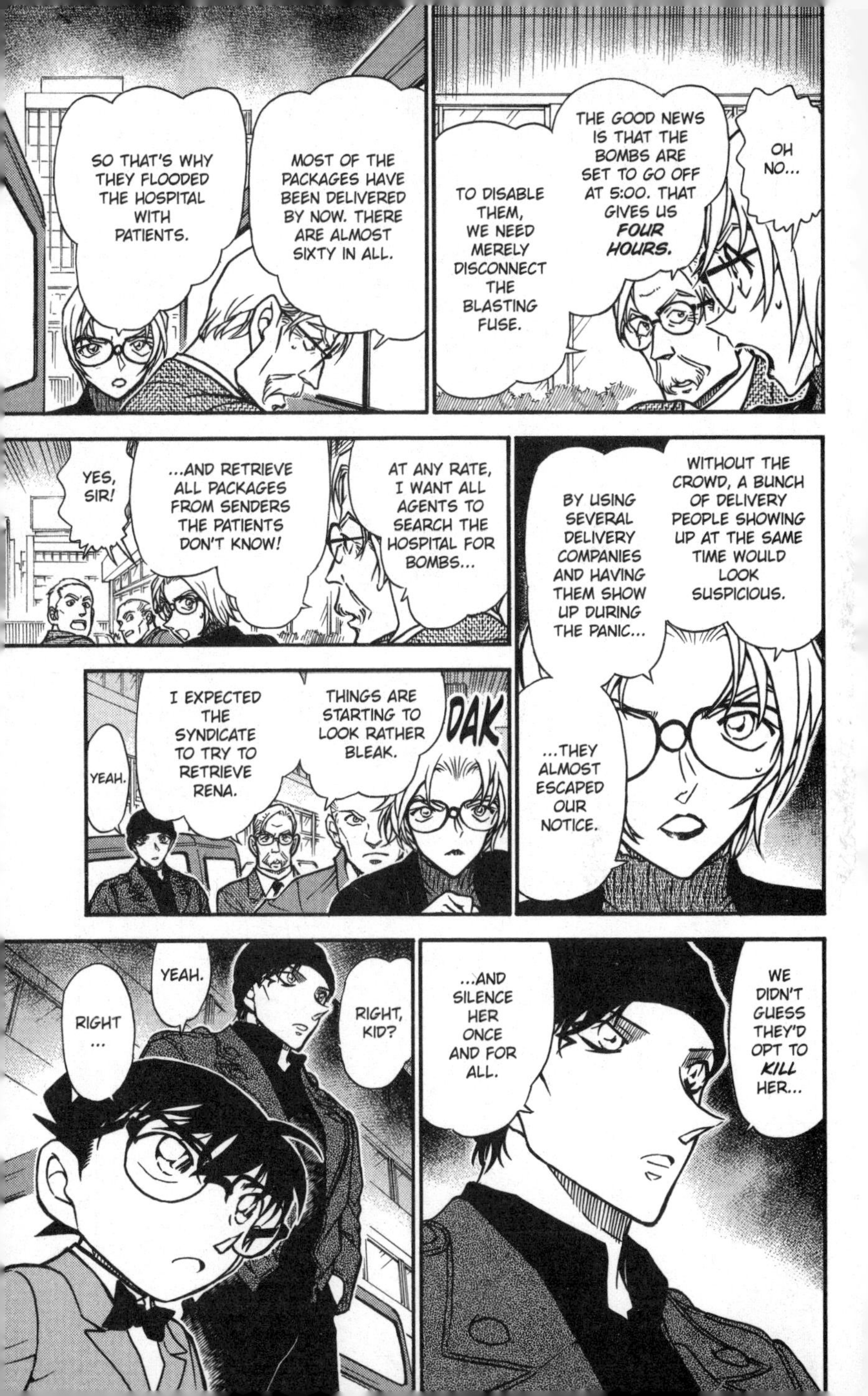
OH NO...
THE GOOD NEWS IS THAT THE BOMBS ARE SET TO GO OFF AT 5:00. THAT GIVES US ***FOUR HOURS.***
TO DISABLE THEM, WE NEED MERELY DISCONNECT THE BLASTING FUSE.
MOST OF THE PACKAGES HAVE BEEN DELIVERED BY NOW. THERE ARE ALMOST SIXTY IN ALL.
SO THAT'S WHY THEY FLOODED THE HOSPITAL WITH PATIENTS.
WITHOUT THE CROWD, A BUNCH OF DELIVERY PEOPLE SHOWING UP AT THE SAME TIME WOULD LOOK SUSPICIOUS.
BY USING SEVERAL DELIVERY COMPANIES AND HAVING THEM SHOW UP DURING THE PANIC...
...THEY ALMOST ESCAPED OUR NOTICE.
AT ANY RATE, I WANT ALL AGENTS TO SEARCH THE HOSPITAL FOR BOMBS...
...AND RETRIEVE ALL PACKAGES FROM SENDERS THE PATIENTS DON'T KNOW!
YES, SIR!
DAK
THINGS ARE STARTING TO LOOK RATHER BLEAK.
I EXPECTED THE SYNDICATE TO TRY TO RETRIEVE RENA.
YEAH.
WE DIDN'T GUESS THEY'D OPT TO ***KILL*** HER...
...AND SILENCE HER ONCE AND FOR ALL.
RIGHT, KID?
YEAH.
RIGHT...

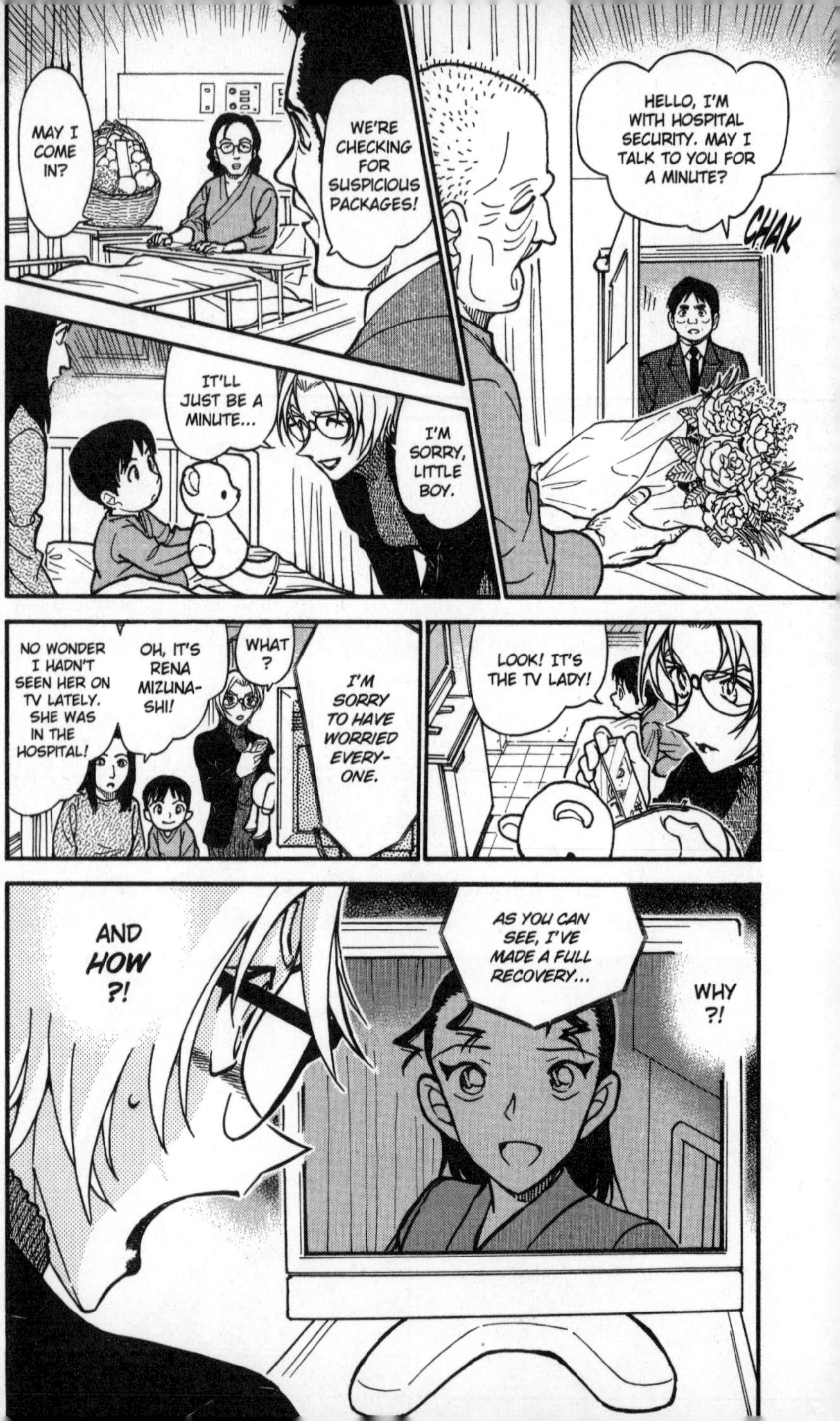
HELLO, I'M WITH HOSPITAL SECURITY. MAY I TALK TO YOU FOR A MINUTE?
CHAK
WE'RE CHECKING FOR SUSPICIOUS PACKAGES!
MAY I COME IN?
I'M SORRY, LITTLE BOY.
IT'LL JUST BE A MINUTE...
LOOK! IT'S THE TV LADY!
I'M SORRY TO HAVE WORRIED EVERY-ONE.
WHAT?
OH, IT'S RENA MIZUNA-SHI!
NO WONDER I HADN'T SEEN HER ON TV LATELY. SHE WAS IN THE HOSPITAL!
AS YOU CAN SEE, I'VE MADE A FULL RECOVERY...
WHY?!
AND HOW?!

FILE 5: LAST RESORT

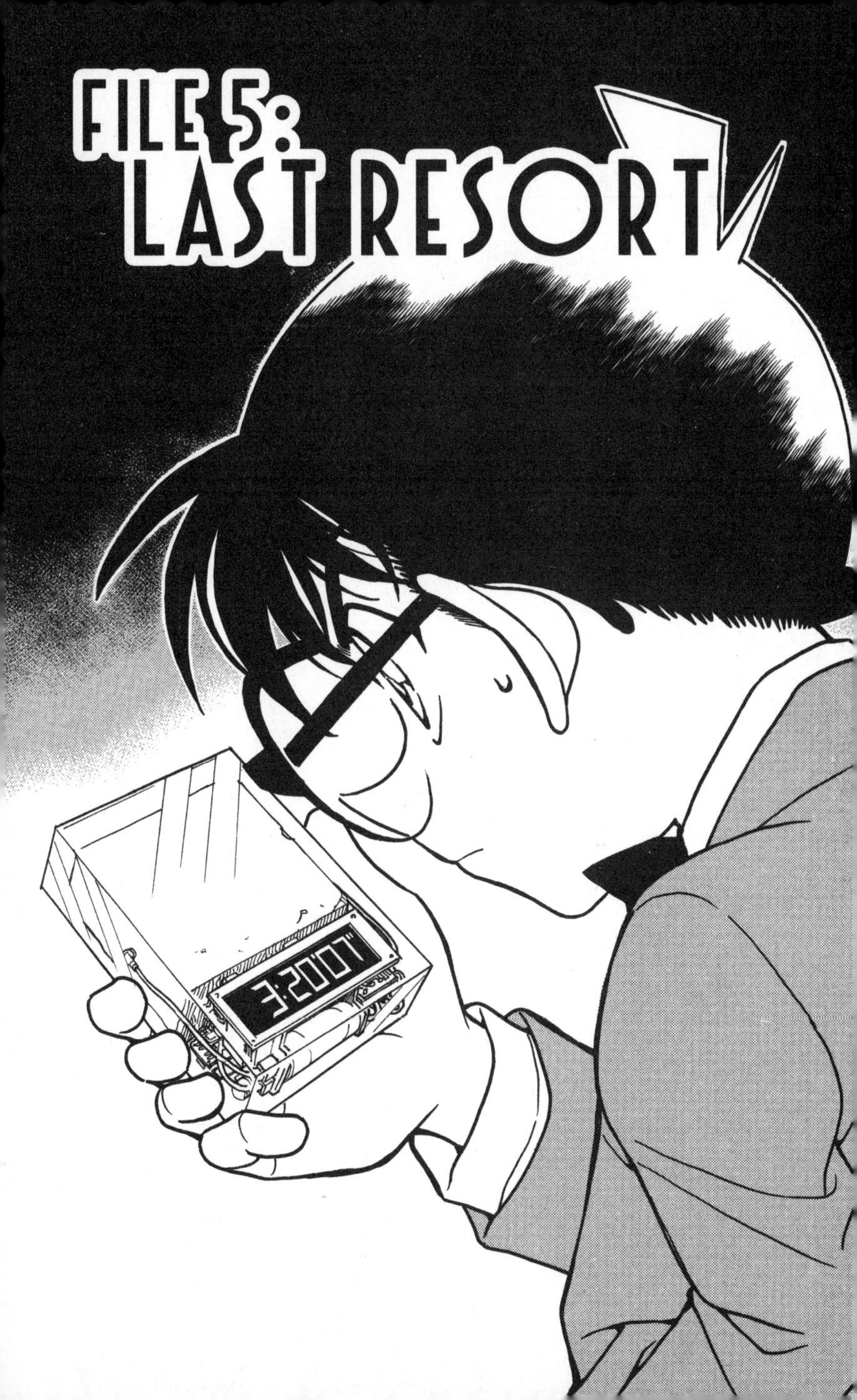
3:20:07

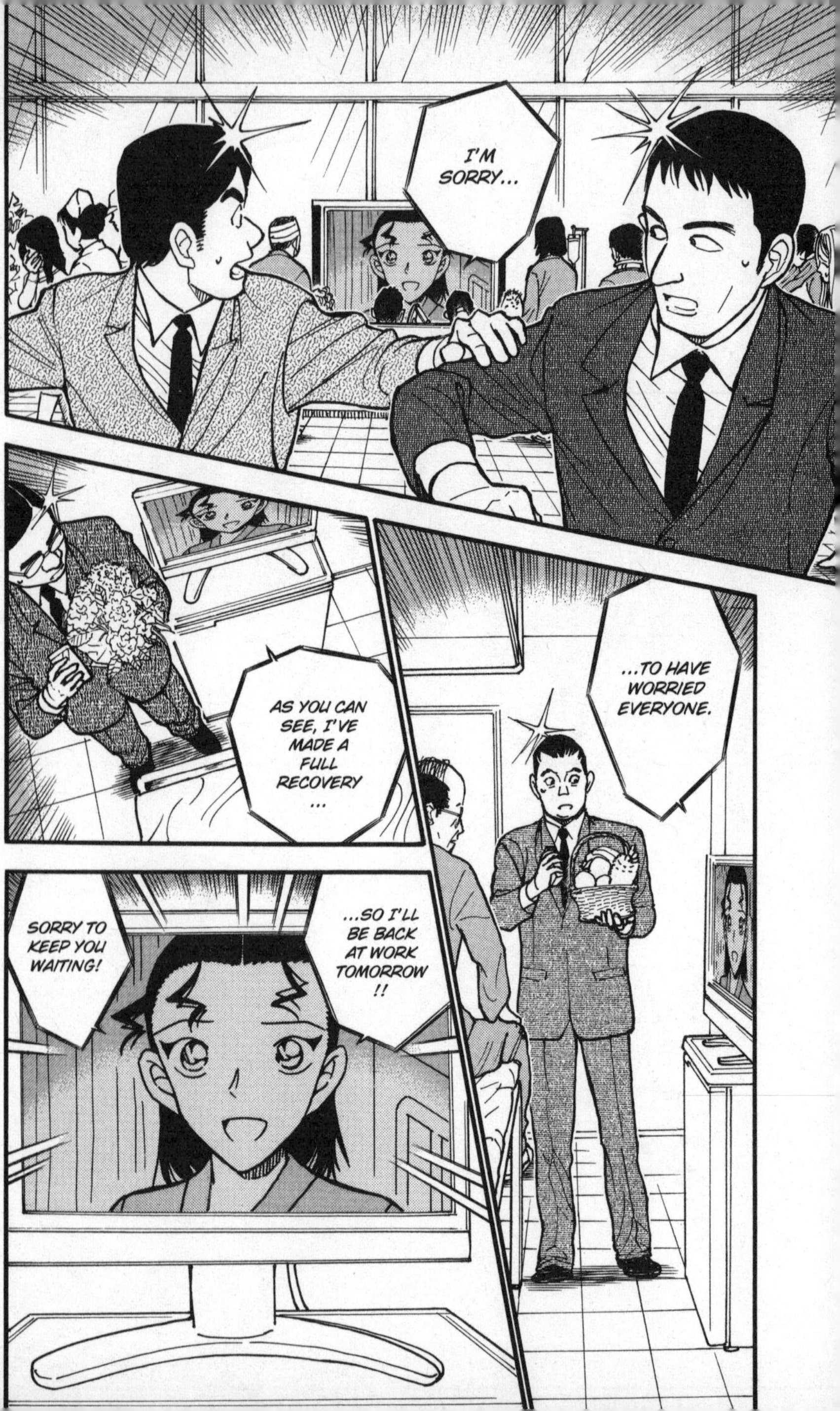
I'M SORRY...
...TO HAVE WORRIED EVERYONE.
AS YOU CAN SEE, I'VE MADE A FULL RECOVERY...
...SO I'LL BE BACK AT WORK TOMORROW!!
SORRY TO KEEP YOU WAITING!

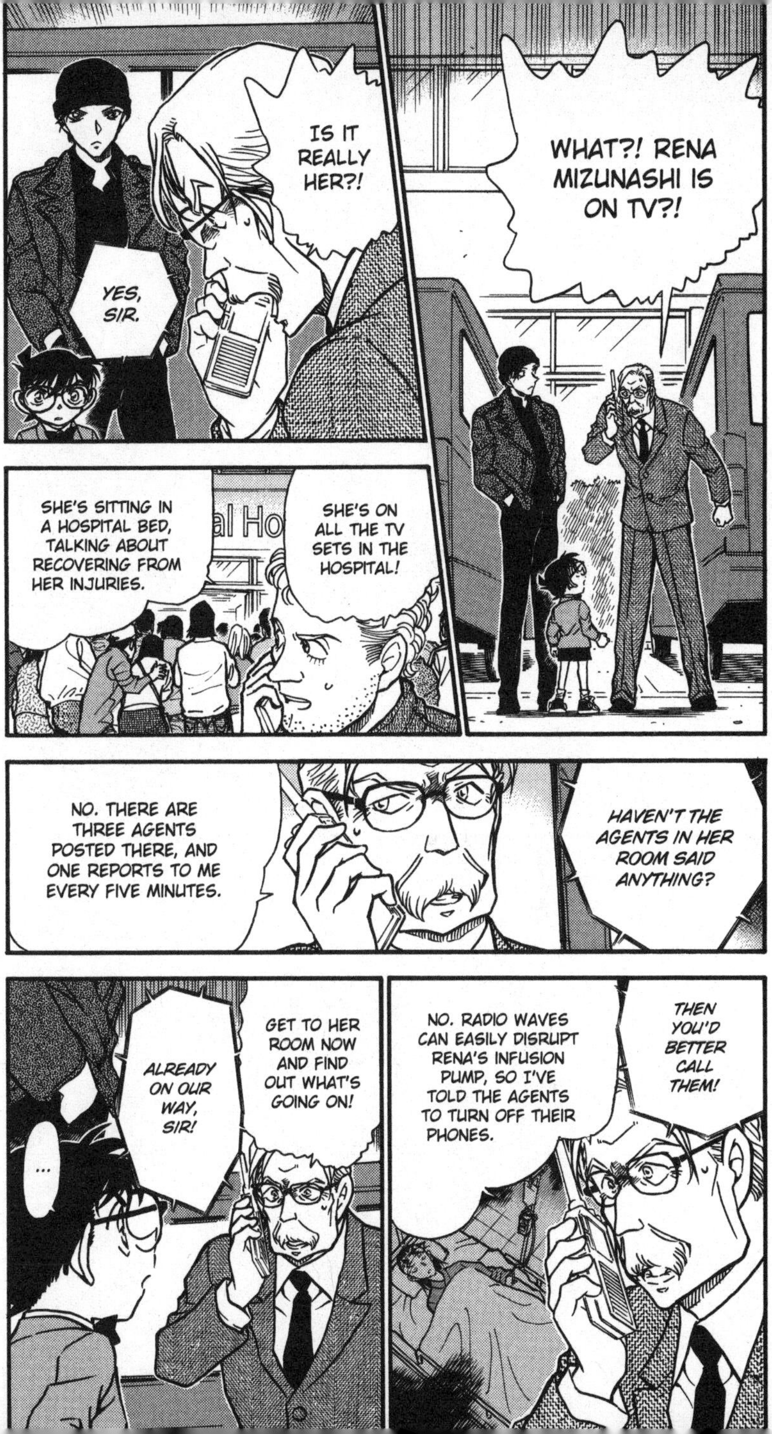
WHAT?! RENA MIZUNASHI IS ON TV?!
IS IT REALLY HER?!
YES, SIR.
SHE'S ON ALL THE TV SETS IN THE HOSPITAL!
SHE'S SITTING IN A HOSPITAL BED, TALKING ABOUT RECOVERING FROM HER INJURIES.
HAVEN'T THE AGENTS IN HER ROOM SAID ANYTHING?
NO. THERE ARE THREE AGENTS POSTED THERE, AND ONE REPORTS TO ME EVERY FIVE MINUTES.
THEN YOU'D BETTER CALL THEM!
NO. RADIO WAVES CAN EASILY DISRUPT RENA'S INFUSION PUMP, SO I'VE TOLD THE AGENTS TO TURN OFF THEIR PHONES.
GET TO HER ROOM NOW AND FIND OUT WHAT'S GOING ON!
ALREADY ON OUR WAY, SIR!
...

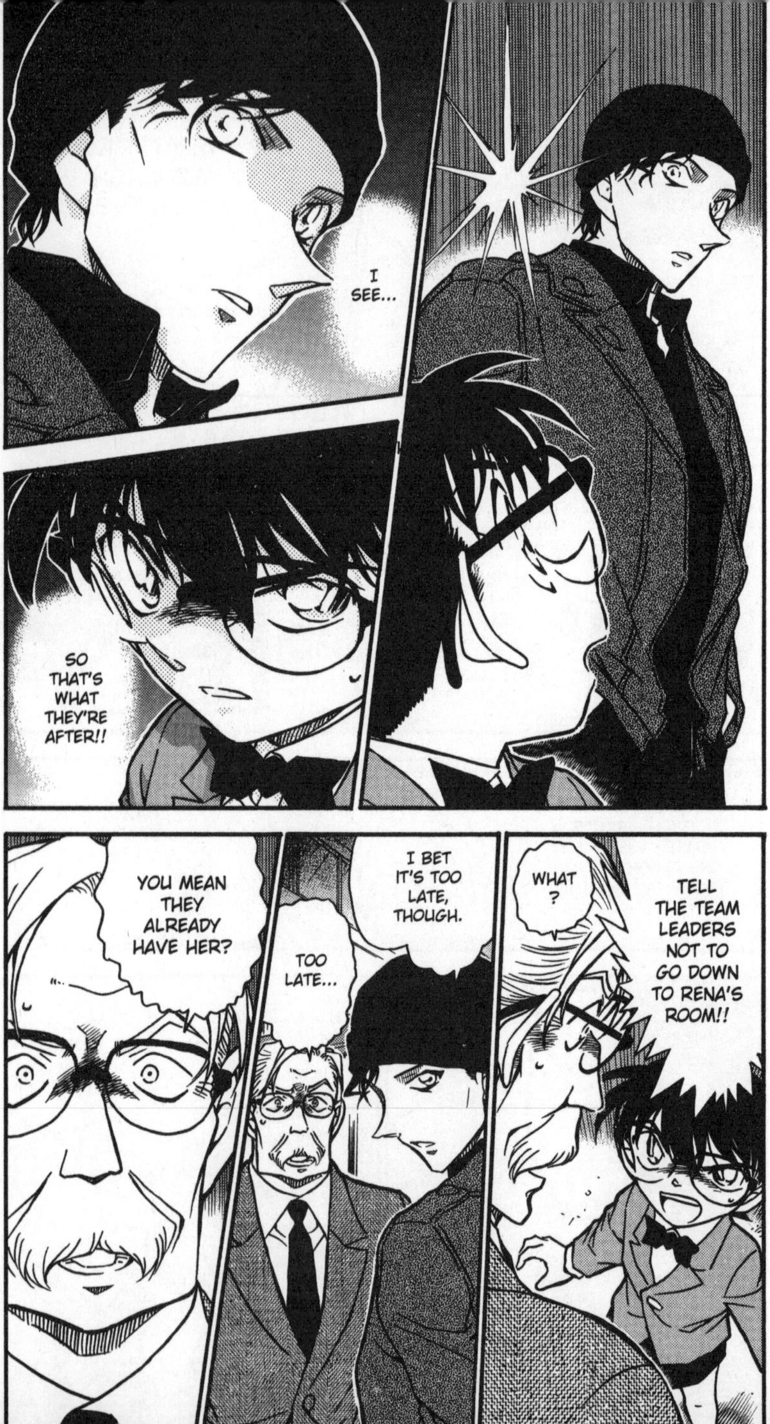
I SEE...
SO THAT'S WHAT THEY'RE AFTER!!
TELL THE TEAM LEADERS NOT TO GO DOWN TO RENA'S ROOM!!
WHAT?
I BET IT'S TOO LATE, THOUGH.
TOO LATE...
YOU MEAN THEY ALREADY HAVE HER?

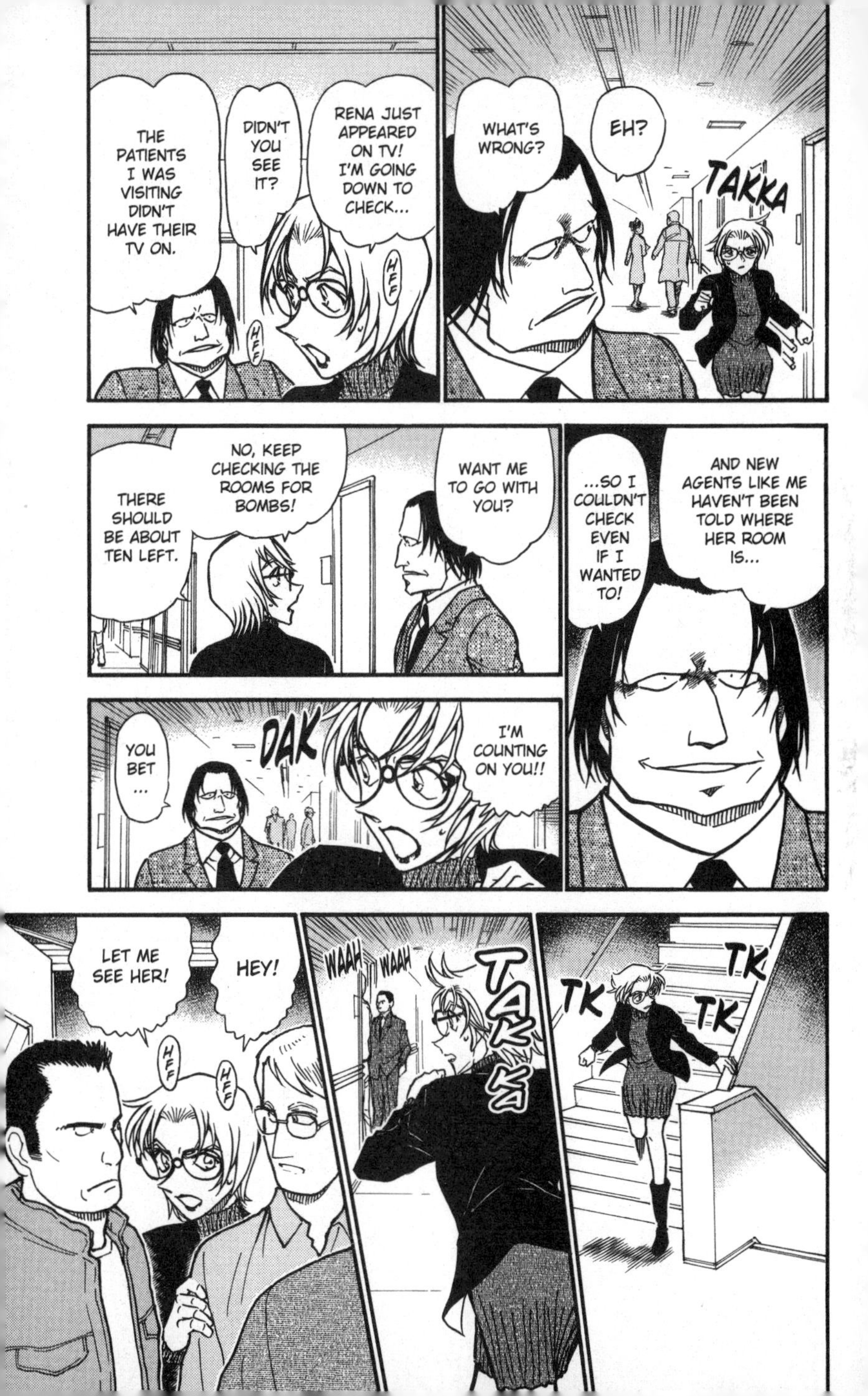
TAKKA
EH?
WHAT'S WRONG?
RENA JUST APPEARED ON TV! I'M GOING DOWN TO CHECK...
HEFF
DIDN'T YOU SEE IT?
THE PATIENTS I WAS VISITING DIDN'T HAVE THEIR TV ON.
HEFF
AND NEW AGENTS LIKE ME HAVEN'T BEEN TOLD WHERE HER ROOM IS...
...SO I COULDN'T CHECK EVEN IF I WANTED TO!
WANT ME TO GO WITH YOU?
NO, KEEP CHECKING THE ROOMS FOR BOMBS!
THERE SHOULD BE ABOUT TEN LEFT.
I'M COUNTING ON YOU!!
DAK
YOU BET ...
TK
TK
TK
TAKKA
WAAH
WAAH
HEY!
HEFF
HEFF
LET ME SEE HER!

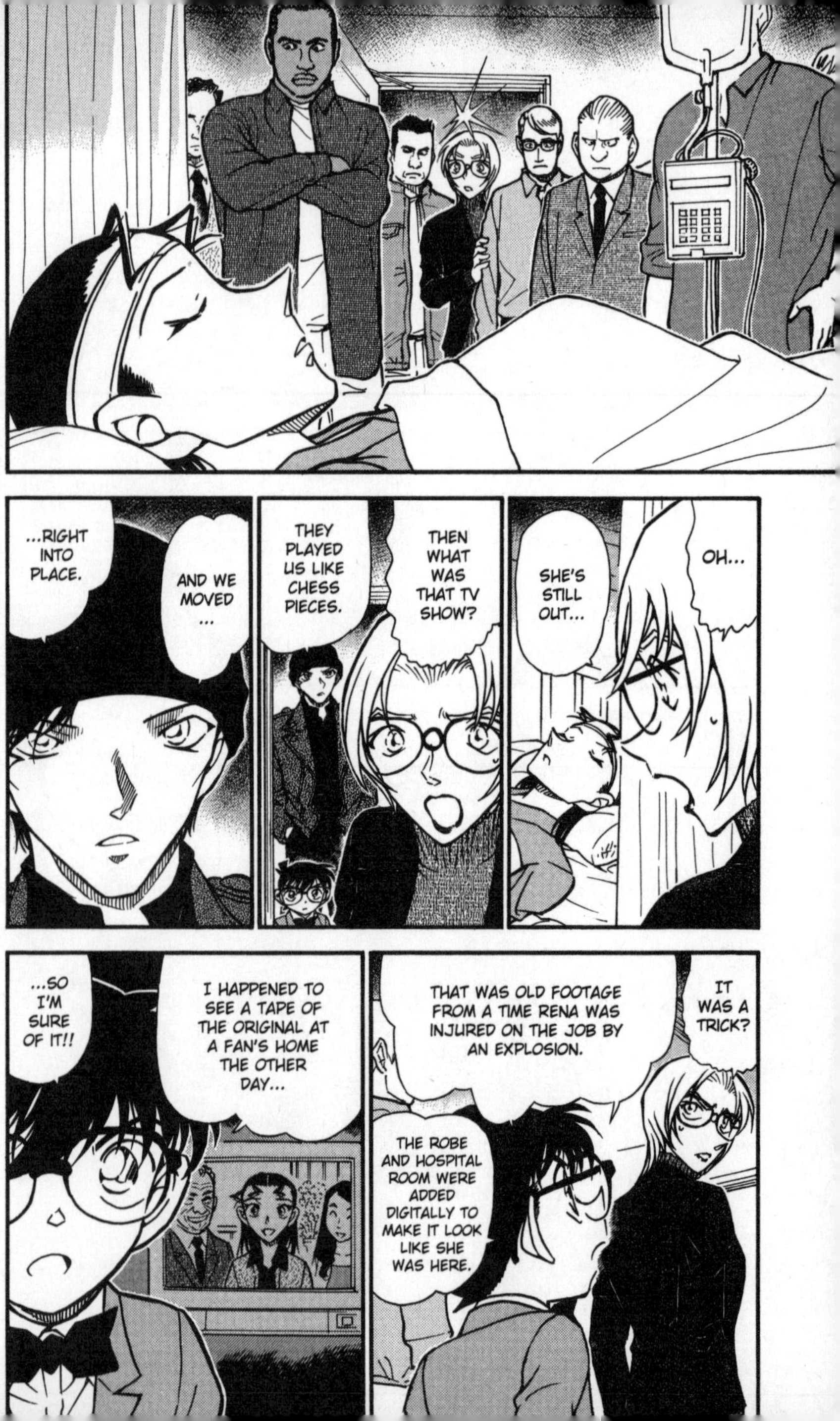
OH...
SHE'S STILL OUT...
THEN WHAT WAS THAT TV SHOW?
THEY PLAYED US LIKE CHESS PIECES.
AND WE MOVED ...
...RIGHT INTO PLACE.
IT WAS A TRICK?
THAT WAS OLD FOOTAGE FROM A TIME RENA WAS INJURED ON THE JOB BY AN EXPLOSION.
THE ROBE AND HOSPITAL ROOM WERE ADDED DIGITALLY TO MAKE IT LOOK LIKE SHE WAS HERE.
I HAPPENED TO SEE A TAPE OF THE ORIGINAL AT A FAN'S HOME THE OTHER DAY...
...SO I'M SURE OF IT!!

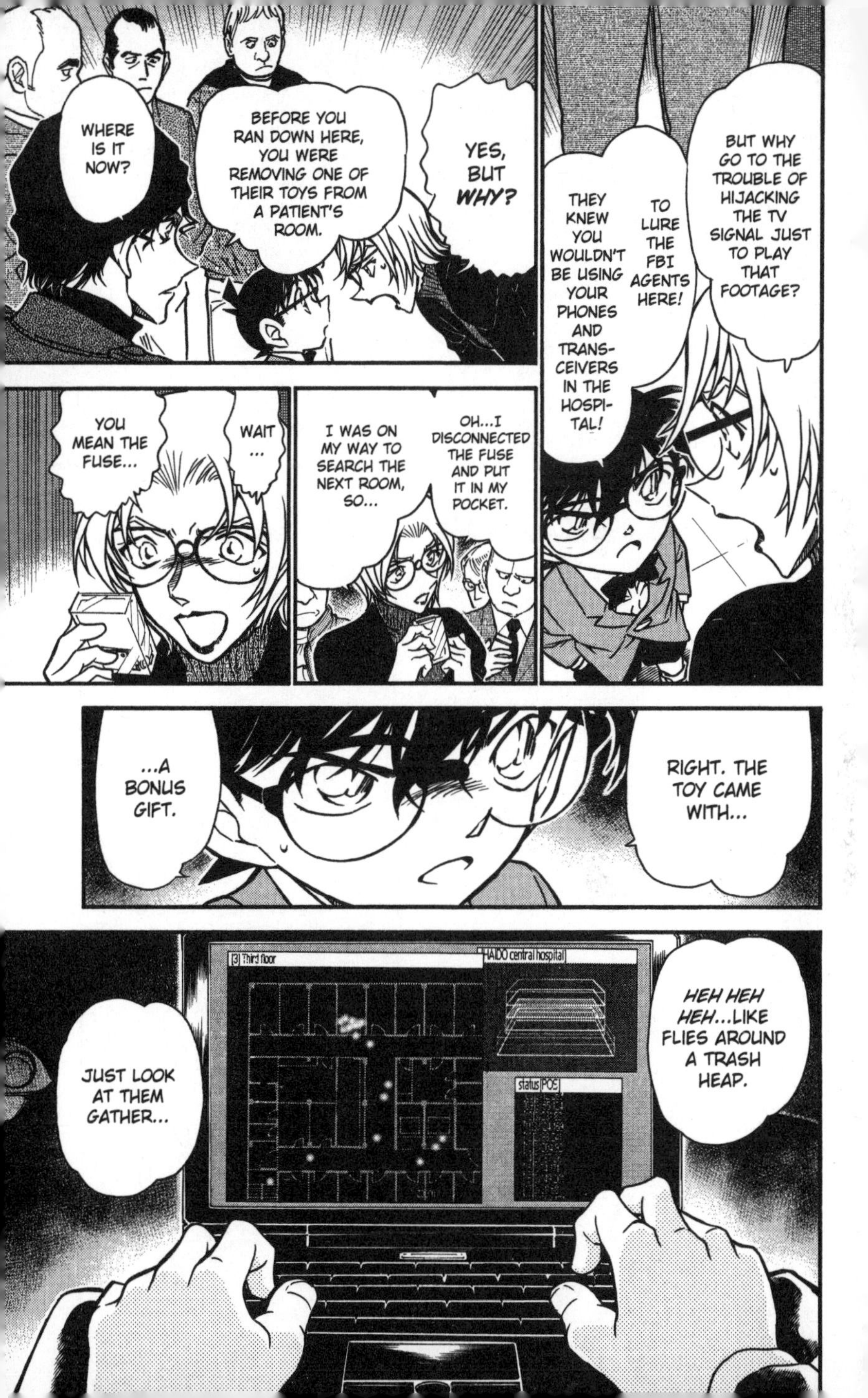
BUT WHY GO TO THE TROUBLE OF HIJACKING THE TV SIGNAL JUST TO PLAY THAT FOOTAGE?
TO LURE THE FBI AGENTS HERE!
THEY KNEW YOU WOULDN'T BE USING YOUR PHONES AND TRANS-CEIVERS IN THE HOSPI-TAL!
YES, BUT *WHY?*
BEFORE YOU RAN DOWN HERE, YOU WERE REMOVING ONE OF THEIR TOYS FROM A PATIENT'S ROOM.
WHERE IS IT NOW?
OH...I DISCONNECTED THE FUSE AND PUT IT IN MY POCKET.
I WAS ON MY WAY TO SEARCH THE NEXT ROOM, SO...
WAIT...
YOU MEAN THE FUSE...
RIGHT. THE TOY CAME WITH...
...A BONUS GIFT.
[3] Third floor
HAIDO central hospital
status POS
HEH HEH HEH...LIKE FLIES AROUND A TRASH HEAP.
JUST LOOK AT THEM GATHER...

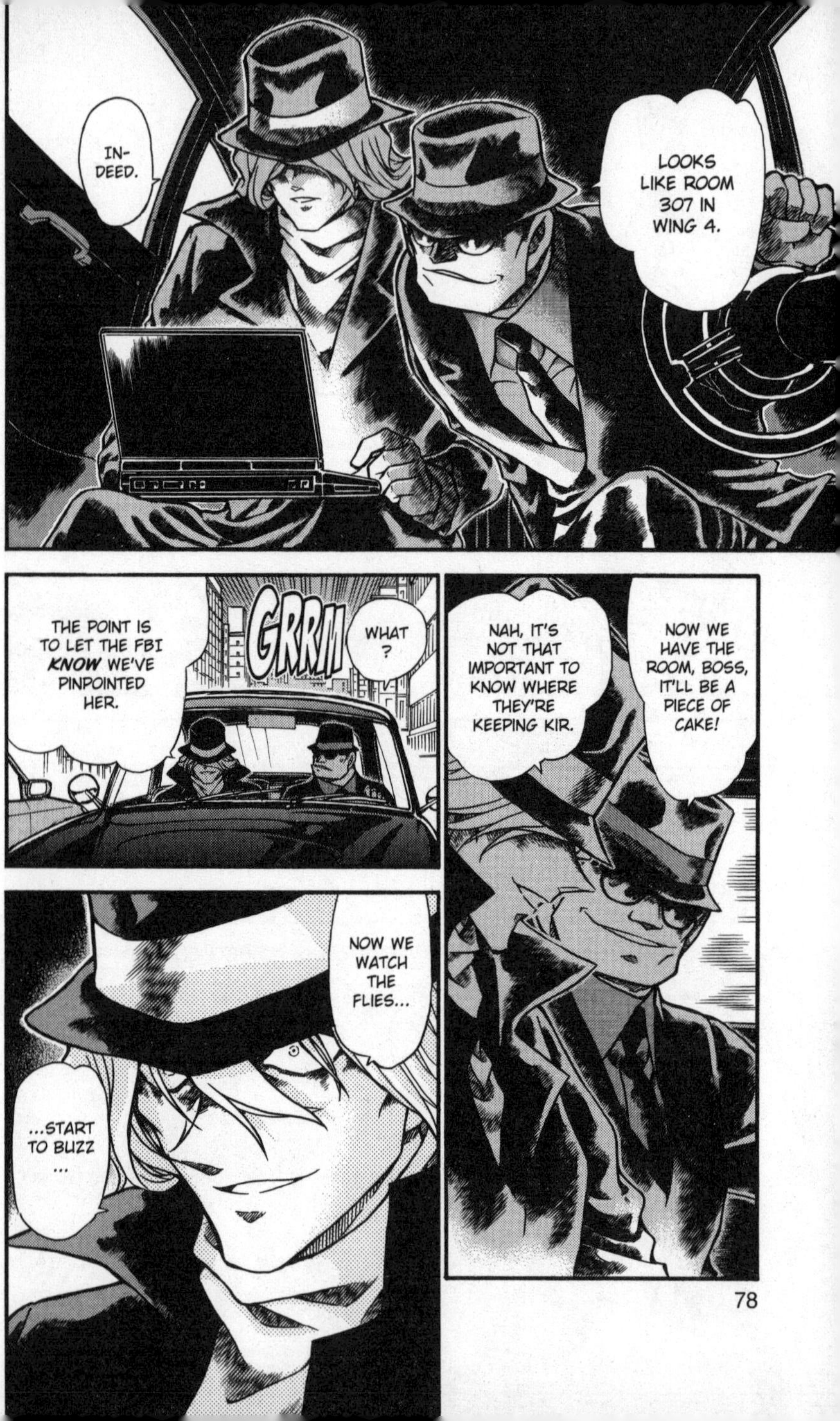
LOOKS LIKE ROOM 307 IN WING 4.
IN-DEED.
NOW WE HAVE THE ROOM, BOSS, IT'LL BE A PIECE OF CAKE!
NAH, IT'S NOT THAT IMPORTANT TO KNOW WHERE THEY'RE KEEPING KIR.
WHAT?
GRRM
THE POINT IS TO LET THE FBI *KNOW* WE'VE PINPOINTED HER.
NOW WE WATCH THE FLIES...
...START TO BUZZ...

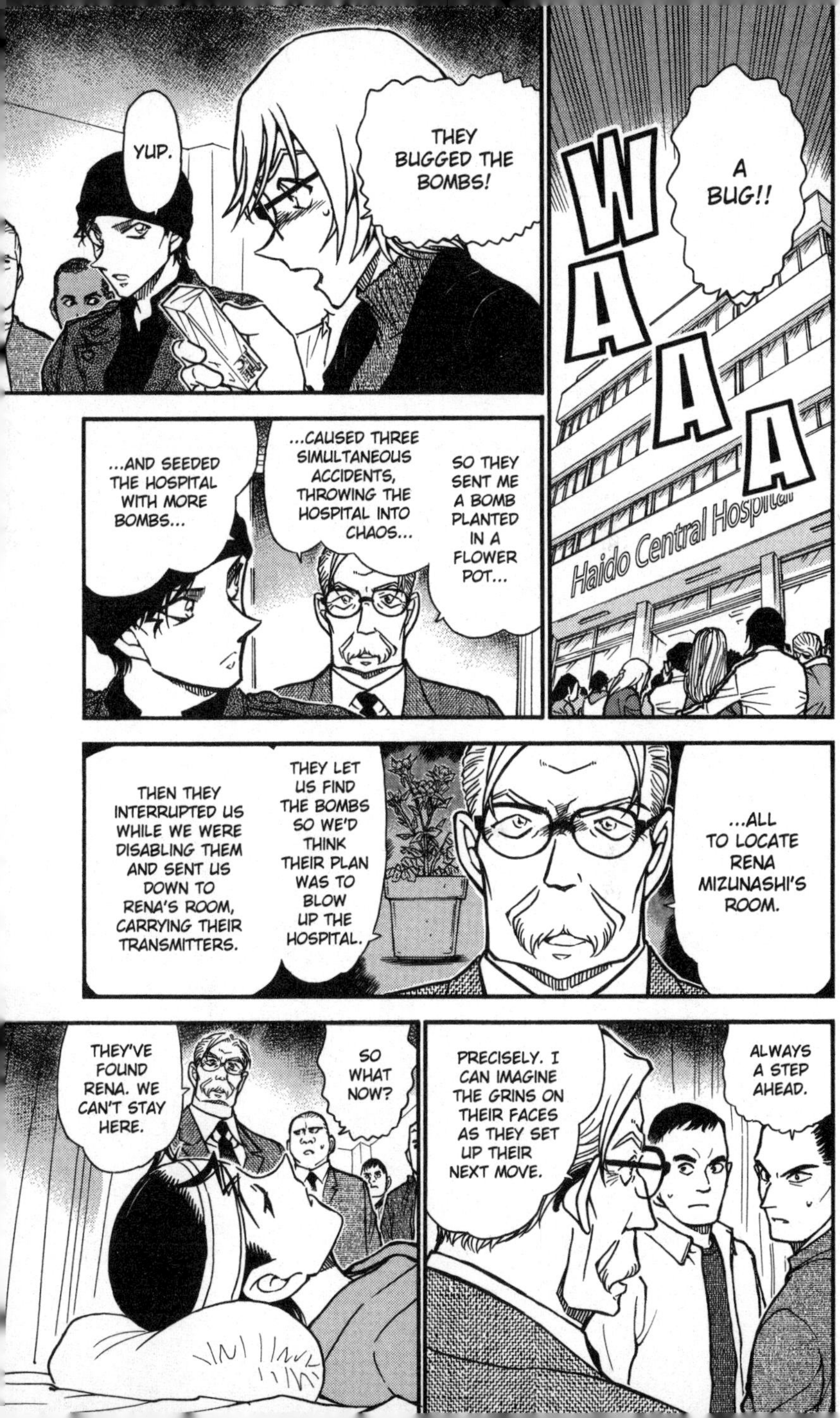
A BUG!!
WAAAA
Haido Central Hospital
THEY BUGGED THE BOMBS!
YUP.
SO THEY SENT ME A BOMB PLANTED IN A FLOWER POT...
...CAUSED THREE SIMULTANEOUS ACCIDENTS, THROWING THE HOSPITAL INTO CHAOS...
...AND SEEDED THE HOSPITAL WITH MORE BOMBS...
...ALL TO LOCATE RENA MIZUNASHI'S ROOM.
THEY LET US FIND THE BOMBS SO WE'D THINK THEIR PLAN WAS TO BLOW UP THE HOSPITAL.
THEN THEY INTERRUPTED US WHILE WE WERE DISABLING THEM AND SENT US DOWN TO RENA'S ROOM, CARRYING THEIR TRANSMITTERS.
ALWAYS A STEP AHEAD.
PRECISELY. I CAN IMAGINE THE GRINS ON THEIR FACES AS THEY SET UP THEIR NEXT MOVE.
SO WHAT NOW?
THEY'VE FOUND RENA. WE CAN'T STAY HERE.

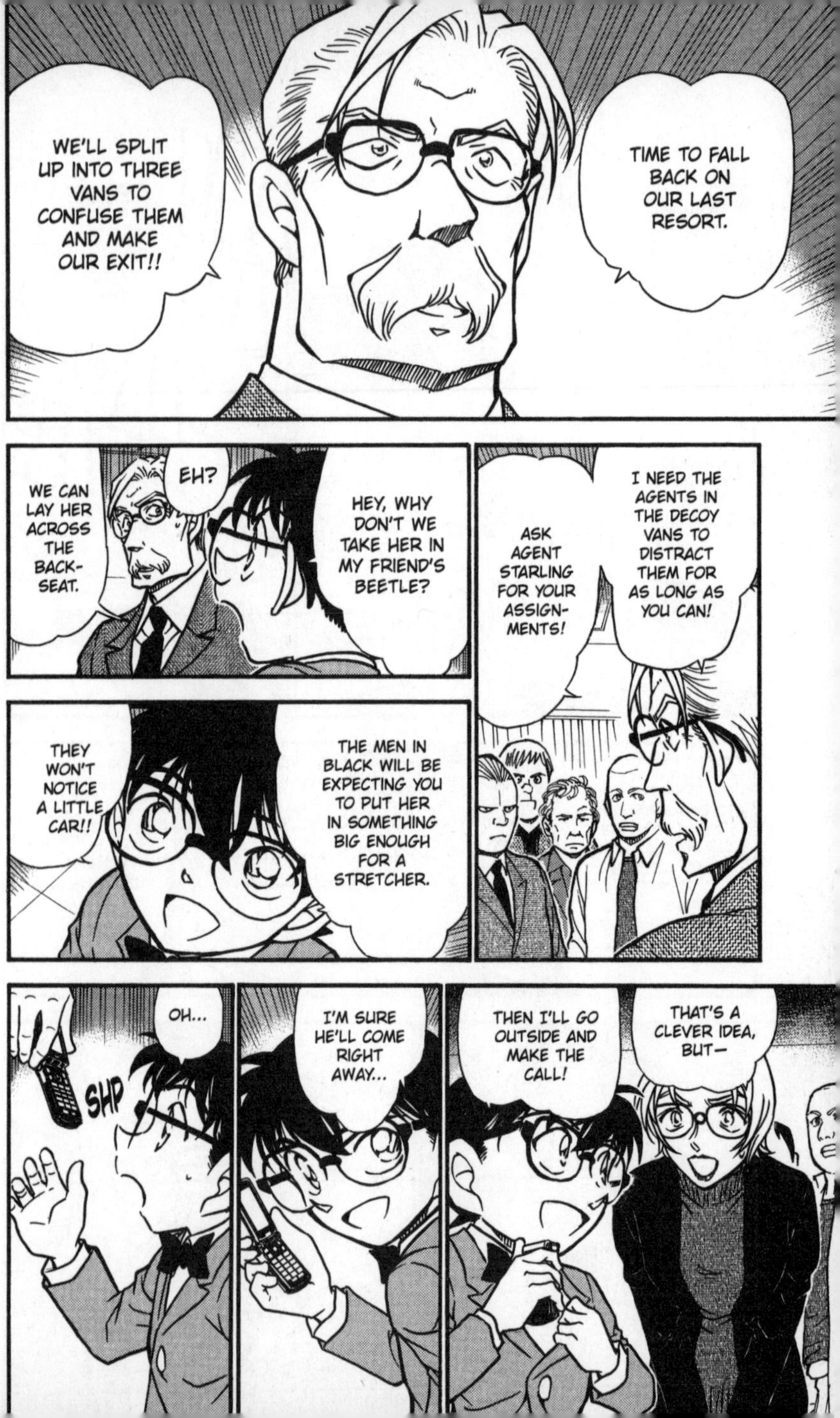
TIME TO FALL BACK ON OUR LAST RESORT.
WE'LL SPLIT UP INTO THREE VANS TO CONFUSE THEM AND MAKE OUR EXIT!!
I NEED THE AGENTS IN THE DECOY VANS TO DISTRACT THEM FOR AS LONG AS YOU CAN!
ASK AGENT STARLING FOR YOUR ASSIGN-MENTS!
HEY, WHY DON'T WE TAKE HER IN MY FRIEND'S BEETLE?
EH?
WE CAN LAY HER ACROSS THE BACK-SEAT.
THE MEN IN BLACK WILL BE EXPECTING YOU TO PUT HER IN SOMETHING BIG ENOUGH FOR A STRETCHER.
THEY WON'T NOTICE A LITTLE CAR!!
THAT'S A CLEVER IDEA, BUT—
THEN I'LL GO OUTSIDE AND MAKE THE CALL!
I'M SURE HE'LL COME RIGHT AWAY...
OH...
SHP

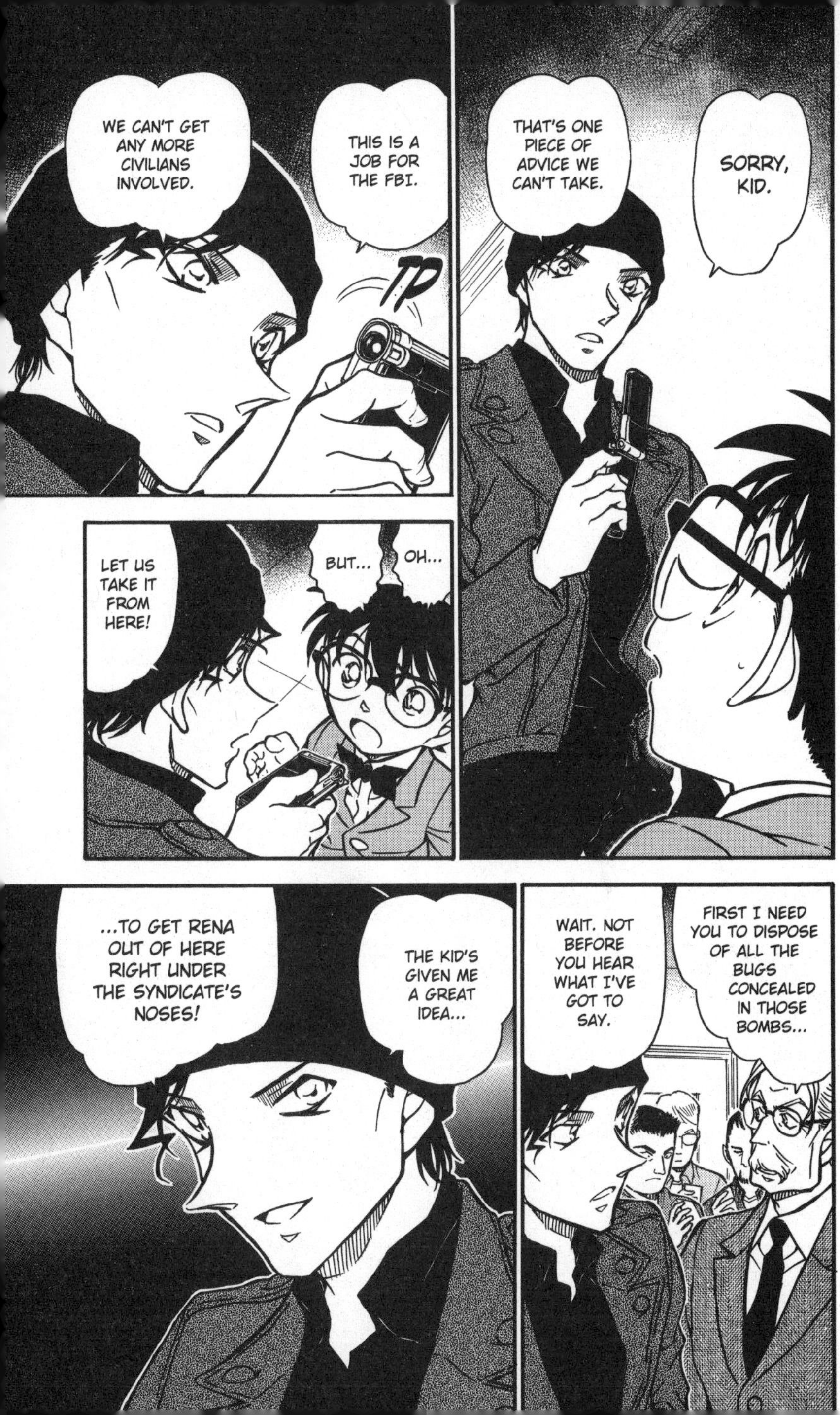
SORRY, KID.
THAT'S ONE PIECE OF ADVICE WE CAN'T TAKE.
THIS IS A JOB FOR THE FBI.
WE CAN'T GET ANY MORE CIVILIANS INVOLVED.
TP
OH...
BUT...
LET US TAKE IT FROM HERE!
FIRST I NEED YOU TO DISPOSE OF ALL THE BUGS CONCEALED IN THOSE BOMBS...
WAIT. NOT BEFORE YOU HEAR WHAT I'VE GOT TO SAY.
THE KID'S GIVEN ME A GREAT IDEA...
...TO GET RENA OUT OF HERE RIGHT UNDER THE SYNDICATE'S NOSES!

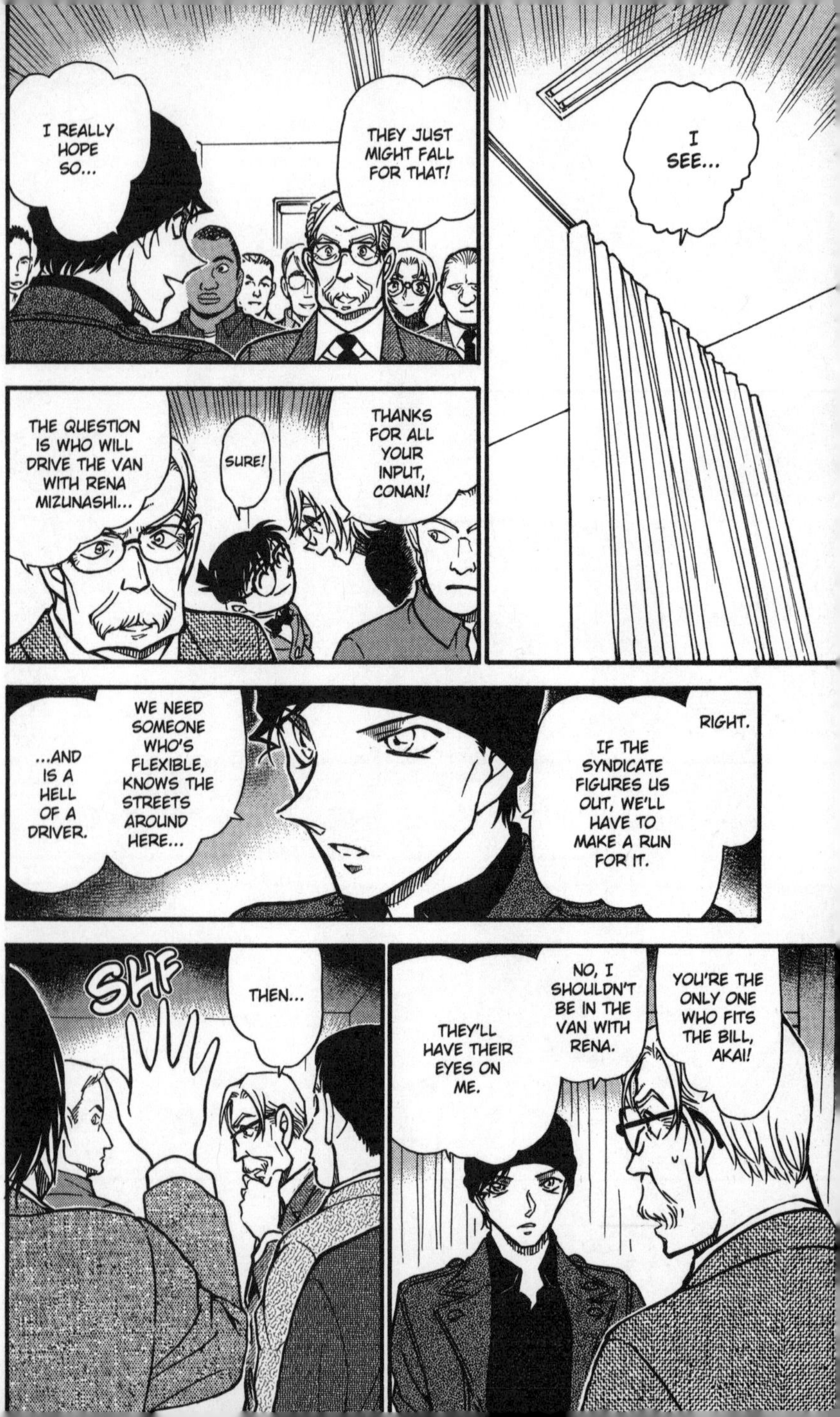
I SEE...
THEY JUST MIGHT FALL FOR THAT!
I REALLY HOPE SO...
THANKS FOR ALL YOUR INPUT, CONAN!
SURE!
THE QUESTION IS WHO WILL DRIVE THE VAN WITH RENA MIZUNASHI...
RIGHT.
IF THE SYNDICATE FIGURES US OUT, WE'LL HAVE TO MAKE A RUN FOR IT.
WE NEED SOMEONE WHO'S FLEXIBLE, KNOWS THE STREETS AROUND HERE...
...AND IS A HELL OF A DRIVER.
YOU'RE THE ONLY ONE WHO FITS THE BILL, AKAI!
NO, I SHOULDN'T BE IN THE VAN WITH RENA.
THEY'LL HAVE THEIR EYES ON ME.
THEN...
SHF

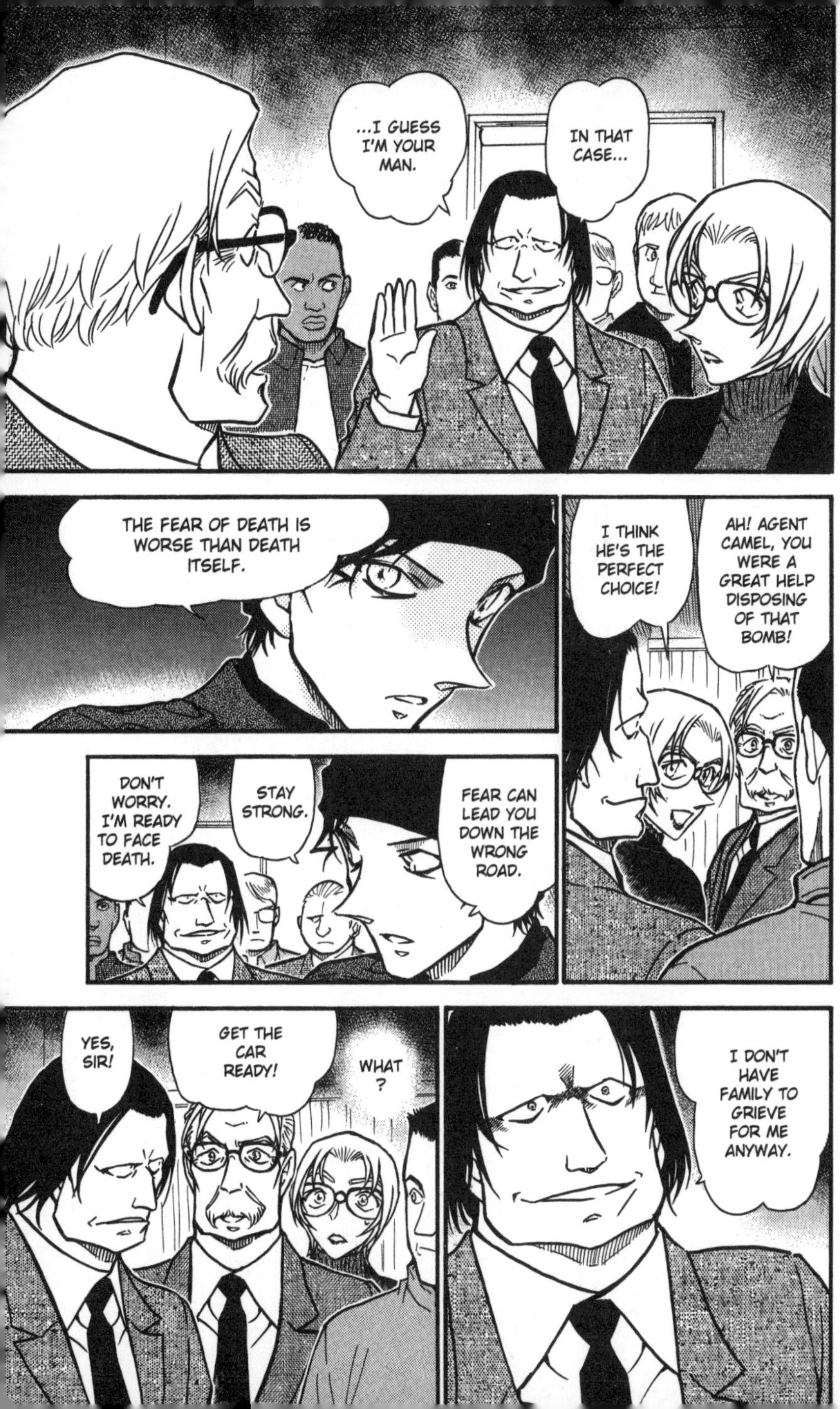
IN THAT CASE...
...I GUESS I'M YOUR MAN.
AH! AGENT CAMEL, YOU WERE A GREAT HELP DISPOSING OF THAT BOMB!
I THINK HE'S THE PERFECT CHOICE!
THE FEAR OF DEATH IS WORSE THAN DEATH ITSELF.
FEAR CAN LEAD YOU DOWN THE WRONG ROAD.
STAY STRONG.
DON'T WORRY. I'M READY TO FACE DEATH.
I DON'T HAVE FAMILY TO GRIEVE FOR ME ANYWAY.
WHAT ?
GET THE CAR READY!
YES, SIR!

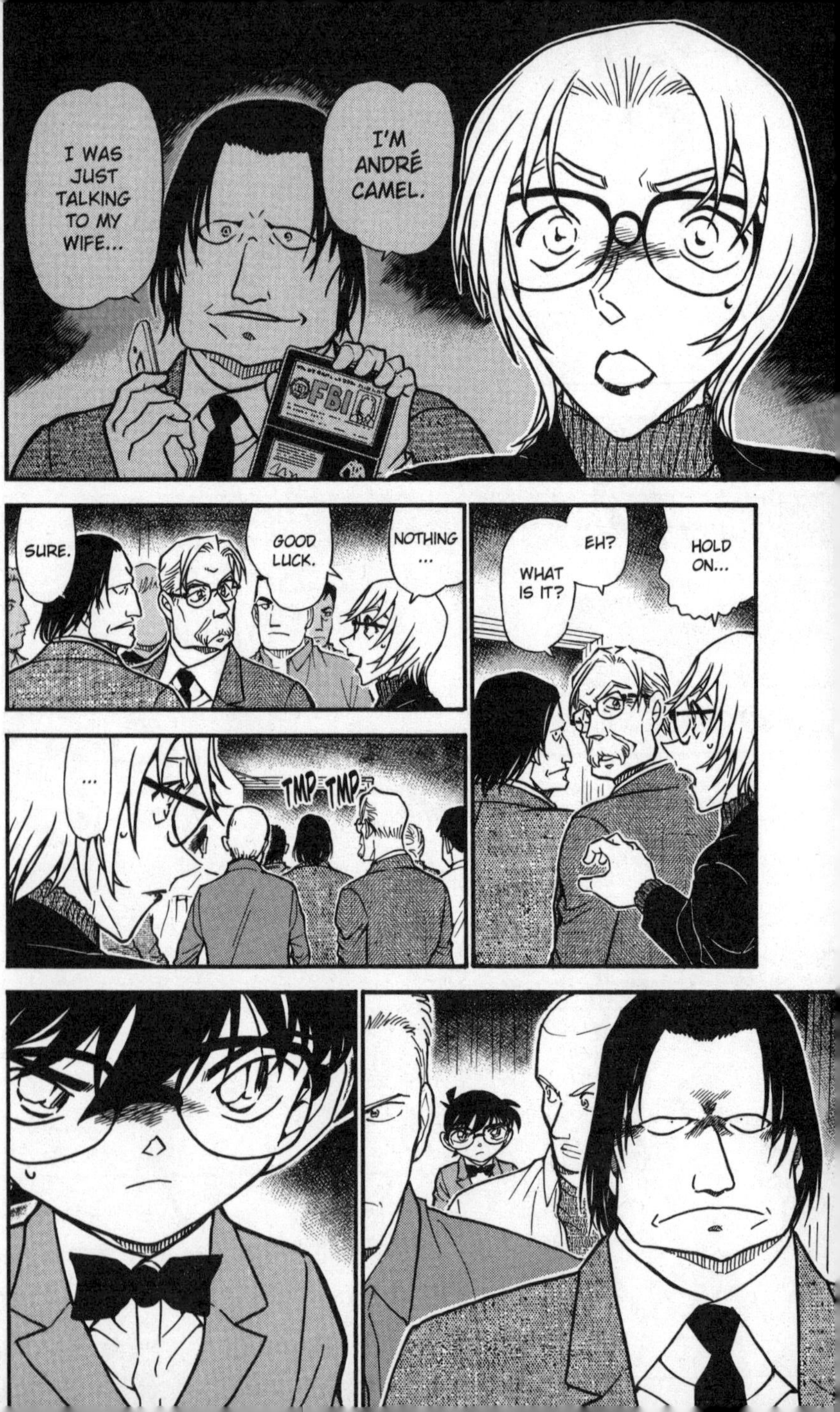
I'M ANDRÉ CAMEL.
I WAS JUST TALKING TO MY WIFE...
HOLD ON...
EH?
WHAT IS IT?
NOTHING...
GOOD LUCK.
SURE.
...
TMP TMP

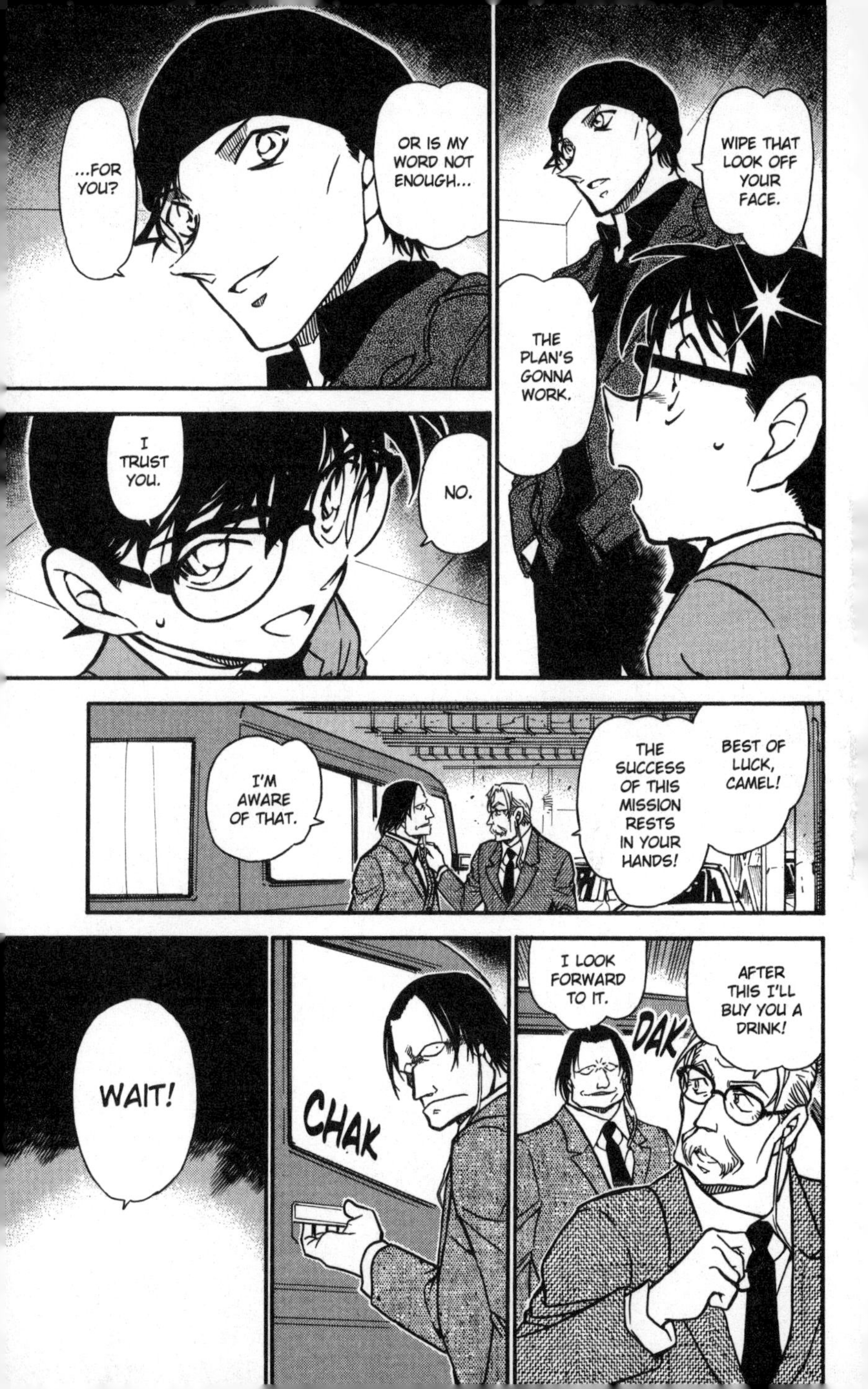
WIPE THAT LOOK OFF YOUR FACE.
THE PLAN'S GONNA WORK.
OR IS MY WORD NOT ENOUGH...
...FOR YOU?
NO.
I TRUST YOU.
BEST OF LUCK, CAMEL!
THE SUCCESS OF THIS MISSION RESTS IN YOUR HANDS!
I'M AWARE OF THAT.
AFTER THIS I'LL BUY YOU A DRINK!
DAK
I LOOK FORWARD TO IT.
CHAK
WAIT!

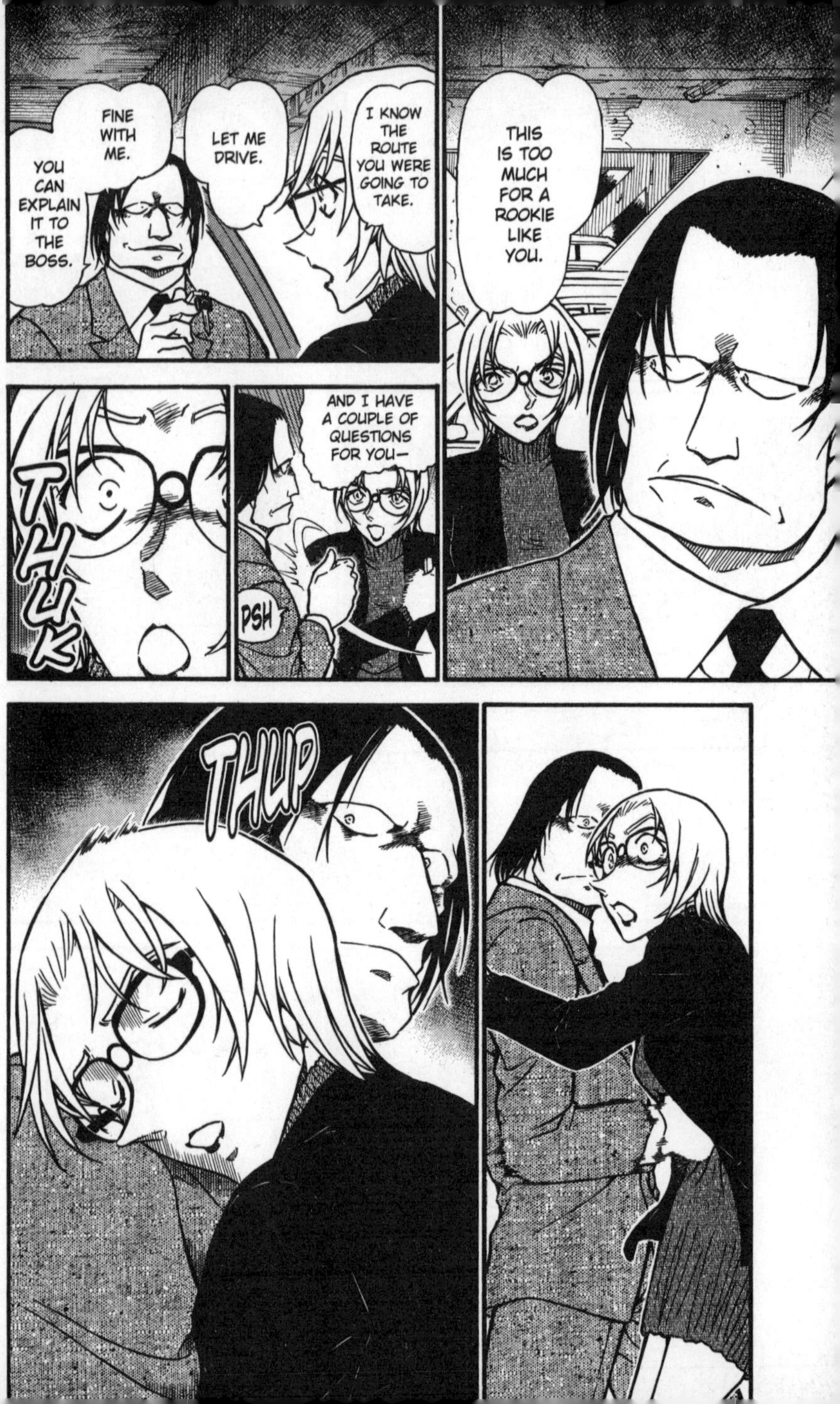
THIS IS TOO MUCH FOR A ROOKIE LIKE YOU.
I KNOW THE ROUTE YOU WERE GOING TO TAKE.
LET ME DRIVE.
FINE WITH ME.
YOU CAN EXPLAIN IT TO THE BOSS.
AND I HAVE A COUPLE OF QUESTIONS FOR YOU—
PSH
THUK
THUP

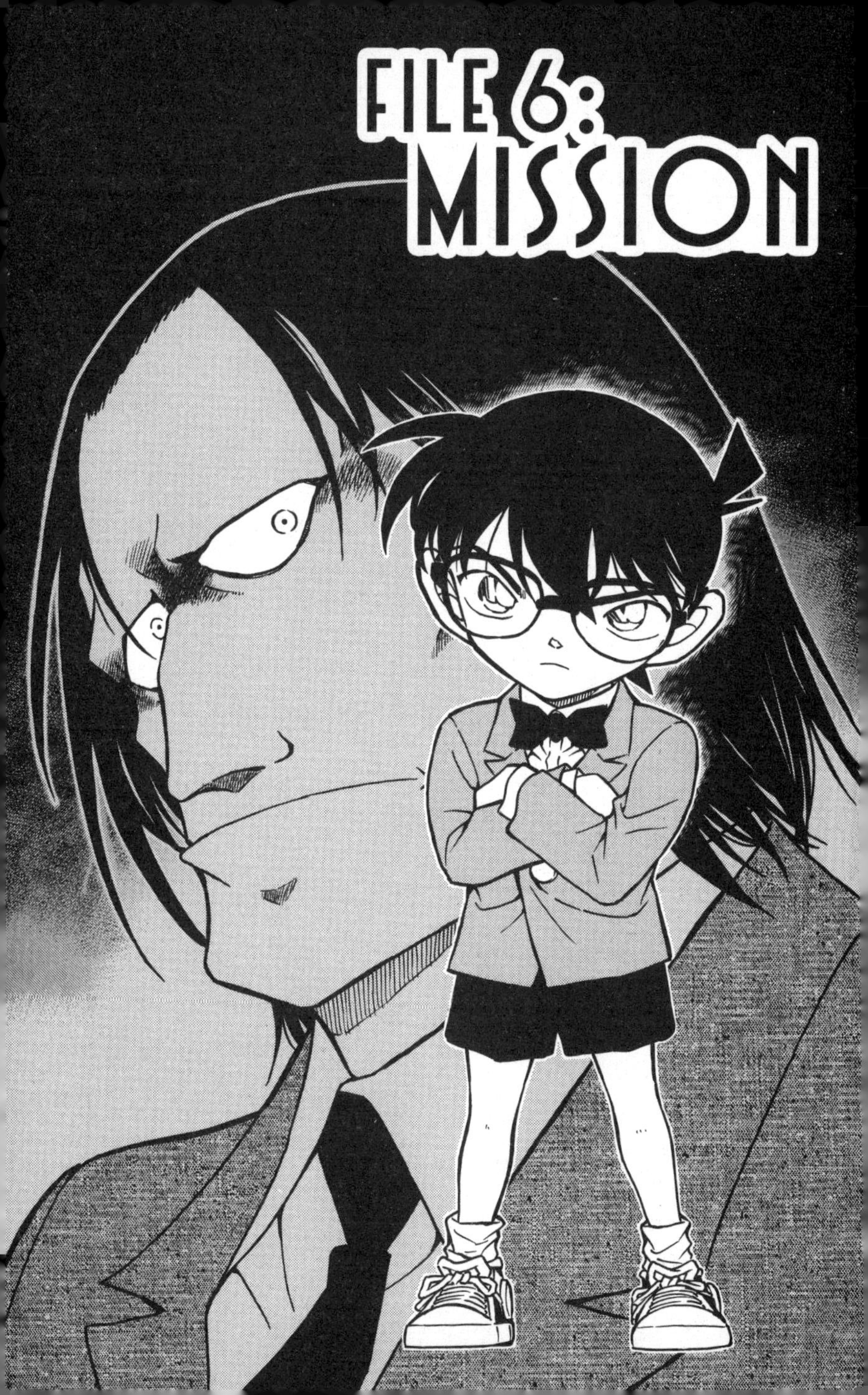
FILE 6:
MISSION

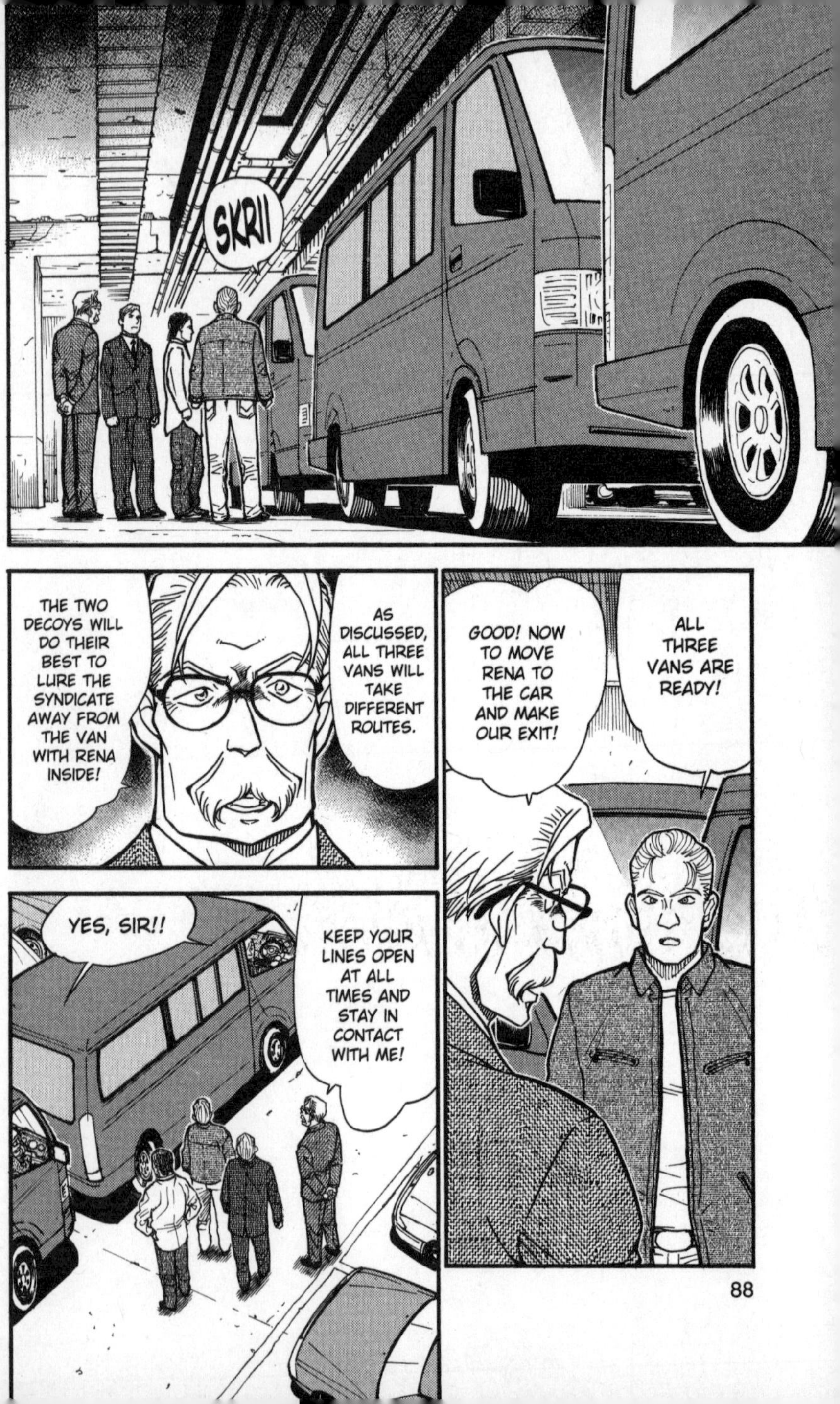
SKRII
ALL THREE VANS ARE READY!
GOOD! NOW TO MOVE RENA TO THE CAR AND MAKE OUR EXIT!
AS DISCUSSED, ALL THREE VANS WILL TAKE DIFFERENT ROUTES.
THE TWO DECOYS WILL DO THEIR BEST TO LURE THE SYNDICATE AWAY FROM THE VAN WITH RENA INSIDE!
KEEP YOUR LINES OPEN AT ALL TIMES AND STAY IN CONTACT WITH ME!
YES, SIR!!

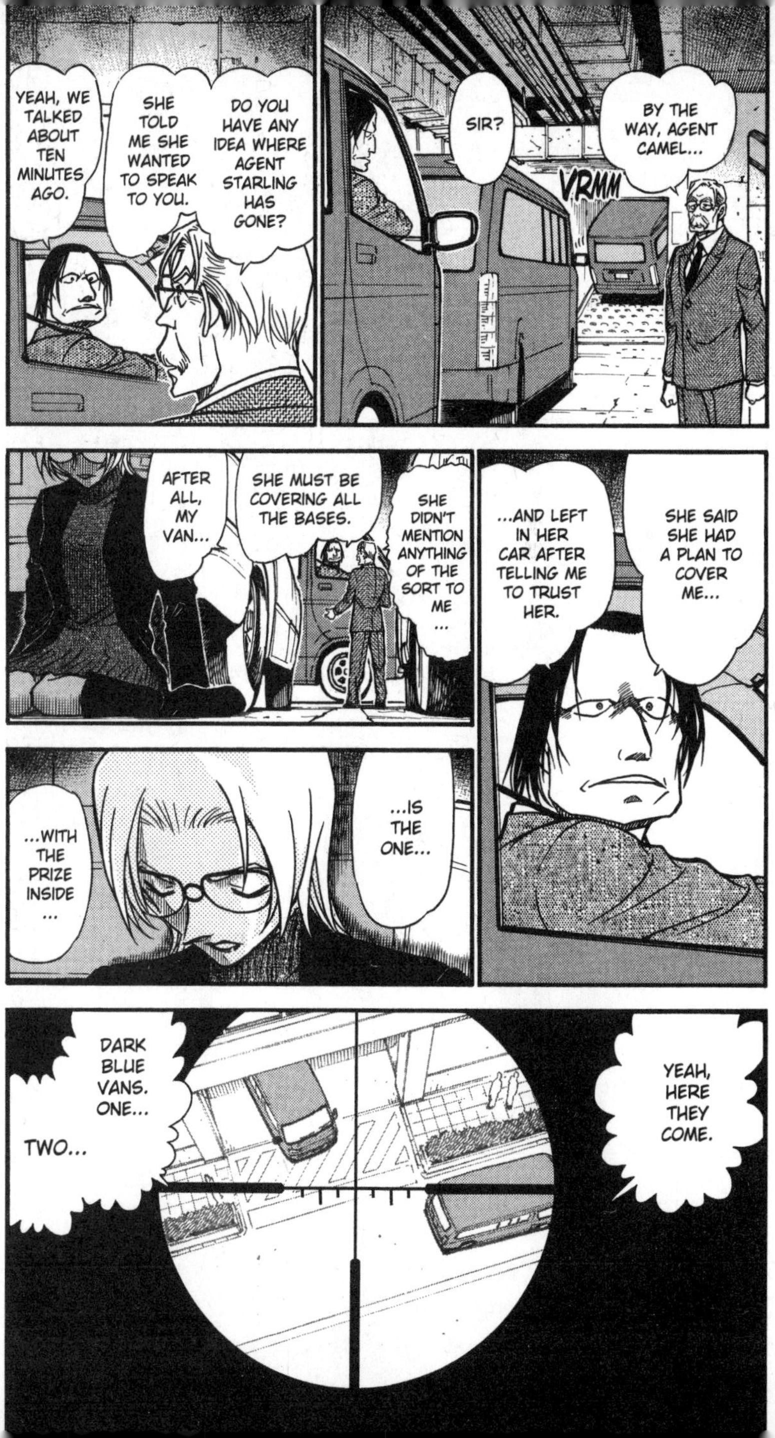
BY THE WAY, AGENT CAMEL...
VRMM
SIR?
DO YOU HAVE ANY IDEA WHERE AGENT STARLING HAS GONE?
SHE TOLD ME SHE WANTED TO SPEAK TO YOU.
YEAH, WE TALKED ABOUT TEN MINUTES AGO.
SHE SAID SHE HAD A PLAN TO COVER ME...
...AND LEFT IN HER CAR AFTER TELLING ME TO TRUST HER.
SHE DIDN'T MENTION ANYTHING OF THE SORT TO ME...
SHE MUST BE COVERING ALL THE BASES.
AFTER ALL, MY VAN...
...IS THE ONE...
...WITH THE PRIZE INSIDE...
YEAH, HERE THEY COME.
DARK BLUE VANS. ONE...
TWO...

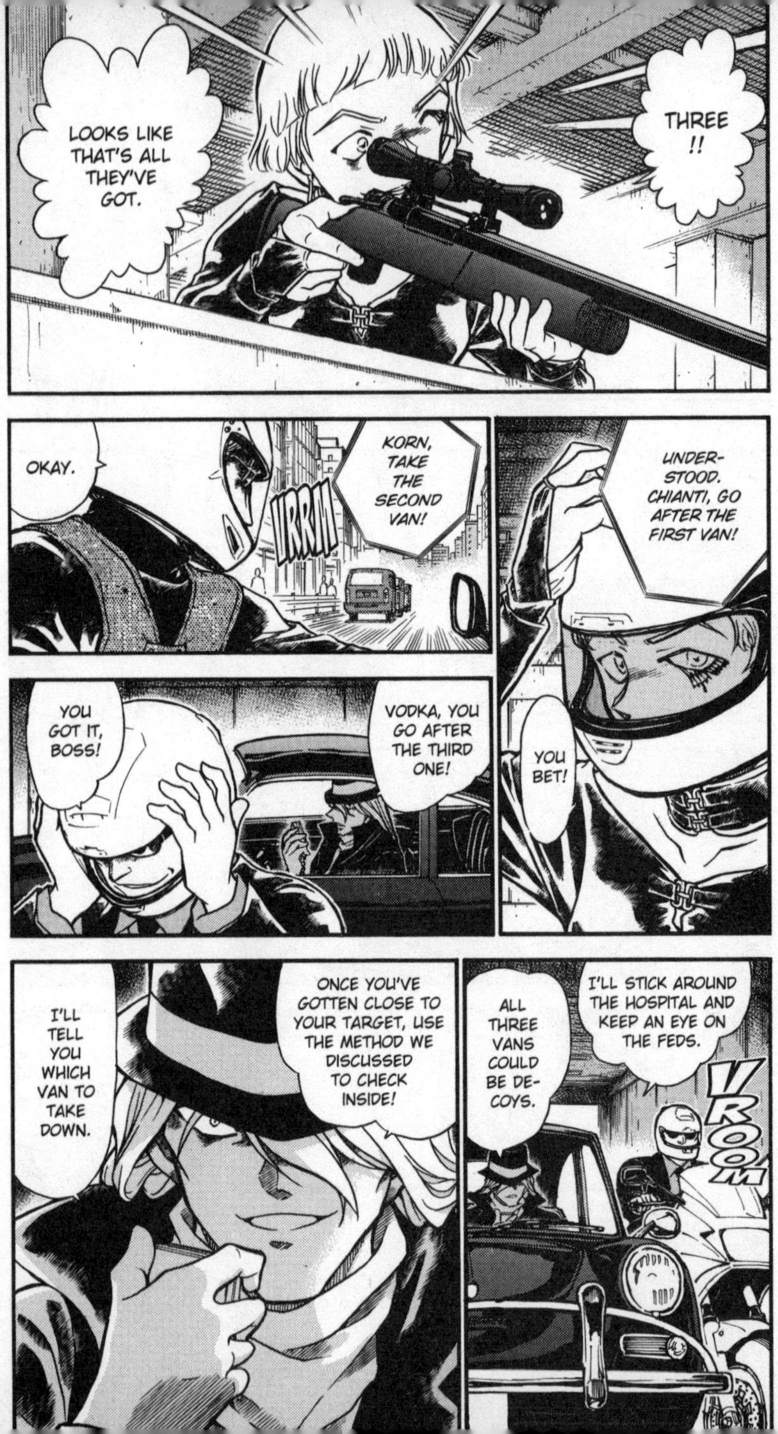
THREE !!
LOOKS LIKE THAT'S ALL THEY'VE GOT.
UNDER-STOOD. CHIANTI, GO AFTER THE FIRST VAN!
YOU BET!
KORN, TAKE THE SECOND VAN!
VRRM
OKAY.
VODKA, YOU GO AFTER THE THIRD ONE!
YOU GOT IT, BOSS!
I'LL STICK AROUND THE HOSPITAL AND KEEP AN EYE ON THE FEDS.
VROOM
ALL THREE VANS COULD BE DE-COYS.
ONCE YOU'VE GOTTEN CLOSE TO YOUR TARGET, USE THE METHOD WE DISCUSSED TO CHECK INSIDE!
I'LL TELL YOU WHICH VAN TO TAKE DOWN.

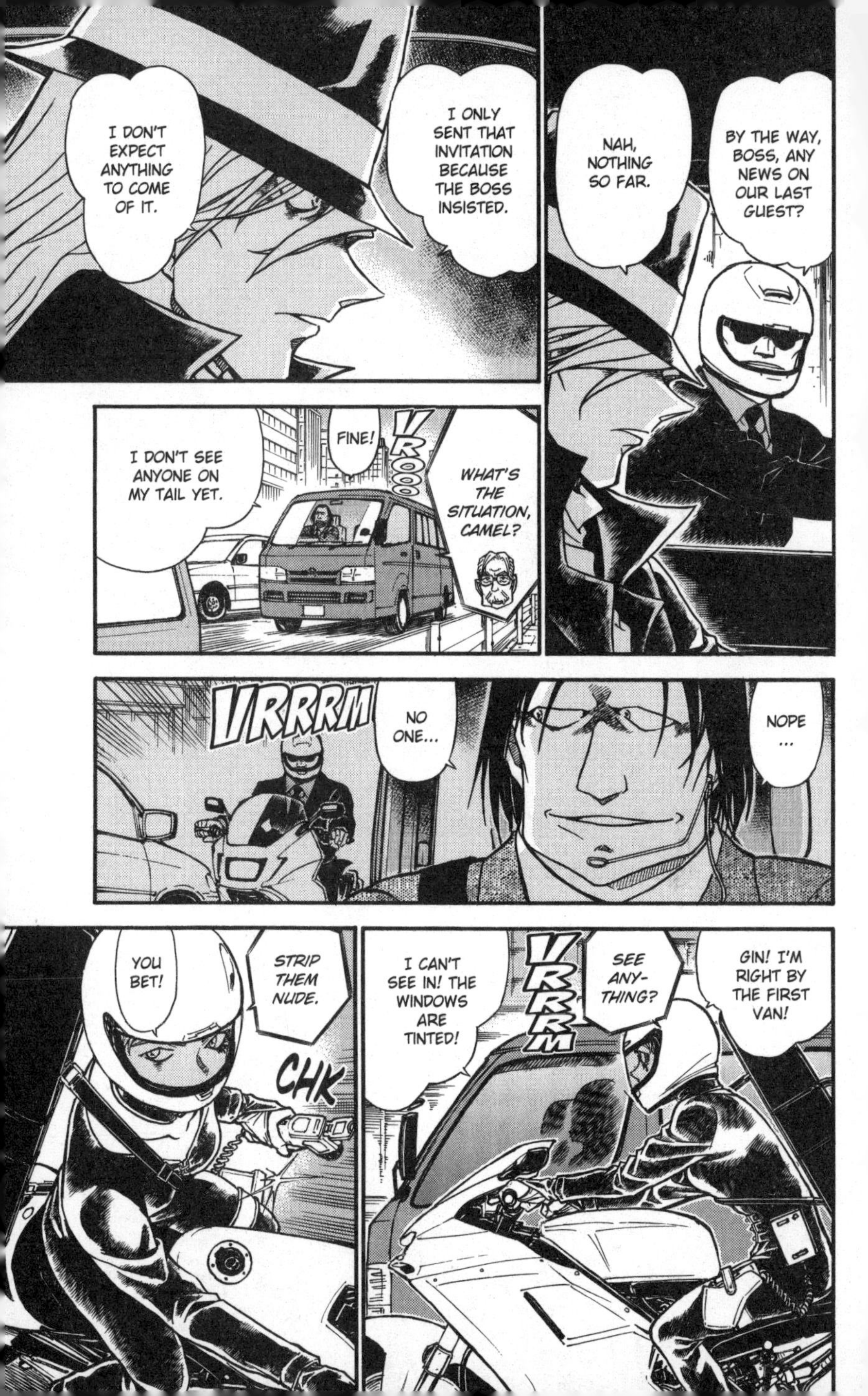
BY THE WAY, BOSS, ANY NEWS ON OUR LAST GUEST?
NAH, NOTHING SO FAR.
I ONLY SENT THAT INVITATION BECAUSE THE BOSS INSISTED.
I DON'T EXPECT ANYTHING TO COME OF IT.
WHAT'S THE SITUATION, CAMEL?
VROOOO
FINE!
I DON'T SEE ANYONE ON MY TAIL YET.
NOPE ...
NO ONE...
VRRRM
GIN! I'M RIGHT BY THE FIRST VAN!
SEE ANY-THING?
VRRRM
I CAN'T SEE IN! THE WINDOWS ARE TINTED!
STRIP THEM NUDE.
YOU BET!
CHK

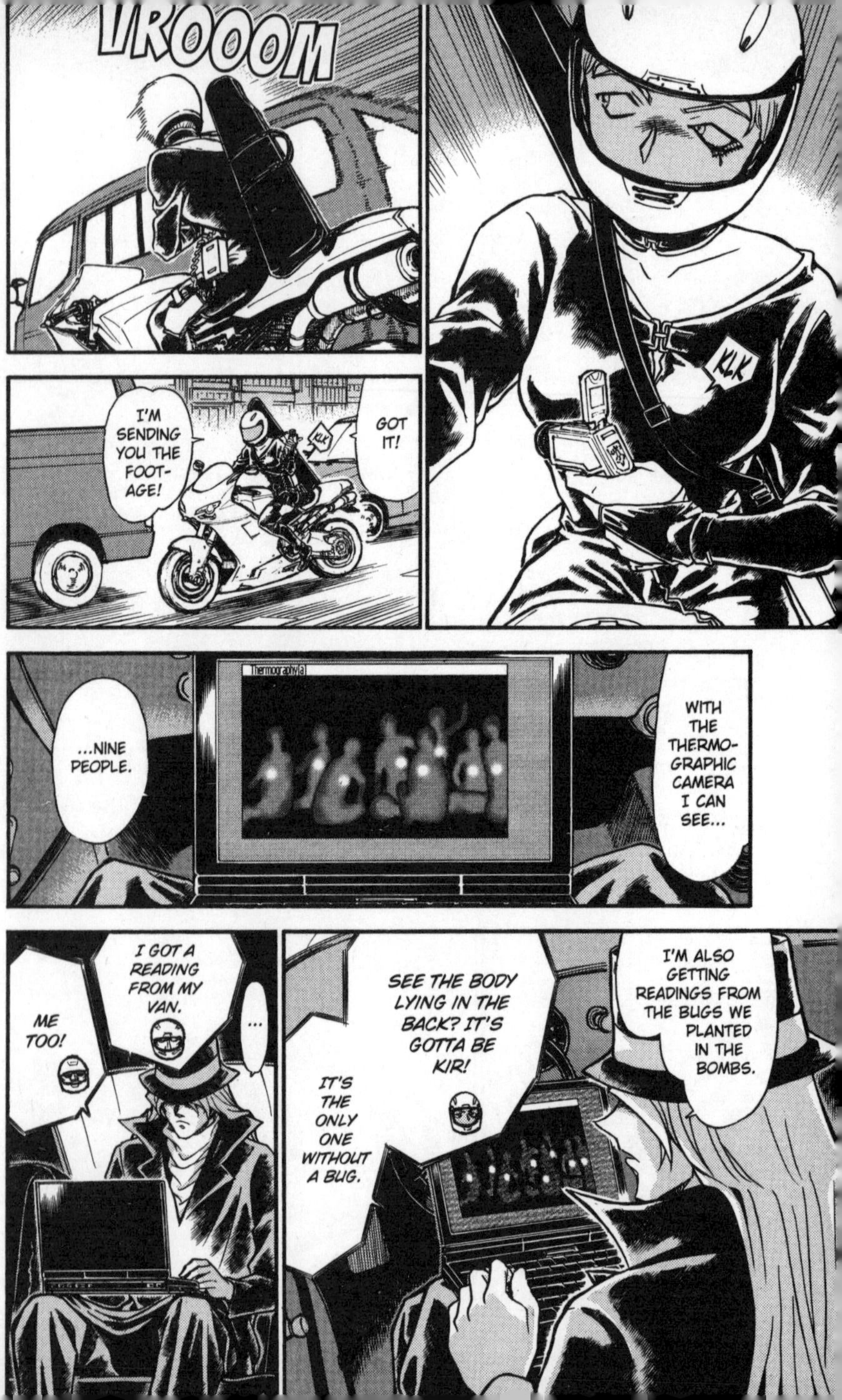
KLK
VROOOM
GOT IT!
I'M SENDING YOU THE FOOTAGE!
KLK
WITH THE THERMOGRAPHIC CAMERA I CAN SEE...
Thermography a
...NINE PEOPLE.
I'M ALSO GETTING READINGS FROM THE BUGS WE PLANTED IN THE BOMBS.
SEE THE BODY LYING IN THE BACK? IT'S GOTTA BE KIR!
IT'S THE ONLY ONE WITHOUT A BUG.
...
I GOT A READING FROM MY VAN.
ME TOO!

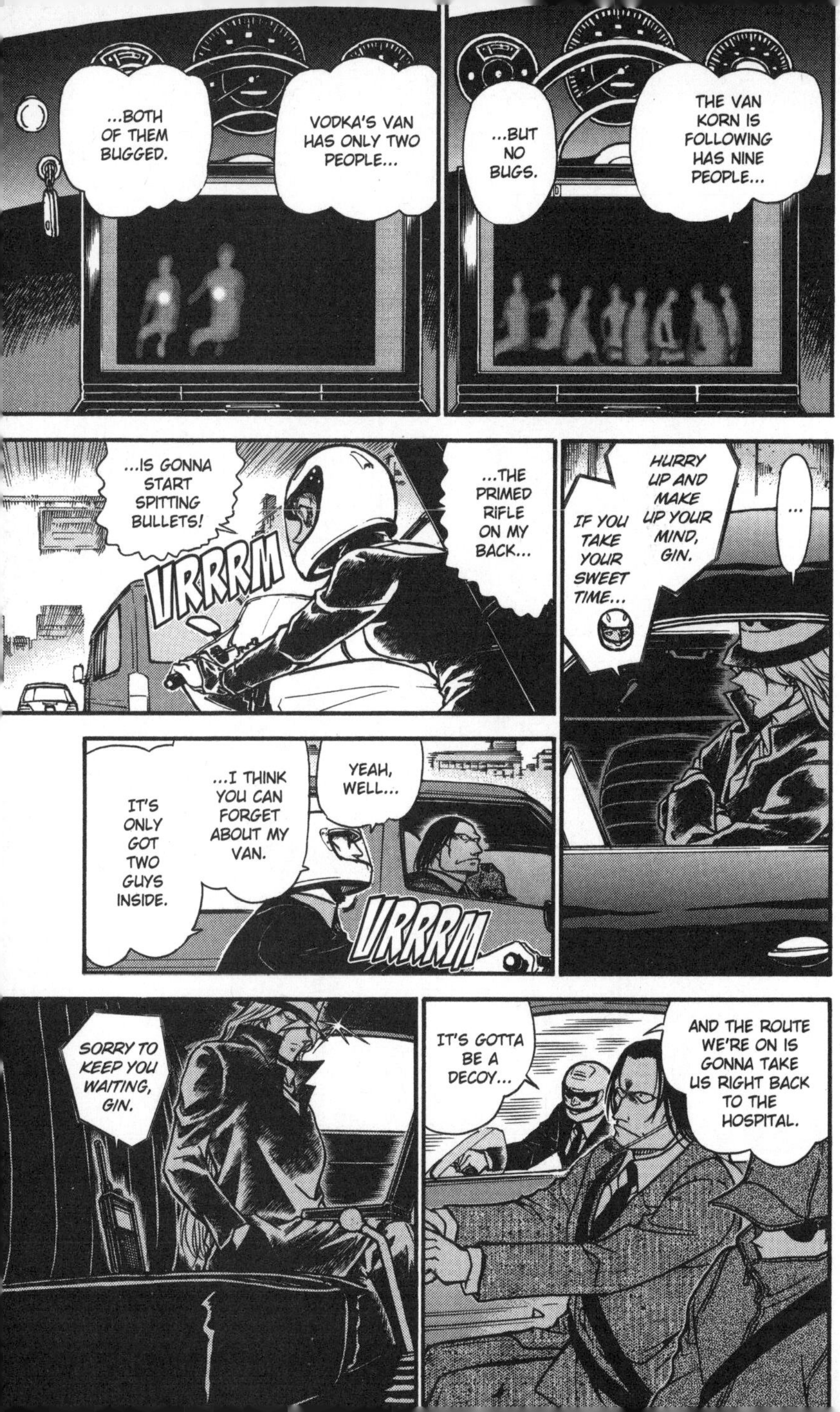
THE VAN KORN IS FOLLOWING HAS NINE PEOPLE...
...BUT NO BUGS.
VODKA'S VAN HAS ONLY TWO PEOPLE...
...BOTH OF THEM BUGGED.
...
HURRY UP AND MAKE UP YOUR MIND, GIN.
IF YOU TAKE YOUR SWEET TIME...
...THE PRIMED RIFLE ON MY BACK...
VRRRM
...IS GONNA START SPITTING BULLETS!
YEAH, WELL...
...I THINK YOU CAN FORGET ABOUT MY VAN.
IT'S ONLY GOT TWO GUYS INSIDE.
VRRRM
AND THE ROUTE WE'RE ON IS GONNA TAKE US RIGHT BACK TO THE HOSPITAL.
IT'S GOTTA BE A DECOY...
SORRY TO KEEP YOU WAITING, GIN.

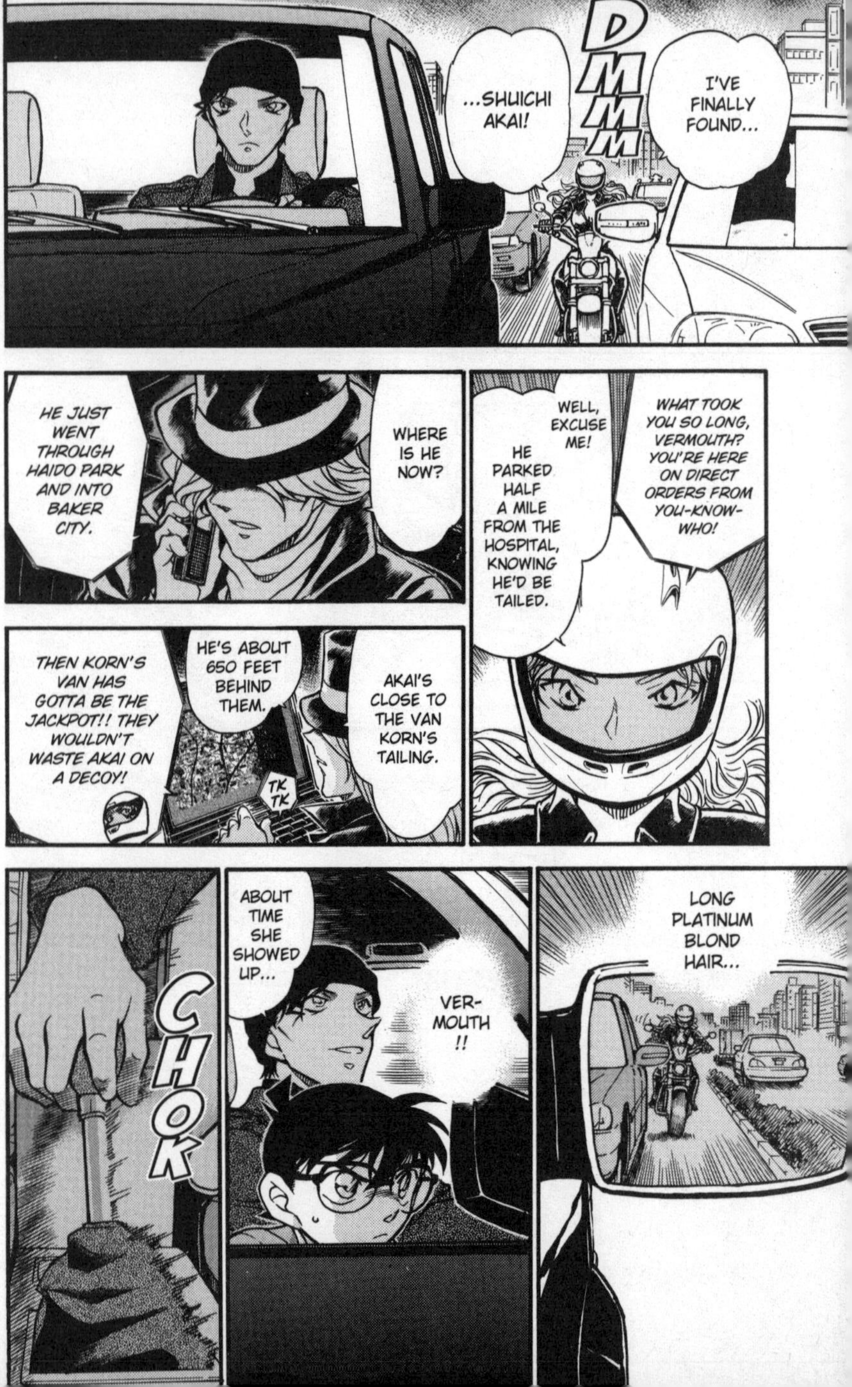
I'VE FINALLY FOUND...
DMMM
...SHUICHI AKAI!
WHAT TOOK YOU SO LONG, VERMOUTH? YOU'RE HERE ON DIRECT ORDERS FROM YOU-KNOW-WHO!
WELL, EXCUSE ME!
HE PARKED HALF A MILE FROM THE HOSPITAL, KNOWING HE'D BE TAILED.
WHERE IS HE NOW?
HE JUST WENT THROUGH HAIDO PARK AND INTO BAKER CITY.
AKAI'S CLOSE TO THE VAN KORN'S TAILING.
TK TK
HE'S ABOUT 650 FEET BEHIND THEM.
THEN KORN'S VAN HAS GOTTA BE THE JACKPOT!! THEY WOULDN'T WASTE AKAI ON A DECOY!
LONG PLATINUM BLOND HAIR...
ABOUT TIME SHE SHOWED UP...
VER-MOUTH!!
CHOK

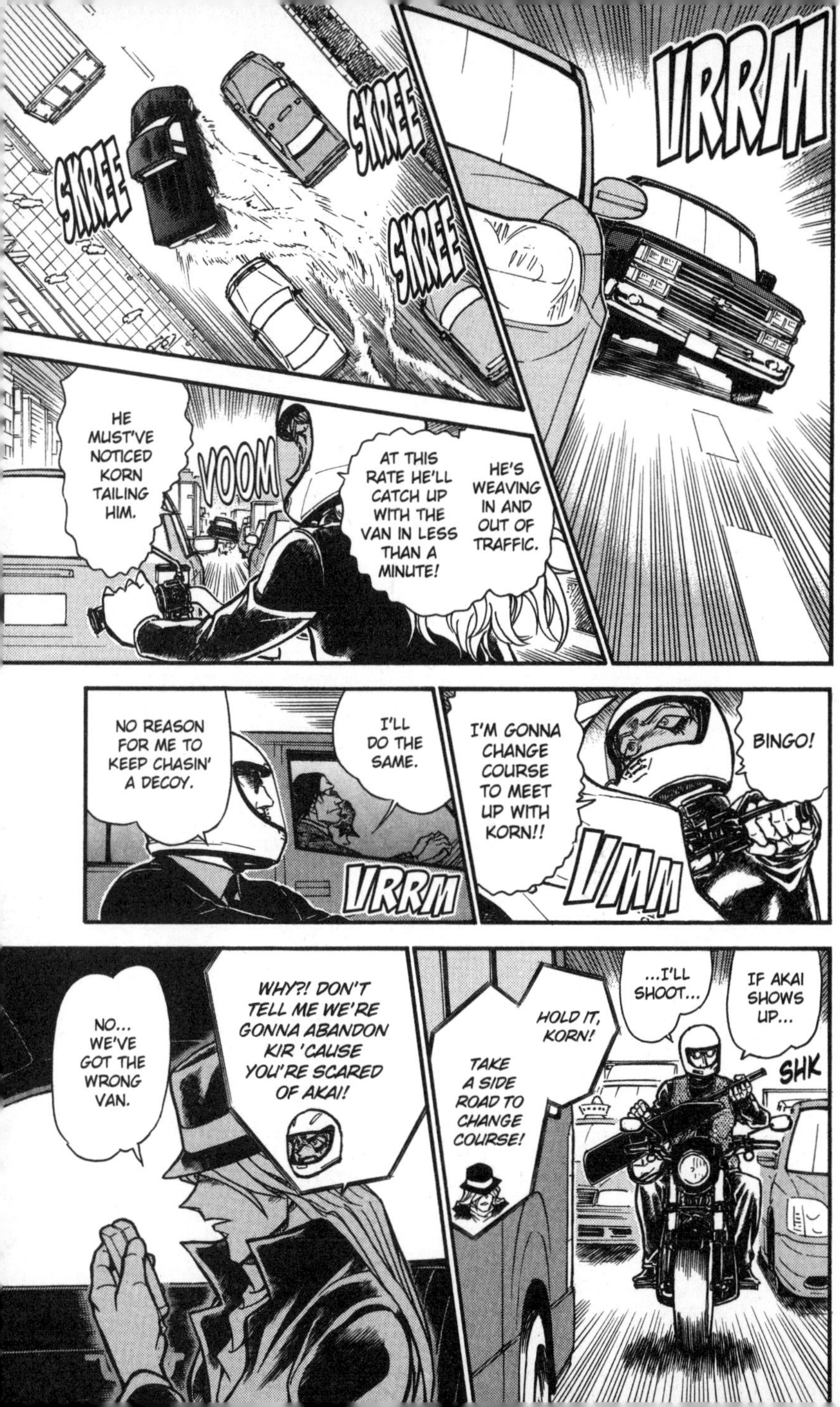
VRRM
SKREE
SKREE
SKREE
HE'S WEAVING IN AND OUT OF TRAFFIC.
AT THIS RATE HE'LL CATCH UP WITH THE VAN IN LESS THAN A MINUTE!
VOOM
HE MUST'VE NOTICED KORN TAILING HIM.
BINGO!
I'M GONNA CHANGE COURSE TO MEET UP WITH KORN!!
VMM
I'LL DO THE SAME.
NO REASON FOR ME TO KEEP CHASIN' A DECOY.
VRRM
IF AKAI SHOWS UP...
...I'LL SHOOT...
SHK
HOLD IT, KORN!
TAKE A SIDE ROAD TO CHANGE COURSE!
WHY?! DON'T TELL ME WE'RE GONNA ABANDON KIR 'CAUSE YOU'RE SCARED OF AKAI!
NO... WE'VE GOT THE WRONG VAN.

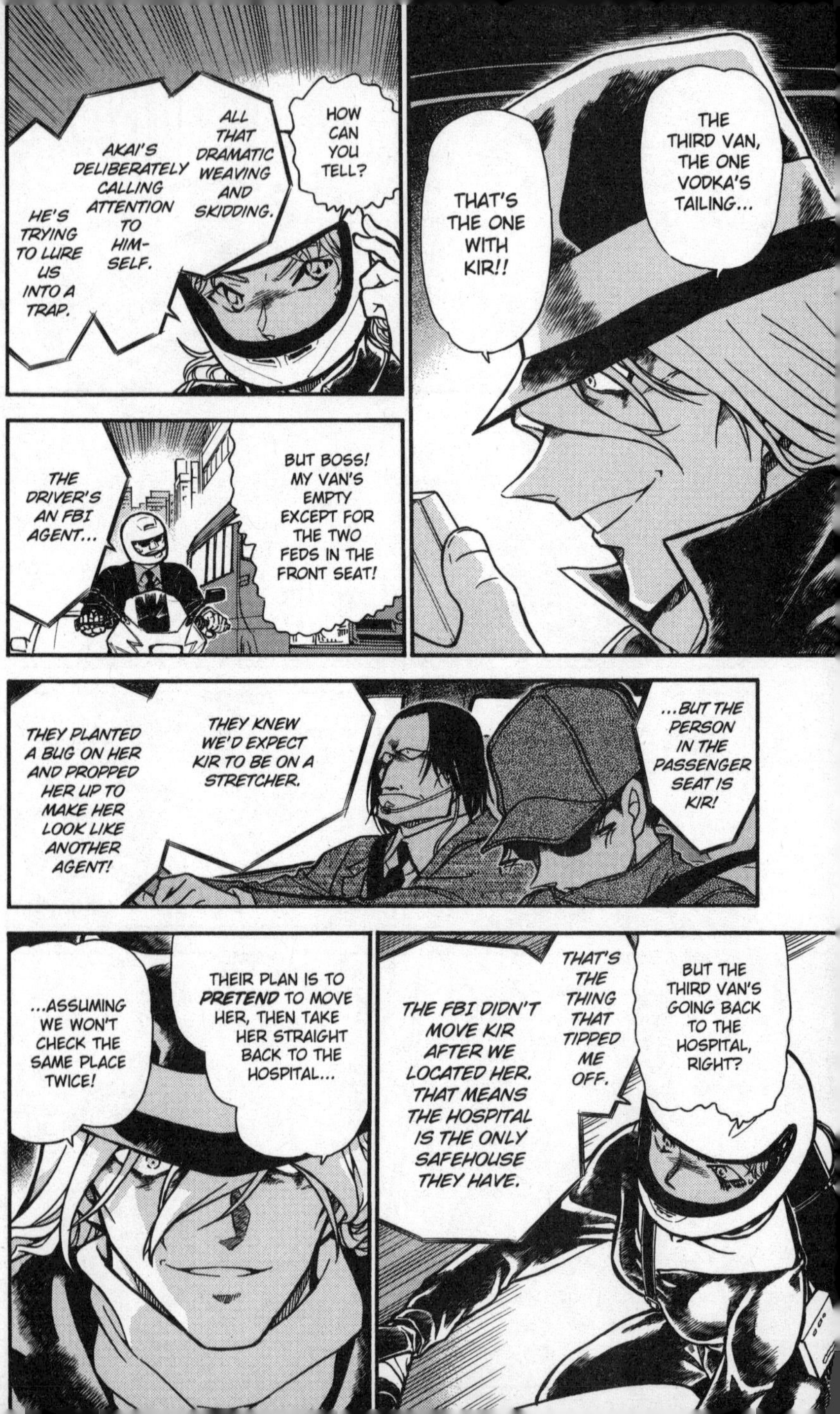
THE THIRD VAN, THE ONE VODKA'S TAILING...
THAT'S THE ONE WITH KIR!!
HOW CAN YOU TELL?
ALL THAT DRAMATIC WEAVING AND SKIDDING.
AKAI'S DELIBERATELY CALLING ATTENTION TO HIMSELF.
HE'S TRYING TO LURE US INTO A TRAP.
BUT BOSS! MY VAN'S EMPTY EXCEPT FOR THE TWO FEDS IN THE FRONT SEAT!
THE DRIVER'S AN FBI AGENT...
...BUT THE PERSON IN THE PASSENGER SEAT IS KIR!
THEY KNEW WE'D EXPECT KIR TO BE ON A STRETCHER.
THEY PLANTED A BUG ON HER AND PROPPED HER UP TO MAKE HER LOOK LIKE ANOTHER AGENT!
BUT THE THIRD VAN'S GOING BACK TO THE HOSPITAL, RIGHT?
THAT'S THE THING THAT TIPPED ME OFF.
THE FBI DIDN'T MOVE KIR AFTER WE LOCATED HER. THAT MEANS THE HOSPITAL IS THE ONLY SAFEHOUSE THEY HAVE.
THEIR PLAN IS TO PRETEND TO MOVE HER, THEN TAKE HER STRAIGHT BACK TO THE HOSPITAL...
...ASSUMING WE WON'T CHECK THE SAME PLACE TWICE!

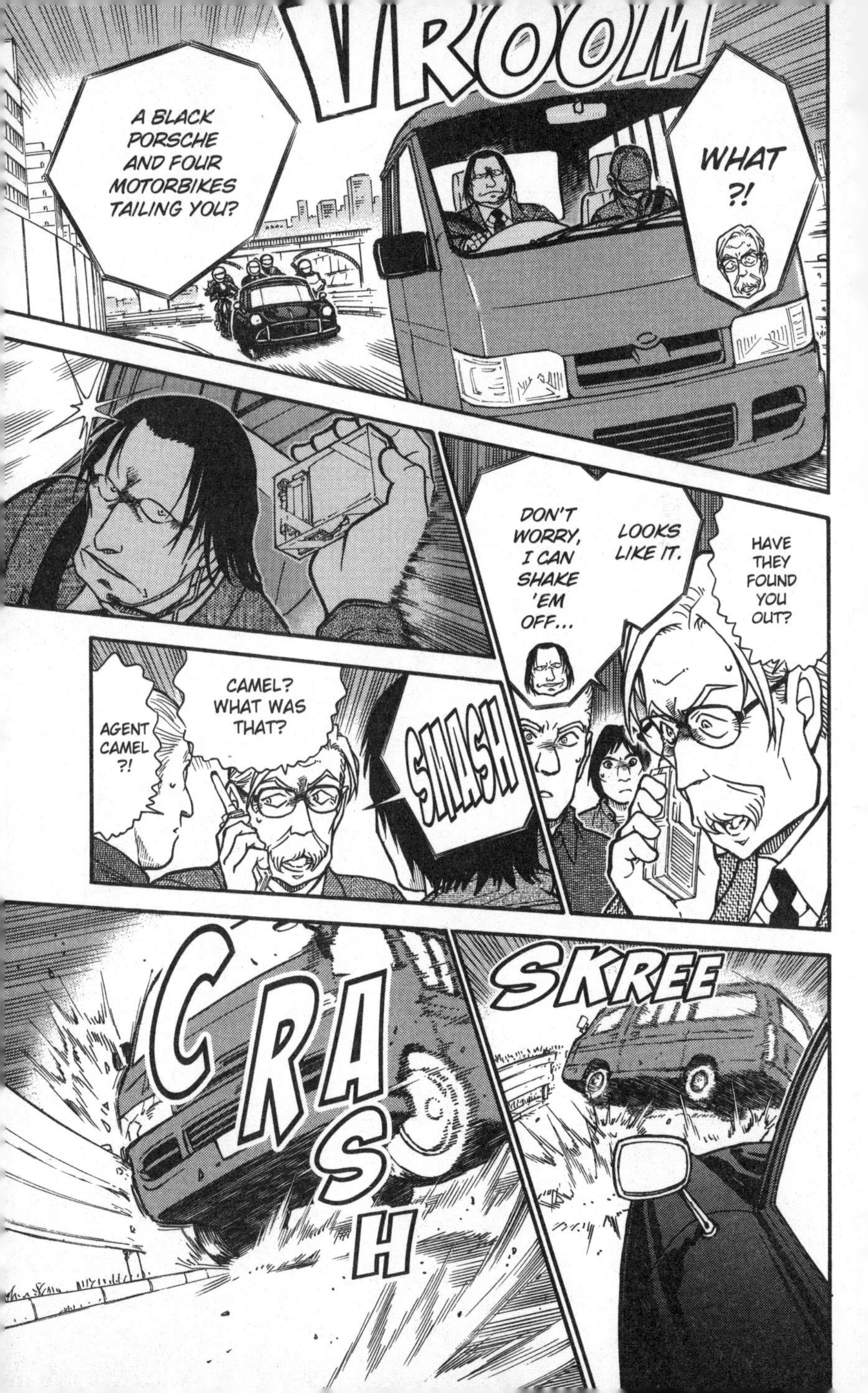
VROOM
WHAT ?!
A BLACK PORSCHE AND FOUR MOTORBIKES TAILING YOU?
HAVE THEY FOUND YOU OUT?
LOOKS LIKE IT.
DON'T WORRY, I CAN SHAKE 'EM OFF...
SMASH
CAMEL? WHAT WAS THAT?
AGENT CAMEL ?!
SKREE
CRASH

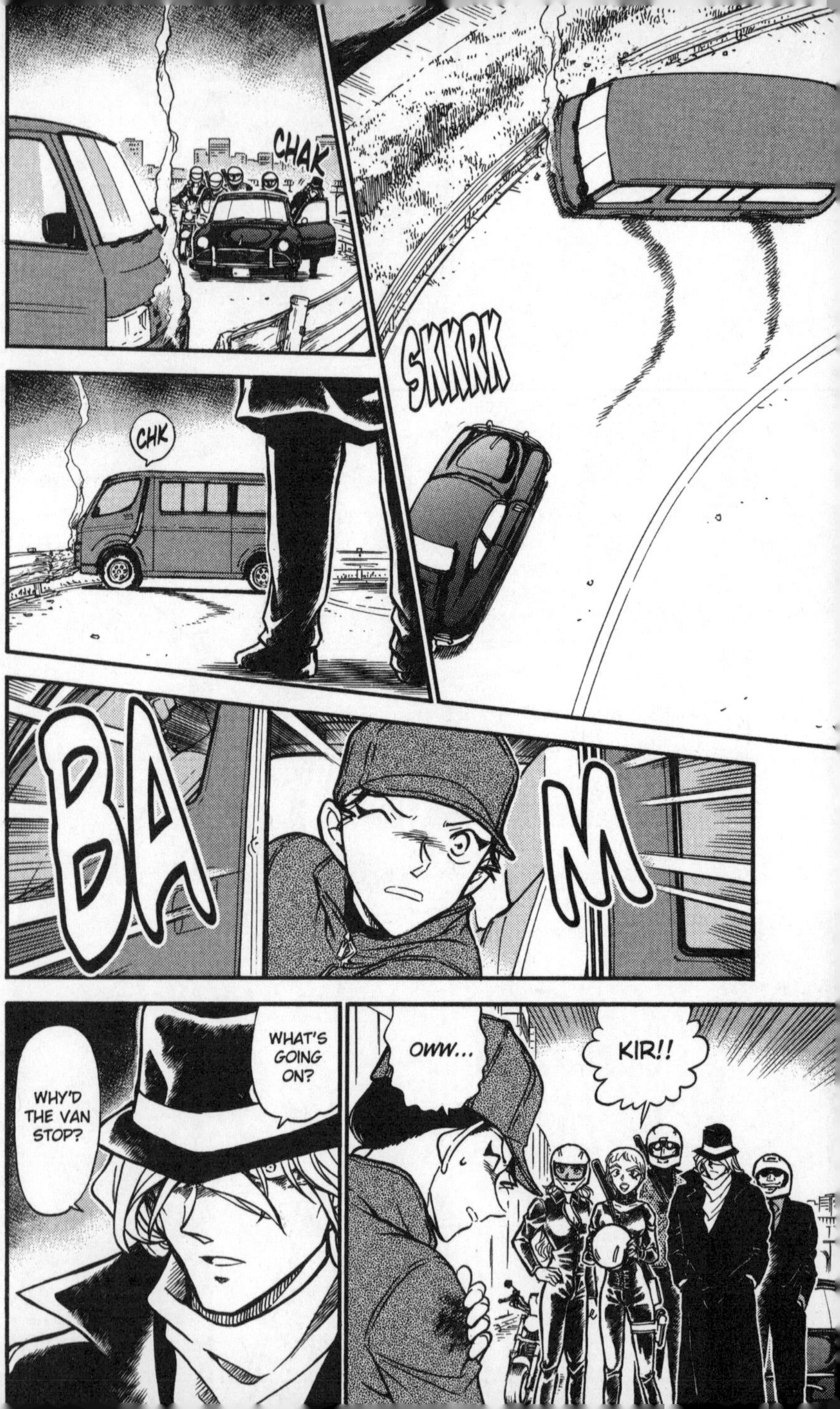
SKKRK
CHAK
CHK
BAM
KIR!!
OWW...
WHAT'S GOING ON?
WHY'D THE VAN STOP?

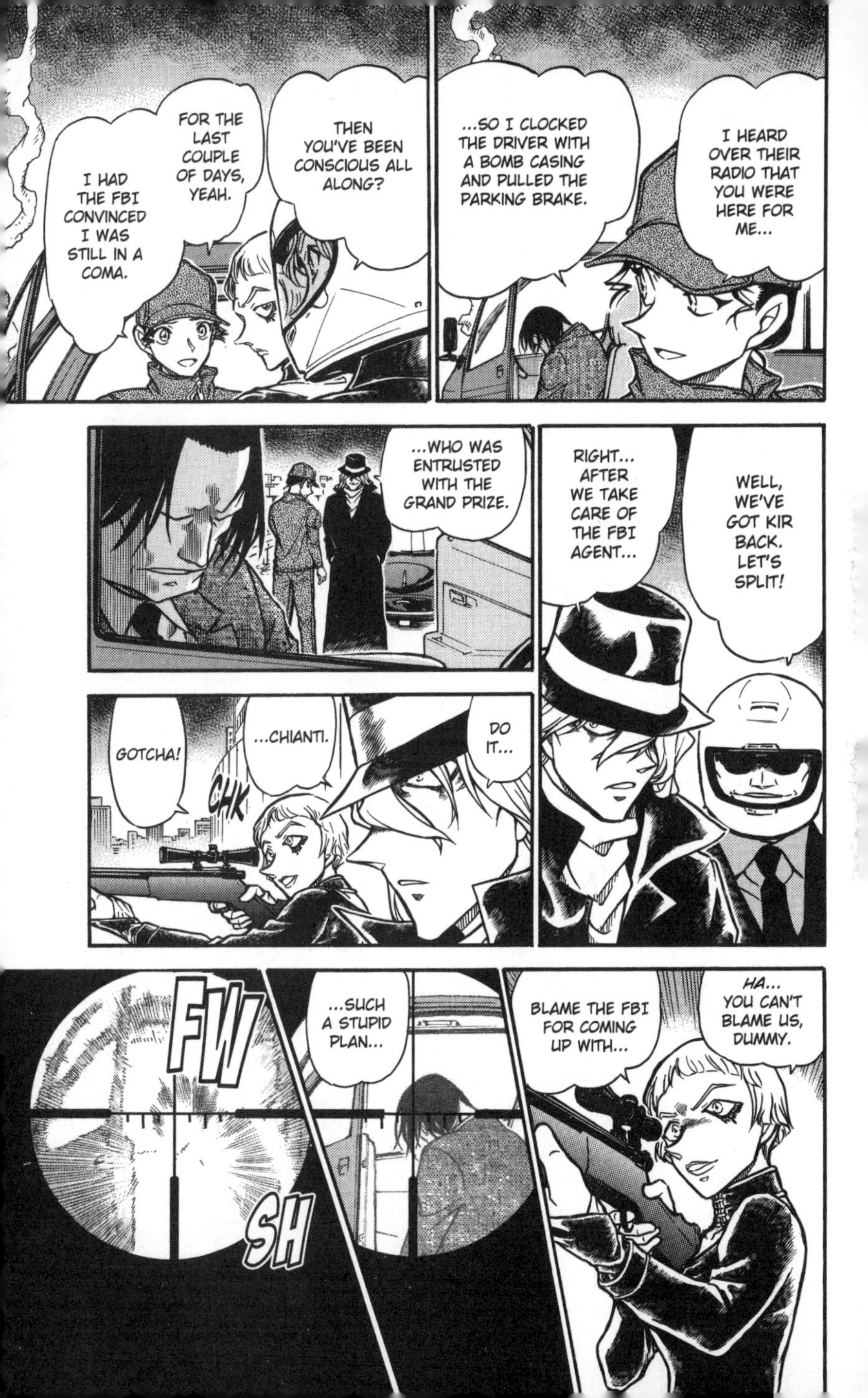
I HEARD OVER THEIR RADIO THAT YOU WERE HERE FOR ME...
...SO I CLOCKED THE DRIVER WITH A BOMB CASING AND PULLED THE PARKING BRAKE.
THEN YOU'VE BEEN CONSCIOUS ALL ALONG?
FOR THE LAST COUPLE OF DAYS, YEAH.
I HAD THE FBI CONVINCED I WAS STILL IN A COMA.
WELL, WE'VE GOT KIR BACK. LET'S SPLIT!
RIGHT... AFTER WE TAKE CARE OF THE FBI AGENT...
...WHO WAS ENTRUSTED WITH THE GRAND PRIZE.
DO IT...
...CHIANTI.
CHK
GOTCHA!
HA... YOU CAN'T BLAME US, DUMMY.
BLAME THE FBI FOR COMING UP WITH...
...SUCH A STUPID PLAN...
FW
SH

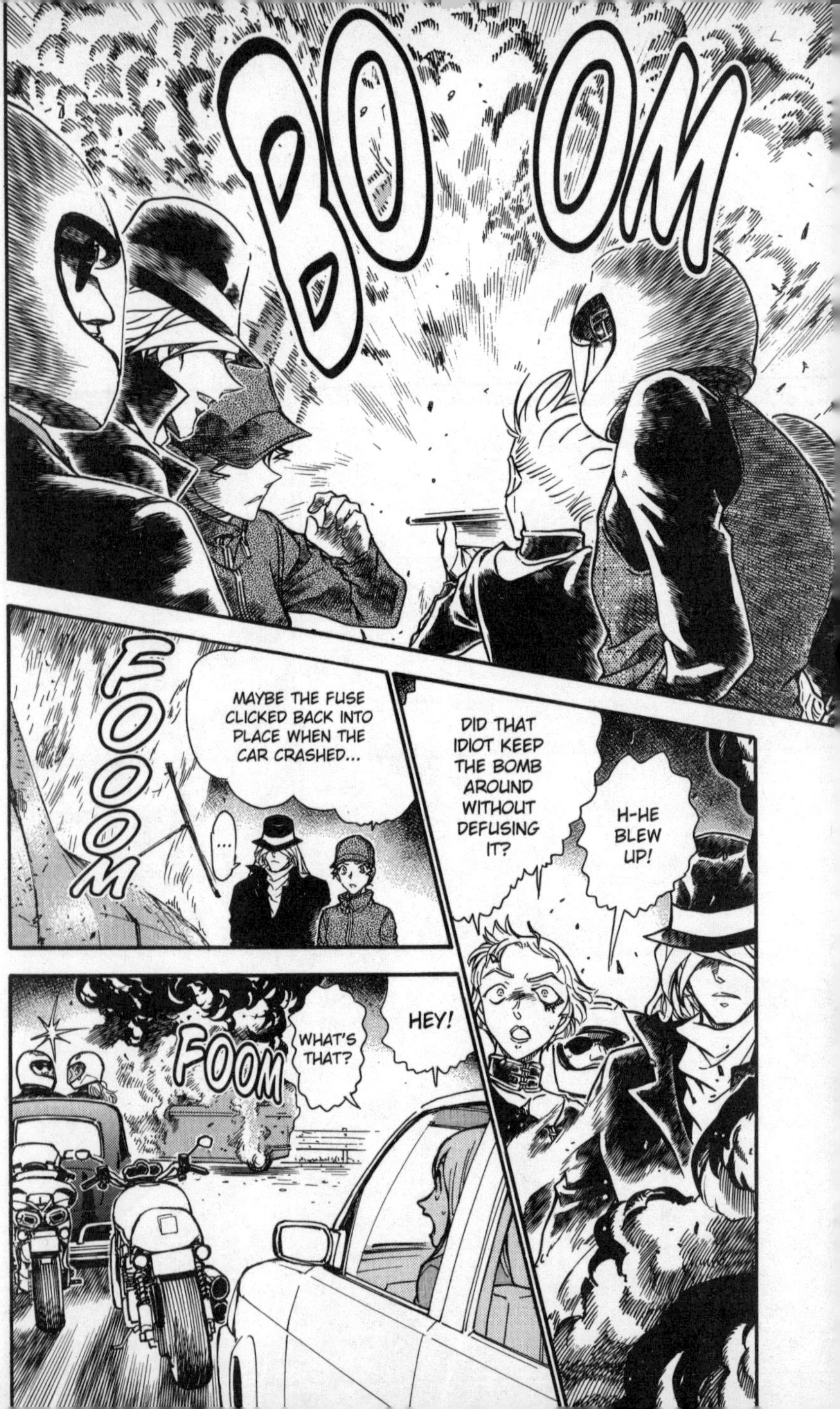
BOOM
H-HE BLEW UP!
DID THAT IDIOT KEEP THE BOMB AROUND WITHOUT DEFUSING IT?
FOOOOOM
MAYBE THE FUSE CLICKED BACK INTO PLACE WHEN THE CAR CRASHED...
...
HEY!
WHAT'S THAT?
FOOM

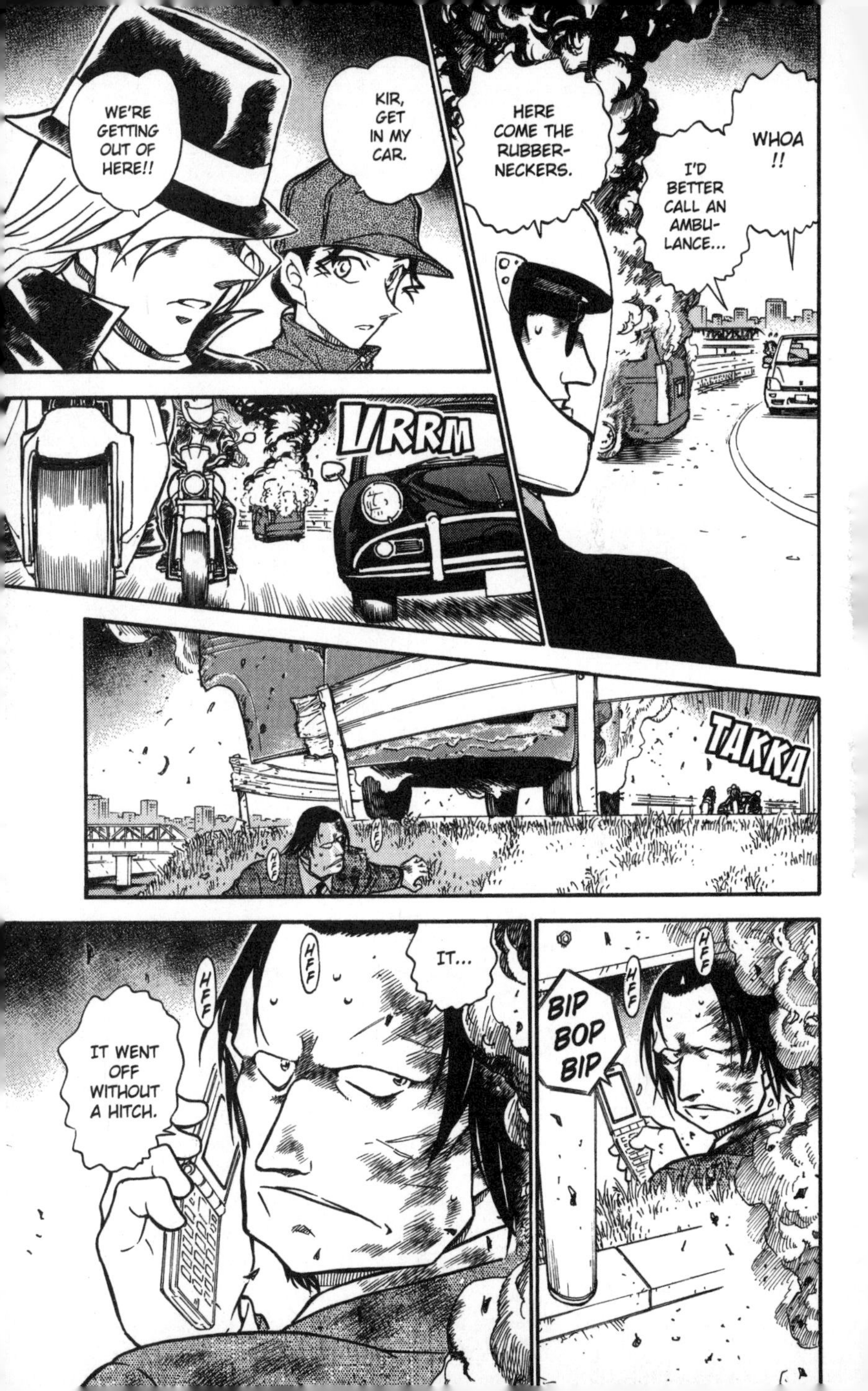
WHOA!!
I'D BETTER CALL AN AMBULANCE...
HERE COME THE RUBBERNECKERS.
KIR, GET IN MY CAR.
WE'RE GETTING OUT OF HERE!!
VRRM
TAKKA
HFF
HFF
BIP BOP BIP
HFF
IT...
HFF
IT WENT OFF WITHOUT A HITCH.

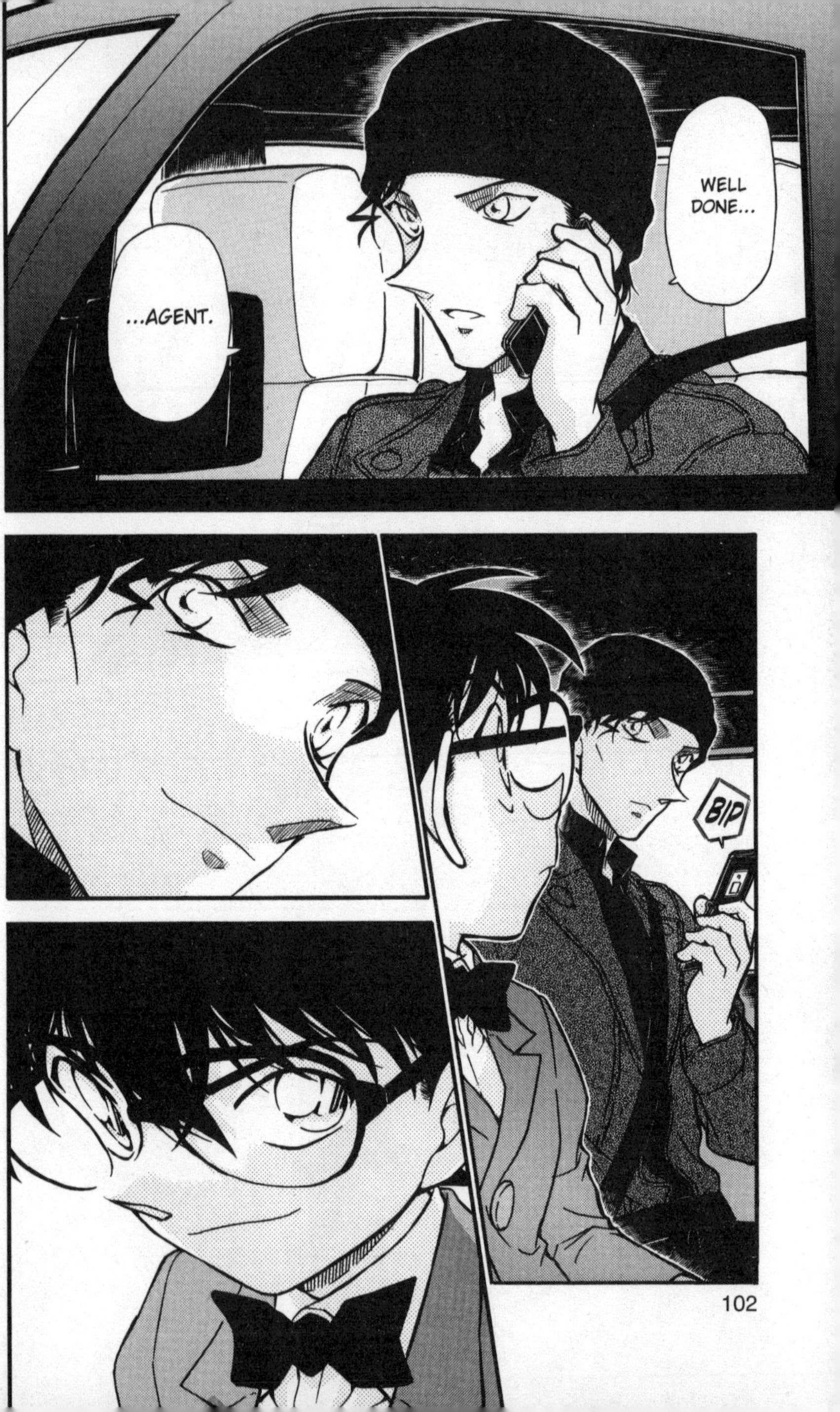
WELL DONE...
...AGENT.
BIP

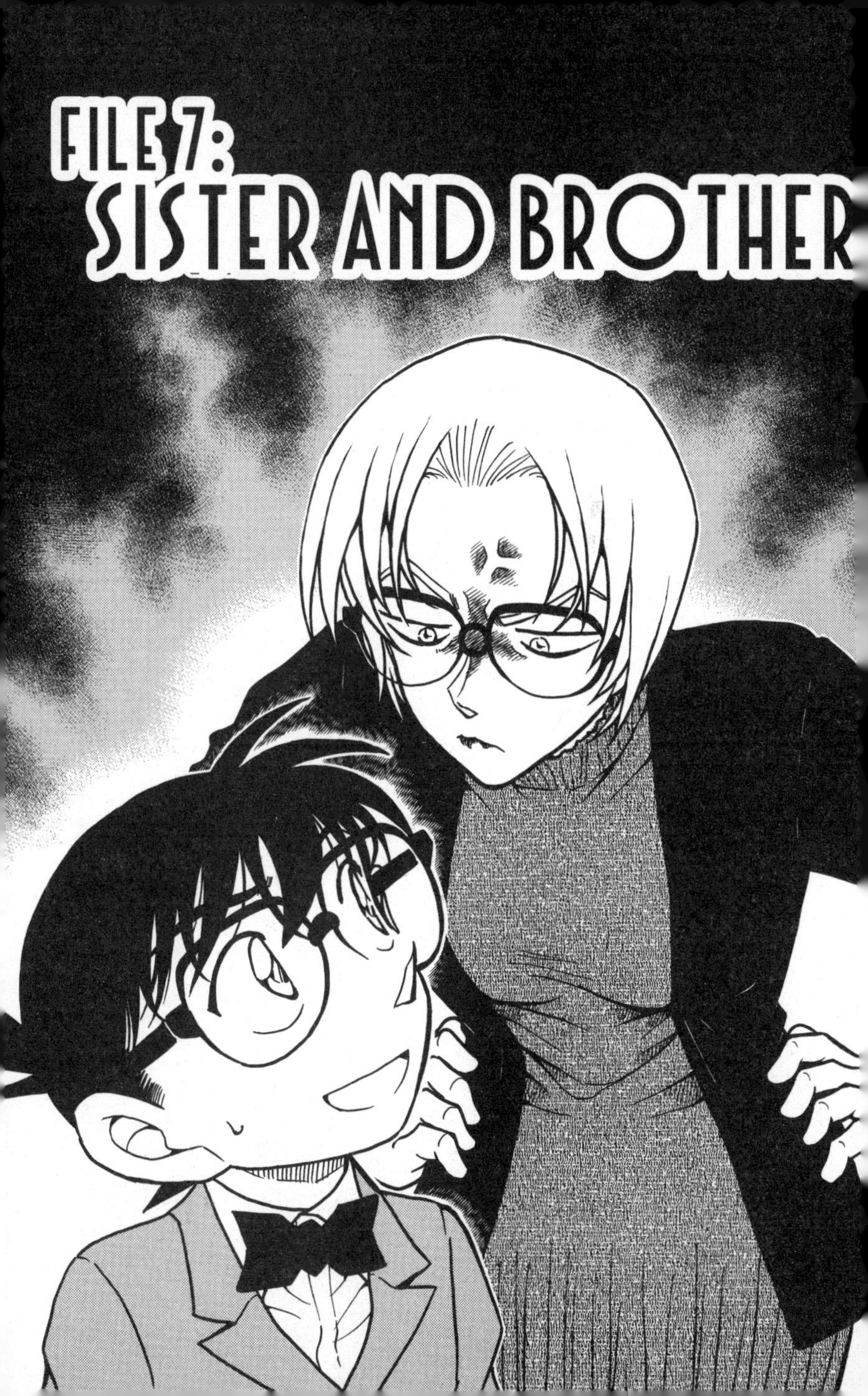
FILE 7:
SISTER AND BROTHER

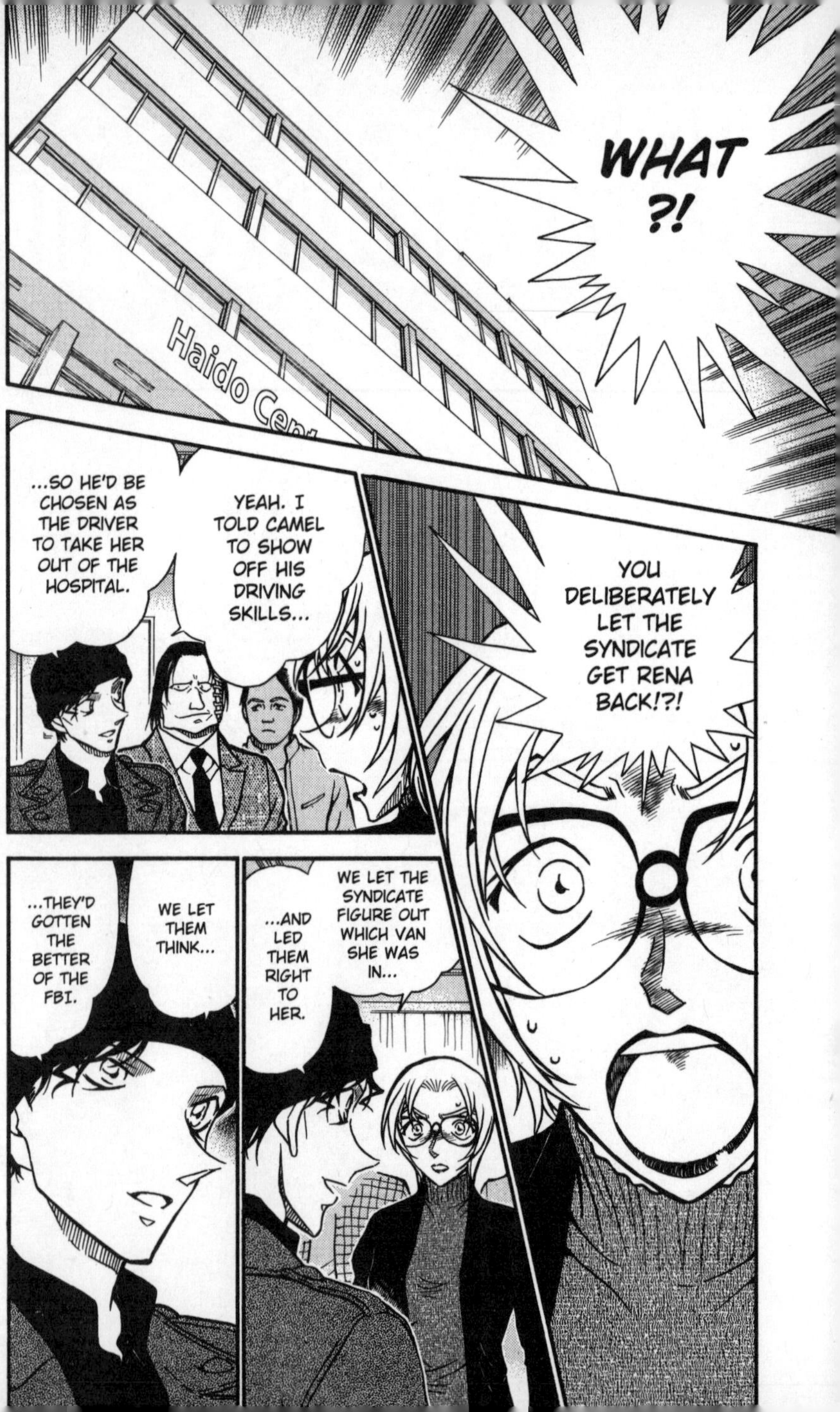
WHAT ?!
Haido Cent
YOU DELIBERATELY LET THE SYNDICATE GET RENA BACK!?!
YEAH. I TOLD CAMEL TO SHOW OFF HIS DRIVING SKILLS...
...SO HE'D BE CHOSEN AS THE DRIVER TO TAKE HER OUT OF THE HOSPITAL.
WE LET THE SYNDICATE FIGURE OUT WHICH VAN SHE WAS IN...
...AND LED THEM RIGHT TO HER.
WE LET THEM THINK...
...THEY'D GOTTEN THE BETTER OF THE FBI.

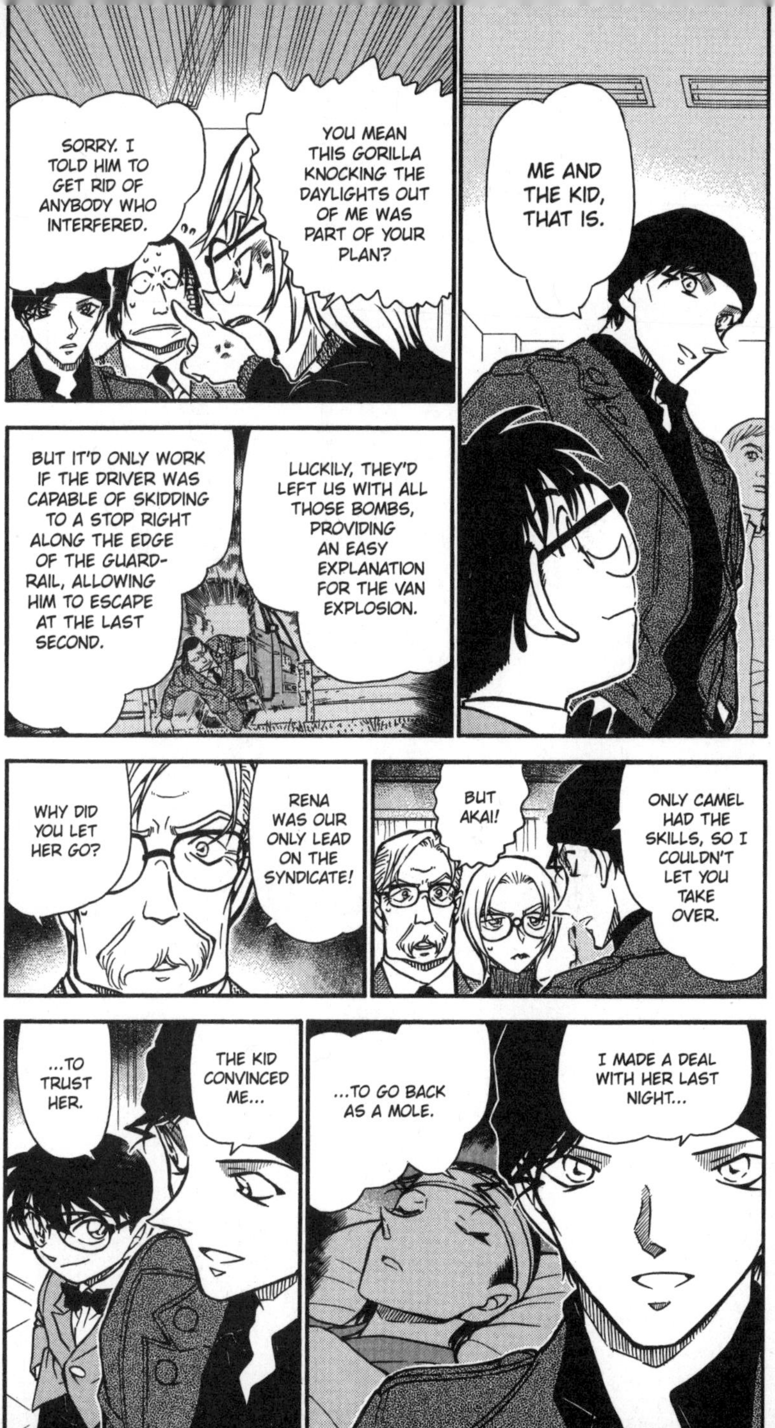
ME AND THE KID, THAT IS.
YOU MEAN THIS GORILLA KNOCKING THE DAYLIGHTS OUT OF ME WAS PART OF YOUR PLAN?
SORRY. I TOLD HIM TO GET RID OF ANYBODY WHO INTERFERED.
LUCKILY, THEY'D LEFT US WITH ALL THOSE BOMBS, PROVIDING AN EASY EXPLANATION FOR THE VAN EXPLOSION.
BUT IT'D ONLY WORK IF THE DRIVER WAS CAPABLE OF SKIDDING TO A STOP RIGHT ALONG THE EDGE OF THE GUARD-RAIL, ALLOWING HIM TO ESCAPE AT THE LAST SECOND.
ONLY CAMEL HAD THE SKILLS, SO I COULDN'T LET YOU TAKE OVER.
BUT AKAI!
RENA WAS OUR ONLY LEAD ON THE SYNDICATE!
WHY DID YOU LET HER GO?
I MADE A DEAL WITH HER LAST NIGHT...
...TO GO BACK AS A MOLE.
THE KID CONVINCED ME...
...TO TRUST HER.

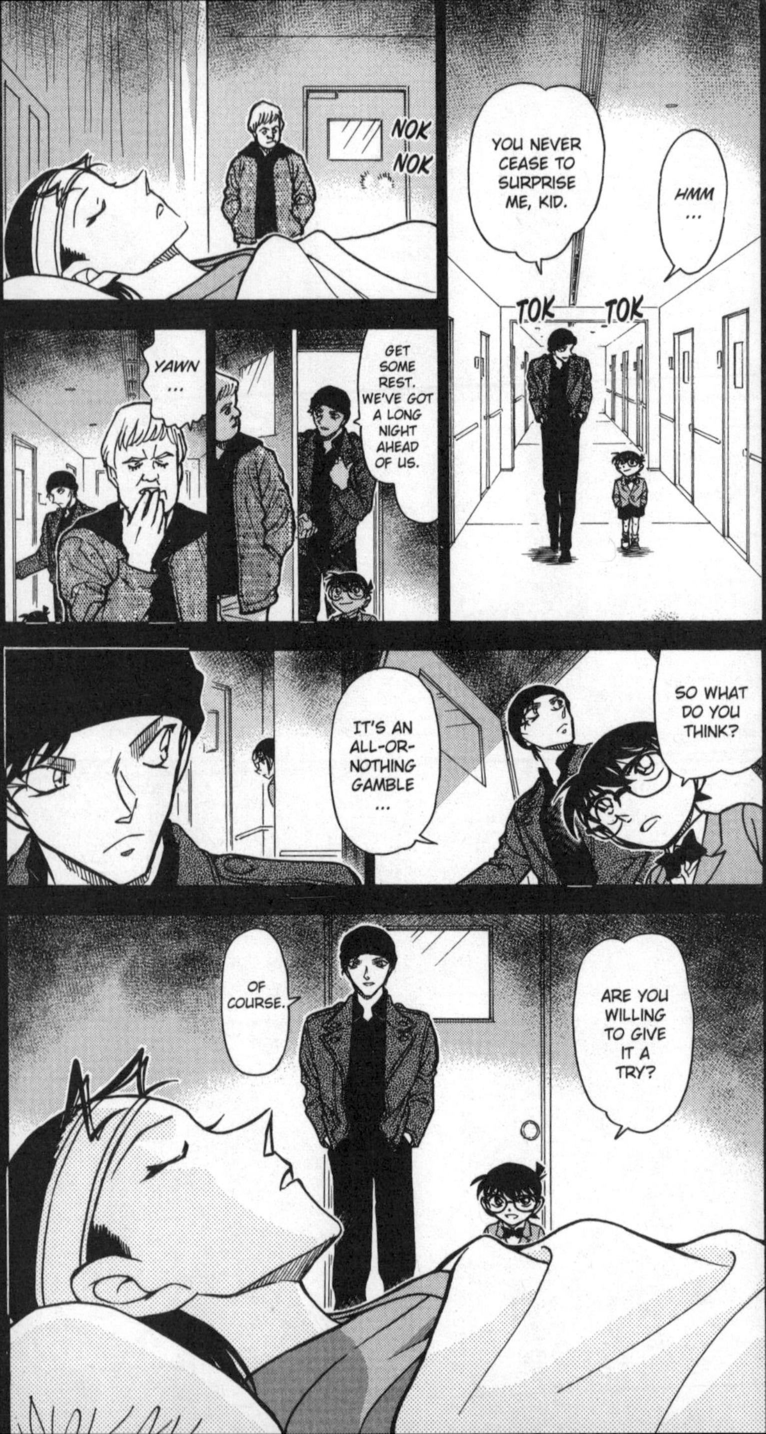
HMM ...
YOU NEVER CEASE TO SURPRISE ME, KID.
TOK TOK
NOK NOK
GET SOME REST. WE'VE GOT A LONG NIGHT AHEAD OF US.
YAWN ...
SO WHAT DO YOU THINK?
IT'S AN ALL-OR-NOTHING GAMBLE ...
ARE YOU WILLING TO GIVE IT A TRY?
OF COURSE.

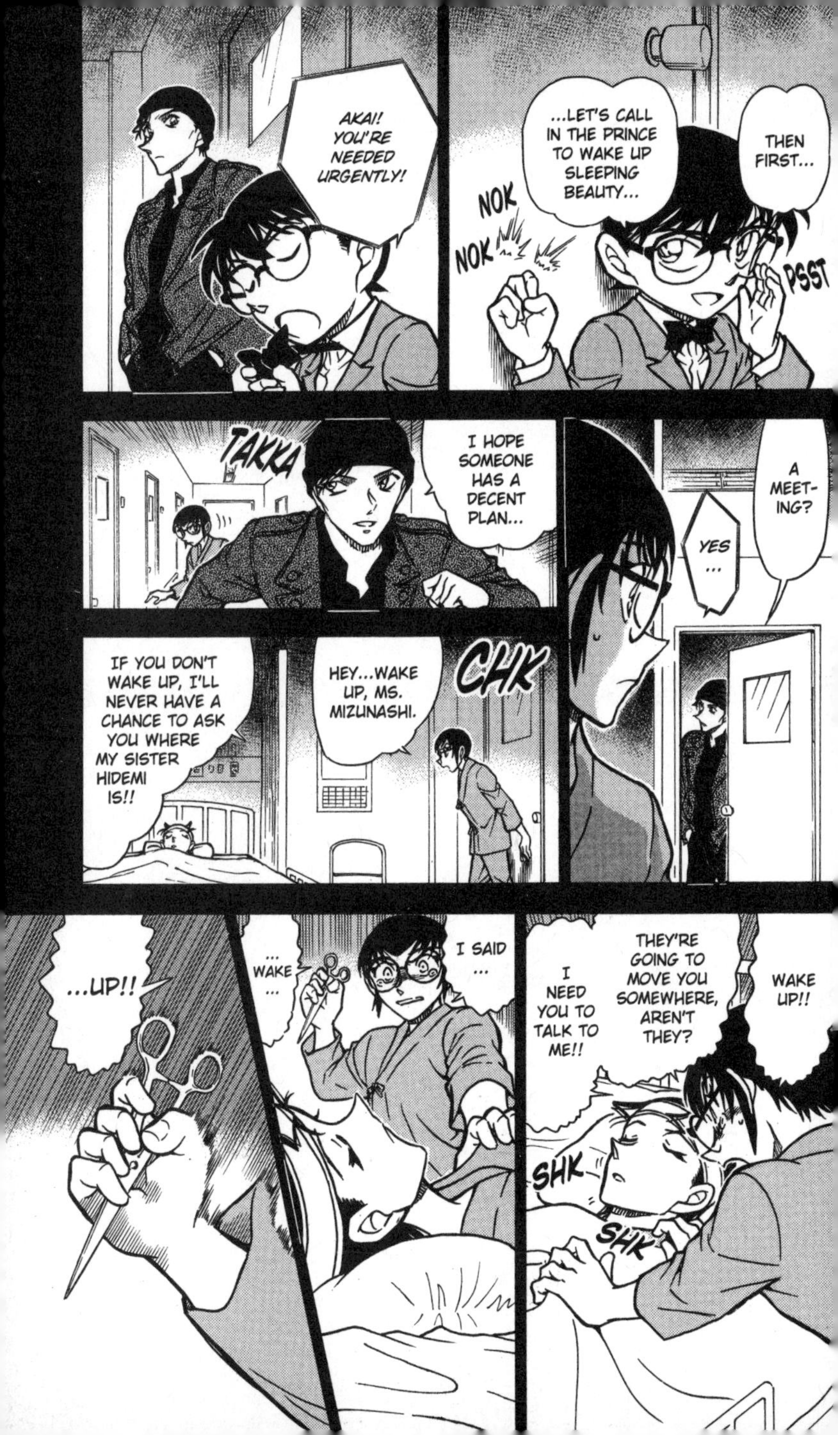
THEN FIRST...
...LET'S CALL IN THE PRINCE TO WAKE UP SLEEPING BEAUTY...
NOK
NOK
PSST
AKAI! YOU'RE NEEDED URGENTLY!
A MEET-ING?
YES ...
TAKKA
I HOPE SOMEONE HAS A DECENT PLAN...
CHK
HEY...WAKE UP, MS. MIZUNASHI.
IF YOU DON'T WAKE UP, I'LL NEVER HAVE A CHANCE TO ASK YOU WHERE MY SISTER HIDEMI IS!!
WAKE UP!!
THEY'RE GOING TO MOVE YOU SOMEWHERE, AREN'T THEY?
I NEED YOU TO TALK TO ME!!
SHK
SHK
I SAID ...
... WAKE ...
...UP!!

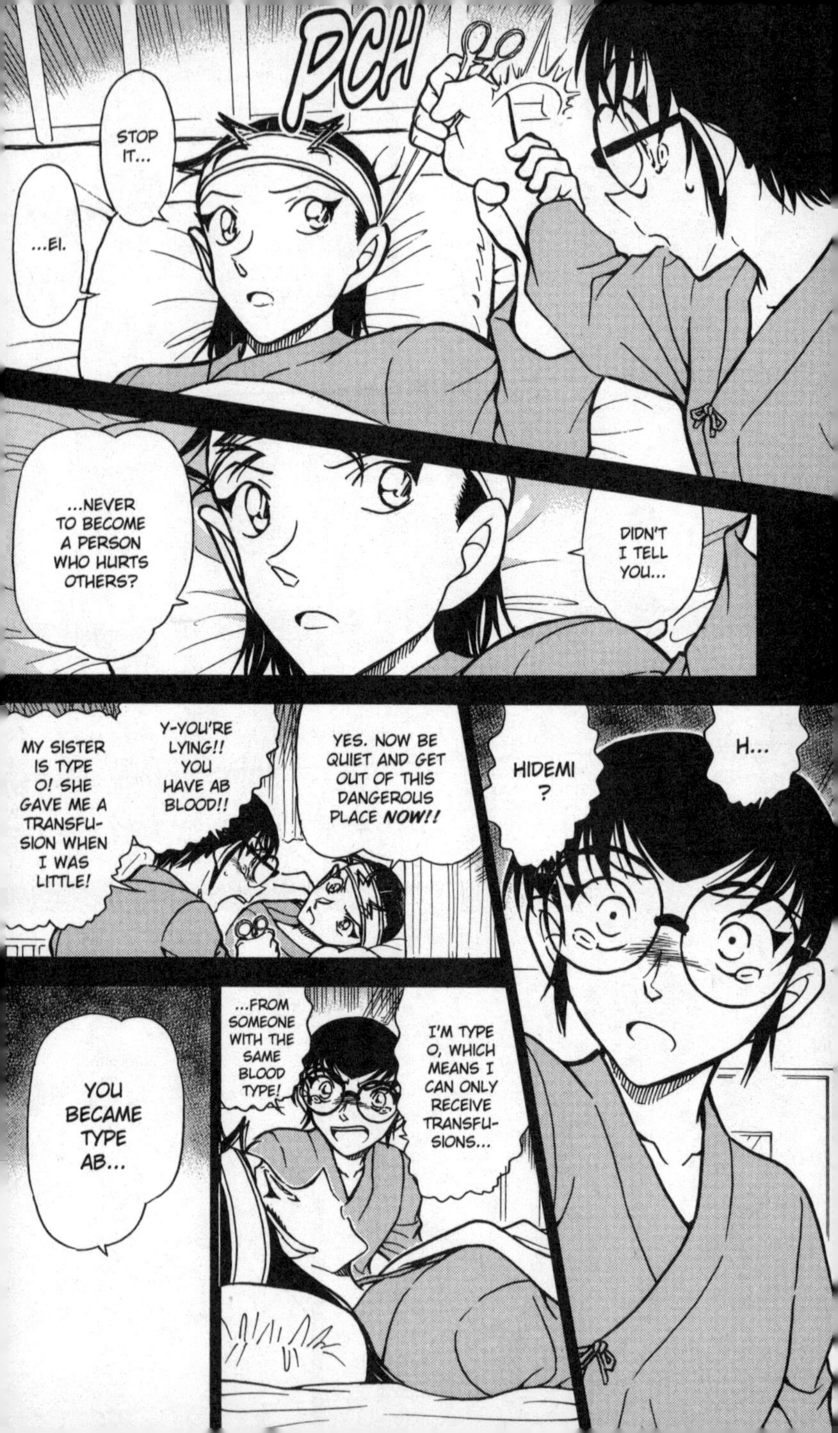
PCH
STOP IT...
...EI.
DIDN'T I TELL YOU...
...NEVER TO BECOME A PERSON WHO HURTS OTHERS?
H...
HIDEMI ?
YES. NOW BE QUIET AND GET OUT OF THIS DANGEROUS PLACE *NOW!!*
Y-YOU'RE LYING!! YOU HAVE AB BLOOD!!
MY SISTER IS TYPE O! SHE GAVE ME A TRANSFUSION WHEN I WAS LITTLE!
I'M TYPE O, WHICH MEANS I CAN ONLY RECEIVE TRANSFUSIONS...
...FROM SOMEONE WITH THE SAME BLOOD TYPE!
YOU BECAME TYPE AB...

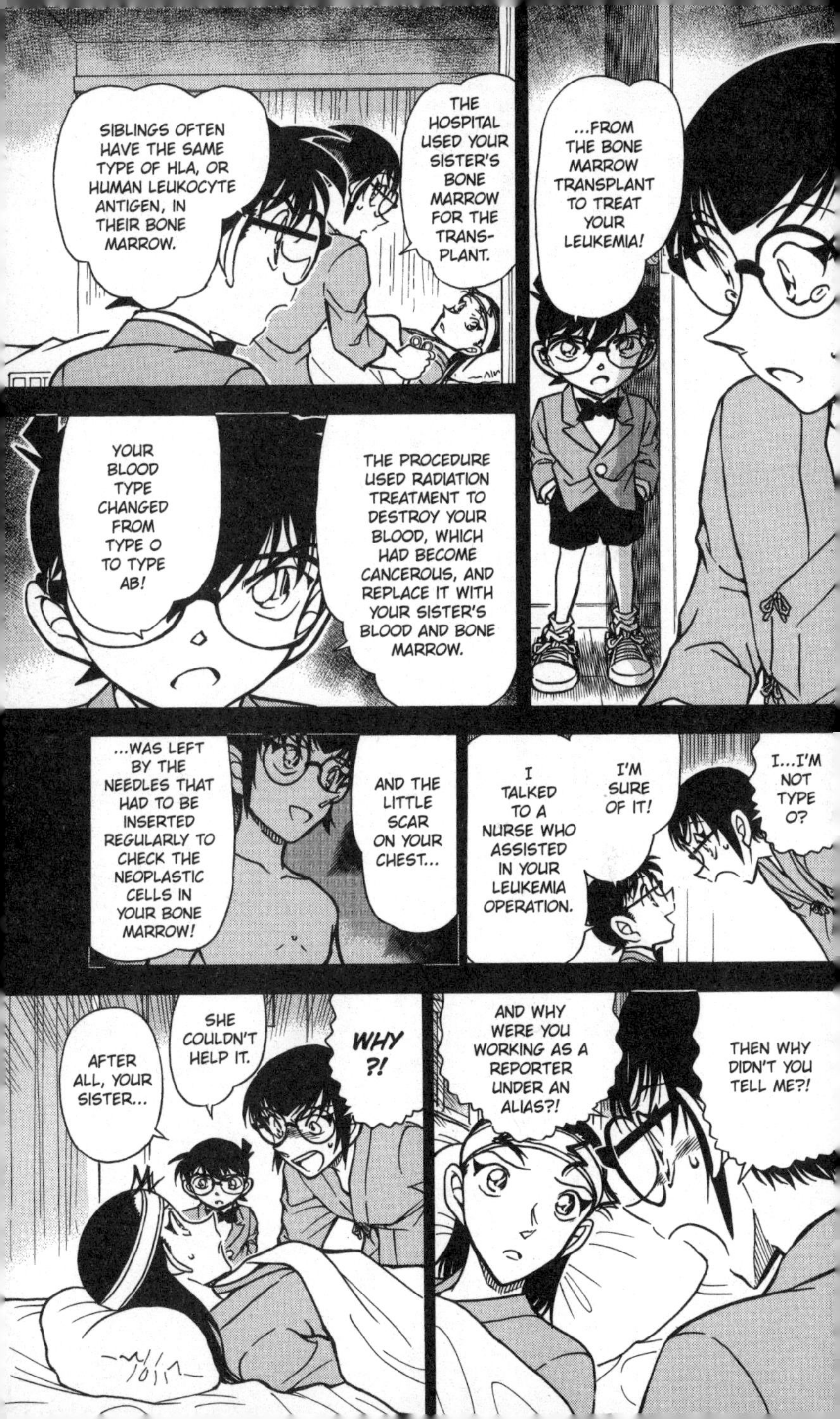
...FROM THE BONE MARROW TRANSPLANT TO TREAT YOUR LEUKEMIA!
THE HOSPITAL USED YOUR SISTER'S BONE MARROW FOR THE TRANS-PLANT.
SIBLINGS OFTEN HAVE THE SAME TYPE OF HLA, OR HUMAN LEUKOCYTE ANTIGEN, IN THEIR BONE MARROW.
THE PROCEDURE USED RADIATION TREATMENT TO DESTROY YOUR BLOOD, WHICH HAD BECOME CANCEROUS, AND REPLACE IT WITH YOUR SISTER'S BLOOD AND BONE MARROW.
YOUR BLOOD TYPE CHANGED FROM TYPE O TO TYPE AB!
I...I'M NOT TYPE O?
I'M SURE OF IT!
I TALKED TO A NURSE WHO ASSISTED IN YOUR LEUKEMIA OPERATION.
AND THE LITTLE SCAR ON YOUR CHEST...
...WAS LEFT BY THE NEEDLES THAT HAD TO BE INSERTED REGULARLY TO CHECK THE NEOPLASTIC CELLS IN YOUR BONE MARROW!
THEN WHY DIDN'T YOU TELL ME?!
AND WHY WERE YOU WORKING AS A REPORTER UNDER AN ALIAS?!
WHY?!
SHE COULDN'T HELP IT.
AFTER ALL, YOUR SISTER...

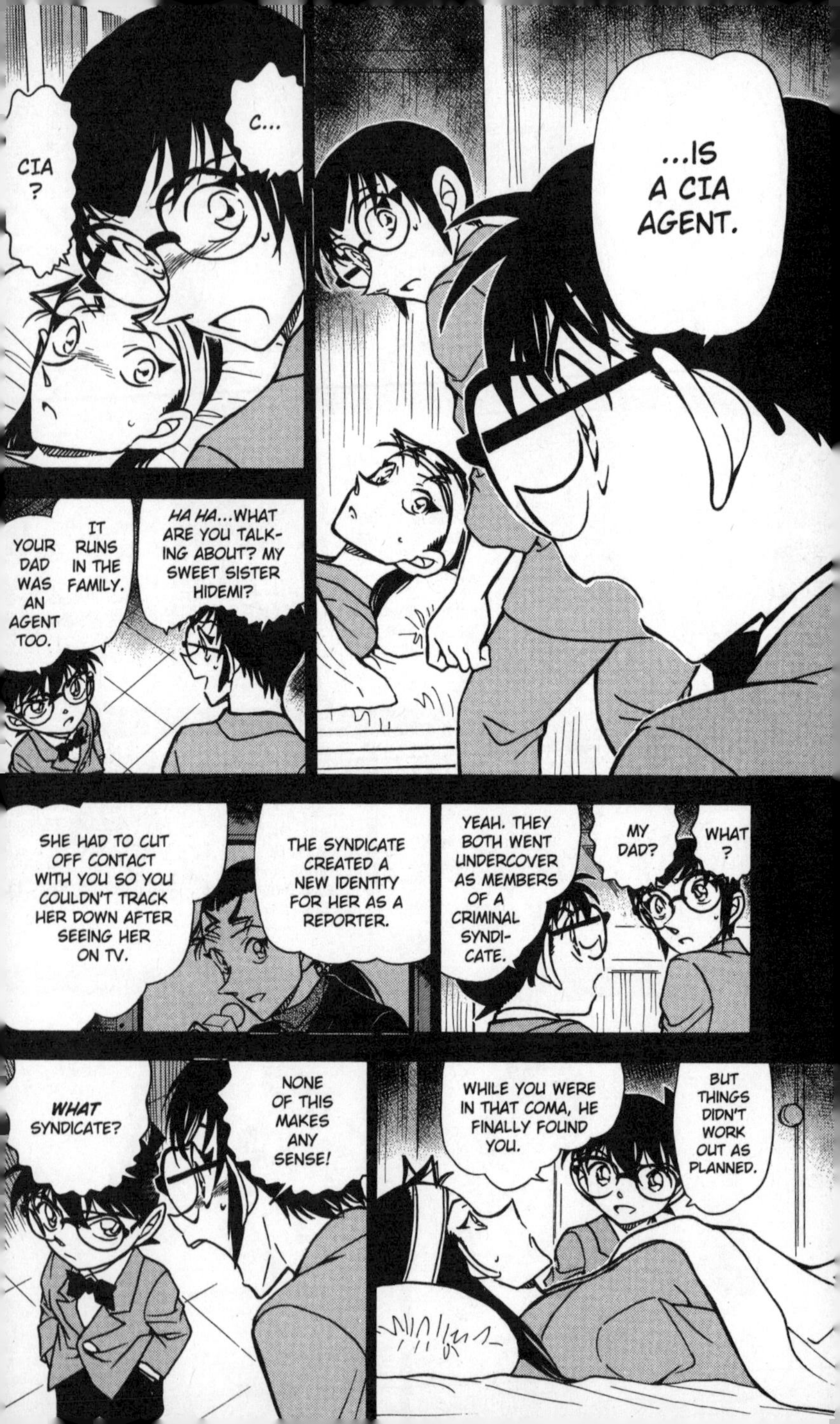
...IS A CIA AGENT.
C...
CIA ?
HA HA...WHAT ARE YOU TALK-ING ABOUT? MY SWEET SISTER HIDEMI?
IT RUNS IN THE FAMILY.
YOUR DAD WAS AN AGENT TOO.
WHAT ?
MY DAD?
YEAH. THEY BOTH WENT UNDERCOVER AS MEMBERS OF A CRIMINAL SYNDI-CATE.
THE SYNDICATE CREATED A NEW IDENTITY FOR HER AS A REPORTER.
SHE HAD TO CUT OFF CONTACT WITH YOU SO YOU COULDN'T TRACK HER DOWN AFTER SEEING HER ON TV.
BUT THINGS DIDN'T WORK OUT AS PLANNED.
WHILE YOU WERE IN THAT COMA, HE FINALLY FOUND YOU.
NONE OF THIS MAKES ANY SENSE!
WHAT SYNDICATE?

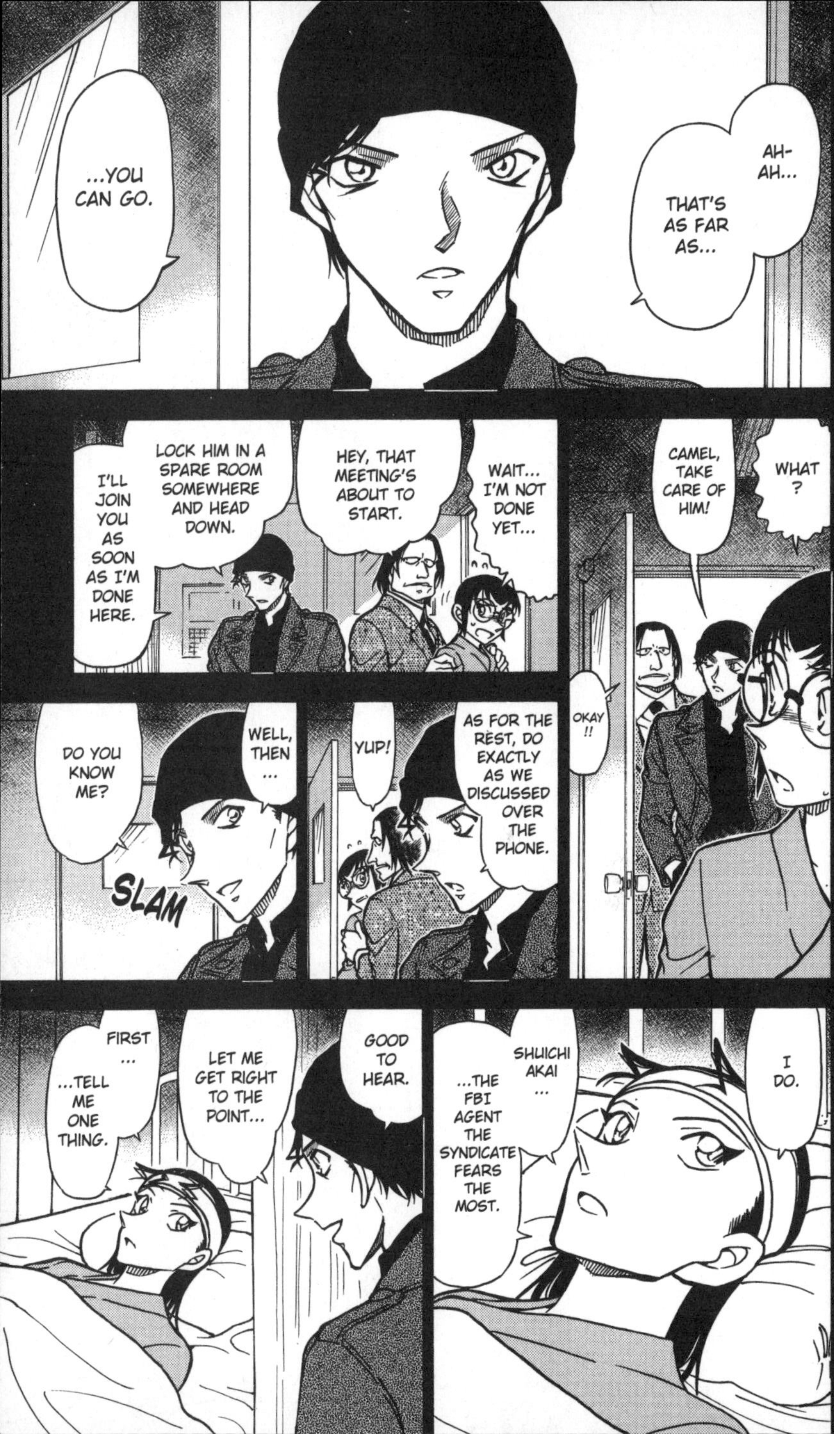
AH-AH... THAT'S AS FAR AS...
...YOU CAN GO.
WHAT?
CAMEL, TAKE CARE OF HIM!
OKAY!!
WAIT... I'M NOT DONE YET...
HEY, THAT MEETING'S ABOUT TO START.
LOCK HIM IN A SPARE ROOM SOMEWHERE AND HEAD DOWN.
I'LL JOIN YOU AS SOON AS I'M DONE HERE.
AS FOR THE REST, DO EXACTLY AS WE DISCUSSED OVER THE PHONE.
YUP!
WELL, THEN ...
SLAM
DO YOU KNOW ME?
I DO.
SHUICHI AKAI ...
...THE FBI AGENT THE SYNDICATE FEARS THE MOST.
GOOD TO HEAR.
LET ME GET RIGHT TO THE POINT...
FIRST ...
...TELL ME ONE THING.

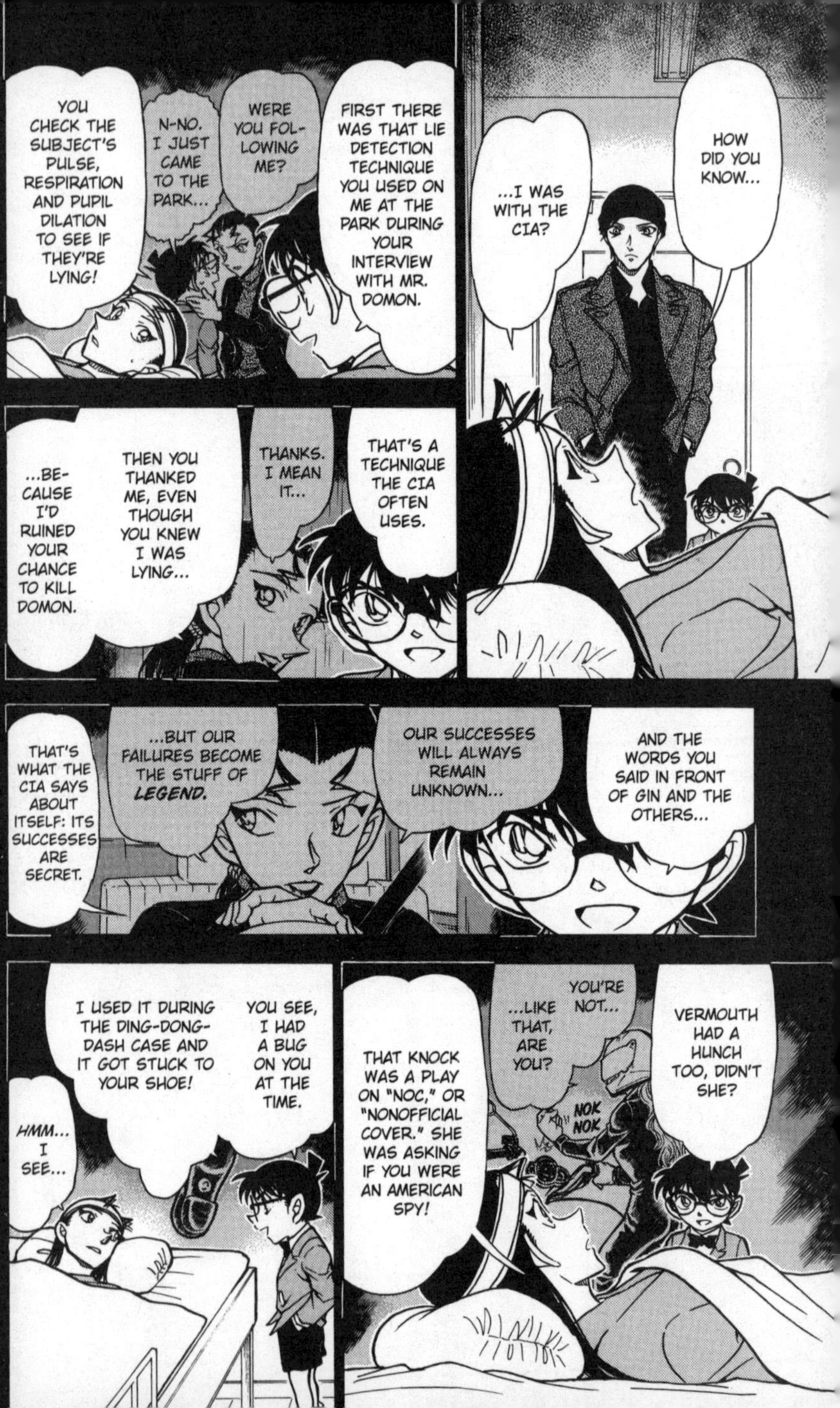
HOW DID YOU KNOW...
...I WAS WITH THE CIA?
FIRST THERE WAS THAT LIE DETECTION TECHNIQUE YOU USED ON ME AT THE PARK DURING YOUR INTERVIEW WITH MR. DOMON.
WERE YOU FOL-LOWING ME?
N-NO. I JUST CAME TO THE PARK...
YOU CHECK THE SUBJECT'S PULSE, RESPIRATION AND PUPIL DILATION TO SEE IF THEY'RE LYING!
THAT'S A TECHNIQUE THE CIA OFTEN USES.
THANKS. I MEAN IT...
THEN YOU THANKED ME, EVEN THOUGH YOU KNEW I WAS LYING...
...BE-CAUSE I'D RUINED YOUR CHANCE TO KILL DOMON.
AND THE WORDS YOU SAID IN FRONT OF GIN AND THE OTHERS...
OUR SUCCESSES WILL ALWAYS REMAIN UNKNOWN...
...BUT OUR FAILURES BECOME THE STUFF OF *LEGEND.*
THAT'S WHAT THE CIA SAYS ABOUT ITSELF: ITS SUCCESSES ARE SECRET.
VERMOUTH HAD A HUNCH TOO, DIDN'T SHE?
YOU'RE NOT...
...LIKE THAT, ARE YOU?
NOK NOK
THAT KNOCK WAS A PLAY ON "NOC," OR "NONOFFICIAL COVER." SHE WAS ASKING IF YOU WERE AN AMERICAN SPY!
YOU SEE, I HAD A BUG ON YOU AT THE TIME.
I USED IT DURING THE DING-DONG-DASH CASE AND IT GOT STUCK TO YOUR SHOE!
HMM... I SEE...

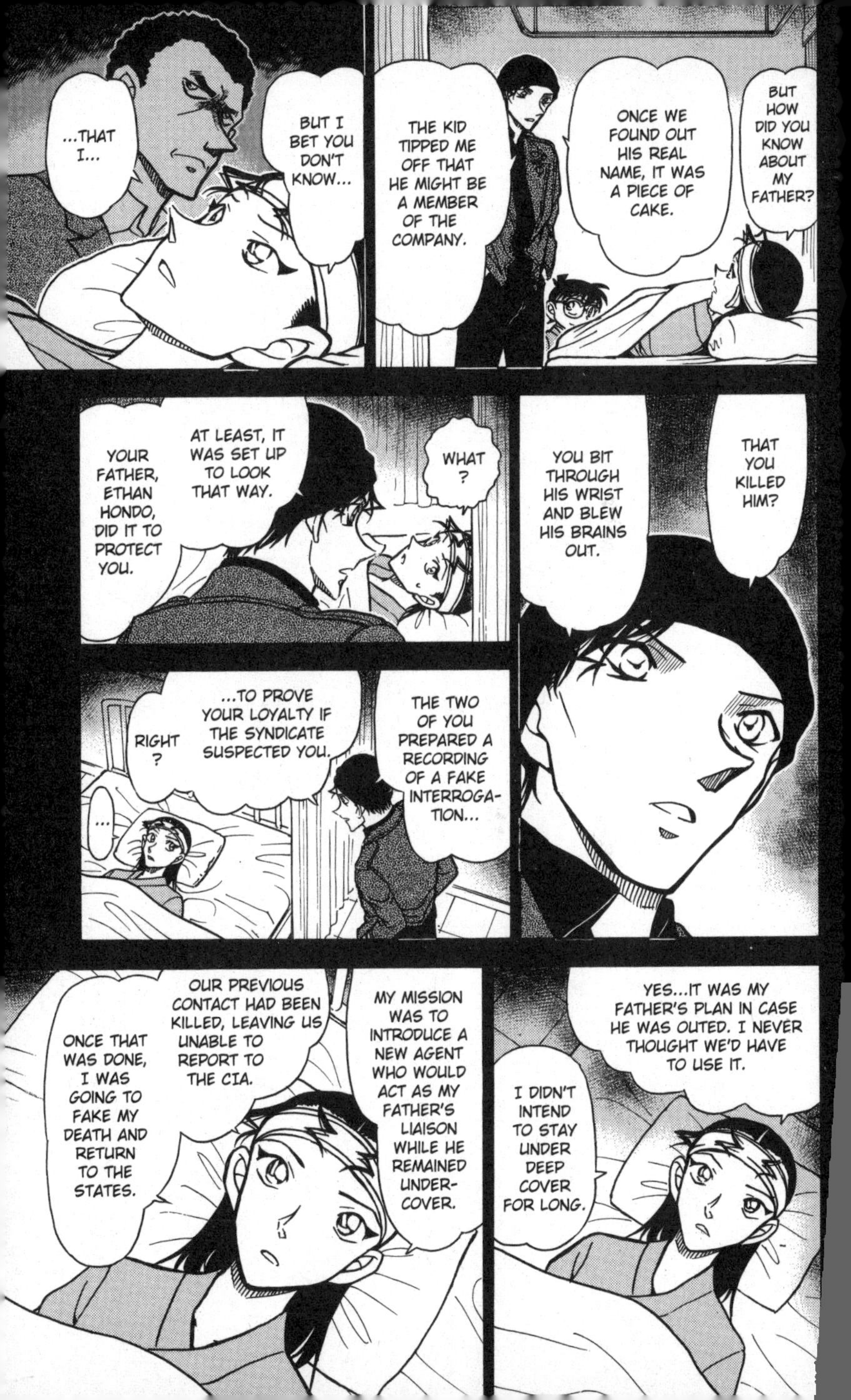
BUT HOW DID YOU KNOW ABOUT MY FATHER?
ONCE WE FOUND OUT HIS REAL NAME, IT WAS A PIECE OF CAKE.
THE KID TIPPED ME OFF THAT HE MIGHT BE A MEMBER OF THE COMPANY.
BUT I BET YOU DON'T KNOW...
...THAT I...
THAT YOU KILLED HIM?
YOU BIT THROUGH HIS WRIST AND BLEW HIS BRAINS OUT.
WHAT?
AT LEAST, IT WAS SET UP TO LOOK THAT WAY.
YOUR FATHER, ETHAN HONDO, DID IT TO PROTECT YOU.
THE TWO OF YOU PREPARED A RECORDING OF A FAKE INTERROGATION...
...TO PROVE YOUR LOYALTY IF THE SYNDICATE SUSPECTED YOU.
RIGHT?
...
YES...IT WAS MY FATHER'S PLAN IN CASE HE WAS OUTED. I NEVER THOUGHT WE'D HAVE TO USE IT.
I DIDN'T INTEND TO STAY UNDER DEEP COVER FOR LONG.
MY MISSION WAS TO INTRODUCE A NEW AGENT WHO WOULD ACT AS MY FATHER'S LIAISON WHILE HE REMAINED UNDERCOVER.
OUR PREVIOUS CONTACT HAD BEEN KILLED, LEAVING US UNABLE TO REPORT TO THE CIA.
ONCE THAT WAS DONE, I WAS GOING TO FAKE MY DEATH AND RETURN TO THE STATES.

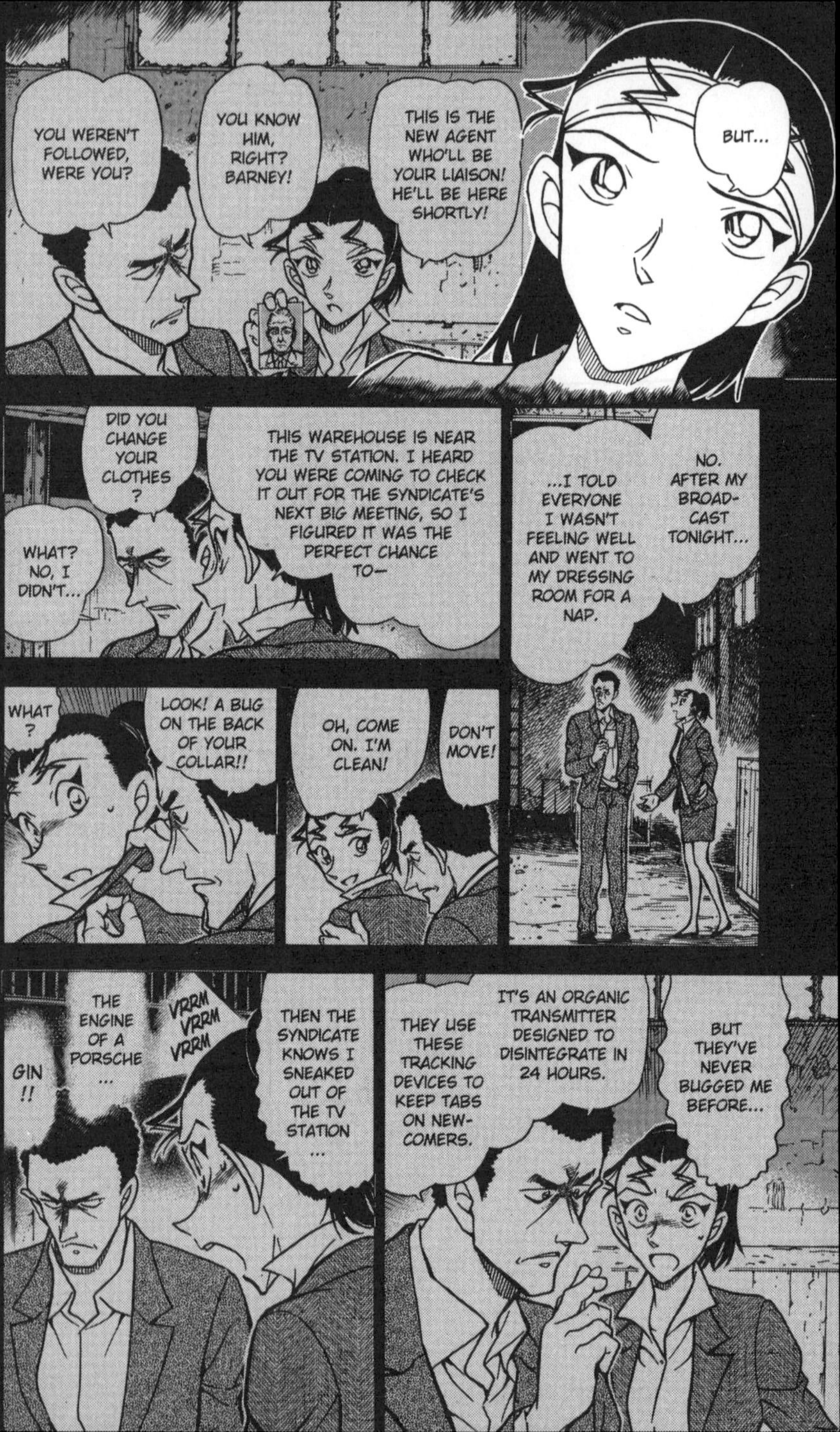
BUT...
THIS IS THE NEW AGENT WHO'LL BE YOUR LIAISON! HE'LL BE HERE SHORTLY!
YOU KNOW HIM, RIGHT? BARNEY!
YOU WEREN'T FOLLOWED, WERE YOU?
NO. AFTER MY BROAD-CAST TONIGHT...
...I TOLD EVERYONE I WASN'T FEELING WELL AND WENT TO MY DRESSING ROOM FOR A NAP.
THIS WAREHOUSE IS NEAR THE TV STATION. I HEARD YOU WERE COMING TO CHECK IT OUT FOR THE SYNDICATE'S NEXT BIG MEETING, SO I FIGURED IT WAS THE PERFECT CHANCE TO—
DID YOU CHANGE YOUR CLOTHES?
WHAT? NO, I DIDN'T...
DON'T MOVE!
OH, COME ON. I'M CLEAN!
LOOK! A BUG ON THE BACK OF YOUR COLLAR!!
WHAT?
BUT THEY'VE NEVER BUGGED ME BEFORE...
IT'S AN ORGANIC TRANSMITTER DESIGNED TO DISINTEGRATE IN 24 HOURS.
THEY USE THESE TRACKING DEVICES TO KEEP TABS ON NEW-COMERS.
THEN THE SYNDICATE KNOWS I SNEAKED OUT OF THE TV STATION...
VRRM VRRM VRRM
THE ENGINE OF A PORSCHE...
GIN!!

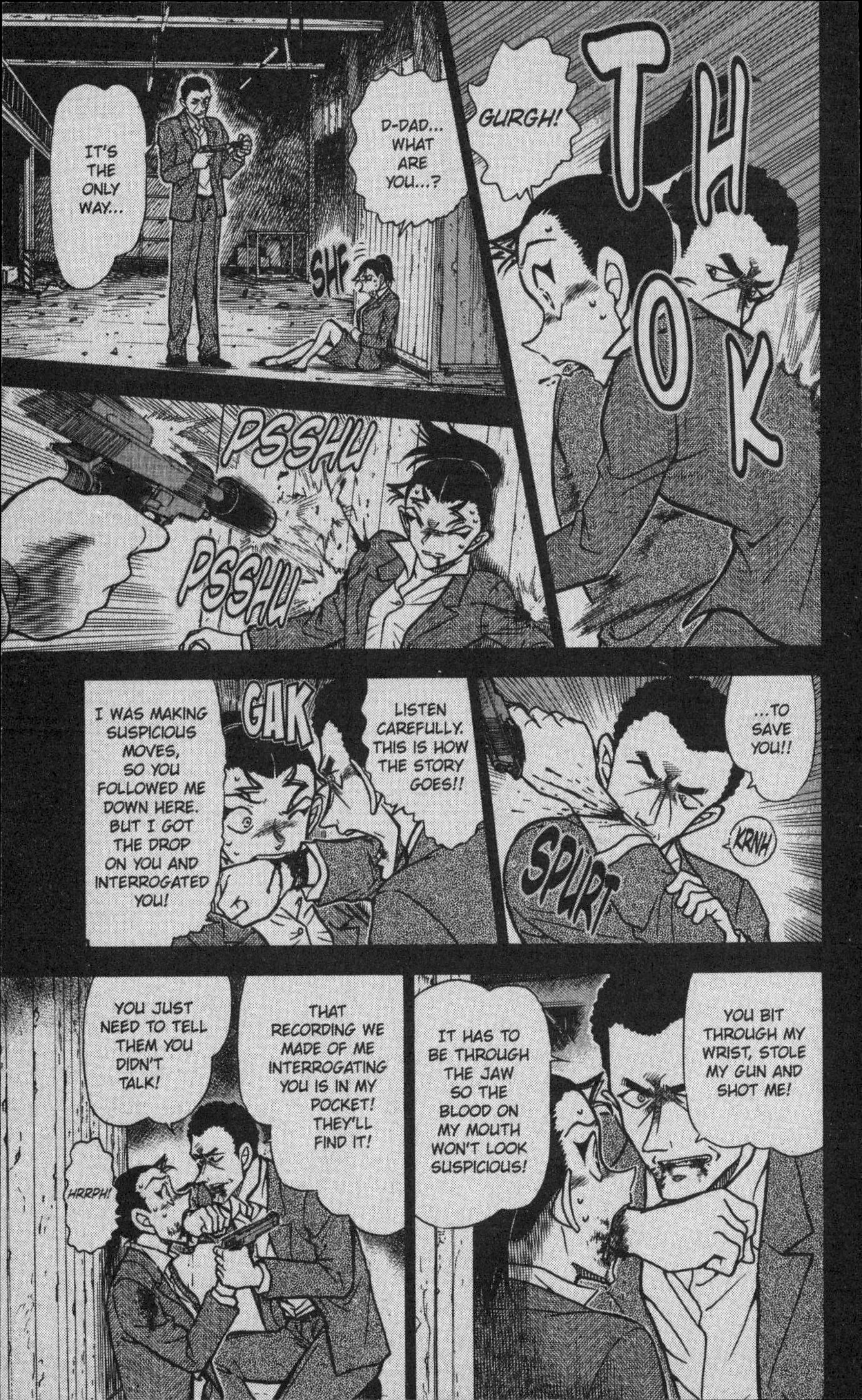
GURGH!
THOK
D-DAD... WHAT ARE YOU...?
IT'S THE ONLY WAY...
SHF
PSSHU
PSSHU
...TO SAVE YOU!!
SPURT
KRNH
LISTEN CAREFULLY. THIS IS HOW THE STORY GOES!!
GAK
I WAS MAKING SUSPICIOUS MOVES, SO YOU FOLLOWED ME DOWN HERE. BUT I GOT THE DROP ON YOU AND INTERROGATED YOU!
YOU BIT THROUGH MY WRIST, STOLE MY GUN AND SHOT ME!
IT HAS TO BE THROUGH THE JAW SO THE BLOOD ON MY MOUTH WON'T LOOK SUSPICIOUS!
THAT RECORDING WE MADE OF ME INTERROGATING YOU IS IN MY POCKET! THEY'LL FIND IT!
YOU JUST NEED TO TELL THEM YOU DIDN'T TALK!
HRRPH!

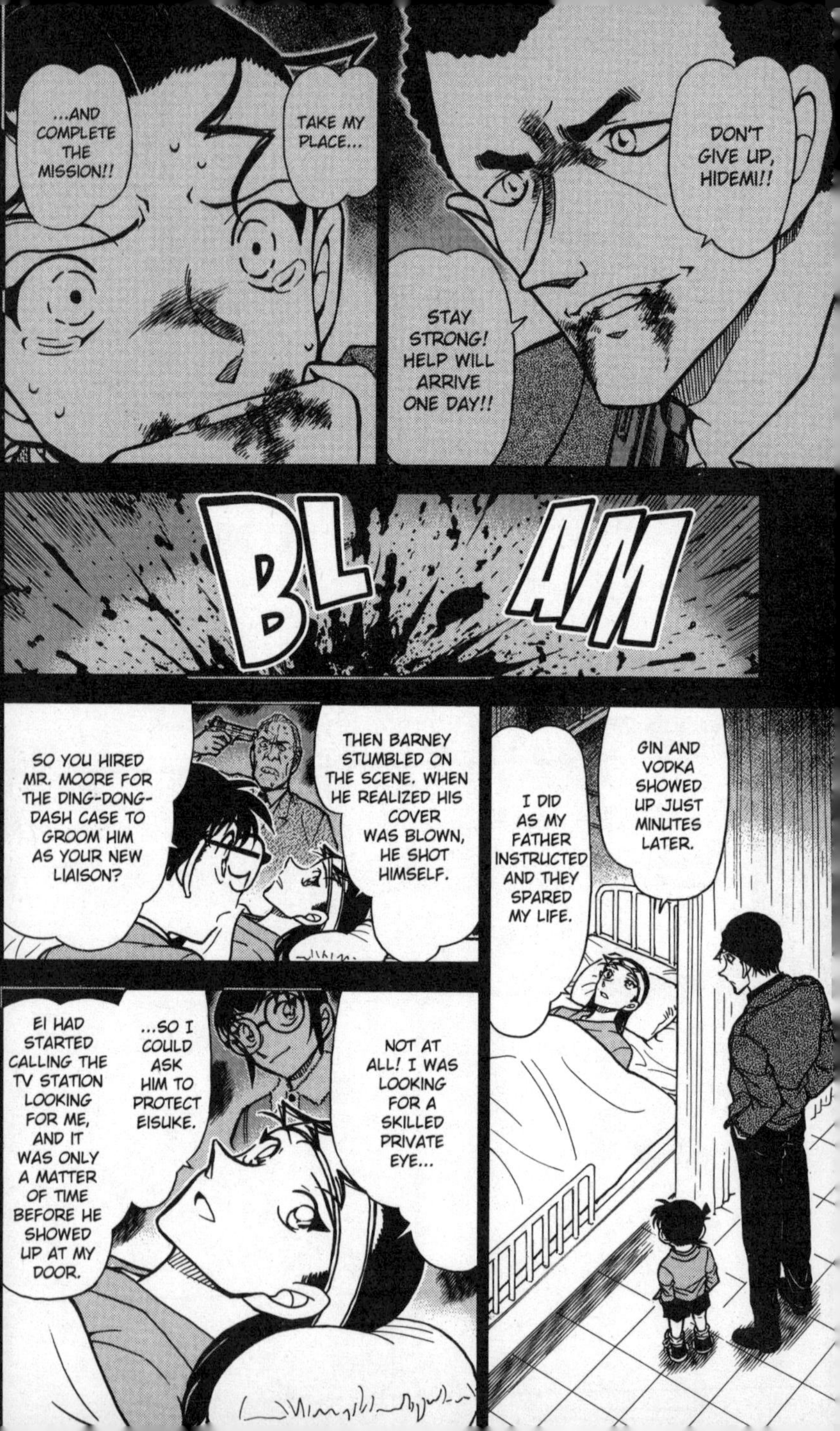
DON'T GIVE UP, HIDEMI!!
STAY STRONG! HELP WILL ARRIVE ONE DAY!!
TAKE MY PLACE...
...AND COMPLETE THE MISSION!!
BLAM
GIN AND VODKA SHOWED UP JUST MINUTES LATER.
I DID AS MY FATHER INSTRUCTED AND THEY SPARED MY LIFE.
THEN BARNEY STUMBLED ON THE SCENE. WHEN HE REALIZED HIS COVER WAS BLOWN, HE SHOT HIMSELF.
SO YOU HIRED MR. MOORE FOR THE DING-DONG-DASH CASE TO GROOM HIM AS YOUR NEW LIAISON?
NOT AT ALL! I WAS LOOKING FOR A SKILLED PRIVATE EYE...
...SO I COULD ASK HIM TO PROTECT EISUKE.
EI HAD STARTED CALLING THE TV STATION LOOKING FOR ME, AND IT WAS ONLY A MATTER OF TIME BEFORE HE SHOWED UP AT MY DOOR.

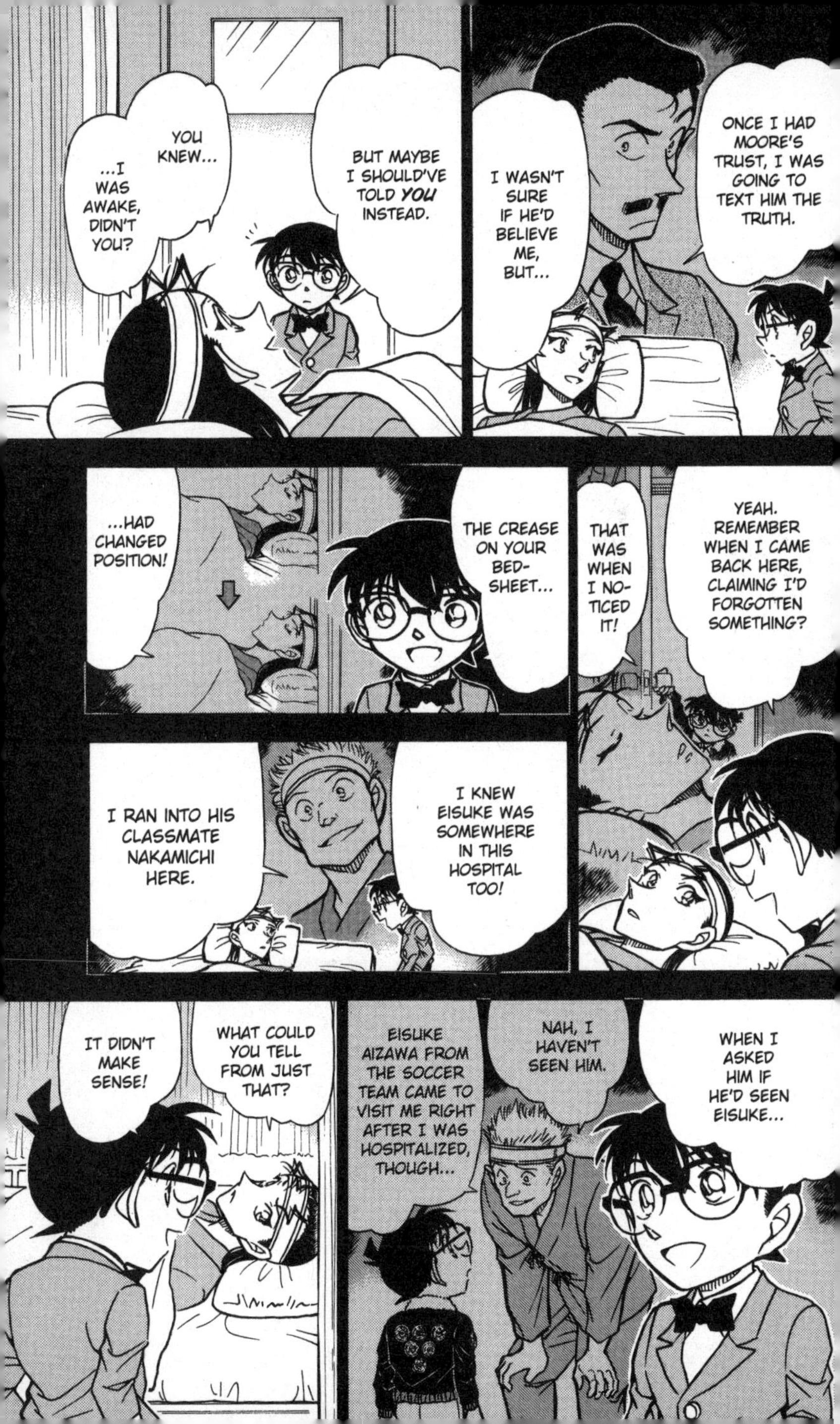
ONCE I HAD MOORE'S TRUST, I WAS GOING TO TEXT HIM THE TRUTH.
I WASN'T SURE IF HE'D BELIEVE ME, BUT...
BUT MAYBE I SHOULD'VE TOLD *YOU* INSTEAD.
YOU KNEW...
...I WAS AWAKE, DIDN'T YOU?
YEAH. REMEMBER WHEN I CAME BACK HERE, CLAIMING I'D FORGOTTEN SOMETHING?
THAT WAS WHEN I NOTICED IT!
THE CREASE ON YOUR BEDSHEET...
...HAD CHANGED POSITION!
I KNEW EISUKE WAS SOMEWHERE IN THIS HOSPITAL TOO!
I RAN INTO HIS CLASSMATE NAKAMICHI HERE.
WHEN I ASKED HIM IF HE'D SEEN EISUKE...
NAH, I HAVEN'T SEEN HIM.
EISUKE AIZAWA FROM THE SOCCER TEAM CAME TO VISIT ME RIGHT AFTER I WAS HOSPITALIZED, THOUGH...
WHAT COULD YOU TELL FROM JUST THAT?
IT DIDN'T MAKE SENSE!

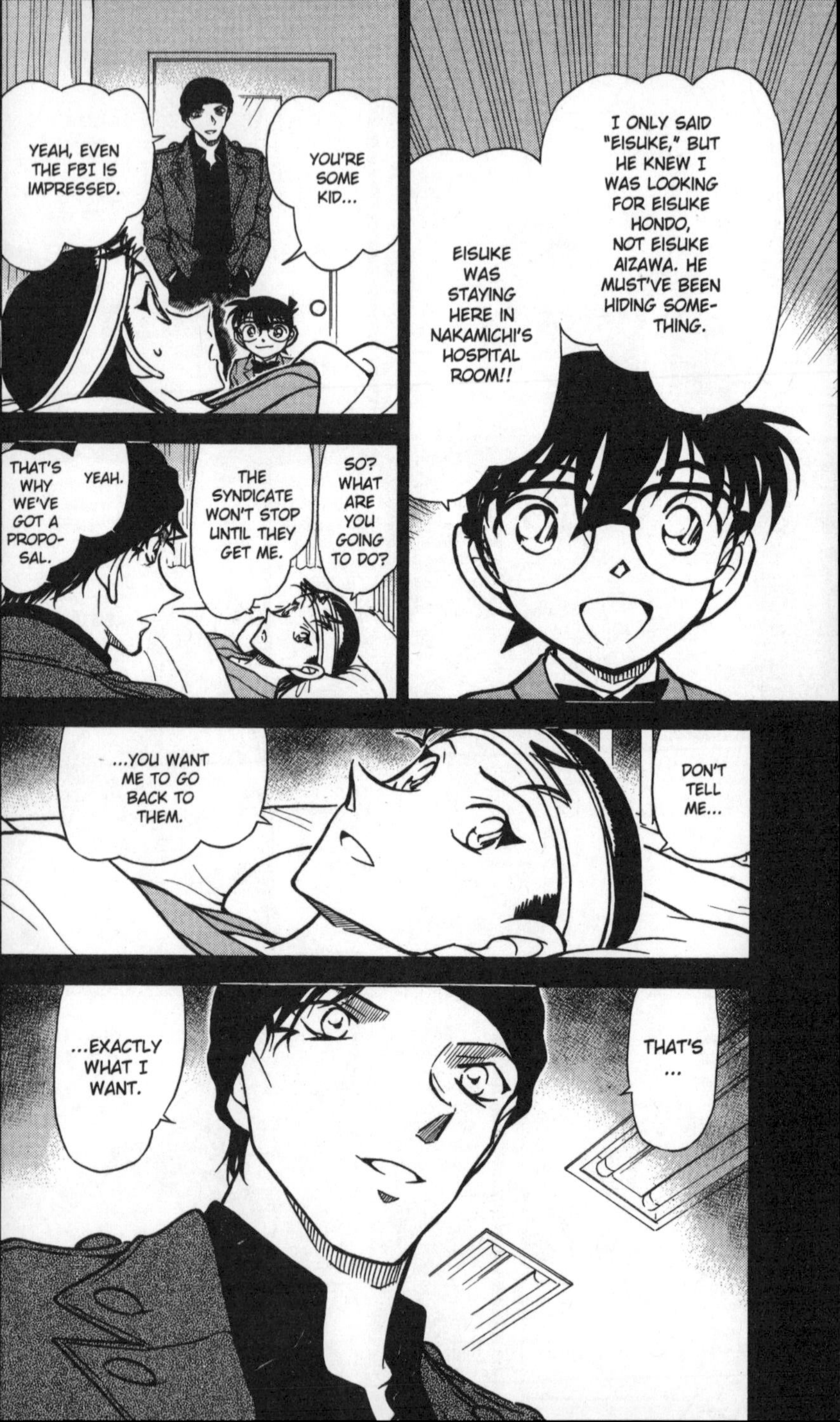
I ONLY SAID "EISUKE," BUT HE KNEW I WAS LOOKING FOR EISUKE HONDO, NOT EISUKE AIZAWA. HE MUST'VE BEEN HIDING SOME-THING.
EISUKE WAS STAYING HERE IN NAKAMICHI'S HOSPITAL ROOM!!
YOU'RE SOME KID...
YEAH, EVEN THE FBI IS IMPRESSED.
SO? WHAT ARE YOU GOING TO DO?
THE SYNDICATE WON'T STOP UNTIL THEY GET ME.
YEAH.
THAT'S WHY WE'VE GOT A PROPO-SAL.
DON'T TELL ME...
...YOU WANT ME TO GO BACK TO THEM.
THAT'S...
...EXACTLY WHAT I WANT.

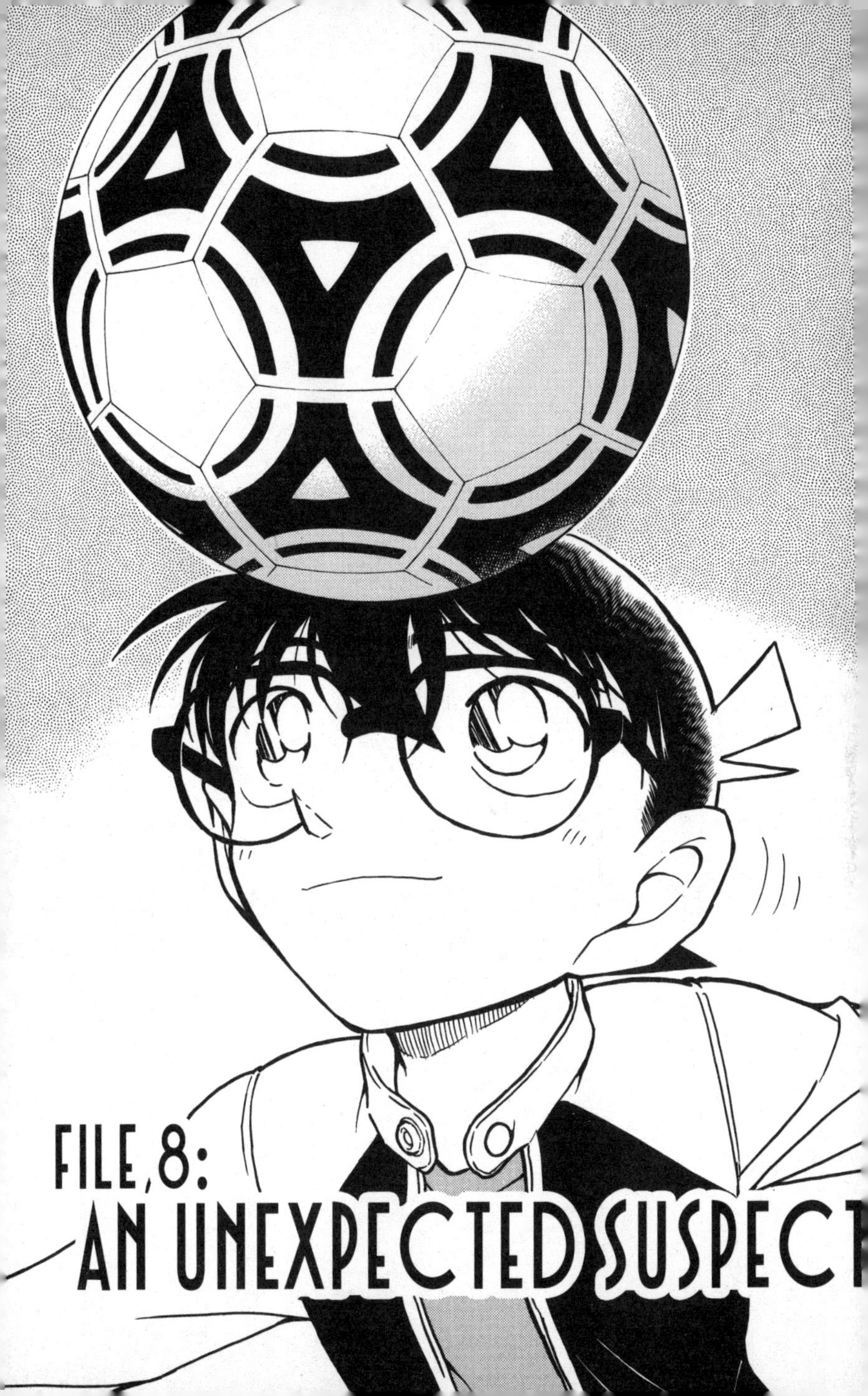
FILE 8:
AN UNEXPECTED SUSPECT

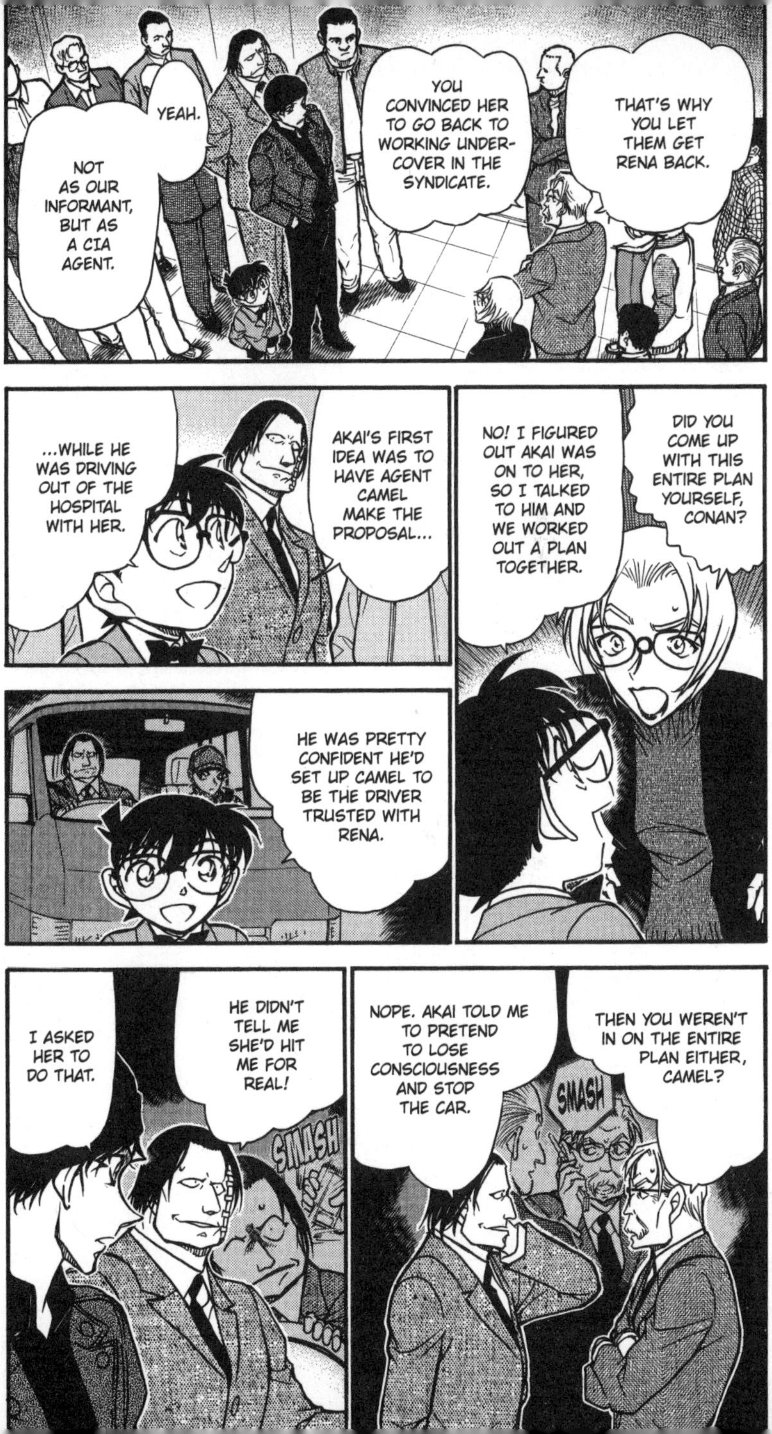
THAT'S WHY YOU LET THEM GET RENA BACK.
YOU CONVINCED HER TO GO BACK TO WORKING UNDER-COVER IN THE SYNDICATE.
YEAH.
NOT AS OUR INFORMANT, BUT AS A CIA AGENT.
DID YOU COME UP WITH THIS ENTIRE PLAN YOURSELF, CONAN?
NO! I FIGURED OUT AKAI WAS ON TO HER, SO I TALKED TO HIM AND WE WORKED OUT A PLAN TOGETHER.
AKAI'S FIRST IDEA WAS TO HAVE AGENT CAMEL MAKE THE PROPOSAL...
...WHILE HE WAS DRIVING OUT OF THE HOSPITAL WITH HER.
HE WAS PRETTY CONFIDENT HE'D SET UP CAMEL TO BE THE DRIVER TRUSTED WITH RENA.
THEN YOU WEREN'T IN ON THE ENTIRE PLAN EITHER, CAMEL?
NOPE. AKAI TOLD ME TO PRETEND TO LOSE CONSCIOUSNESS AND STOP THE CAR.
SMASH
HE DIDN'T TELL ME SHE'D HIT ME FOR REAL!
I ASKED HER TO DO THAT.
SMASH

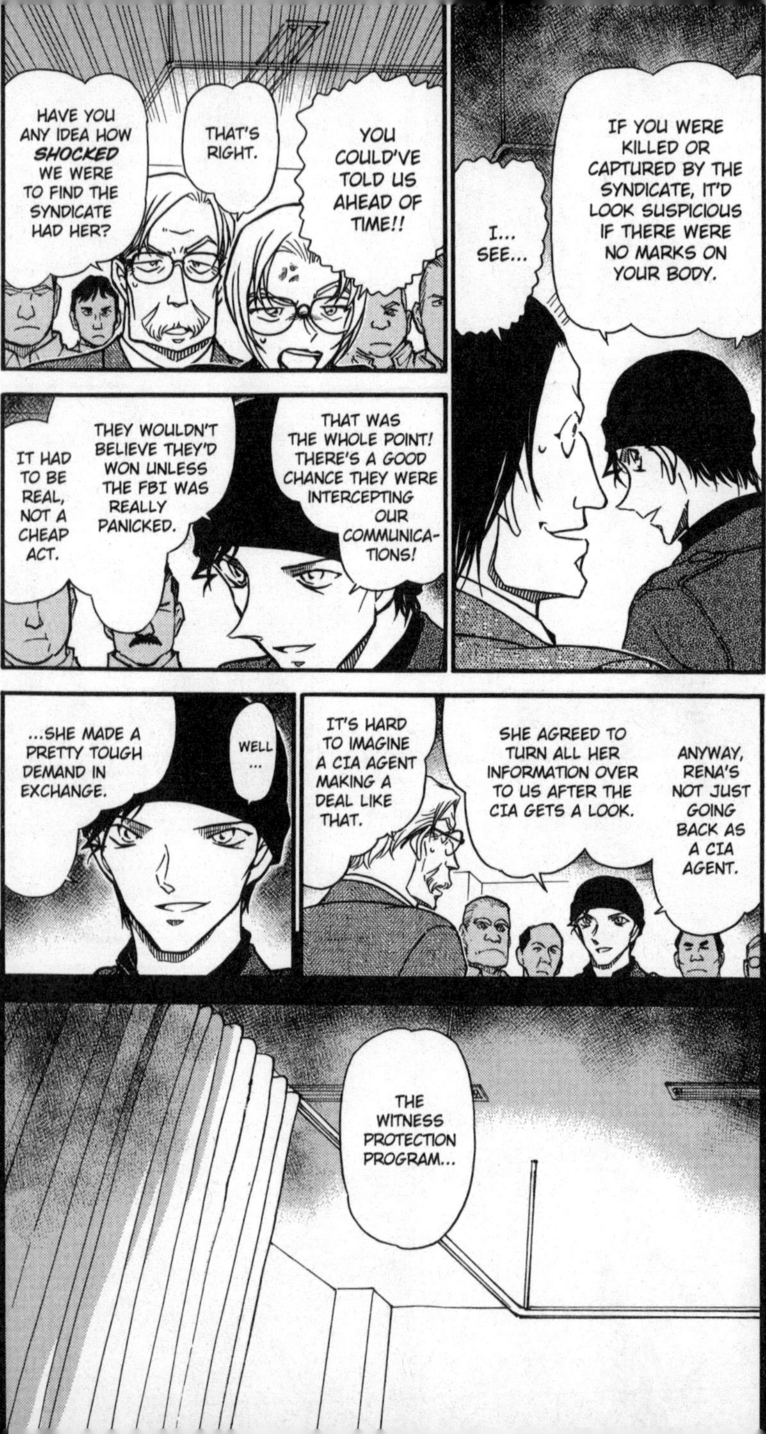
IF YOU WERE KILLED OR CAPTURED BY THE SYNDICATE, IT'D LOOK SUSPICIOUS IF THERE WERE NO MARKS ON YOUR BODY.
I... SEE...
YOU COULD'VE TOLD US AHEAD OF TIME!!
THAT'S RIGHT.
HAVE YOU ANY IDEA HOW SHOCKED WE WERE TO FIND THE SYNDICATE HAD HER?
THAT WAS THE WHOLE POINT! THERE'S A GOOD CHANCE THEY WERE INTERCEPTING OUR COMMUNICATIONS!
THEY WOULDN'T BELIEVE THEY'D WON UNLESS THE FBI WAS REALLY PANICKED.
IT HAD TO BE REAL, NOT A CHEAP ACT.
ANYWAY, RENA'S NOT JUST GOING BACK AS A CIA AGENT.
SHE AGREED TO TURN ALL HER INFORMATION OVER TO US AFTER THE CIA GETS A LOOK.
IT'S HARD TO IMAGINE A CIA AGENT MAKING A DEAL LIKE THAT.
WELL...
...SHE MADE A PRETTY TOUGH DEMAND IN EXCHANGE.
THE WITNESS PROTECTION PROGRAM...

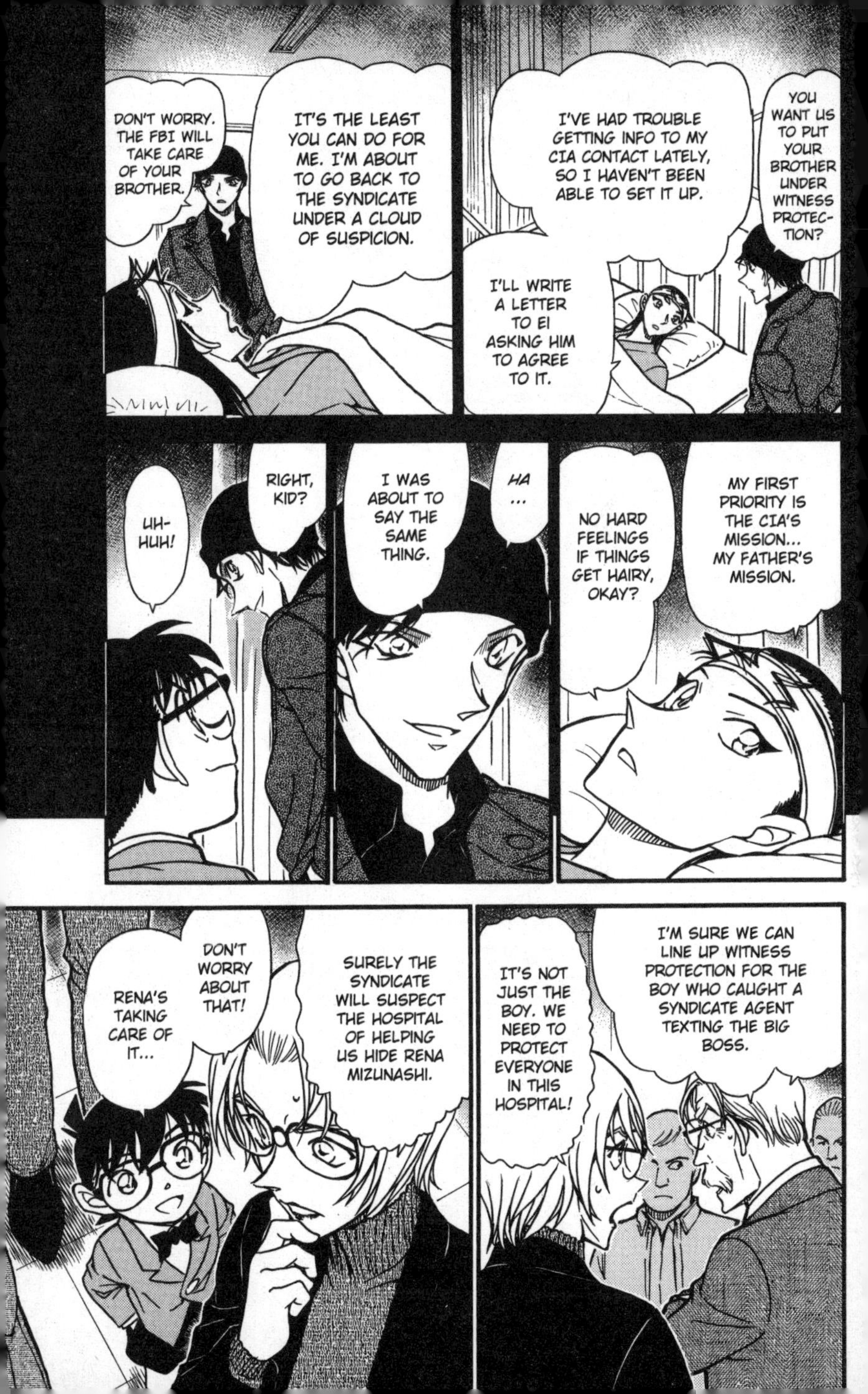
YOU WANT US TO PUT YOUR BROTHER UNDER WITNESS PROTECTION?
I'VE HAD TROUBLE GETTING INFO TO MY CIA CONTACT LATELY, SO I HAVEN'T BEEN ABLE TO SET IT UP.
I'LL WRITE A LETTER TO EI ASKING HIM TO AGREE TO IT.
IT'S THE LEAST YOU CAN DO FOR ME. I'M ABOUT TO GO BACK TO THE SYNDICATE UNDER A CLOUD OF SUSPICION.
DON'T WORRY. THE FBI WILL TAKE CARE OF YOUR BROTHER.
MY FIRST PRIORITY IS THE CIA'S MISSION... MY FATHER'S MISSION.
NO HARD FEELINGS IF THINGS GET HAIRY, OKAY?
HA...
I WAS ABOUT TO SAY THE SAME THING.
RIGHT, KID?
UH-HUH!
I'M SURE WE CAN LINE UP WITNESS PROTECTION FOR THE BOY WHO CAUGHT A SYNDICATE AGENT TEXTING THE BIG BOSS.
IT'S NOT JUST THE BOY. WE NEED TO PROTECT EVERYONE IN THIS HOSPITAL!
SURELY THE SYNDICATE WILL SUSPECT THE HOSPITAL OF HELPING US HIDE RENA MIZUNASHI.
DON'T WORRY ABOUT THAT!
RENA'S TAKING CARE OF IT...

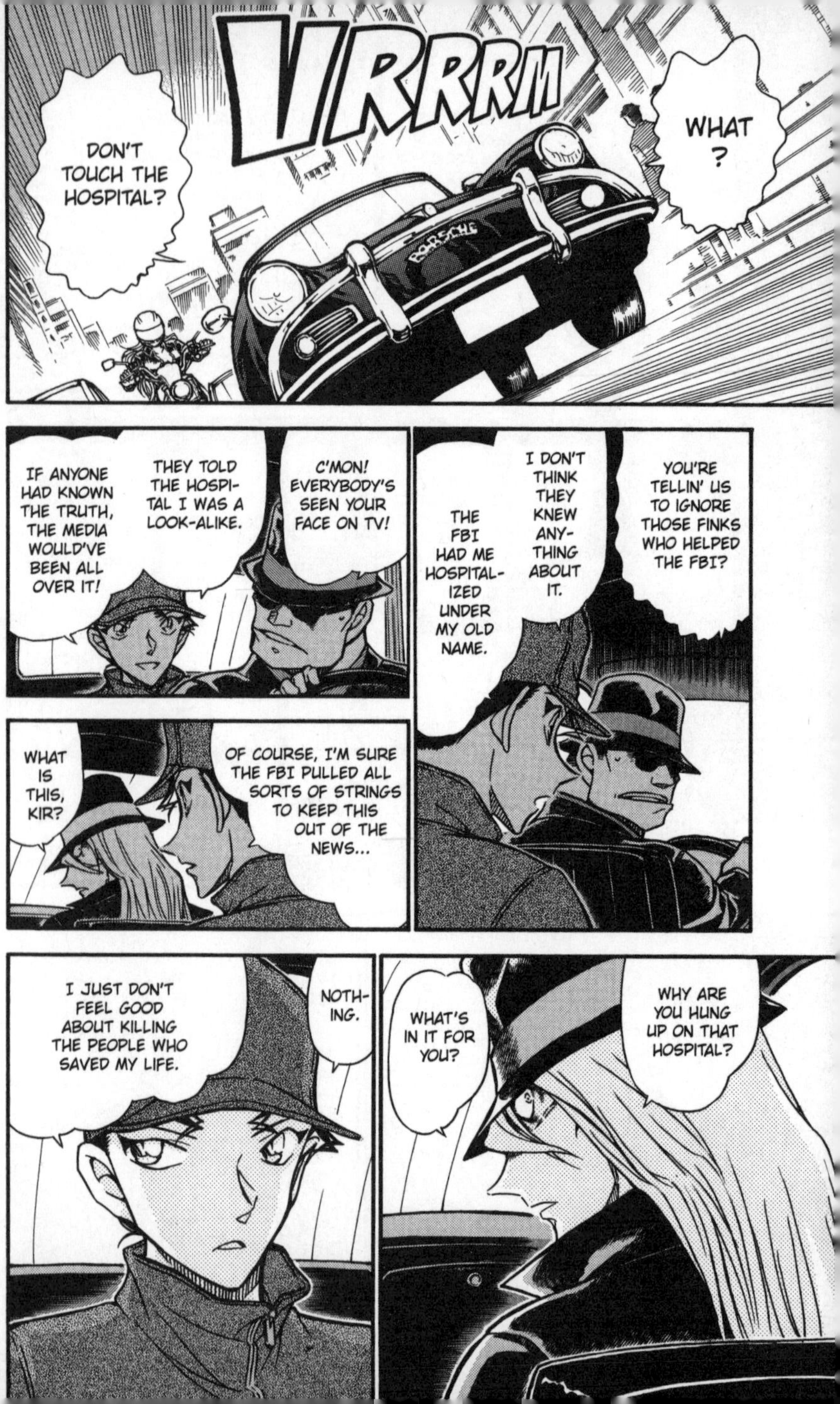
WHAT ?
VRRRRM
DON'T TOUCH THE HOSPITAL?
YOU'RE TELLIN' US TO IGNORE THOSE FINKS WHO HELPED THE FBI?
I DON'T THINK THEY KNEW ANYTHING ABOUT IT.
THE FBI HAD ME HOSPITALIZED UNDER MY OLD NAME.
C'MON! EVERYBODY'S SEEN YOUR FACE ON TV!
THEY TOLD THE HOSPITAL I WAS A LOOK-ALIKE.
IF ANYONE HAD KNOWN THE TRUTH, THE MEDIA WOULD'VE BEEN ALL OVER IT!
OF COURSE, I'M SURE THE FBI PULLED ALL SORTS OF STRINGS TO KEEP THIS OUT OF THE NEWS...
WHAT IS THIS, KIR?
WHY ARE YOU HUNG UP ON THAT HOSPITAL?
WHAT'S IN IT FOR YOU?
NOTHING.
I JUST DON'T FEEL GOOD ABOUT KILLING THE PEOPLE WHO SAVED MY LIFE.

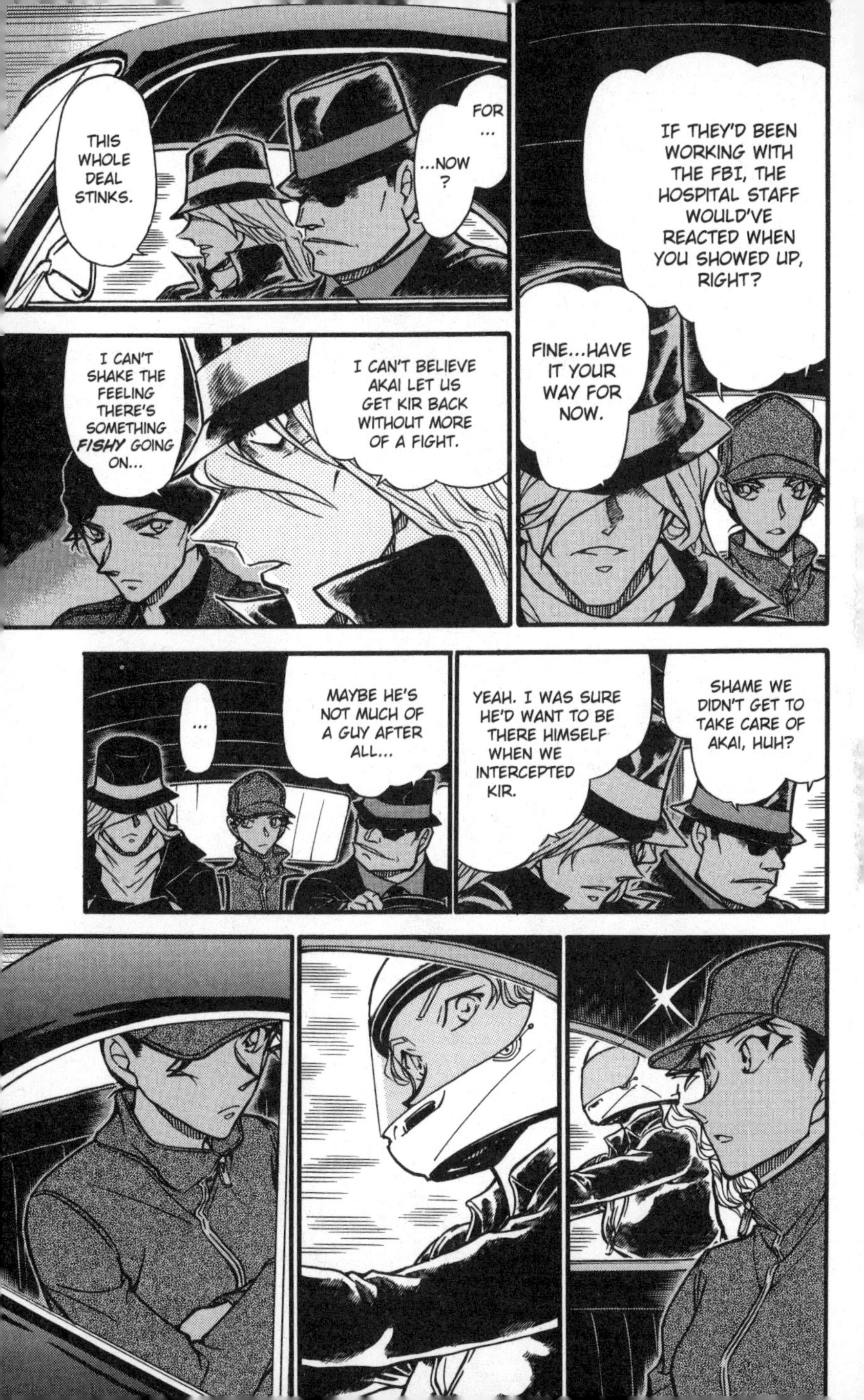
IF THEY'D BEEN WORKING WITH THE FBI, THE HOSPITAL STAFF WOULD'VE REACTED WHEN YOU SHOWED UP, RIGHT?
FINE...HAVE IT YOUR WAY FOR NOW.
FOR ...
...NOW ?
THIS WHOLE DEAL STINKS.
I CAN'T BELIEVE AKAI LET US GET KIR BACK WITHOUT MORE OF A FIGHT.
I CAN'T SHAKE THE FEELING THERE'S SOMETHING *FISHY* GOING ON...
SHAME WE DIDN'T GET TO TAKE CARE OF AKAI, HUH?
YEAH. I WAS SURE HE'D WANT TO BE THERE HIMSELF WHEN WE INTERCEPTED KIR.
MAYBE HE'S NOT MUCH OF A GUY AFTER ALL...
...

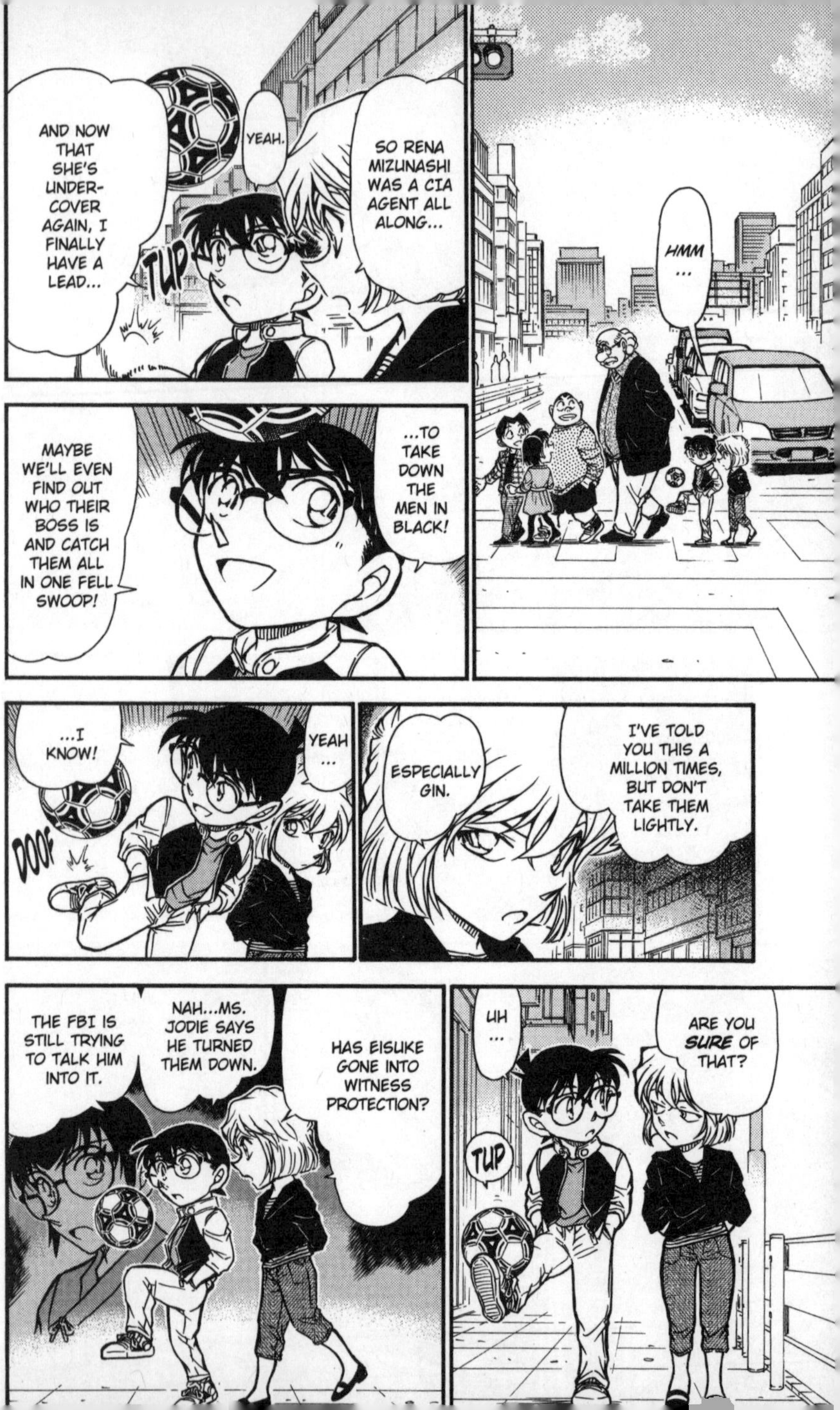
HMM...
SO RENA MIZUNASHI WAS A CIA AGENT ALL ALONG...
YEAH.
AND NOW THAT SHE'S UNDER-COVER AGAIN, I FINALLY HAVE A LEAD...
TUP
...TO TAKE DOWN THE MEN IN BLACK!
MAYBE WE'LL EVEN FIND OUT WHO THEIR BOSS IS AND CATCH THEM ALL IN ONE FELL SWOOP!
I'VE TOLD YOU THIS A MILLION TIMES, BUT DON'T TAKE THEM LIGHTLY.
ESPECIALLY GIN.
YEAH...
...I KNOW!
DOOF
ARE YOU ***SURE*** OF THAT?
UH...
TUP
HAS EISUKE GONE INTO WITNESS PROTECTION?
NAH...MS. JODIE SAYS HE TURNED THEM DOWN.
THE FBI IS STILL TRYING TO TALK HIM INTO IT.

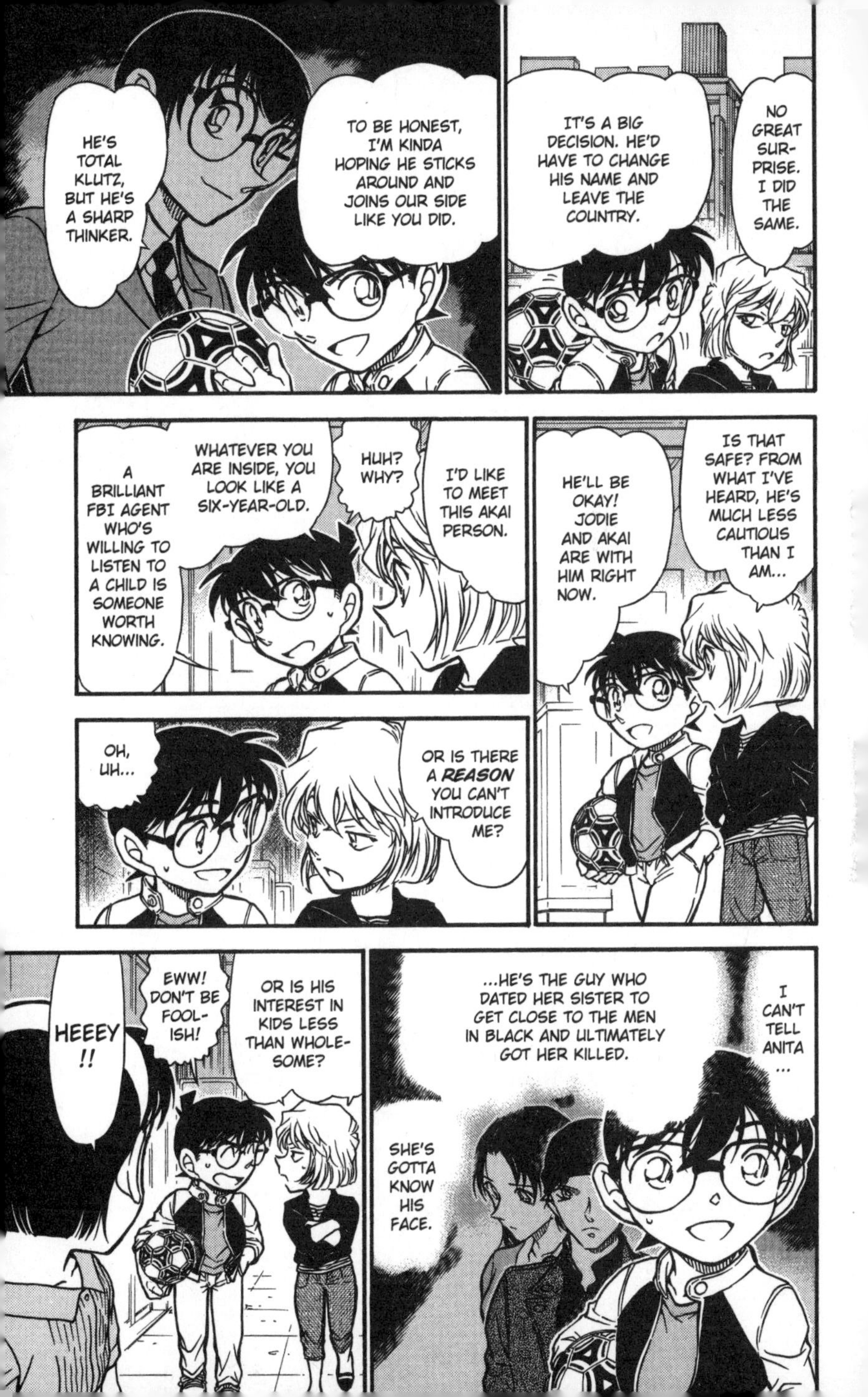
NO GREAT SURPRISE. I DID THE SAME.
IT'S A BIG DECISION. HE'D HAVE TO CHANGE HIS NAME AND LEAVE THE COUNTRY.
TO BE HONEST, I'M KINDA HOPING HE STICKS AROUND AND JOINS OUR SIDE LIKE YOU DID.
HE'S TOTAL KLUTZ, BUT HE'S A SHARP THINKER.
IS THAT SAFE? FROM WHAT I'VE HEARD, HE'S MUCH LESS CAUTIOUS THAN I AM...
HE'LL BE OKAY! JODIE AND AKAI ARE WITH HIM RIGHT NOW.
I'D LIKE TO MEET THIS AKAI PERSON.
HUH? WHY?
WHATEVER YOU ARE INSIDE, YOU LOOK LIKE A SIX-YEAR-OLD.
A BRILLIANT FBI AGENT WHO'S WILLING TO LISTEN TO A CHILD IS SOMEONE WORTH KNOWING.
OR IS THERE A ***REASON*** YOU CAN'T INTRODUCE ME?
OH, UH...
I CAN'T TELL ANITA...
...HE'S THE GUY WHO DATED HER SISTER TO GET CLOSE TO THE MEN IN BLACK AND ULTIMATELY GOT HER KILLED.
SHE'S GOTTA KNOW HIS FACE.
OR IS HIS INTEREST IN KIDS LESS THAN WHOLESOME?
EWW! DON'T BE FOOLISH!
HEEEY!!

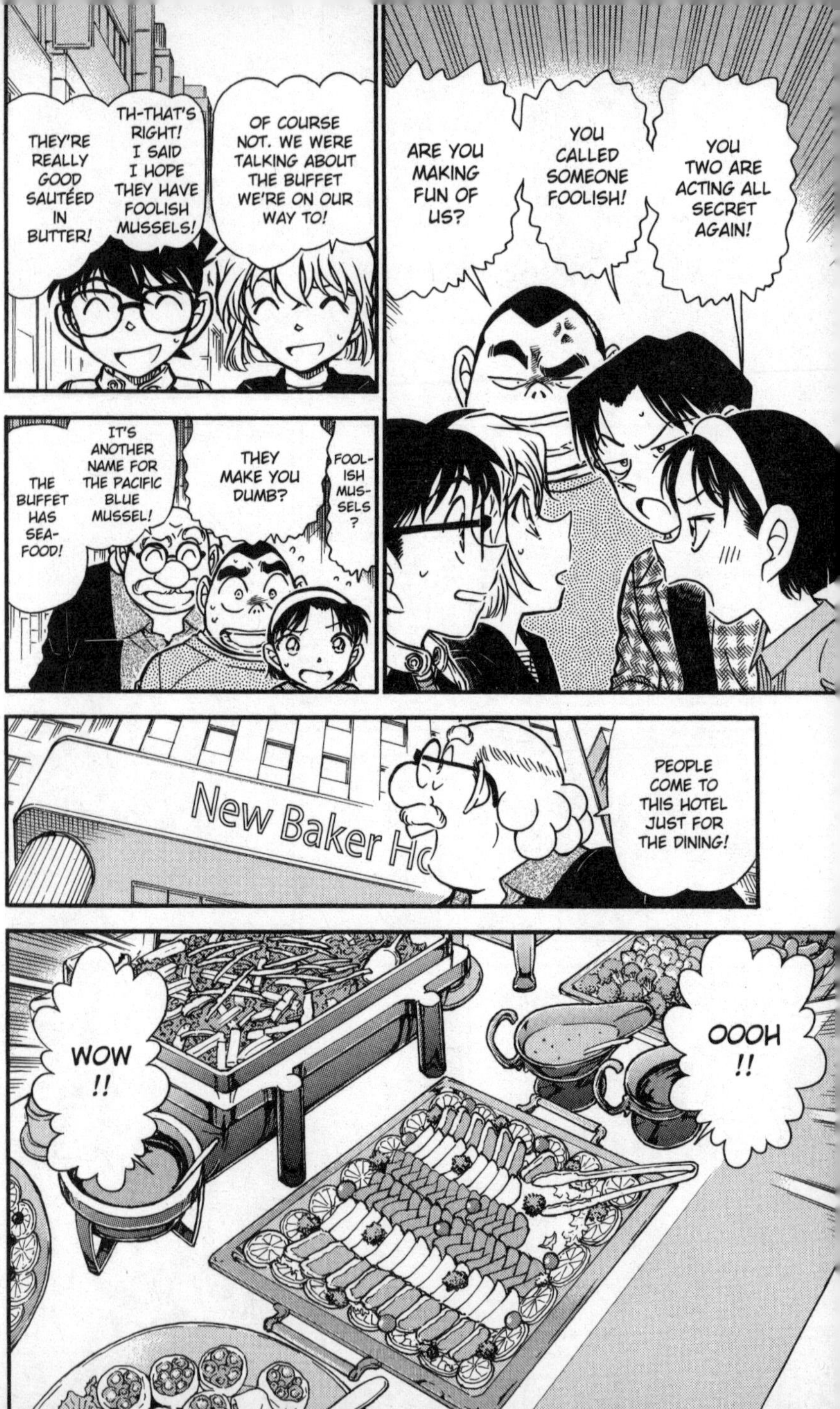
YOU TWO ARE ACTING ALL SECRET AGAIN!
YOU CALLED SOMEONE FOOLISH!
ARE YOU MAKING FUN OF US?
OF COURSE NOT. WE WERE TALKING ABOUT THE BUFFET WE'RE ON OUR WAY TO!
TH-THAT'S RIGHT! I SAID I HOPE THEY HAVE FOOLISH MUSSELS!
THEY'RE REALLY GOOD SAUTÉED IN BUTTER!
FOOL-ISH MUS-SELS?
THEY MAKE YOU DUMB?
IT'S ANOTHER NAME FOR THE PACIFIC BLUE MUSSEL!
THE BUFFET HAS SEA-FOOD!
PEOPLE COME TO THIS HOTEL JUST FOR THE DINING!
New Baker Ho
OOOH !!
WOW !!

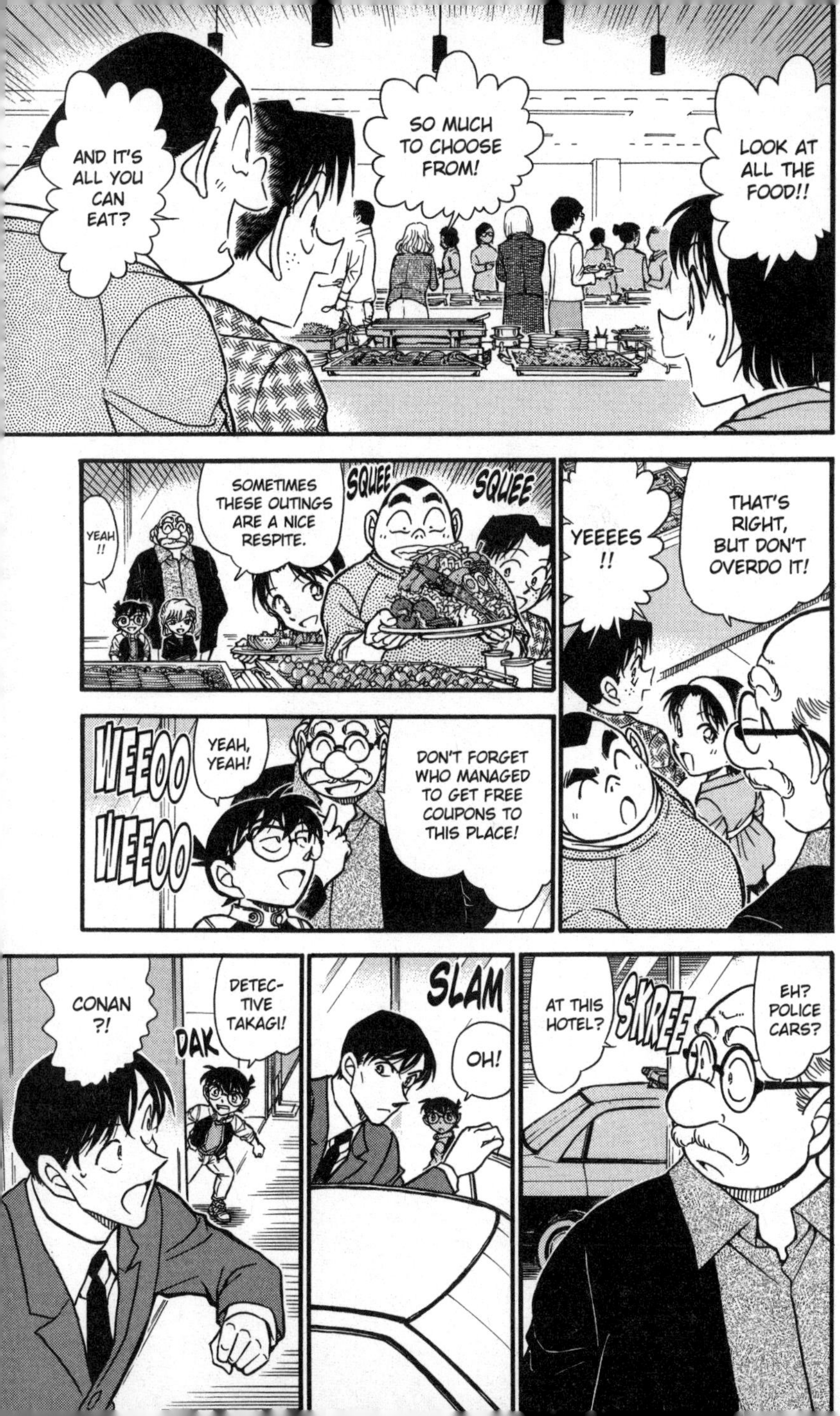
LOOK AT ALL THE FOOD!!
SO MUCH TO CHOOSE FROM!
AND IT'S ALL YOU CAN EAT?
THAT'S RIGHT, BUT DON'T OVERDO IT!
YEEEES !!
SQUEE
SQUEE
SOMETIMES THESE OUTINGS ARE A NICE RESPITE.
YEAH !!
DON'T FORGET WHO MANAGED TO GET FREE COUPONS TO THIS PLACE!
YEAH, YEAH!
WEEOO
WEEOO
EH? POLICE CARS?
SKREE
AT THIS HOTEL?
SLAM
OH!
DETEC-TIVE TAKAGI!
DAK
CONAN ?!

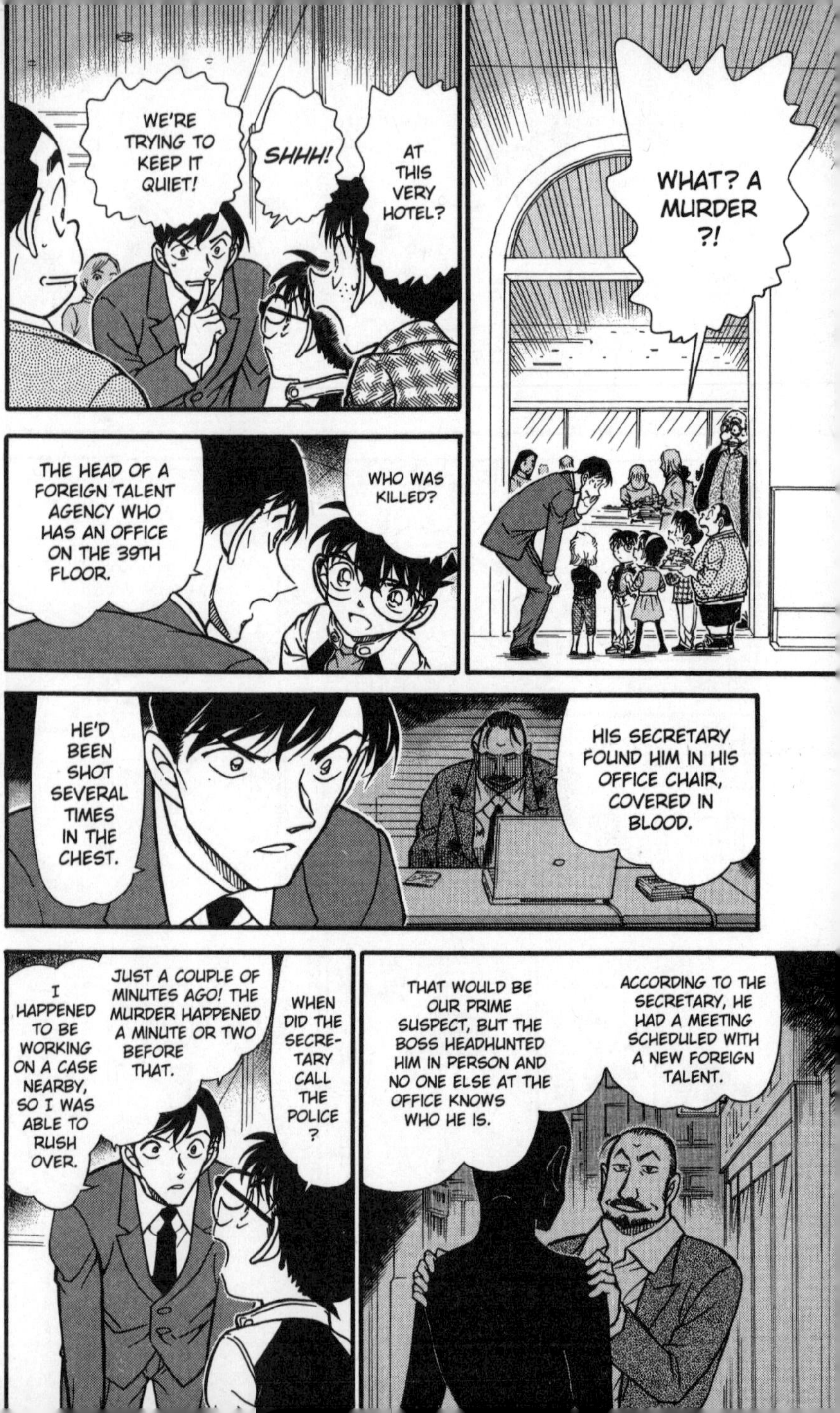
WHAT? A MURDER ?!
AT THIS VERY HOTEL?
SHHH!
WE'RE TRYING TO KEEP IT QUIET!
WHO WAS KILLED?
THE HEAD OF A FOREIGN TALENT AGENCY WHO HAS AN OFFICE ON THE 39TH FLOOR.
HIS SECRETARY FOUND HIM IN HIS OFFICE CHAIR, COVERED IN BLOOD.
HE'D BEEN SHOT SEVERAL TIMES IN THE CHEST.
ACCORDING TO THE SECRETARY, HE HAD A MEETING SCHEDULED WITH A NEW FOREIGN TALENT.
THAT WOULD BE OUR PRIME SUSPECT, BUT THE BOSS HEADHUNTED HIM IN PERSON AND NO ONE ELSE AT THE OFFICE KNOWS WHO HE IS.
WHEN DID THE SECRE-TARY CALL THE POLICE?
JUST A COUPLE OF MINUTES AGO! THE MURDER HAPPENED A MINUTE OR TWO BEFORE THAT.
I HAPPENED TO BE WORKING ON A CASE NEARBY, SO I WAS ABLE TO RUSH OVER.

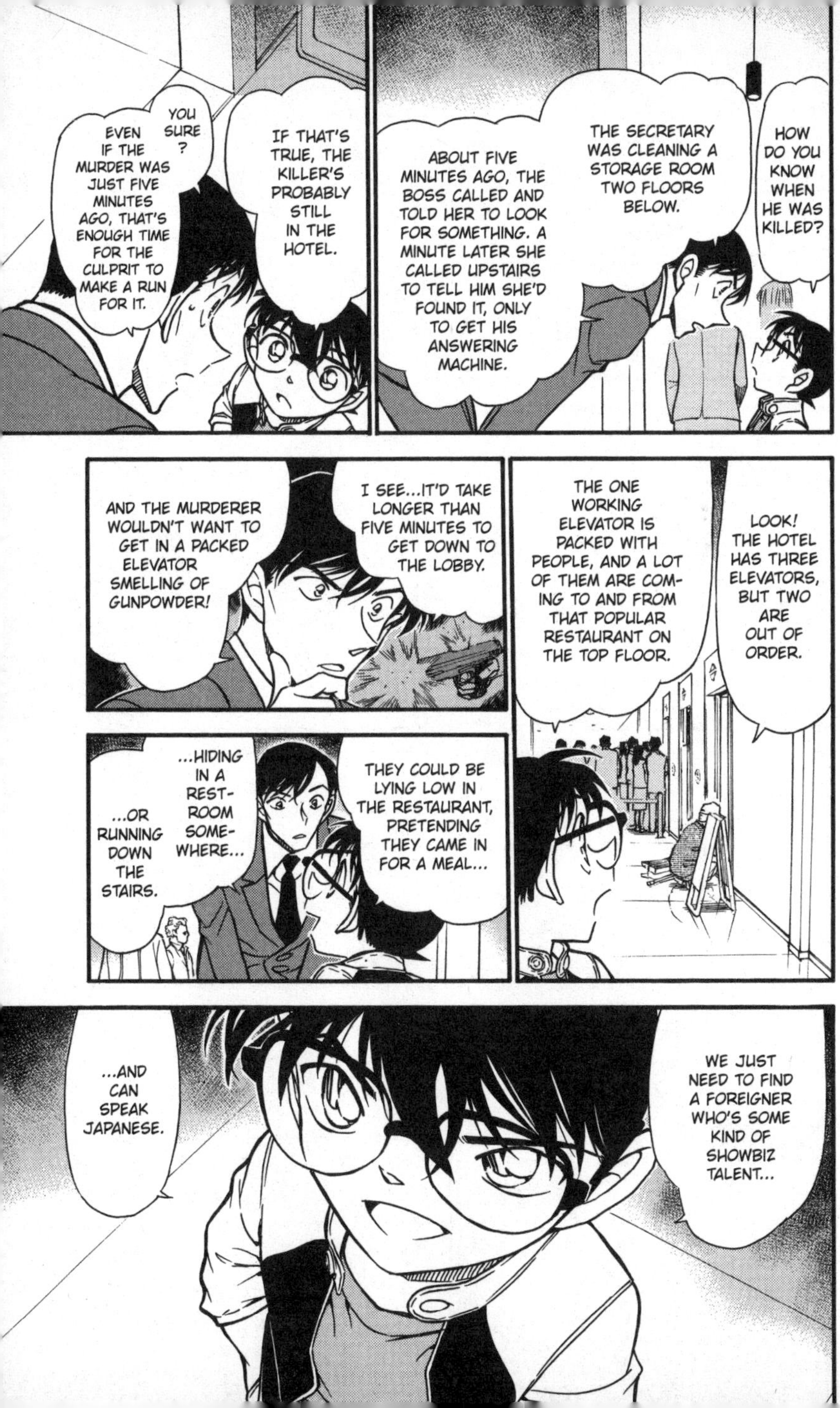
HOW DO YOU KNOW WHEN HE WAS KILLED?
THE SECRETARY WAS CLEANING A STORAGE ROOM TWO FLOORS BELOW.
ABOUT FIVE MINUTES AGO, THE BOSS CALLED AND TOLD HER TO LOOK FOR SOMETHING. A MINUTE LATER SHE CALLED UPSTAIRS TO TELL HIM SHE'D FOUND IT, ONLY TO GET HIS ANSWERING MACHINE.
IF THAT'S TRUE, THE KILLER'S PROBABLY STILL IN THE HOTEL.
YOU SURE?
EVEN IF THE MURDER WAS JUST FIVE MINUTES AGO, THAT'S ENOUGH TIME FOR THE CULPRIT TO MAKE A RUN FOR IT.
LOOK! THE HOTEL HAS THREE ELEVATORS, BUT TWO ARE OUT OF ORDER.
THE ONE WORKING ELEVATOR IS PACKED WITH PEOPLE, AND A LOT OF THEM ARE COMING TO AND FROM THAT POPULAR RESTAURANT ON THE TOP FLOOR.
I SEE...IT'D TAKE LONGER THAN FIVE MINUTES TO GET DOWN TO THE LOBBY.
AND THE MURDERER WOULDN'T WANT TO GET IN A PACKED ELEVATOR SMELLING OF GUNPOWDER!
THEY COULD BE LYING LOW IN THE RESTAURANT, PRETENDING THEY CAME IN FOR A MEAL...
...HIDING IN A REST-ROOM SOME-WHERE...
...OR RUNNING DOWN THE STAIRS.
WE JUST NEED TO FIND A FOREIGNER WHO'S SOME KIND OF SHOWBIZ TALENT...
...AND CAN SPEAK JAPANESE.

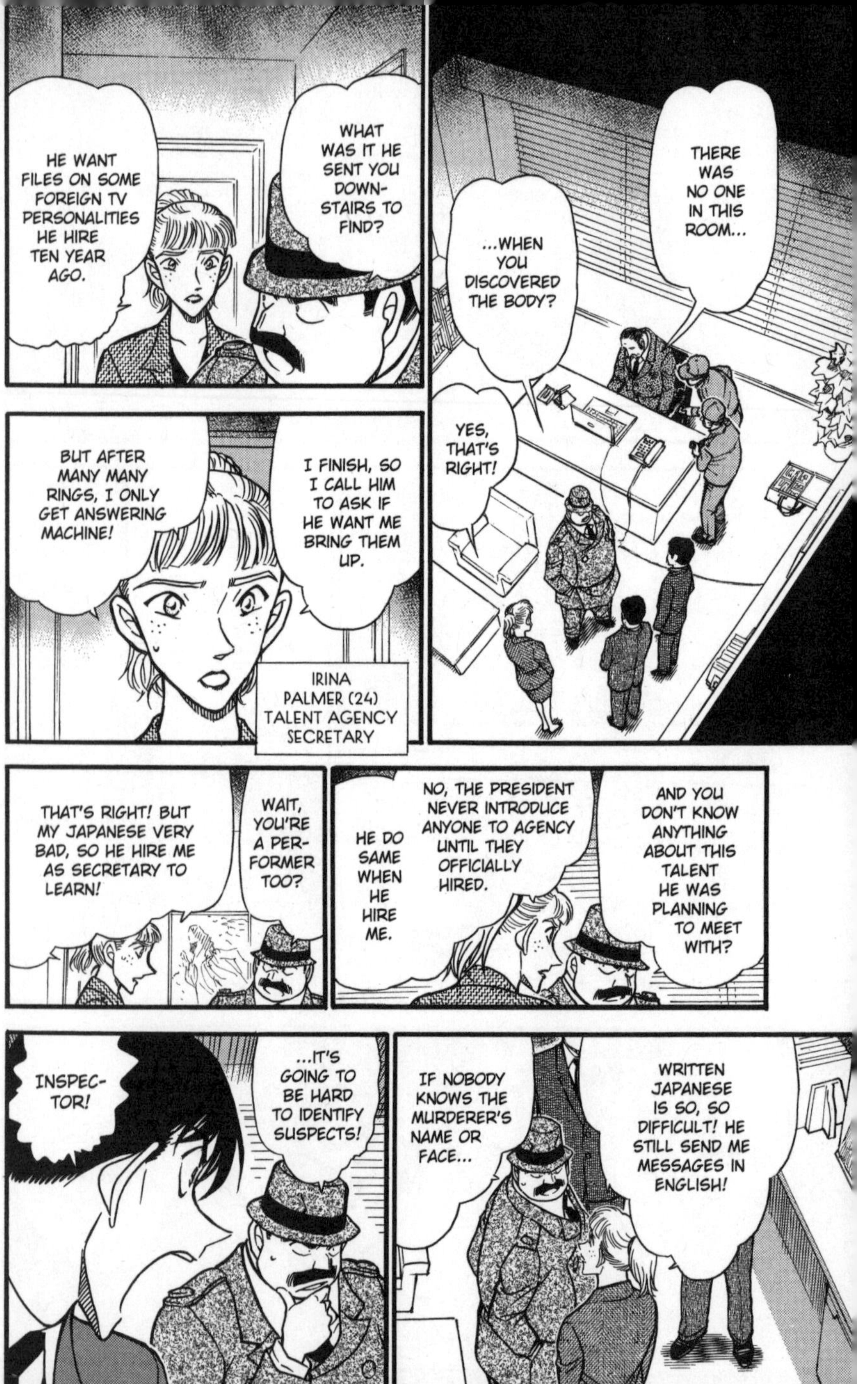
THERE WAS NO ONE IN THIS ROOM...
...WHEN YOU DISCOVERED THE BODY?
YES, THAT'S RIGHT!
WHAT WAS IT HE SENT YOU DOWN-STAIRS TO FIND?
HE WANT FILES ON SOME FOREIGN TV PERSONALITIES HE HIRE TEN YEAR AGO.
I FINISH, SO I CALL HIM TO ASK IF HE WANT ME BRING THEM UP.
BUT AFTER MANY MANY RINGS, I ONLY GET ANSWERING MACHINE!
IRINA PALMER (24) TALENT AGENCY SECRETARY
AND YOU DON'T KNOW ANYTHING ABOUT THIS TALENT HE WAS PLANNING TO MEET WITH?
NO, THE PRESIDENT NEVER INTRODUCE ANYONE TO AGENCY UNTIL THEY OFFICIALLY HIRED.
HE DO SAME WHEN HE HIRE ME.
WAIT, YOU'RE A PER-FORMER TOO?
THAT'S RIGHT! BUT MY JAPANESE VERY BAD, SO HE HIRE ME AS SECRETARY TO LEARN!
WRITTEN JAPANESE IS SO, SO DIFFICULT! HE STILL SEND ME MESSAGES IN ENGLISH!
IF NOBODY KNOWS THE MURDERER'S NAME OR FACE...
...IT'S GOING TO BE HARD TO IDENTIFY SUSPECTS!
INSPEC-TOR!

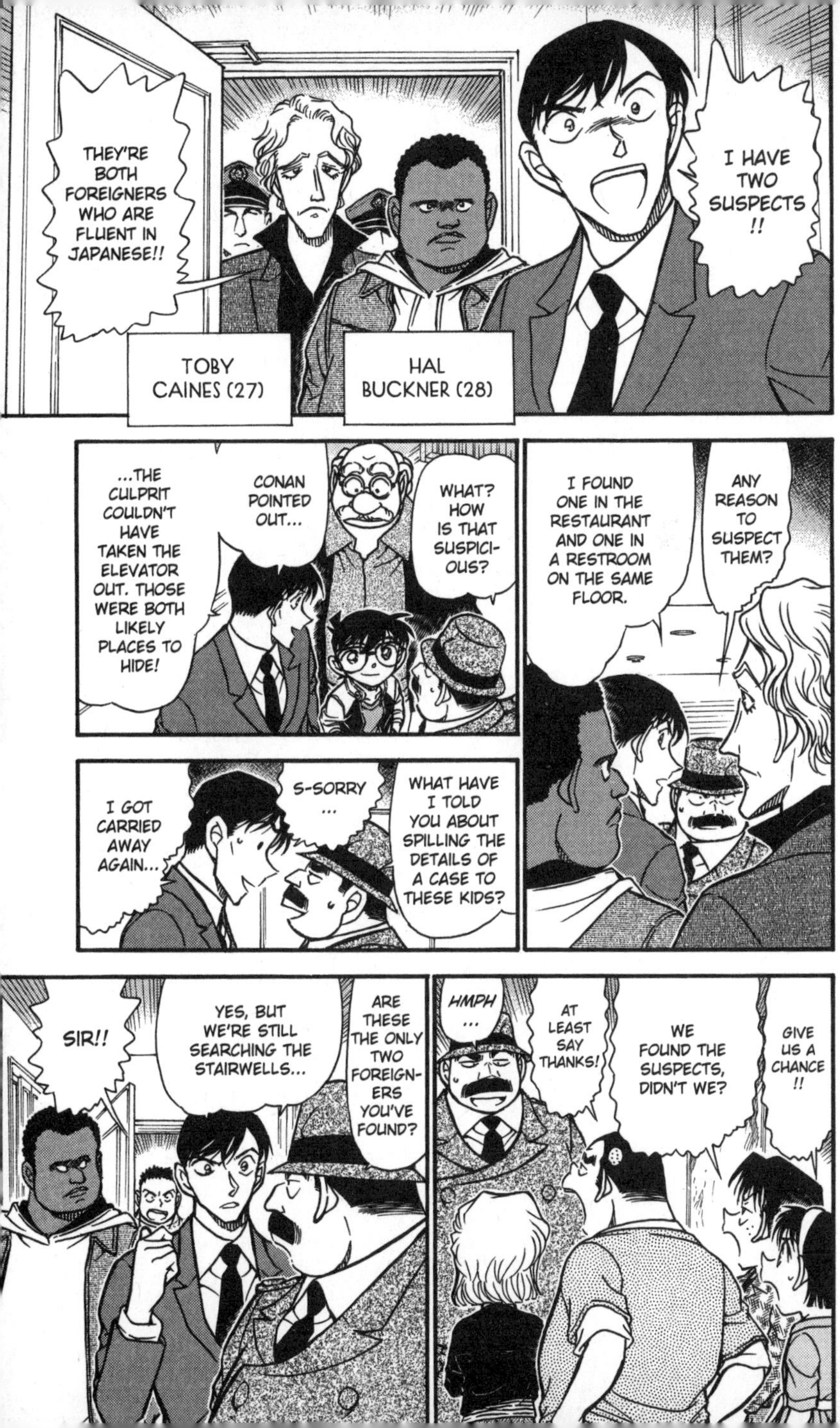
I HAVE TWO SUSPECTS!!
THEY'RE BOTH FOREIGNERS WHO ARE FLUENT IN JAPANESE!!
HAL BUCKNER (28)
TOBY CAINES (27)
ANY REASON TO SUSPECT THEM?
I FOUND ONE IN THE RESTAURANT AND ONE IN A RESTROOM ON THE SAME FLOOR.
WHAT? HOW IS THAT SUSPICIOUS?
CONAN POINTED OUT...
...THE CULPRIT COULDN'T HAVE TAKEN THE ELEVATOR OUT. THOSE WERE BOTH LIKELY PLACES TO HIDE!
WHAT HAVE I TOLD YOU ABOUT SPILLING THE DETAILS OF A CASE TO THESE KIDS?
S-SORRY...
I GOT CARRIED AWAY AGAIN...
GIVE US A CHANCE!!
WE FOUND THE SUSPECTS, DIDN'T WE?
AT LEAST SAY THANKS!
HMPH...
ARE THESE THE ONLY TWO FOREIGNERS YOU'VE FOUND?
YES, BUT WE'RE STILL SEARCHING THE STAIRWELLS...
SIR!!

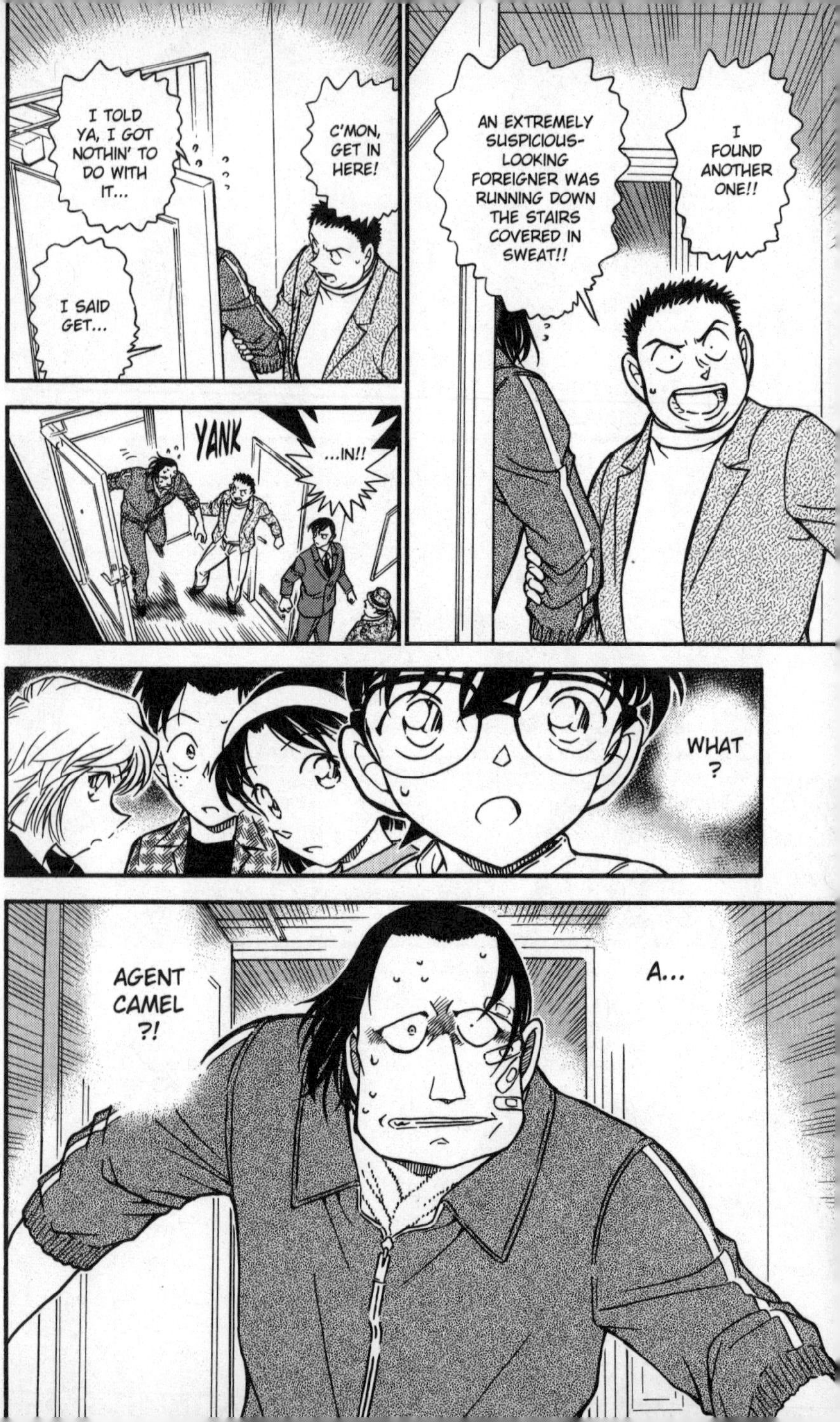
I FOUND ANOTHER ONE!!
AN EXTREMELY SUSPICIOUS-LOOKING FOREIGNER WAS RUNNING DOWN THE STAIRS COVERED IN SWEAT!!
C'MON, GET IN HERE!
I TOLD YA, I GOT NOTHIN' TO DO WITH IT...
I SAID GET...
...IN!!
YANK
WHAT?
A...
AGENT CAMEL?!

FILE 9: FRIDAY THE 13TH

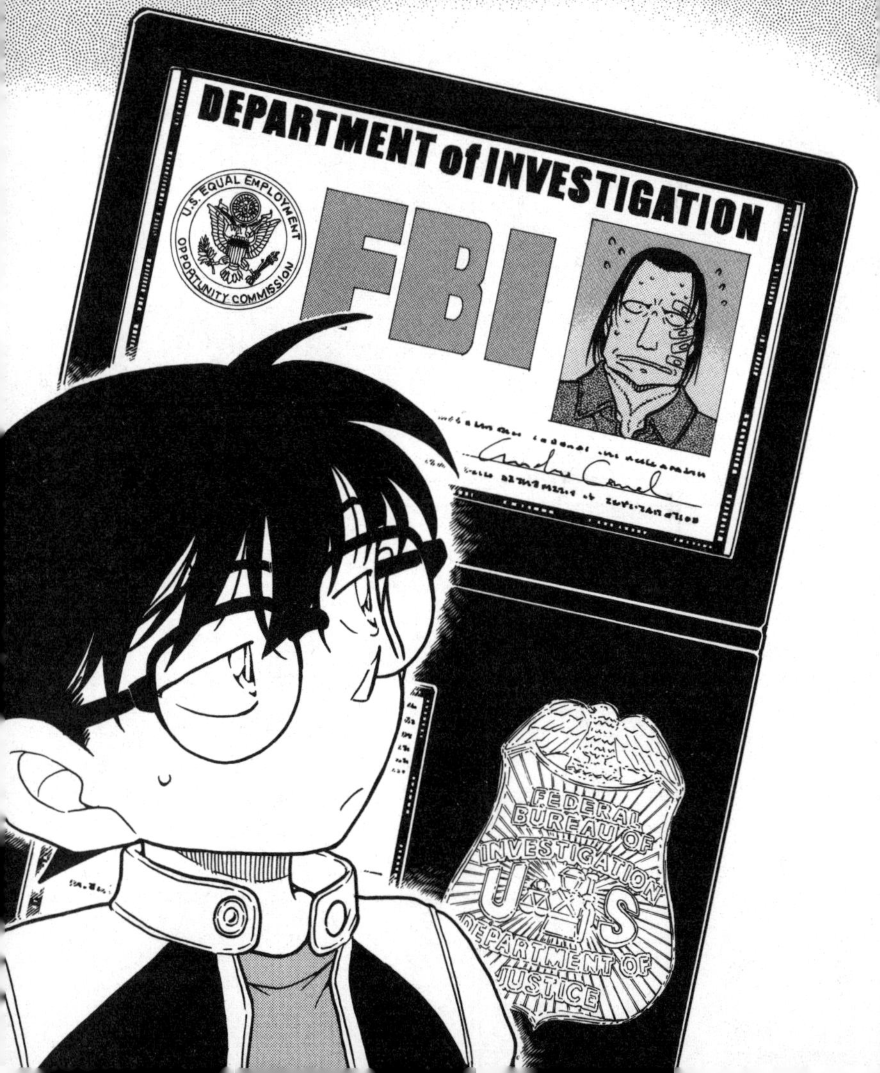
DEPARTMENT of INVESTIGATION
U.S. EQUAL EMPLOYMENT OPPORTUNITY COMMISSION
FBI
FEDERAL BUREAU OF INVESTIGATION
U S
DEPARTMENT OF JUSTICE

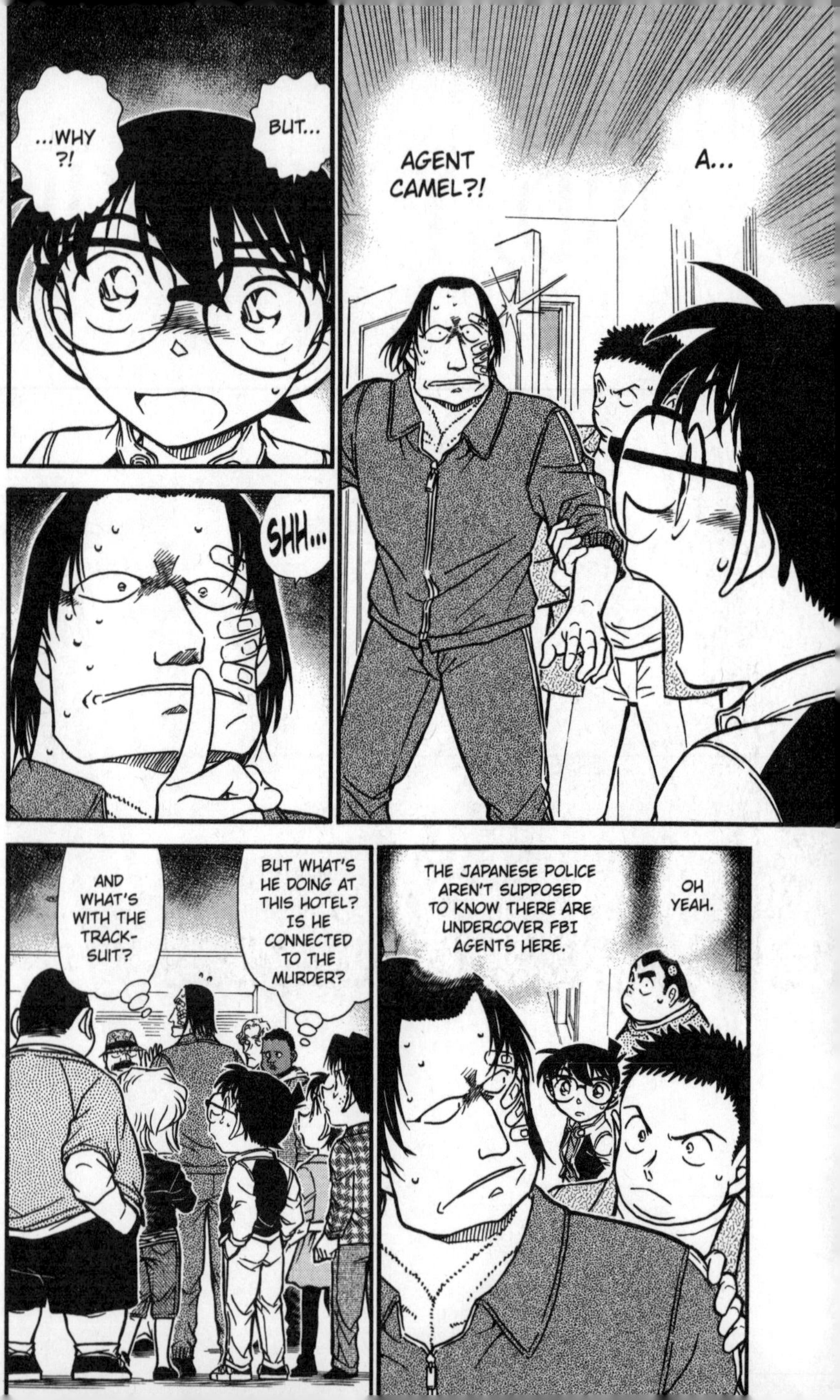
A...
AGENT CAMEL?!
BUT...
...WHY ?!
SHH...
OH YEAH.
THE JAPANESE POLICE AREN'T SUPPOSED TO KNOW THERE ARE UNDERCOVER FBI AGENTS HERE.
BUT WHAT'S HE DOING AT THIS HOTEL? IS HE CONNECTED TO THE MURDER?
AND WHAT'S WITH THE TRACK-SUIT?

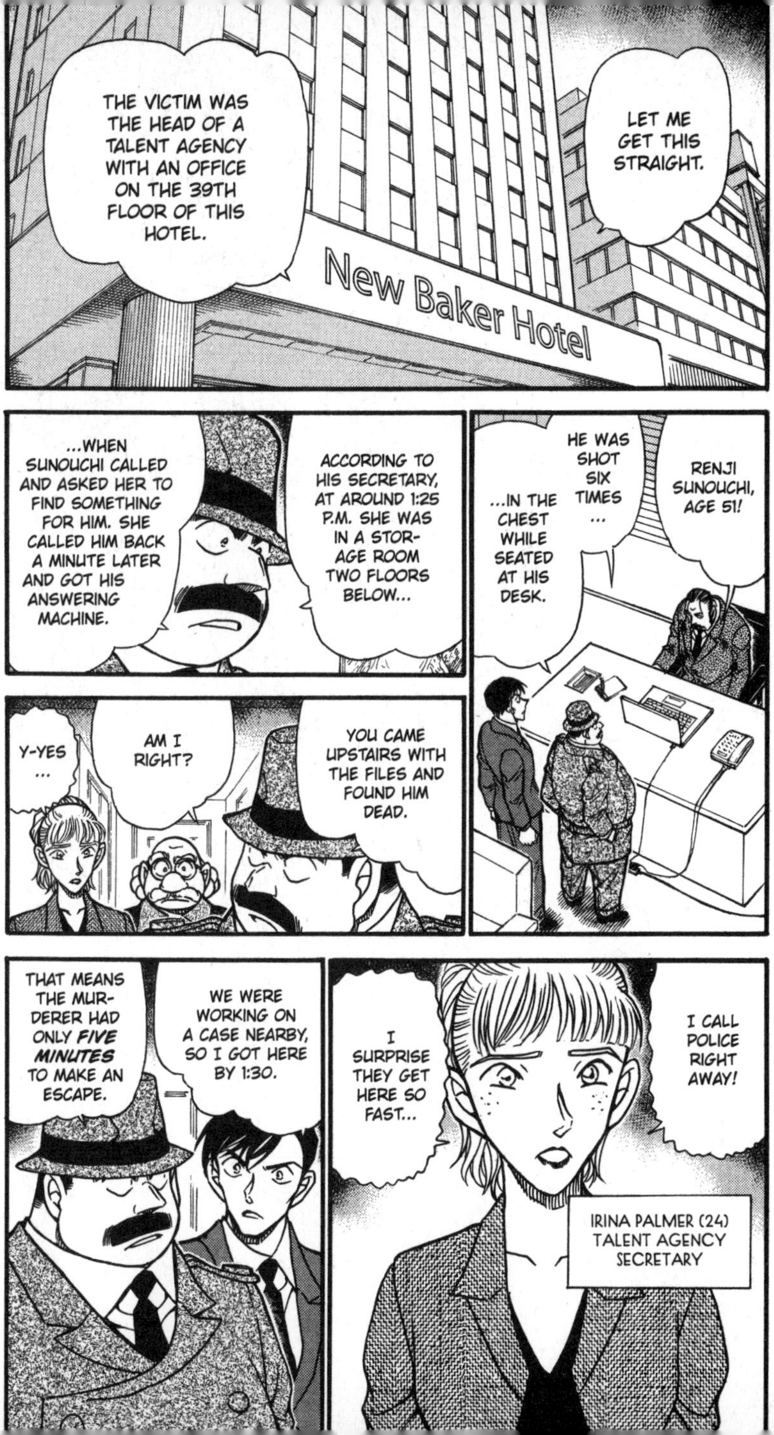
LET ME GET THIS STRAIGHT.
THE VICTIM WAS THE HEAD OF A TALENT AGENCY WITH AN OFFICE ON THE 39TH FLOOR OF THIS HOTEL.
New Baker Hotel
RENJI SUNOUCHI, AGE 51!
HE WAS SHOT SIX TIMES ...
...IN THE CHEST WHILE SEATED AT HIS DESK.
ACCORDING TO HIS SECRETARY, AT AROUND 1:25 P.M. SHE WAS IN A STORAGE ROOM TWO FLOORS BELOW...
...WHEN SUNOUCHI CALLED AND ASKED HER TO FIND SOMETHING FOR HIM. SHE CALLED HIM BACK A MINUTE LATER AND GOT HIS ANSWERING MACHINE.
YOU CAME UPSTAIRS WITH THE FILES AND FOUND HIM DEAD.
AM I RIGHT?
Y-YES ...
I CALL POLICE RIGHT AWAY!
I SURPRISE THEY GET HERE SO FAST...
IRINA PALMER (24) TALENT AGENCY SECRETARY
WE WERE WORKING ON A CASE NEARBY, SO I GOT HERE BY 1:30.
THAT MEANS THE MURDERER HAD ONLY *FIVE MINUTES* TO MAKE AN ESCAPE.

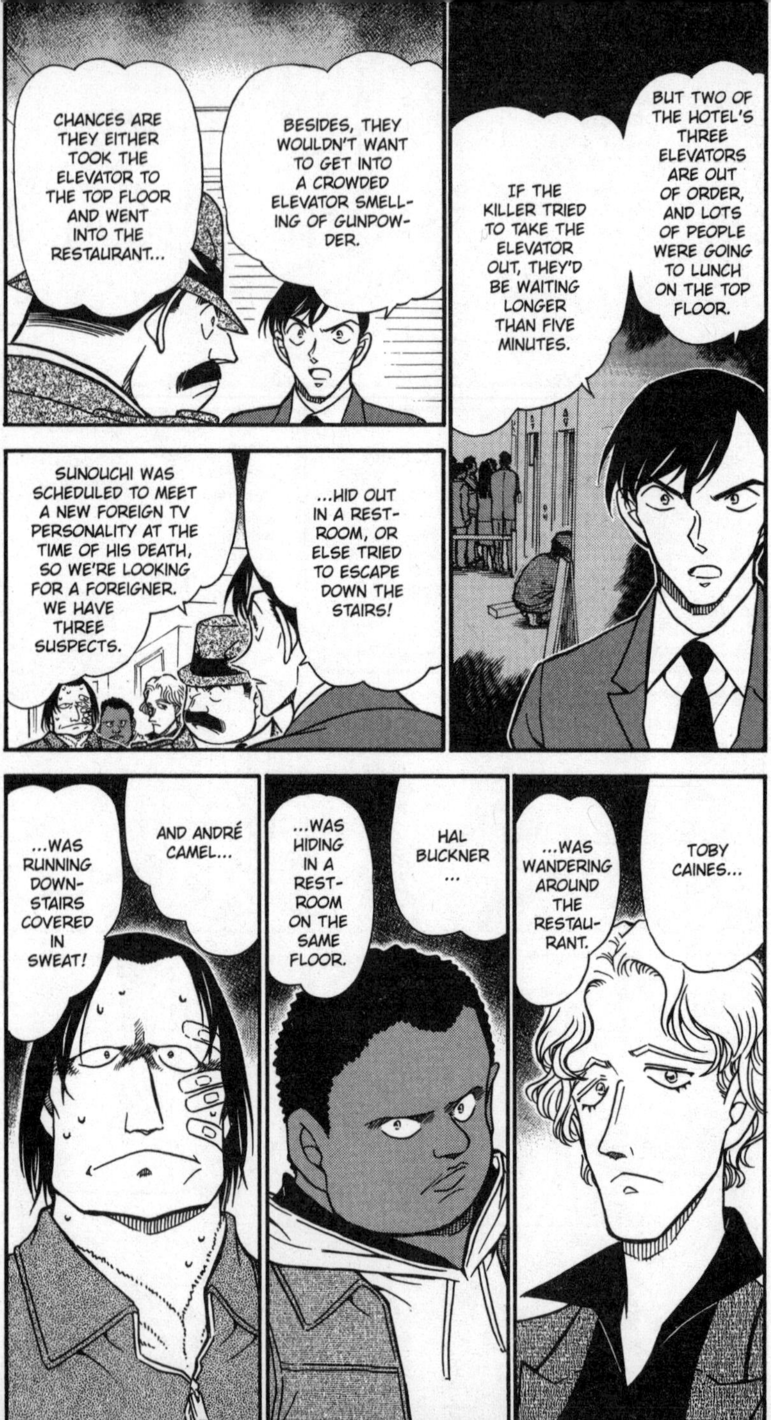
BUT TWO OF THE HOTEL'S THREE ELEVATORS ARE OUT OF ORDER, AND LOTS OF PEOPLE WERE GOING TO LUNCH ON THE TOP FLOOR.
IF THE KILLER TRIED TO TAKE THE ELEVATOR OUT, THEY'D BE WAITING LONGER THAN FIVE MINUTES.
BESIDES, THEY WOULDN'T WANT TO GET INTO A CROWDED ELEVATOR SMELL-ING OF GUNPOW-DER.
CHANCES ARE THEY EITHER TOOK THE ELEVATOR TO THE TOP FLOOR AND WENT INTO THE RESTAURANT...
...HID OUT IN A REST-ROOM, OR ELSE TRIED TO ESCAPE DOWN THE STAIRS!
SUNOUCHI WAS SCHEDULED TO MEET A NEW FOREIGN TV PERSONALITY AT THE TIME OF HIS DEATH, SO WE'RE LOOKING FOR A FOREIGNER. WE HAVE THREE SUSPECTS.
TOBY CAINES...
...WAS WANDERING AROUND THE RESTAU-RANT.
HAL BUCKNER ...
...WAS HIDING IN A REST-ROOM ON THE SAME FLOOR.
AND ANDRÉ CAMEL...
...WAS RUNNING DOWN-STAIRS COVERED IN SWEAT!

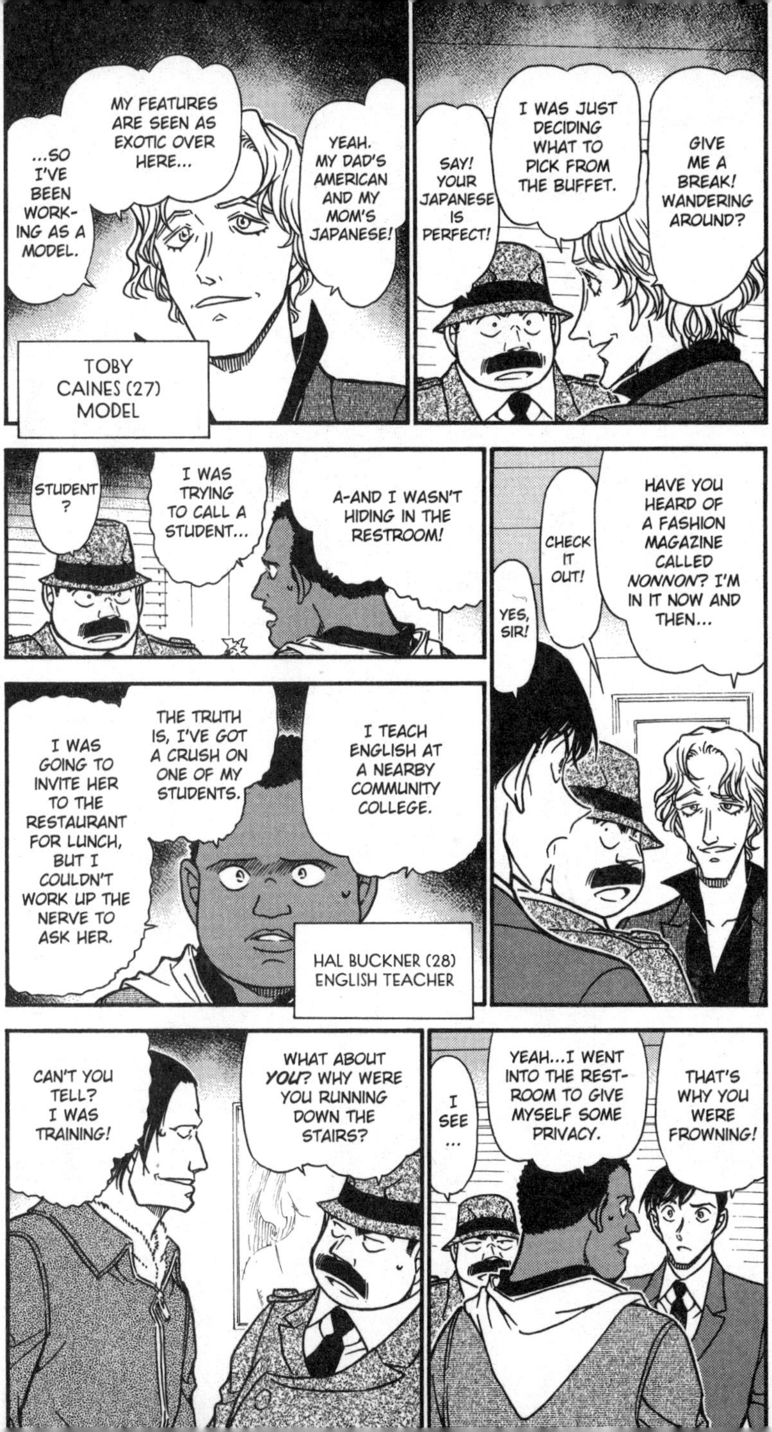

GIVE ME A BREAK! WANDERING AROUND?
I WAS JUST DECIDING WHAT TO PICK FROM THE BUFFET.
SAY! YOUR JAPANESE IS PERFECT!
YEAH. MY DAD'S AMERICAN AND MY MOM'S JAPANESE!
MY FEATURES ARE SEEN AS EXOTIC OVER HERE...
...SO I'VE BEEN WORK-ING AS A MODEL.
TOBY CAINES (27) MODEL
HAVE YOU HEARD OF A FASHION MAGAZINE CALLED *NONNON*? I'M IN IT NOW AND THEN...
CHECK IT OUT!
YES, SIR!
A-AND I WASN'T HIDING IN THE RESTROOM!
I WAS TRYING TO CALL A STUDENT...
STUDENT?
I TEACH ENGLISH AT A NEARBY COMMUNITY COLLEGE.
THE TRUTH IS, I'VE GOT A CRUSH ON ONE OF MY STUDENTS.
I WAS GOING TO INVITE HER TO THE RESTAURANT FOR LUNCH, BUT I COULDN'T WORK UP THE NERVE TO ASK HER.
HAL BUCKNER (28) ENGLISH TEACHER
THAT'S WHY YOU WERE FROWNING!
YEAH...I WENT INTO THE REST-ROOM TO GIVE MYSELF SOME PRIVACY.
I SEE...
WHAT ABOUT ***YOU***? WHY WERE YOU RUNNING DOWN THE STAIRS?
CAN'T YOU TELL? I WAS TRAINING!

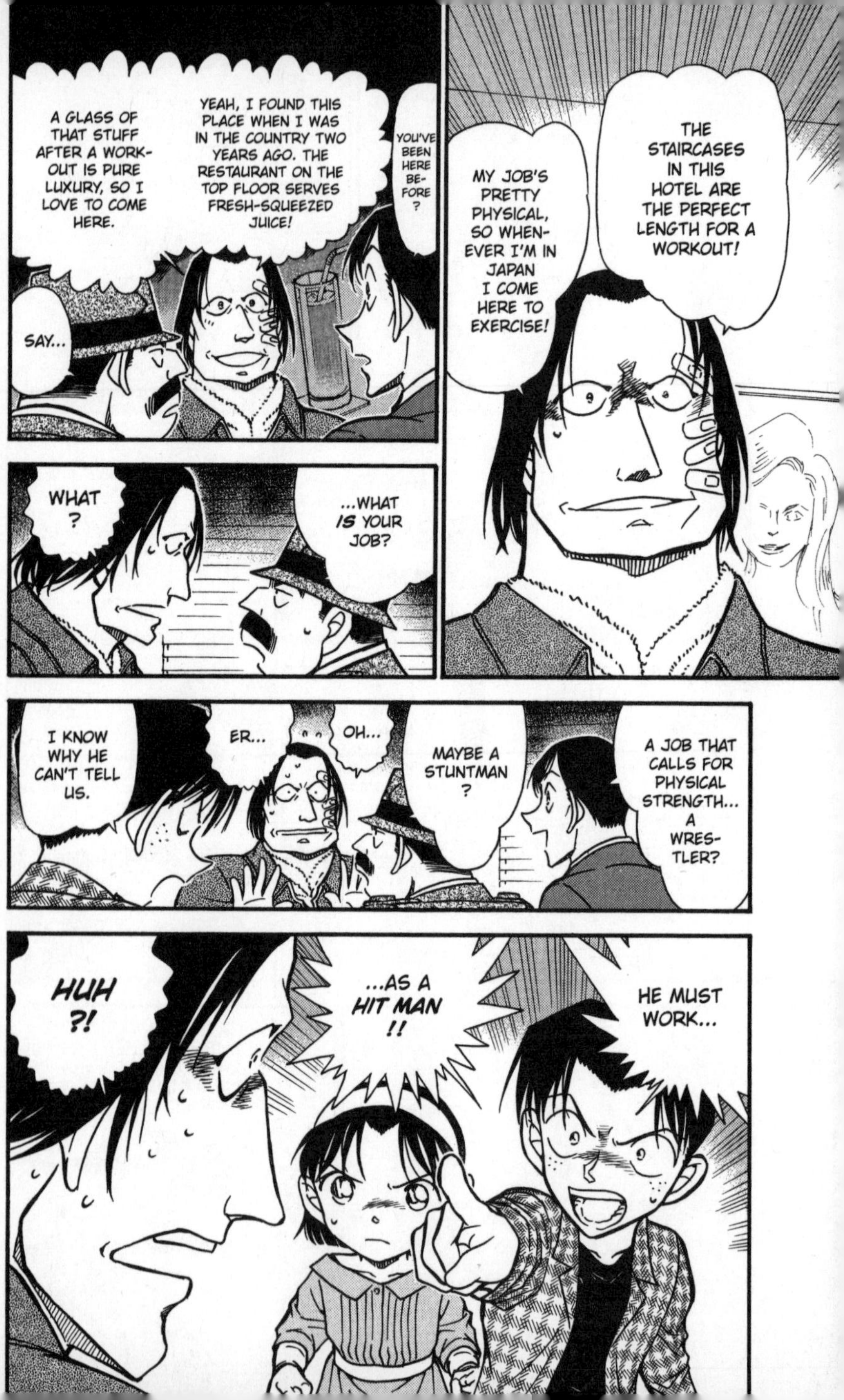
THE STAIRCASES IN THIS HOTEL ARE THE PERFECT LENGTH FOR A WORKOUT!
MY JOB'S PRETTY PHYSICAL, SO WHENEVER I'M IN JAPAN I COME HERE TO EXERCISE!
YOU'VE BEEN HERE BEFORE?
YEAH, I FOUND THIS PLACE WHEN I WAS IN THE COUNTRY TWO YEARS AGO. THE RESTAURANT ON THE TOP FLOOR SERVES FRESH-SQUEEZED JUICE!
A GLASS OF THAT STUFF AFTER A WORKOUT IS PURE LUXURY, SO I LOVE TO COME HERE.
SAY...
...WHAT *IS* YOUR JOB?
WHAT?
A JOB THAT CALLS FOR PHYSICAL STRENGTH... A WRESTLER?
MAYBE A STUNTMAN?
OH...
ER...
I KNOW WHY HE CAN'T TELL US.
HE MUST WORK...
...AS A ***HIT MAN***!!
***HUH*?!**

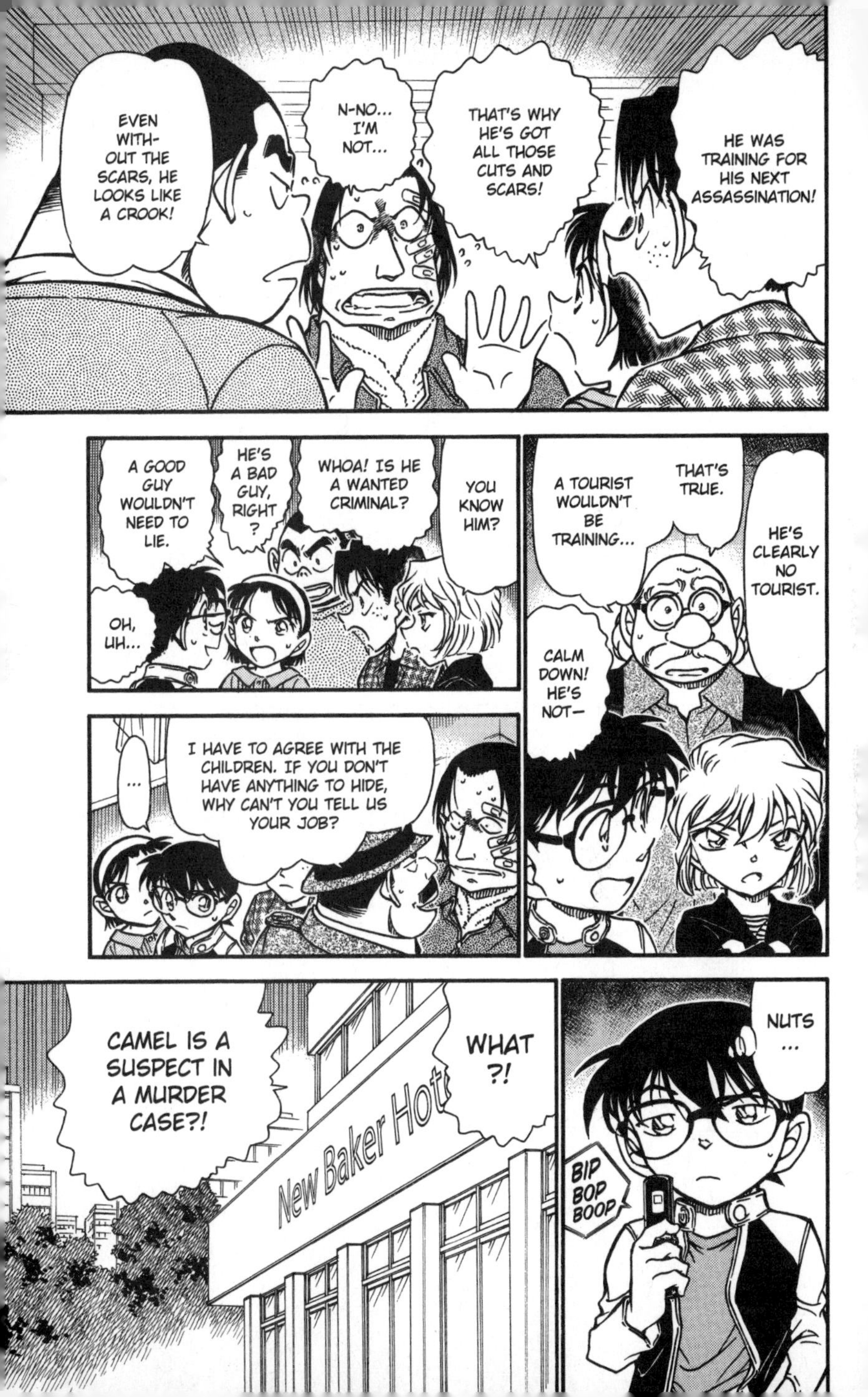
HE WAS TRAINING FOR HIS NEXT ASSASSINATION!
THAT'S WHY HE'S GOT ALL THOSE CUTS AND SCARS!
N-NO... I'M NOT...
EVEN WITH-OUT THE SCARS, HE LOOKS LIKE A CROOK!
HE'S CLEARLY NO TOURIST.
THAT'S TRUE.
A TOURIST WOULDN'T BE TRAINING...
CALM DOWN! HE'S NOT—
YOU KNOW HIM?
WHOA! IS HE A WANTED CRIMINAL?
HE'S A BAD GUY, RIGHT?
A GOOD GUY WOULDN'T NEED TO LIE.
OH, UH...
I HAVE TO AGREE WITH THE CHILDREN. IF YOU DON'T HAVE ANYTHING TO HIDE, WHY CAN'T YOU TELL US YOUR JOB?
...
NUTS...
BIP BOP BOOP
WHAT?!
CAMEL IS A SUSPECT IN A MURDER CASE?!
New Baker Hot

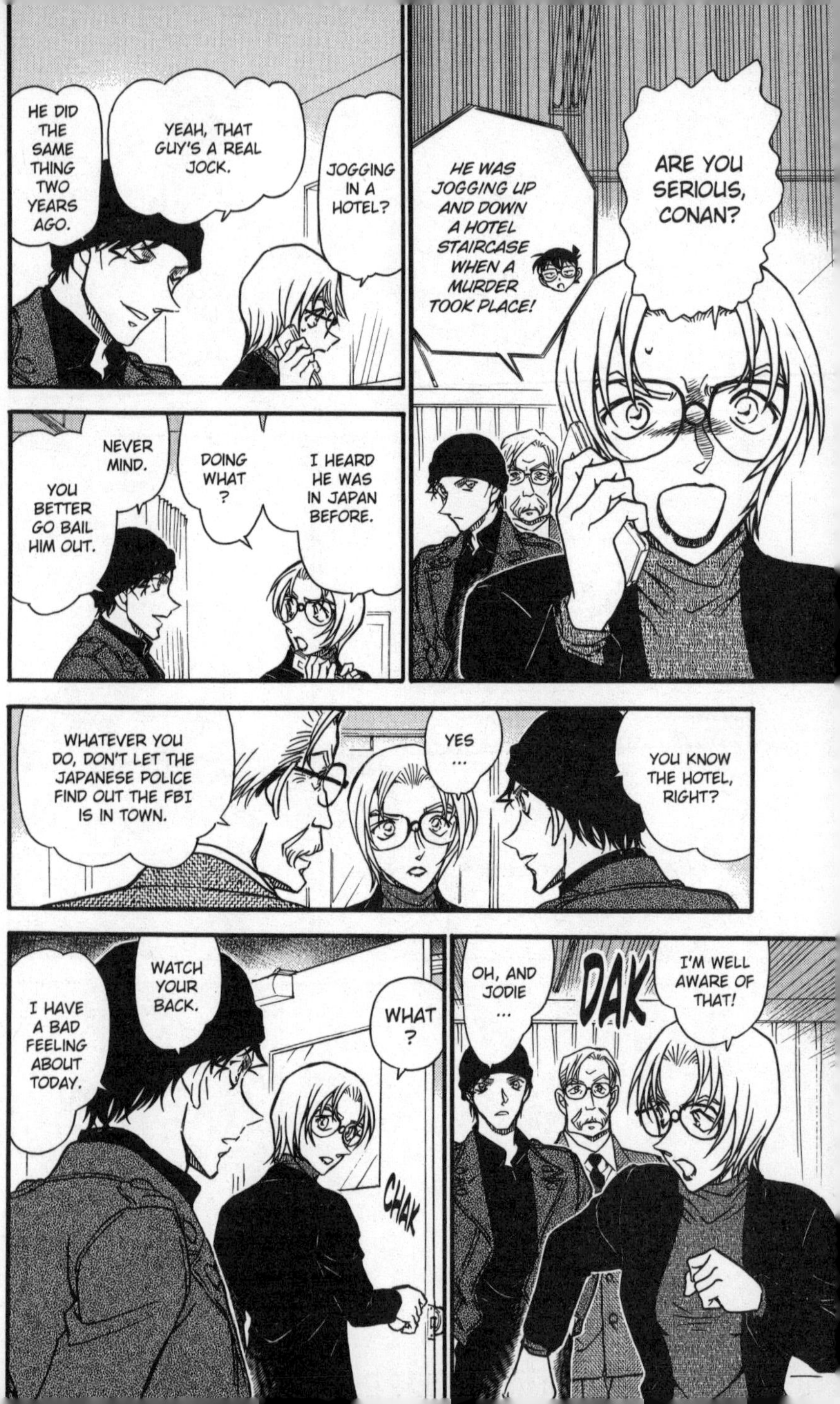
ARE YOU SERIOUS, CONAN?
HE WAS JOGGING UP AND DOWN A HOTEL STAIRCASE WHEN A MURDER TOOK PLACE!
JOGGING IN A HOTEL?
YEAH, THAT GUY'S A REAL JOCK.
HE DID THE SAME THING TWO YEARS AGO.
I HEARD HE WAS IN JAPAN BEFORE.
DOING WHAT?
NEVER MIND.
YOU BETTER GO BAIL HIM OUT.
YOU KNOW THE HOTEL, RIGHT?
YES ...
WHATEVER YOU DO, DON'T LET THE JAPANESE POLICE FIND OUT THE FBI IS IN TOWN.
I'M WELL AWARE OF THAT!
DAK
OH, AND JODIE ...
WHAT?
WATCH YOUR BACK.
I HAVE A BAD FEELING ABOUT TODAY.
CHAK

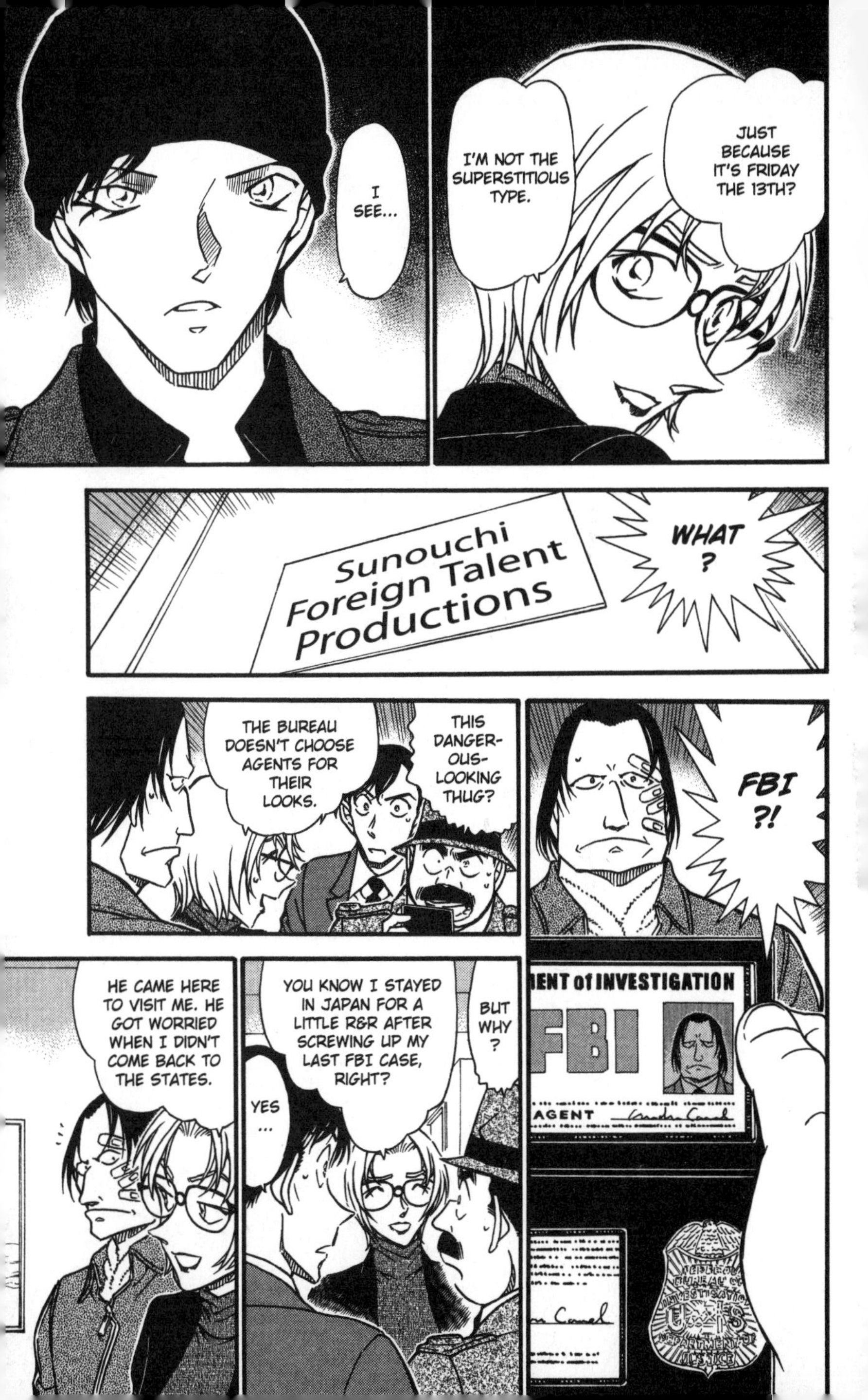
JUST BECAUSE IT'S FRIDAY THE 13TH?
I'M NOT THE SUPERSTITIOUS TYPE.
I SEE...
WHAT?
Sunouchi Foreign Talent Productions
FBI?!
ENT of INVESTIGATION
FBI
AGENT
THIS DANGEROUS-LOOKING THUG?
THE BUREAU DOESN'T CHOOSE AGENTS FOR THEIR LOOKS.
BUT WHY?
YOU KNOW I STAYED IN JAPAN FOR A LITTLE R&R AFTER SCREWING UP MY LAST FBI CASE, RIGHT?
YES...
HE CAME HERE TO VISIT ME. HE GOT WORRIED WHEN I DIDN'T COME BACK TO THE STATES.

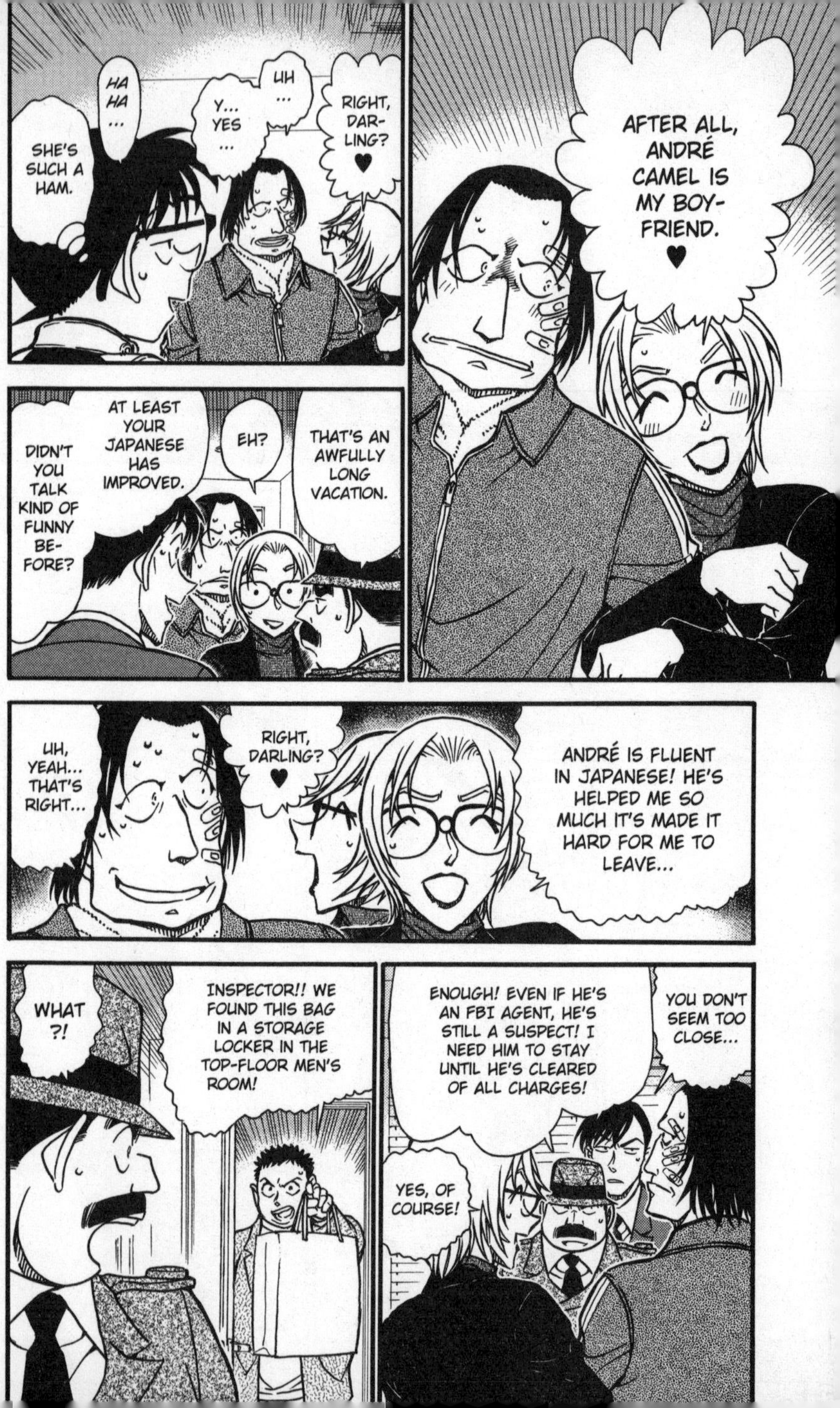
AFTER ALL, ANDRÉ CAMEL IS MY BOYFRIEND. ♥
RIGHT, DARLING? ♥
UH ...
Y... YES ...
HA HA ...
SHE'S SUCH A HAM.
THAT'S AN AWFULLY LONG VACATION.
EH?
AT LEAST YOUR JAPANESE HAS IMPROVED.
DIDN'T YOU TALK KIND OF FUNNY BEFORE?
ANDRÉ IS FLUENT IN JAPANESE! HE'S HELPED ME SO MUCH IT'S MADE IT HARD FOR ME TO LEAVE...
RIGHT, DARLING? ♥
UH, YEAH... THAT'S RIGHT...
YOU DON'T SEEM TOO CLOSE...
ENOUGH! EVEN IF HE'S AN FBI AGENT, HE'S STILL A SUSPECT! I NEED HIM TO STAY UNTIL HE'S CLEARED OF ALL CHARGES!
YES, OF COURSE!
INSPECTOR!! WE FOUND THIS BAG IN A STORAGE LOCKER IN THE TOP-FLOOR MEN'S ROOM!
WHAT?!

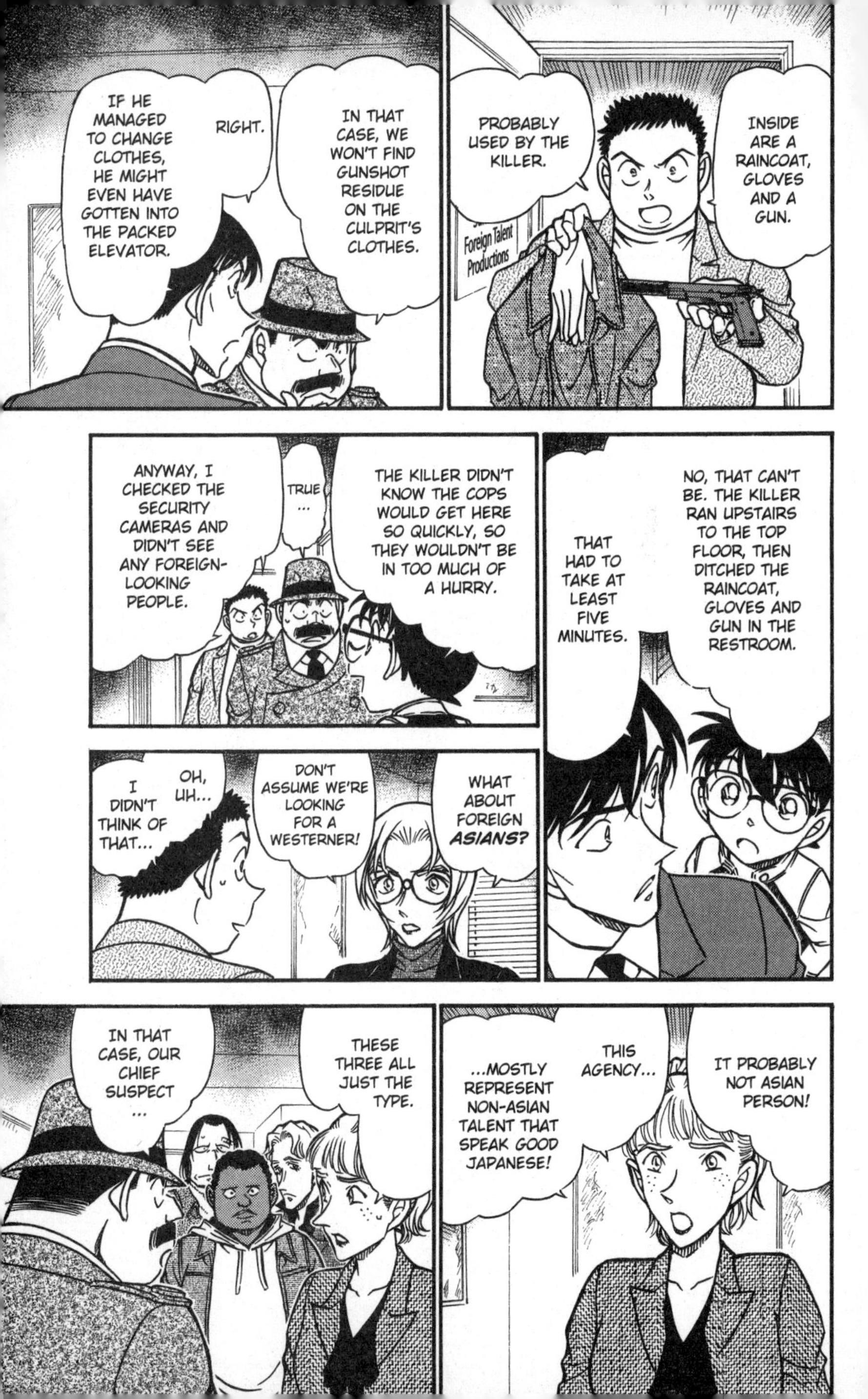
INSIDE ARE A RAINCOAT, GLOVES AND A GUN.
PROBABLY USED BY THE KILLER.
Foreign Talent Productions
IN THAT CASE, WE WON'T FIND GUNSHOT RESIDUE ON THE CULPRIT'S CLOTHES.
RIGHT.
IF HE MANAGED TO CHANGE CLOTHES, HE MIGHT EVEN HAVE GOTTEN INTO THE PACKED ELEVATOR.
NO, THAT CAN'T BE. THE KILLER RAN UPSTAIRS TO THE TOP FLOOR, THEN DITCHED THE RAINCOAT, GLOVES AND GUN IN THE RESTROOM.
THAT HAD TO TAKE AT LEAST FIVE MINUTES.
THE KILLER DIDN'T KNOW THE COPS WOULD GET HERE SO QUICKLY, SO THEY WOULDN'T BE IN TOO MUCH OF A HURRY.
TRUE...
ANYWAY, I CHECKED THE SECURITY CAMERAS AND DIDN'T SEE ANY FOREIGN-LOOKING PEOPLE.
WHAT ABOUT FOREIGN ***ASIANS?***
DON'T ASSUME WE'RE LOOKING FOR A WESTERNER!
OH, UH...
I DIDN'T THINK OF THAT...
IT PROBABLY NOT ASIAN PERSON!
THIS AGENCY...
...MOSTLY REPRESENT NON-ASIAN TALENT THAT SPEAK GOOD JAPANESE!
THESE THREE ALL JUST THE TYPE.
IN THAT CASE, OUR CHIEF SUSPECT...

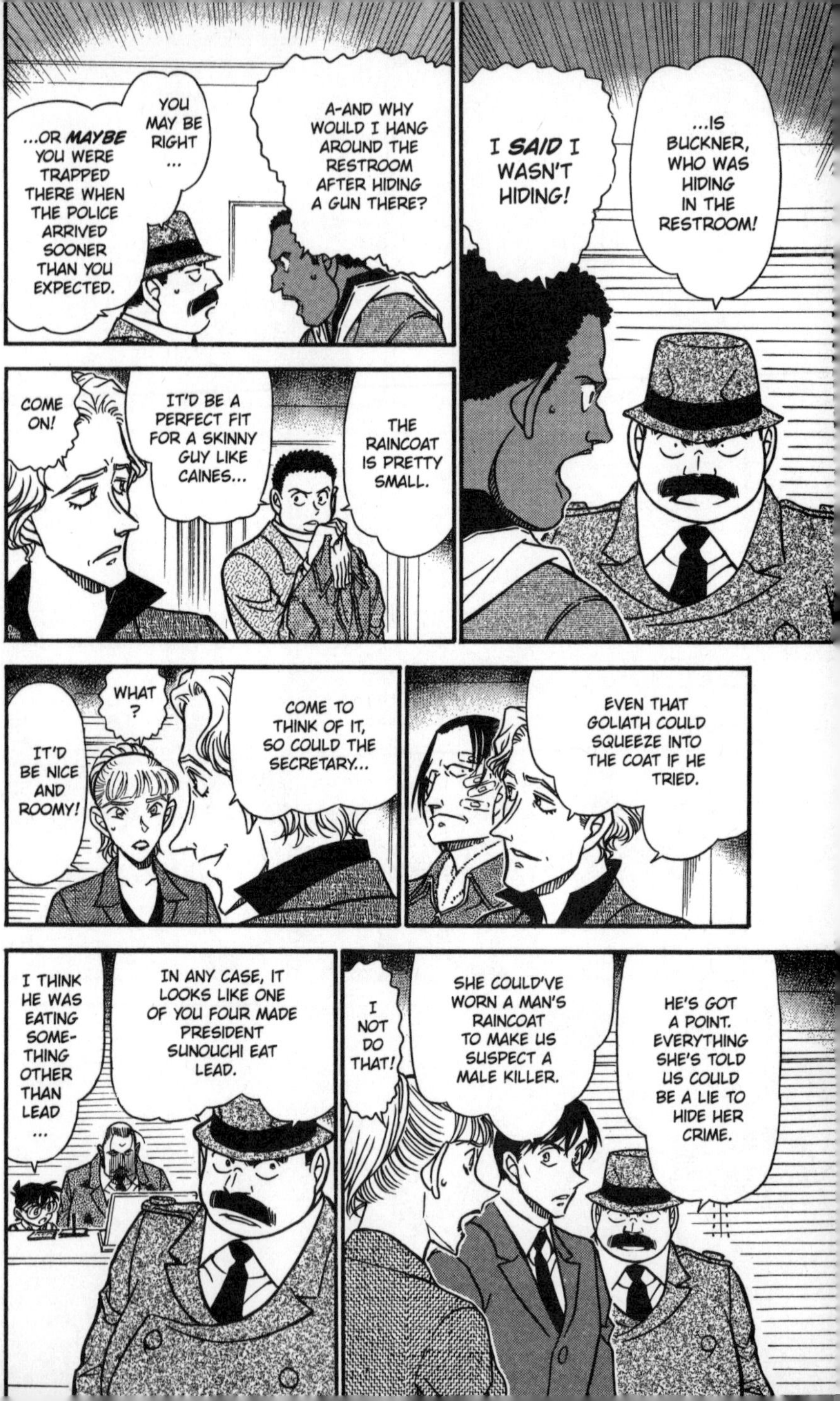
...IS BUCKNER, WHO WAS HIDING IN THE RESTROOM!
I *SAID* I WASN'T HIDING!
A-AND WHY WOULD I HANG AROUND THE RESTROOM AFTER HIDING A GUN THERE?
YOU MAY BE RIGHT...
...OR *MAYBE* YOU WERE TRAPPED THERE WHEN THE POLICE ARRIVED SOONER THAN YOU EXPECTED.
THE RAINCOAT IS PRETTY SMALL.
IT'D BE A PERFECT FIT FOR A SKINNY GUY LIKE CAINES...
COME ON!
EVEN THAT GOLIATH COULD SQUEEZE INTO THE COAT IF HE TRIED.
COME TO THINK OF IT, SO COULD THE SECRETARY...
WHAT?
IT'D BE NICE AND ROOMY!
HE'S GOT A POINT. EVERYTHING SHE'S TOLD US COULD BE A LIE TO HIDE HER CRIME.
SHE COULD'VE WORN A MAN'S RAINCOAT TO MAKE US SUSPECT A MALE KILLER.
I NOT DO THAT!
IN ANY CASE, IT LOOKS LIKE ONE OF YOU FOUR MADE PRESIDENT SUNOUCHI EAT LEAD.
I THINK HE WAS EATING SOME-THING OTHER THAN LEAD...

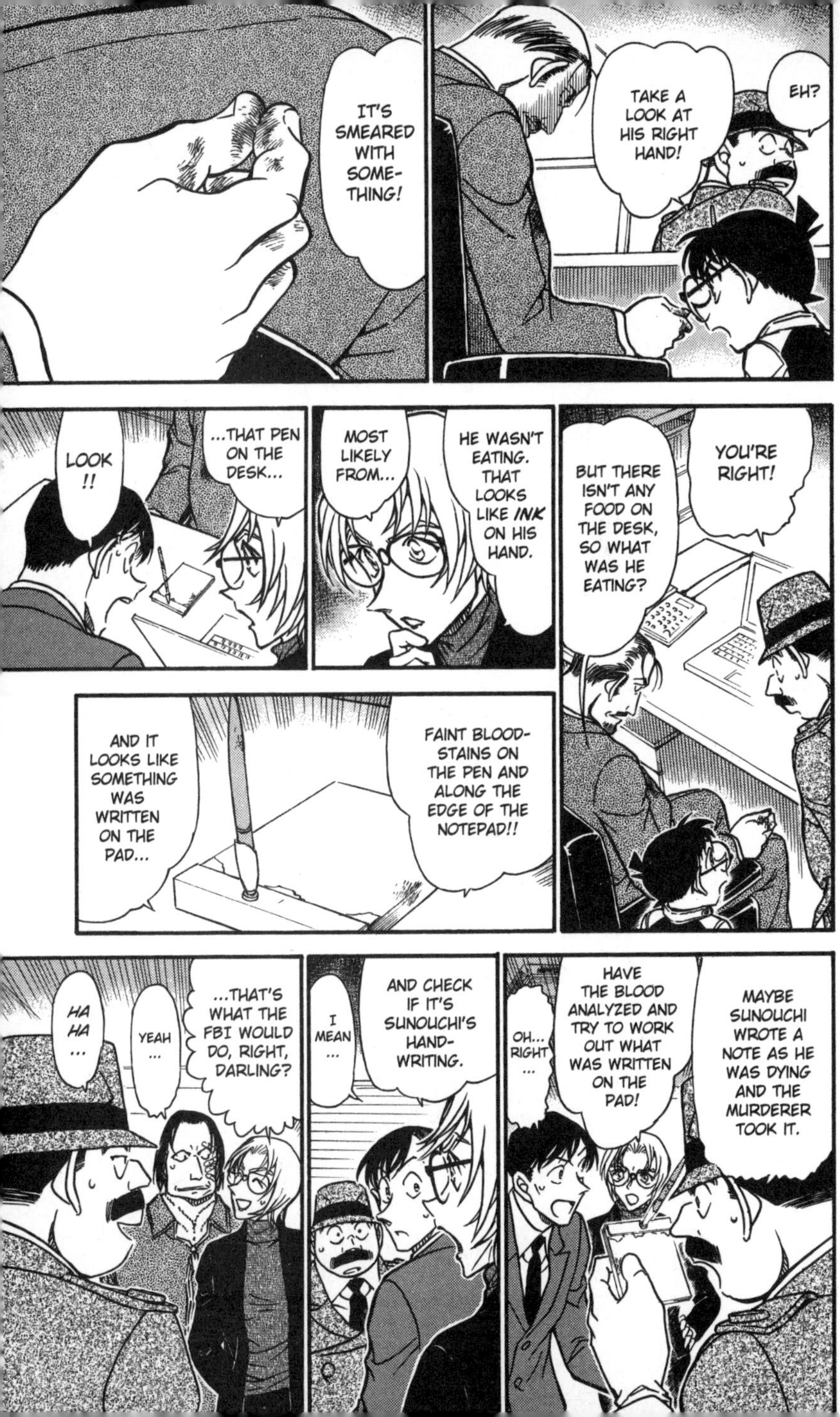
EH?
TAKE A LOOK AT HIS RIGHT HAND!
IT'S SMEARED WITH SOME-THING!
YOU'RE RIGHT!
BUT THERE ISN'T ANY FOOD ON THE DESK, SO WHAT WAS HE EATING?
HE WASN'T EATING. THAT LOOKS LIKE *INK* ON HIS HAND.
MOST LIKELY FROM...
...THAT PEN ON THE DESK...
LOOK!!
FAINT BLOOD-STAINS ON THE PEN AND ALONG THE EDGE OF THE NOTEPAD!!
AND IT LOOKS LIKE SOMETHING WAS WRITTEN ON THE PAD...
MAYBE SUNOUCHI WROTE A NOTE AS HE WAS DYING AND THE MURDERER TOOK IT.
HAVE THE BLOOD ANALYZED AND TRY TO WORK OUT WHAT WAS WRITTEN ON THE PAD!
OH... RIGHT...
AND CHECK IF IT'S SUNOUCHI'S HAND-WRITING.
I MEAN...
...THAT'S WHAT THE FBI WOULD DO, RIGHT, DARLING?
YEAH...
HA HA...

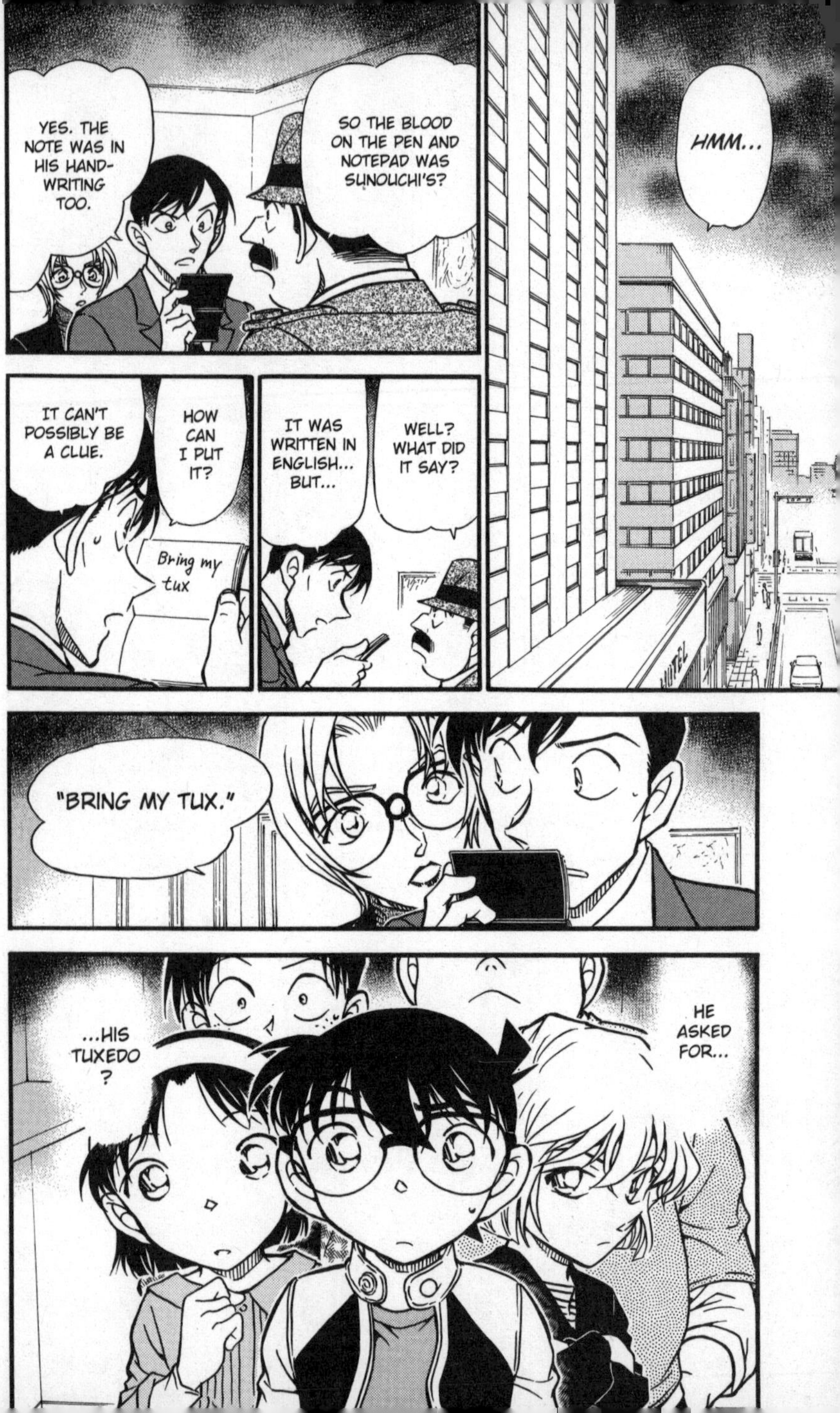
HMM...
SO THE BLOOD ON THE PEN AND NOTEPAD WAS SUNOUCHI'S?
YES. THE NOTE WAS IN HIS HAND-WRITING TOO.
WELL? WHAT DID IT SAY?
IT WAS WRITTEN IN ENGLISH... BUT...
HOW CAN I PUT IT?
IT CAN'T POSSIBLY BE A CLUE.
Bring my tux
"BRING MY TUX."
HE ASKED FOR...
...HIS TUXEDO ?

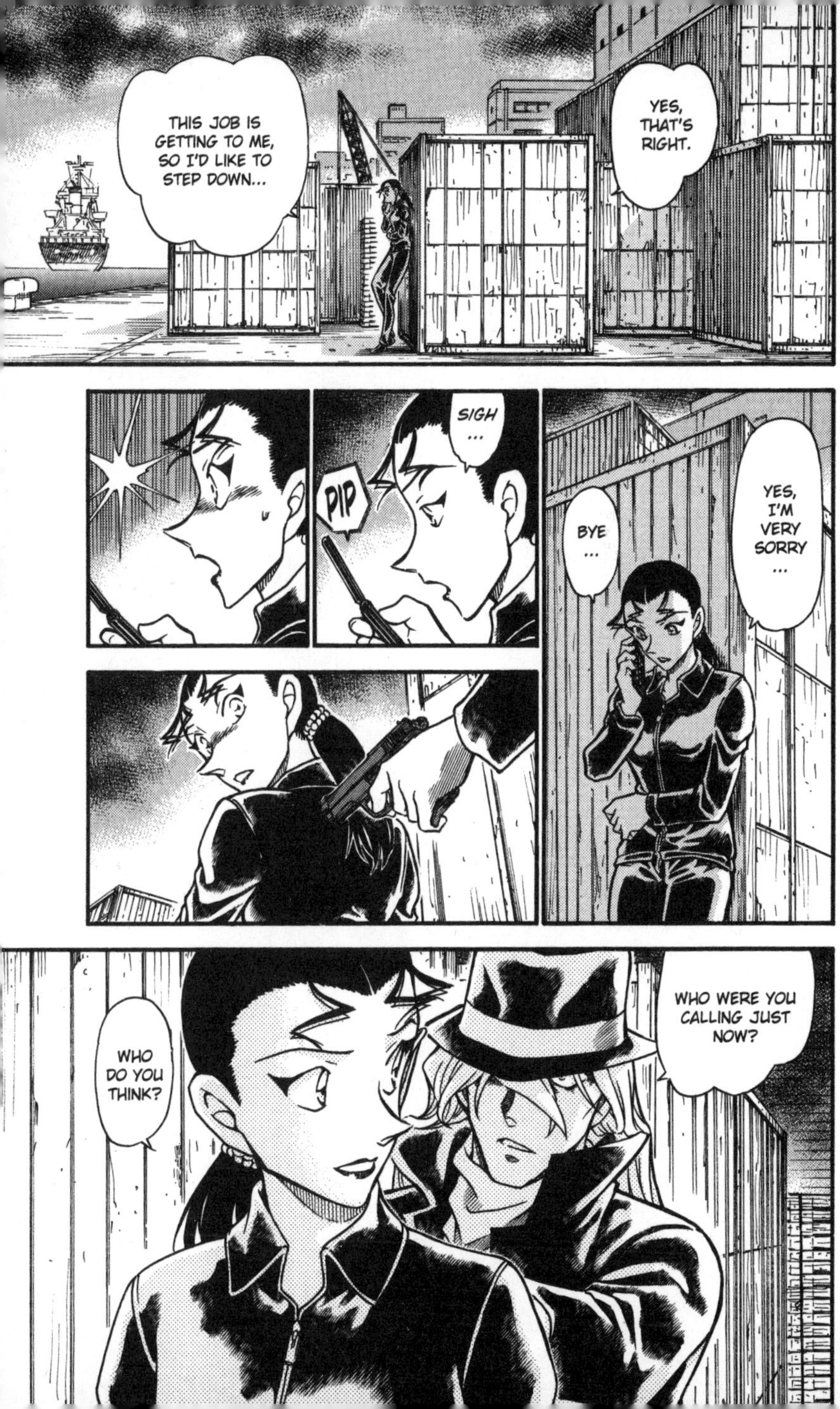
YES, THAT'S RIGHT.
THIS JOB IS GETTING TO ME, SO I'D LIKE TO STEP DOWN...
YES, I'M VERY SORRY...
BYE...
SIGH...
PIP
WHO WERE YOU CALLING JUST NOW?
WHO DO YOU THINK?

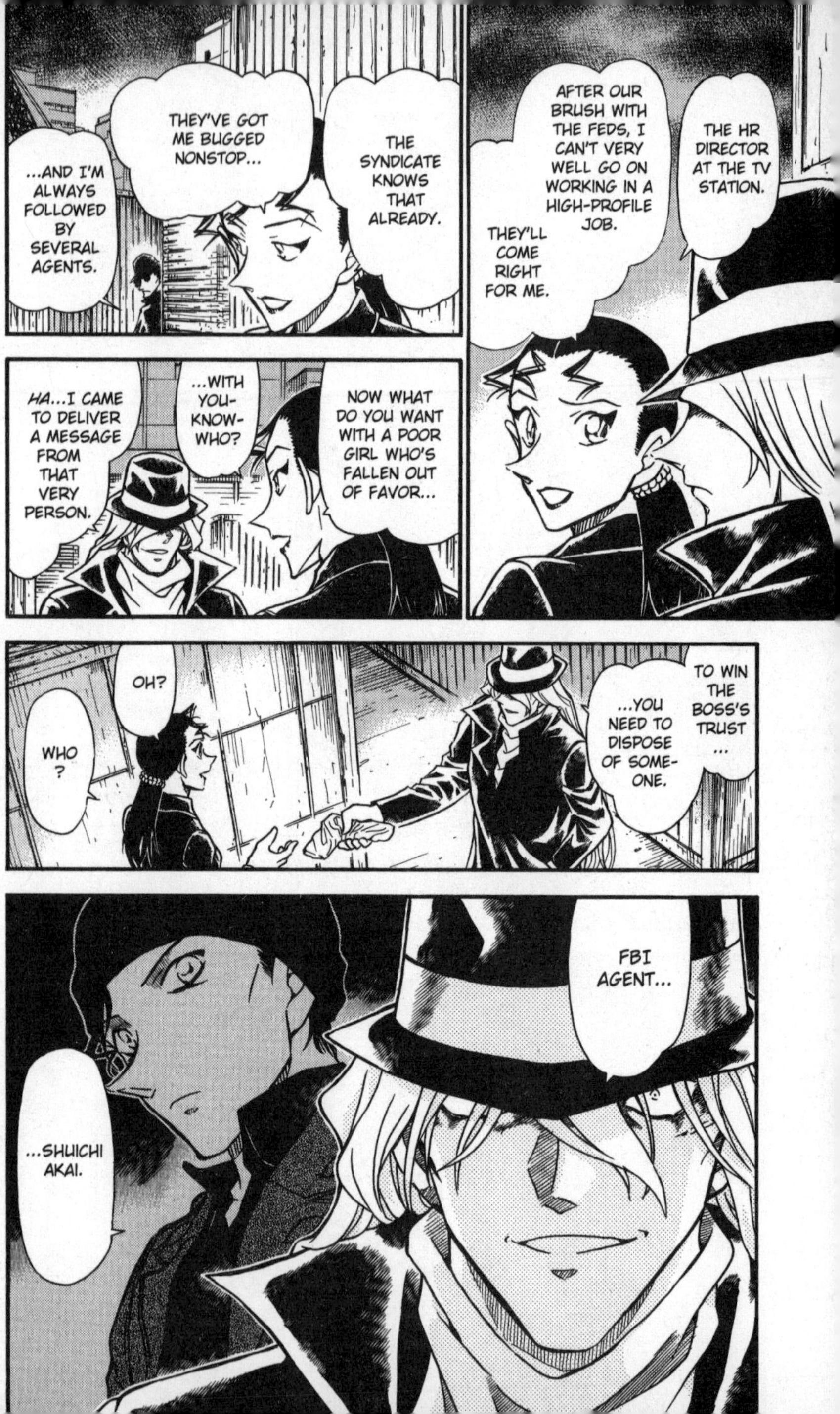
THE HR DIRECTOR AT THE TV STATION.
AFTER OUR BRUSH WITH THE FEDS, I CAN'T VERY WELL GO ON WORKING IN A HIGH-PROFILE JOB.
THEY'LL COME RIGHT FOR ME.
THE SYNDICATE KNOWS THAT ALREADY.
THEY'VE GOT ME BUGGED NONSTOP...
...AND I'M ALWAYS FOLLOWED BY SEVERAL AGENTS.
NOW WHAT DO YOU WANT WITH A POOR GIRL WHO'S FALLEN OUT OF FAVOR...
...WITH YOU-KNOW-WHO?
HA...I CAME TO DELIVER A MESSAGE FROM THAT VERY PERSON.
TO WIN THE BOSS'S TRUST...
...YOU NEED TO DISPOSE OF SOME-ONE.
OH?
WHO?
FBI AGENT...
...SHUICHI AKAI.

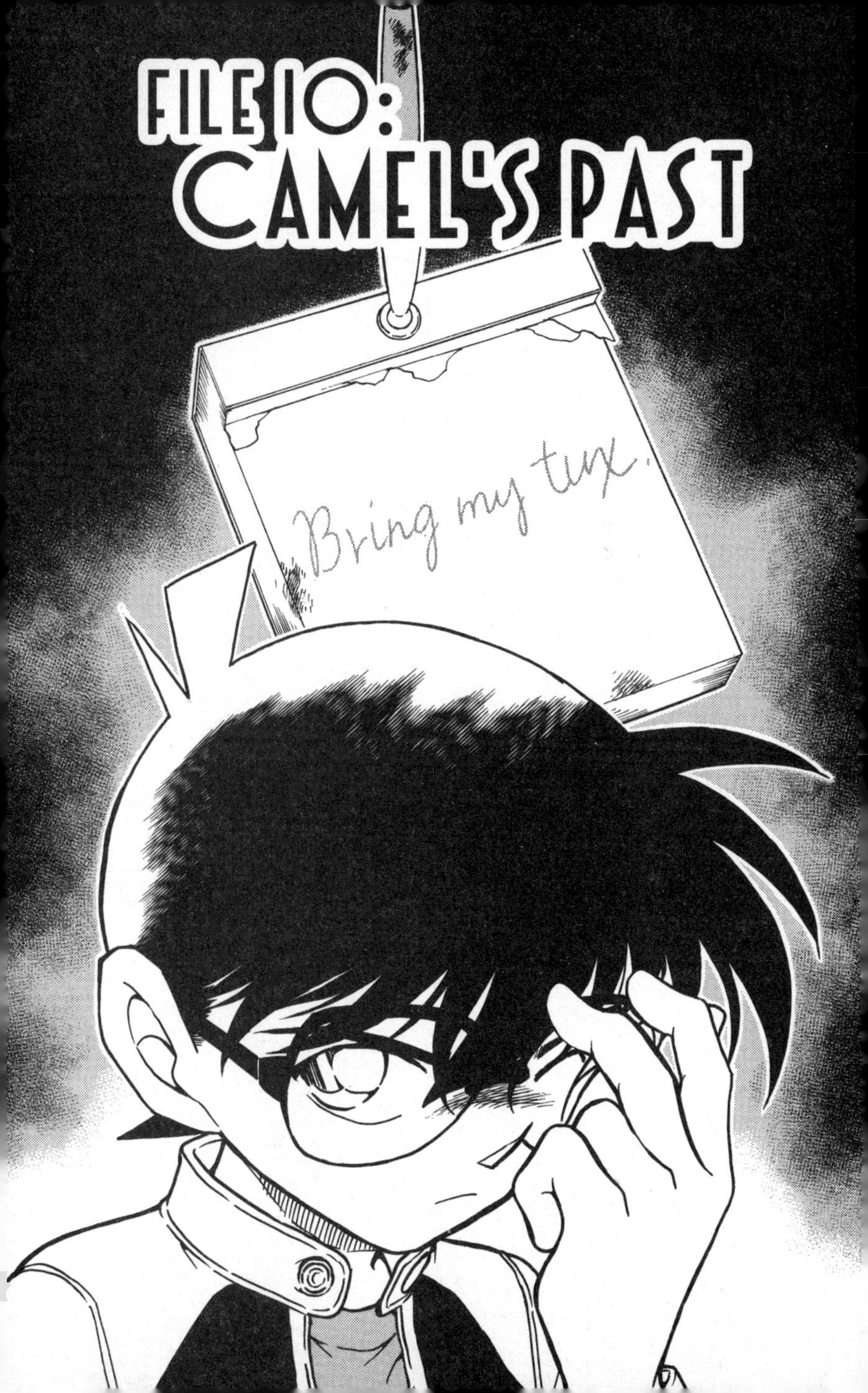
FILE 10:
CAMEL'S PAST
Bring my tux.

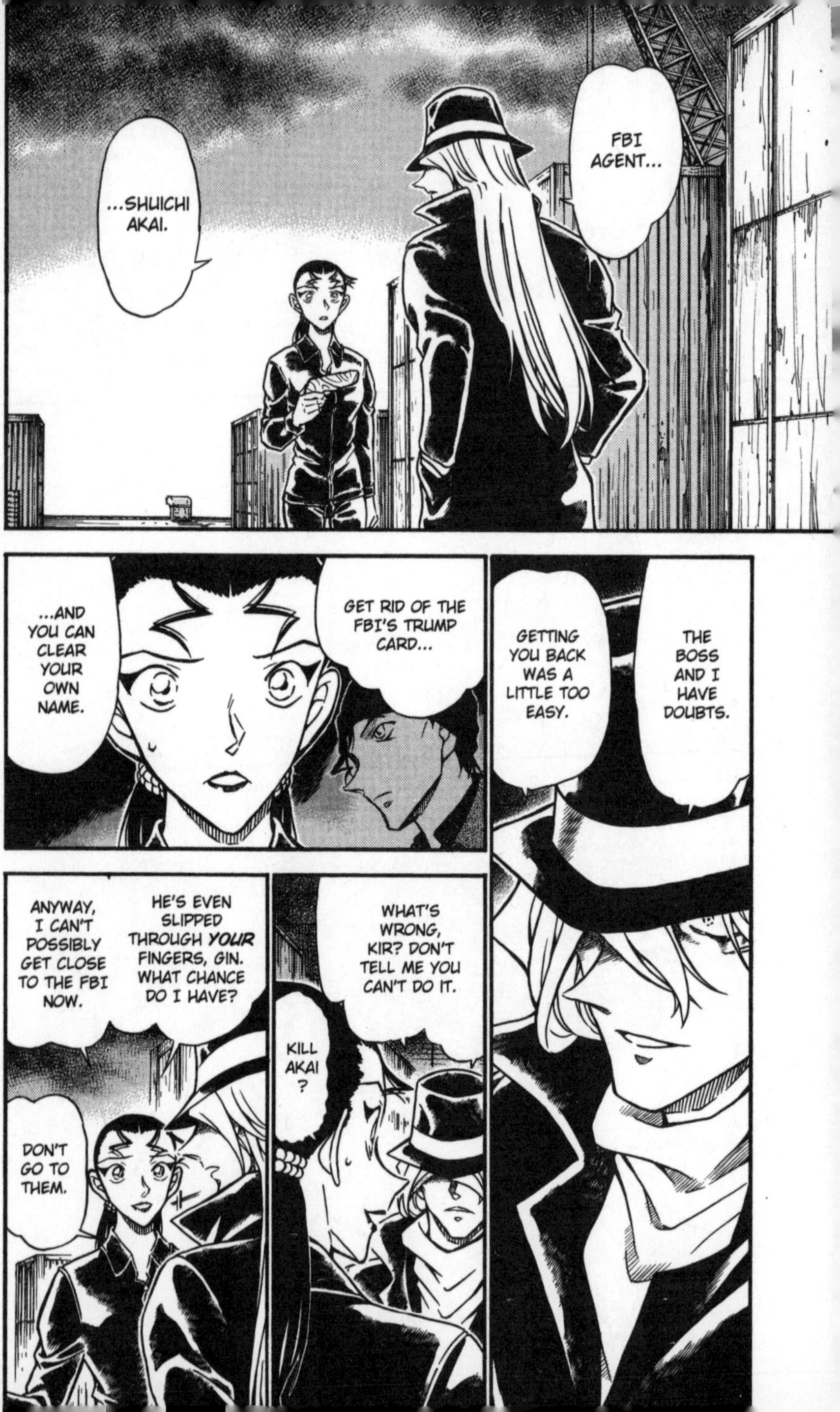
FBI AGENT...
...SHUICHI AKAI.
THE BOSS AND I HAVE DOUBTS.
GETTING YOU BACK WAS A LITTLE TOO EASY.
GET RID OF THE FBI'S TRUMP CARD...
...AND YOU CAN CLEAR YOUR OWN NAME.
WHAT'S WRONG, KIR? DON'T TELL ME YOU CAN'T DO IT.
KILL AKAI?
HE'S EVEN SLIPPED THROUGH *YOUR* FINGERS, GIN. WHAT CHANCE DO I HAVE?
ANYWAY, I CAN'T POSSIBLY GET CLOSE TO THE FBI NOW.
DON'T GO TO THEM.

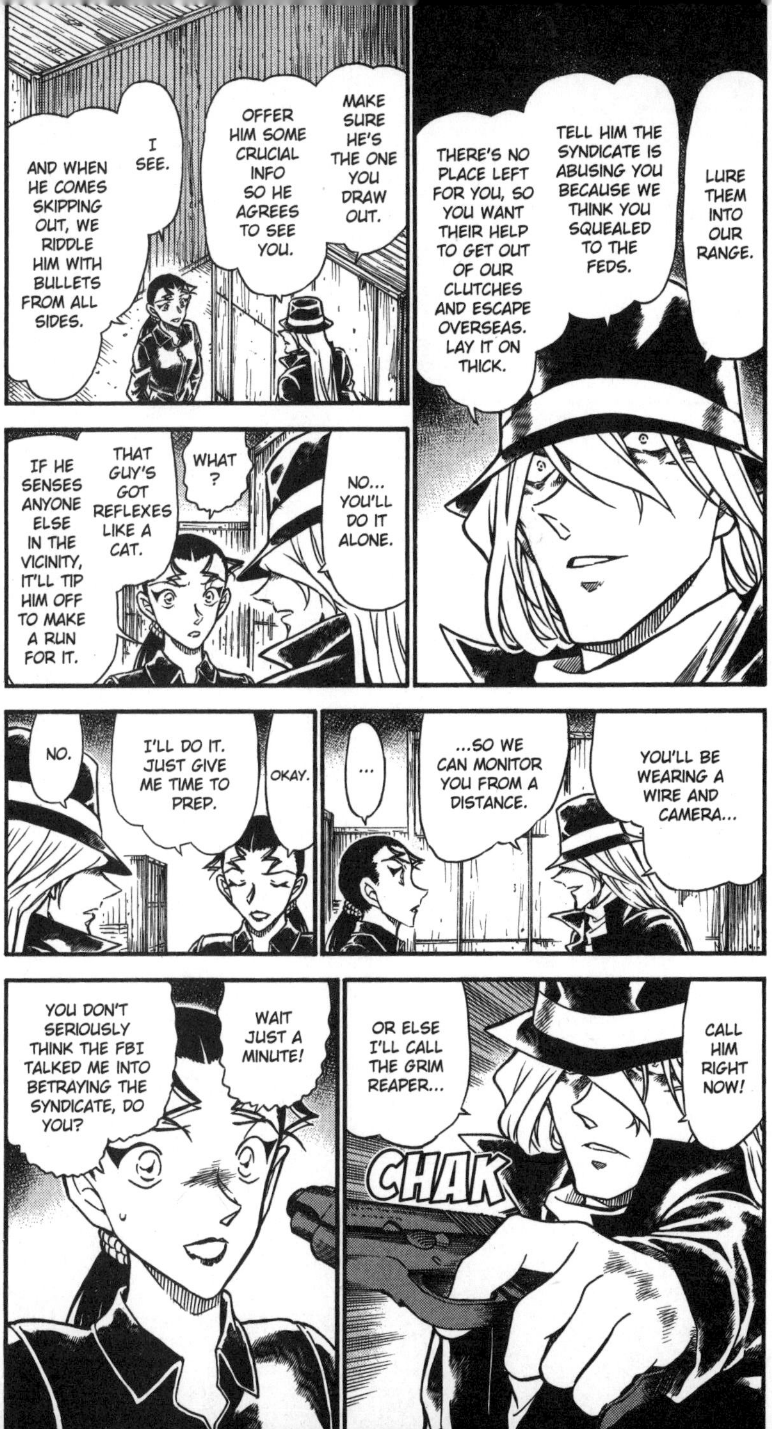
LURE THEM INTO OUR RANGE.
TELL HIM THE SYNDICATE IS ABUSING YOU BECAUSE WE THINK YOU SQUEALED TO THE FEDS.
THERE'S NO PLACE LEFT FOR YOU, SO YOU WANT THEIR HELP TO GET OUT OF OUR CLUTCHES AND ESCAPE OVERSEAS. LAY IT ON THICK.
MAKE SURE HE'S THE ONE YOU DRAW OUT.
OFFER HIM SOME CRUCIAL INFO SO HE AGREES TO SEE YOU.
I SEE.
AND WHEN HE COMES SKIPPING OUT, WE RIDDLE HIM WITH BULLETS FROM ALL SIDES.
NO... YOU'LL DO IT ALONE.
WHAT?
THAT GUY'S GOT REFLEXES LIKE A CAT.
IF HE SENSES ANYONE ELSE IN THE VICINITY, IT'LL TIP HIM OFF TO MAKE A RUN FOR IT.
YOU'LL BE WEARING A WIRE AND CAMERA...
...SO WE CAN MONITOR YOU FROM A DISTANCE.
...
OKAY.
I'LL DO IT. JUST GIVE ME TIME TO PREP.
NO.
CALL HIM RIGHT NOW!
OR ELSE I'LL CALL THE GRIM REAPER...
CHAK
WAIT JUST A MINUTE!
YOU DON'T SERIOUSLY THINK THE FBI TALKED ME INTO BETRAYING THE SYNDICATE, DO YOU?

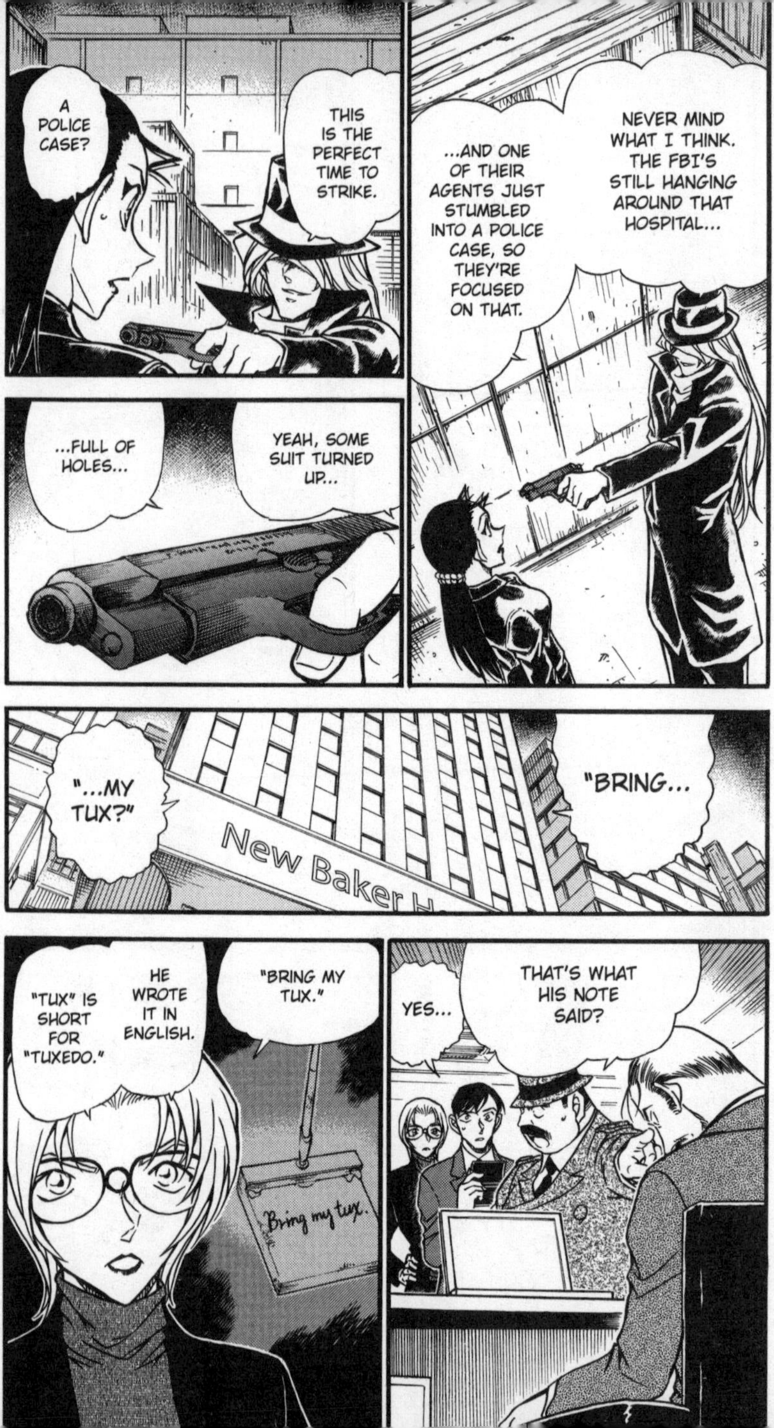
NEVER MIND WHAT I THINK. THE FBI'S STILL HANGING AROUND THAT HOSPITAL...
...AND ONE OF THEIR AGENTS JUST STUMBLED INTO A POLICE CASE, SO THEY'RE FOCUSED ON THAT.
THIS IS THE PERFECT TIME TO STRIKE.
A POLICE CASE?
YEAH, SOME SUIT TURNED UP...
...FULL OF HOLES...
"BRING...
"...MY TUX?"
New Baker H
THAT'S WHAT HIS NOTE SAID?
YES...
"BRING MY TUX."
Bring my tux.
HE WROTE IT IN ENGLISH.
"TUX" IS SHORT FOR "TUXEDO."

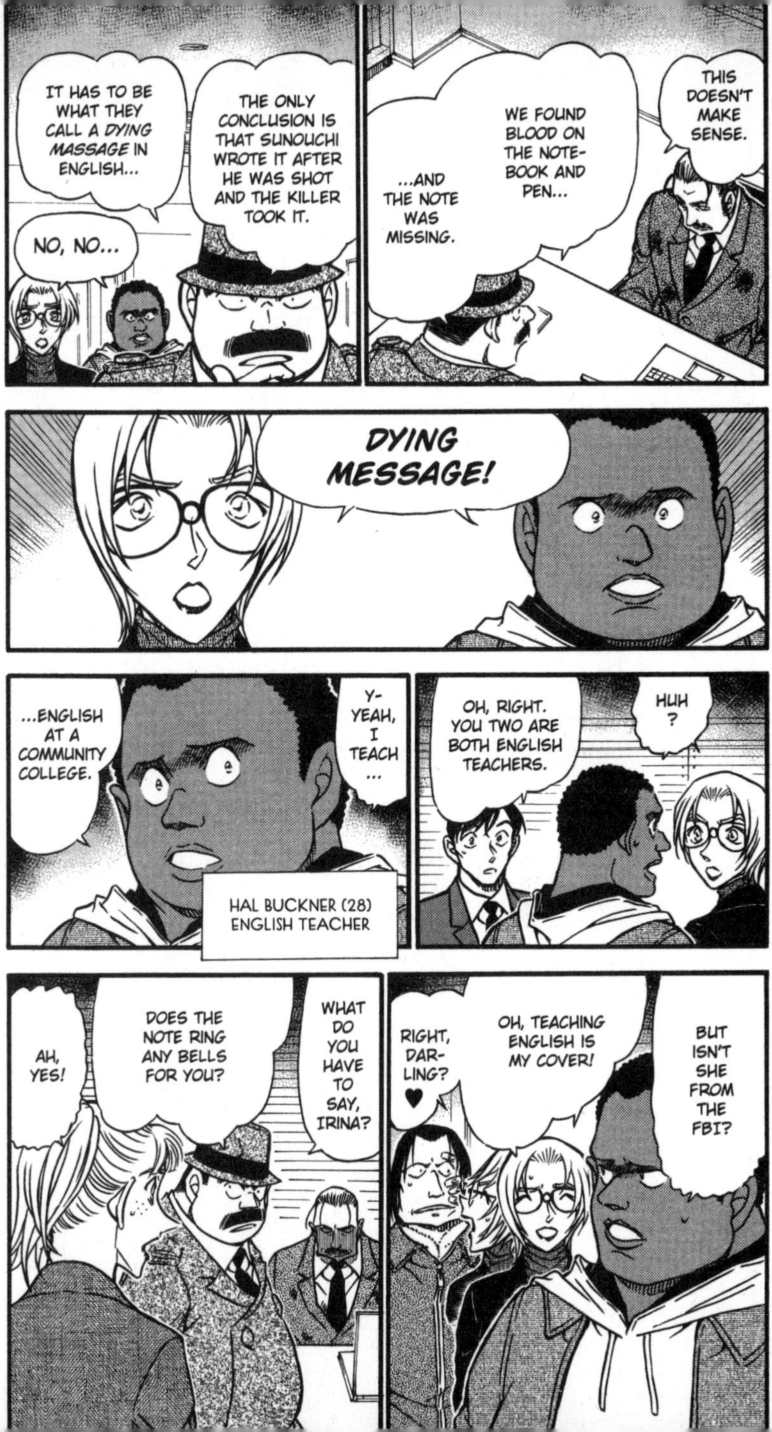
THIS DOESN'T MAKE SENSE.
WE FOUND BLOOD ON THE NOTE-BOOK AND PEN...
...AND THE NOTE WAS MISSING.
THE ONLY CONCLUSION IS THAT SUNOUCHI WROTE IT AFTER HE WAS SHOT AND THE KILLER TOOK IT.
IT HAS TO BE WHAT THEY CALL A *DYING MASSAGE* IN ENGLISH...
NO, NO...
DYING MESSAGE!
HUH ?
OH, RIGHT. YOU TWO ARE BOTH ENGLISH TEACHERS.
Y-YEAH, I TEACH...
...ENGLISH AT A COMMUNITY COLLEGE.
HAL BUCKNER (28) ENGLISH TEACHER
BUT ISN'T SHE FROM THE FBI?
OH, TEACHING ENGLISH IS MY COVER!
RIGHT, DAR-LING? ♥
WHAT DO YOU HAVE TO SAY, IRINA?
DOES THE NOTE RING ANY BELLS FOR YOU?
AH, YES!

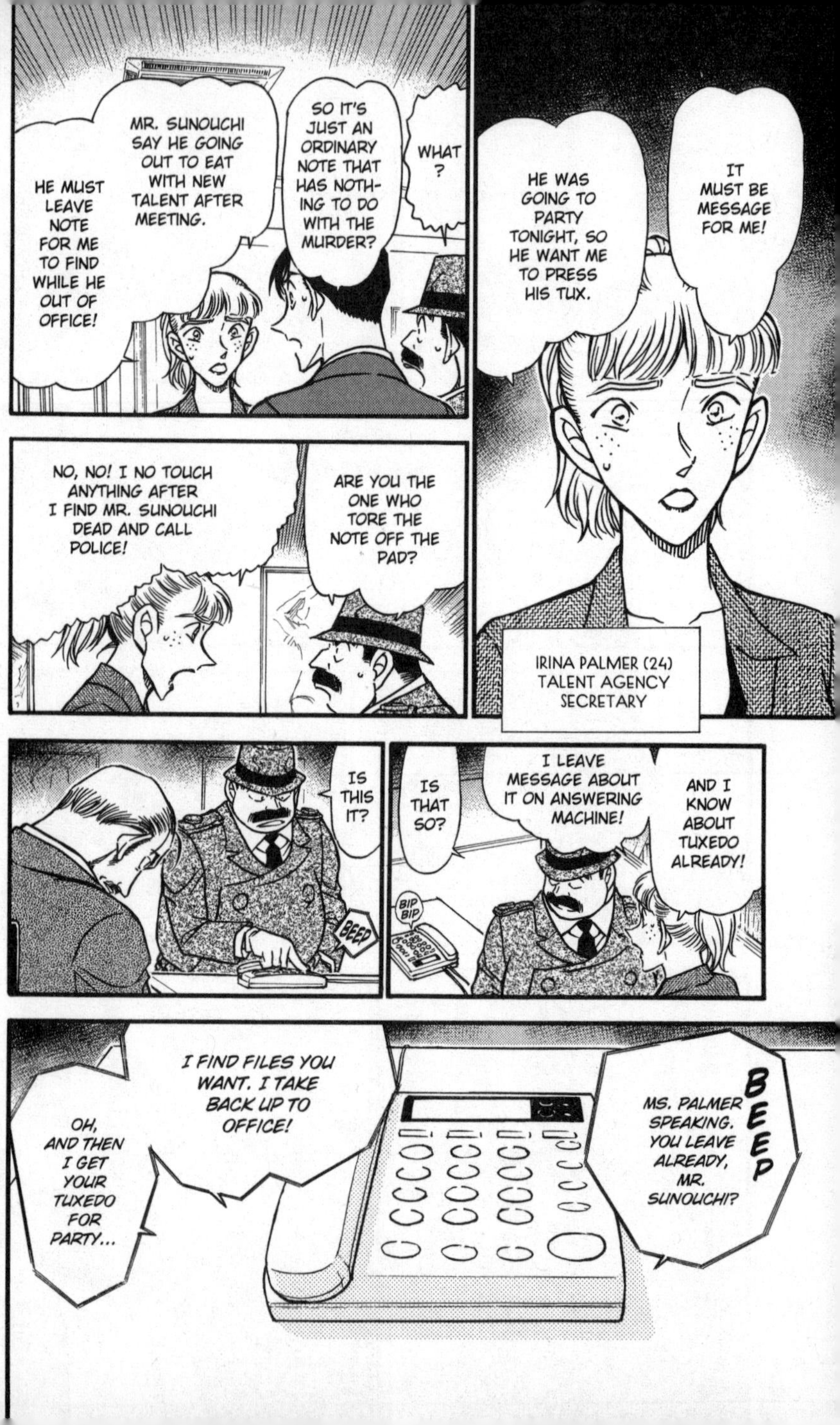
IT MUST BE MESSAGE FOR ME!
HE WAS GOING TO PARTY TONIGHT, SO HE WANT ME TO PRESS HIS TUX.
IRINA PALMER (24) TALENT AGENCY SECRETARY
WHAT?
SO IT'S JUST AN ORDINARY NOTE THAT HAS NOTHING TO DO WITH THE MURDER?
MR. SUNOUCHI SAY HE GOING OUT TO EAT WITH NEW TALENT AFTER MEETING.
HE MUST LEAVE NOTE FOR ME TO FIND WHILE HE OUT OF OFFICE!
ARE YOU THE ONE WHO TORE THE NOTE OFF THE PAD?
NO, NO! I NO TOUCH ANYTHING AFTER I FIND MR. SUNOUCHI DEAD AND CALL POLICE!
AND I KNOW ABOUT TUXEDO ALREADY!
I LEAVE MESSAGE ABOUT IT ON ANSWERING MACHINE!
IS THAT SO?
BIP BIP
IS THIS IT?
BEEP
BEEP
MS. PALMER SPEAKING. YOU LEAVE ALREADY, MR. SUNOUCHI?
I FIND FILES YOU WANT. I TAKE BACK UP TO OFFICE!
OH, AND THEN I GET YOUR TUXEDO FOR PARTY...

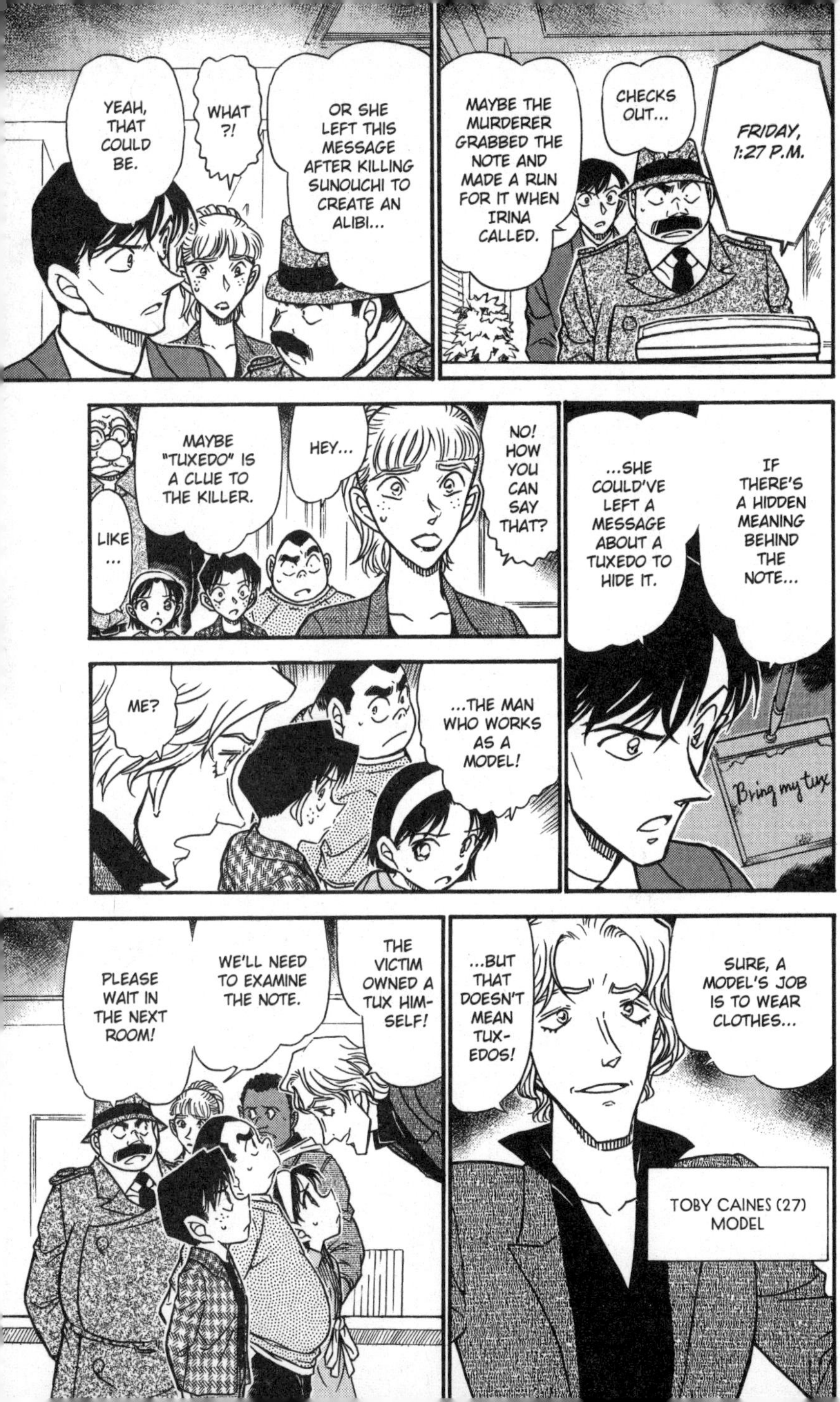
FRIDAY, 1:27 P.M.
CHECKS OUT...
MAYBE THE MURDERER GRABBED THE NOTE AND MADE A RUN FOR IT WHEN IRINA CALLED.
OR SHE LEFT THIS MESSAGE AFTER KILLING SUNOUCHI TO CREATE AN ALIBI...
WHAT?!
YEAH, THAT COULD BE.
IF THERE'S A HIDDEN MEANING BEHIND THE NOTE...
...SHE COULD'VE LEFT A MESSAGE ABOUT A TUXEDO TO HIDE IT.
Bring my tux
NO! HOW YOU CAN SAY THAT?
HEY...
MAYBE "TUXEDO" IS A CLUE TO THE KILLER.
LIKE ...
...THE MAN WHO WORKS AS A MODEL!
ME?
SURE, A MODEL'S JOB IS TO WEAR CLOTHES...
...BUT THAT DOESN'T MEAN TUX-EDOS!
TOBY CAINES (27) MODEL
THE VICTIM OWNED A TUX HIM-SELF!
WE'LL NEED TO EXAMINE THE NOTE.
PLEASE WAIT IN THE NEXT ROOM!

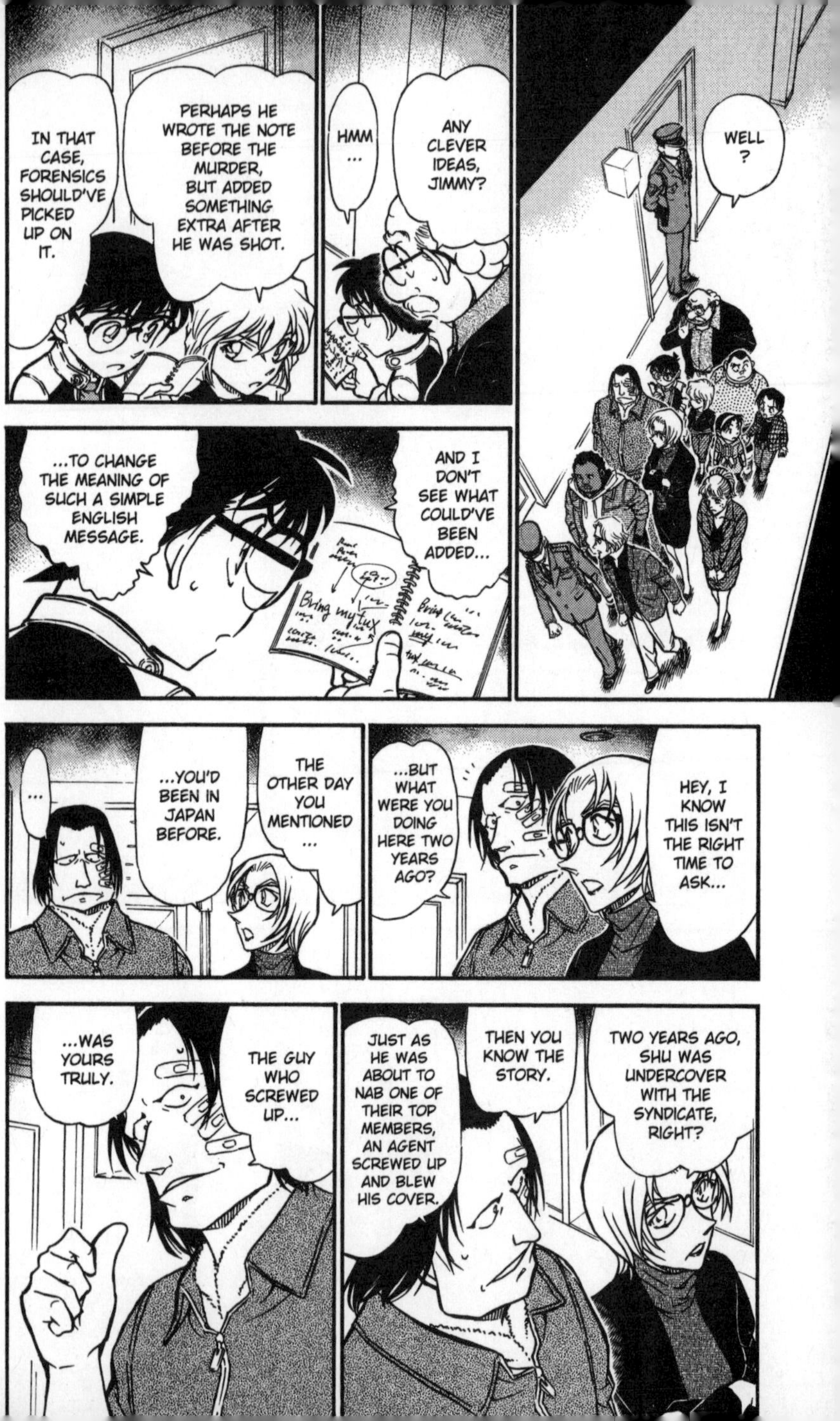
WELL?
ANY CLEVER IDEAS, JIMMY?
HMM...
PERHAPS HE WROTE THE NOTE BEFORE THE MURDER, BUT ADDED SOMETHING EXTRA AFTER HE WAS SHOT.
IN THAT CASE, FORENSICS SHOULD'VE PICKED UP ON IT.
AND I DON'T SEE WHAT COULD'VE BEEN ADDED...
Bring my tux
...TO CHANGE THE MEANING OF SUCH A SIMPLE ENGLISH MESSAGE.
HEY, I KNOW THIS ISN'T THE RIGHT TIME TO ASK...
...BUT WHAT WERE YOU DOING HERE TWO YEARS AGO?
THE OTHER DAY YOU MENTIONED...
...YOU'D BEEN IN JAPAN BEFORE.
...
TWO YEARS AGO, SHU WAS UNDERCOVER WITH THE SYNDICATE, RIGHT?
THEN YOU KNOW THE STORY.
JUST AS HE WAS ABOUT TO NAB ONE OF THEIR TOP MEMBERS, AN AGENT SCREWED UP AND BLEW HIS COVER.
THE GUY WHO SCREWED UP...
...WAS YOURS TRULY.

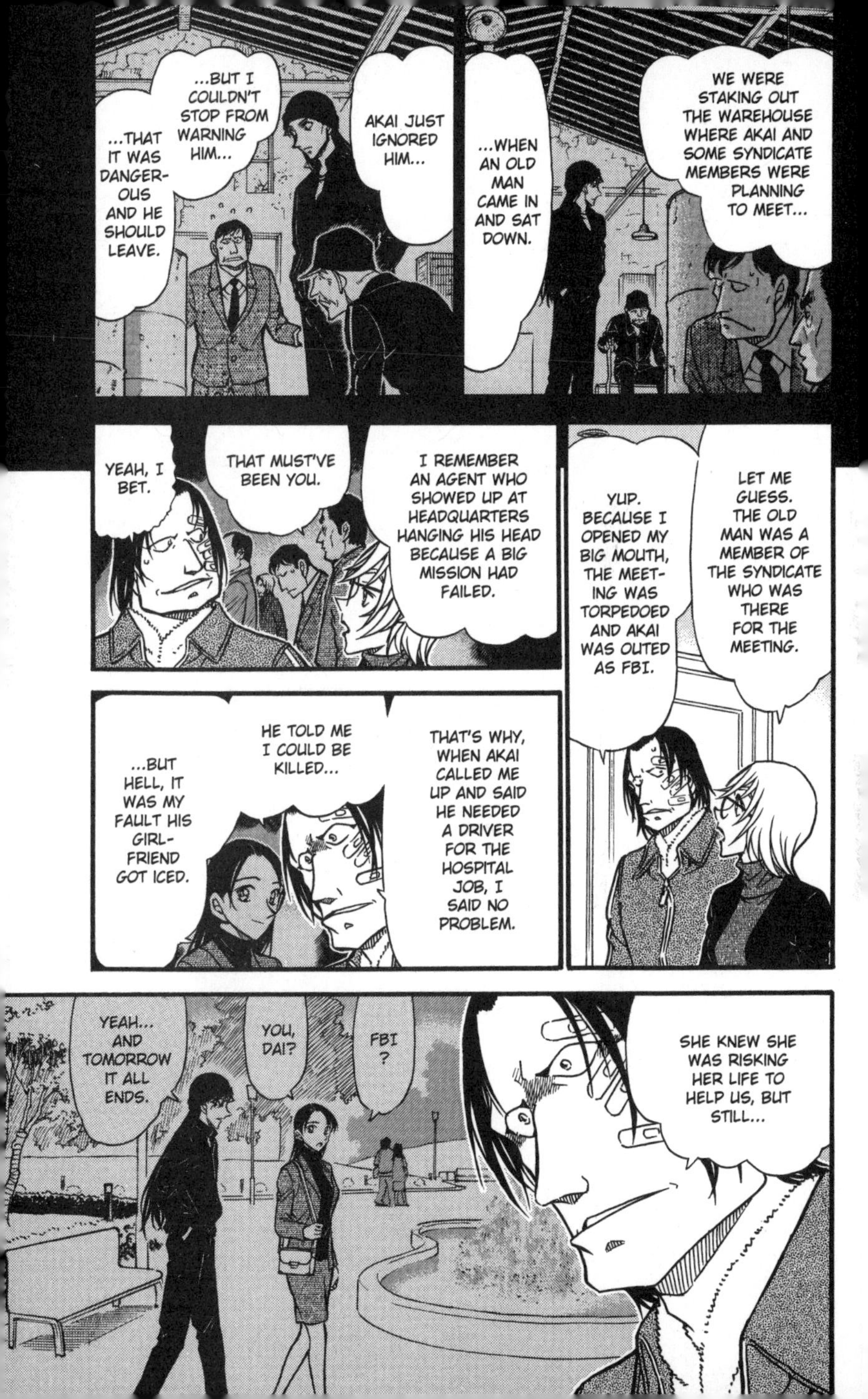
WE WERE STAKING OUT THE WAREHOUSE WHERE AKAI AND SOME SYNDICATE MEMBERS WERE PLANNING TO MEET...
...WHEN AN OLD MAN CAME IN AND SAT DOWN.
AKAI JUST IGNORED HIM...
...BUT I COULDN'T STOP FROM WARNING HIM...
...THAT IT WAS DANGER-OUS AND HE SHOULD LEAVE.
LET ME GUESS. THE OLD MAN WAS A MEMBER OF THE SYNDICATE WHO WAS THERE FOR THE MEETING.
YUP. BECAUSE I OPENED MY BIG MOUTH, THE MEET-ING WAS TORPEDOED AND AKAI WAS OUTED AS FBI.
I REMEMBER AN AGENT WHO SHOWED UP AT HEADQUARTERS HANGING HIS HEAD BECAUSE A BIG MISSION HAD FAILED.
THAT MUST'VE BEEN YOU.
YEAH, I BET.
THAT'S WHY, WHEN AKAI CALLED ME UP AND SAID HE NEEDED A DRIVER FOR THE HOSPITAL JOB, I SAID NO PROBLEM.
HE TOLD ME I COULD BE KILLED...
...BUT HELL, IT WAS MY FAULT HIS GIRL-FRIEND GOT ICED.
SHE KNEW SHE WAS RISKING HER LIFE TO HELP US, BUT STILL...
FBI?
YOU, DAI?
YEAH... AND TOMORROW IT ALL ENDS.

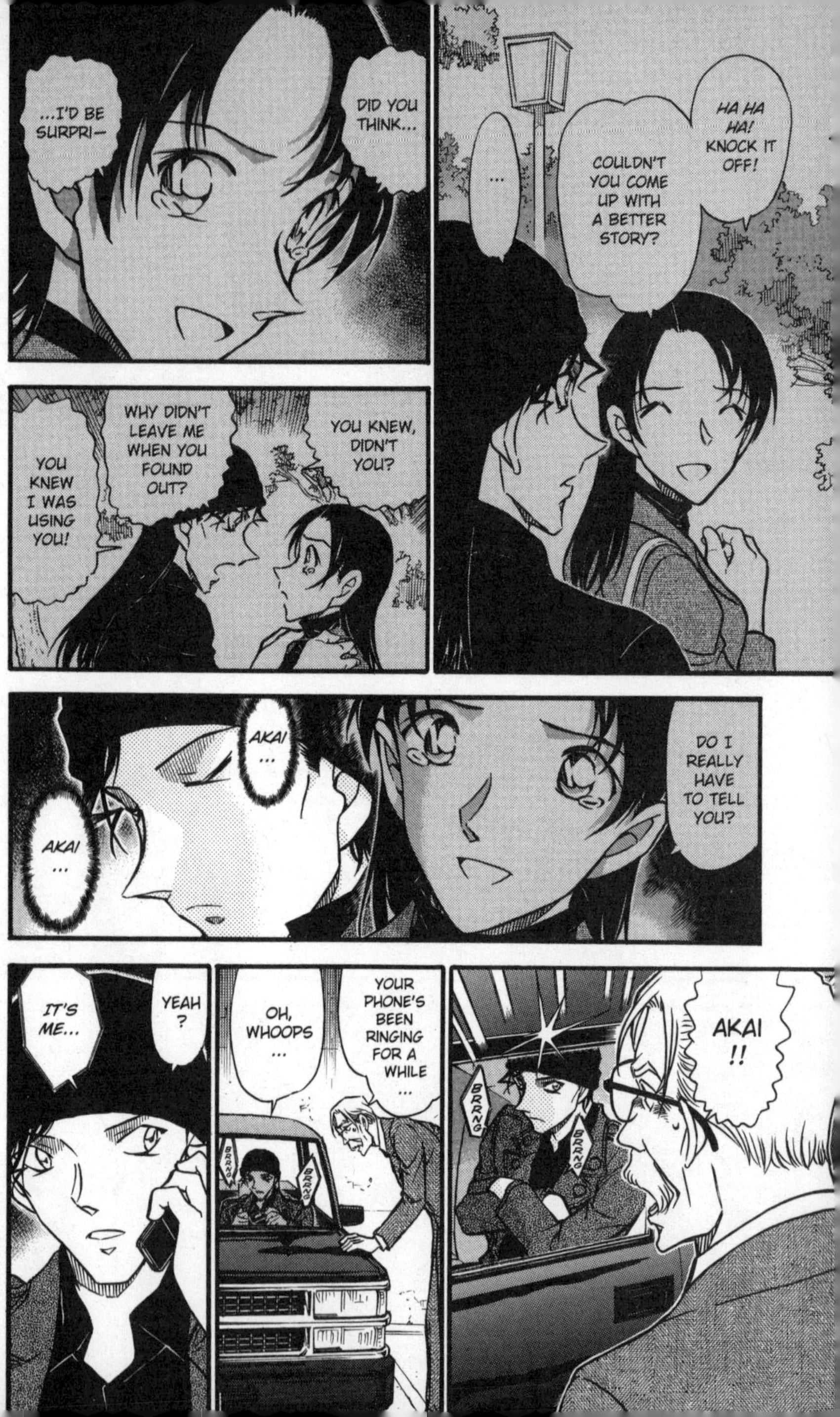
HA HA HA! KNOCK IT OFF!
COULDN'T YOU COME UP WITH A BETTER STORY?
...
DID YOU THINK...
...I'D BE SURPRI—
YOU KNEW, DIDN'T YOU?
WHY DIDN'T LEAVE ME WHEN YOU FOUND OUT?
YOU KNEW I WAS USING YOU!
DO I REALLY HAVE TO TELL YOU?
AKAI ...
AKAI ...
AKAI !!
BRRNG
BRRNG
YOUR PHONE'S BEEN RINGING FOR A WHILE ...
OH, WHOOPS ...
BRRNG
BRRNG
YEAH ?
IT'S ME...

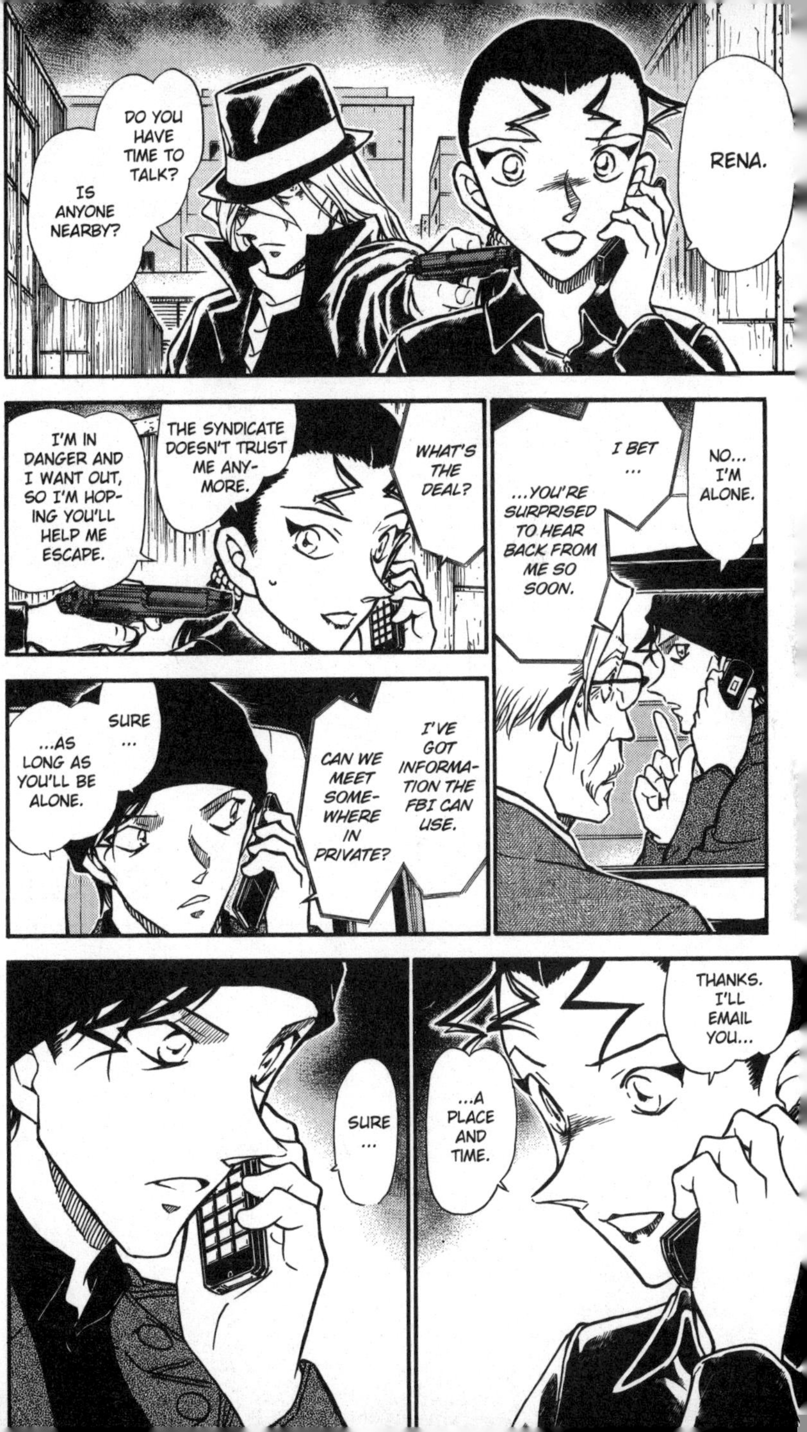
RENA.
DO YOU HAVE TIME TO TALK?
IS ANYONE NEARBY?
NO... I'M ALONE.
I BET ...
...YOU'RE SURPRISED TO HEAR BACK FROM ME SO SOON.
WHAT'S THE DEAL?
THE SYNDICATE DOESN'T TRUST ME ANY-MORE.
I'M IN DANGER AND I WANT OUT, SO I'M HOP-ING YOU'LL HELP ME ESCAPE.
I'VE GOT INFORMA-TION THE FBI CAN USE.
CAN WE MEET SOME-WHERE IN PRIVATE?
SURE ...
...AS LONG AS YOU'LL BE ALONE.
THANKS. I'LL EMAIL YOU...
...A PLACE AND TIME.
SURE ...

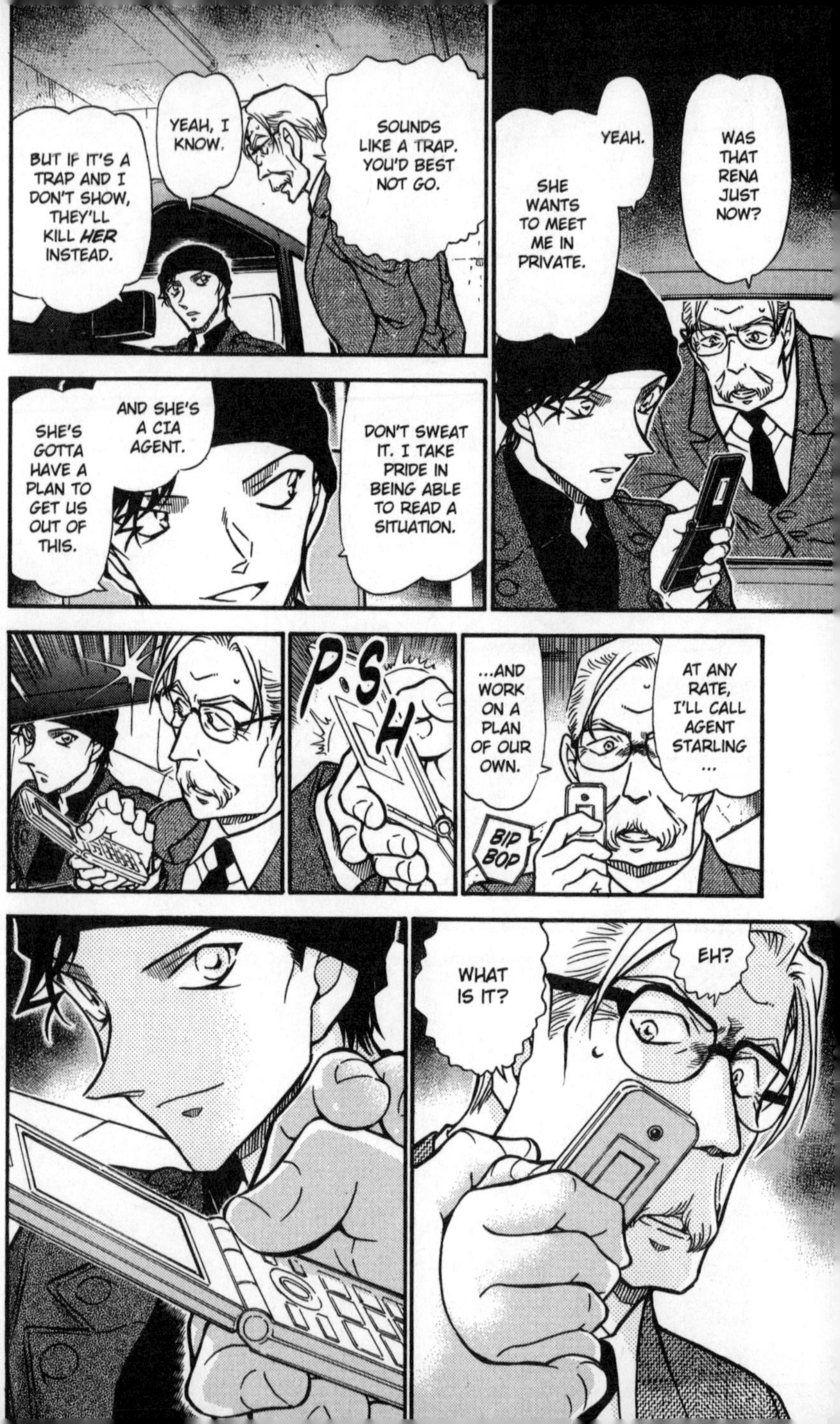
WAS THAT RENA JUST NOW?
YEAH.
SHE WANTS TO MEET ME IN PRIVATE.
SOUNDS LIKE A TRAP. YOU'D BEST NOT GO.
YEAH, I KNOW.
BUT IF IT'S A TRAP AND I DON'T SHOW, THEY'LL KILL *HER* INSTEAD.
DON'T SWEAT IT. I TAKE PRIDE IN BEING ABLE TO READ A SITUATION.
AND SHE'S A CIA AGENT.
SHE'S GOTTA HAVE A PLAN TO GET US OUT OF THIS.
AT ANY RATE, I'LL CALL AGENT STARLING ...
...AND WORK ON A PLAN OF OUR OWN.
BIP BOP
P.S.H
EH?
WHAT IS IT?

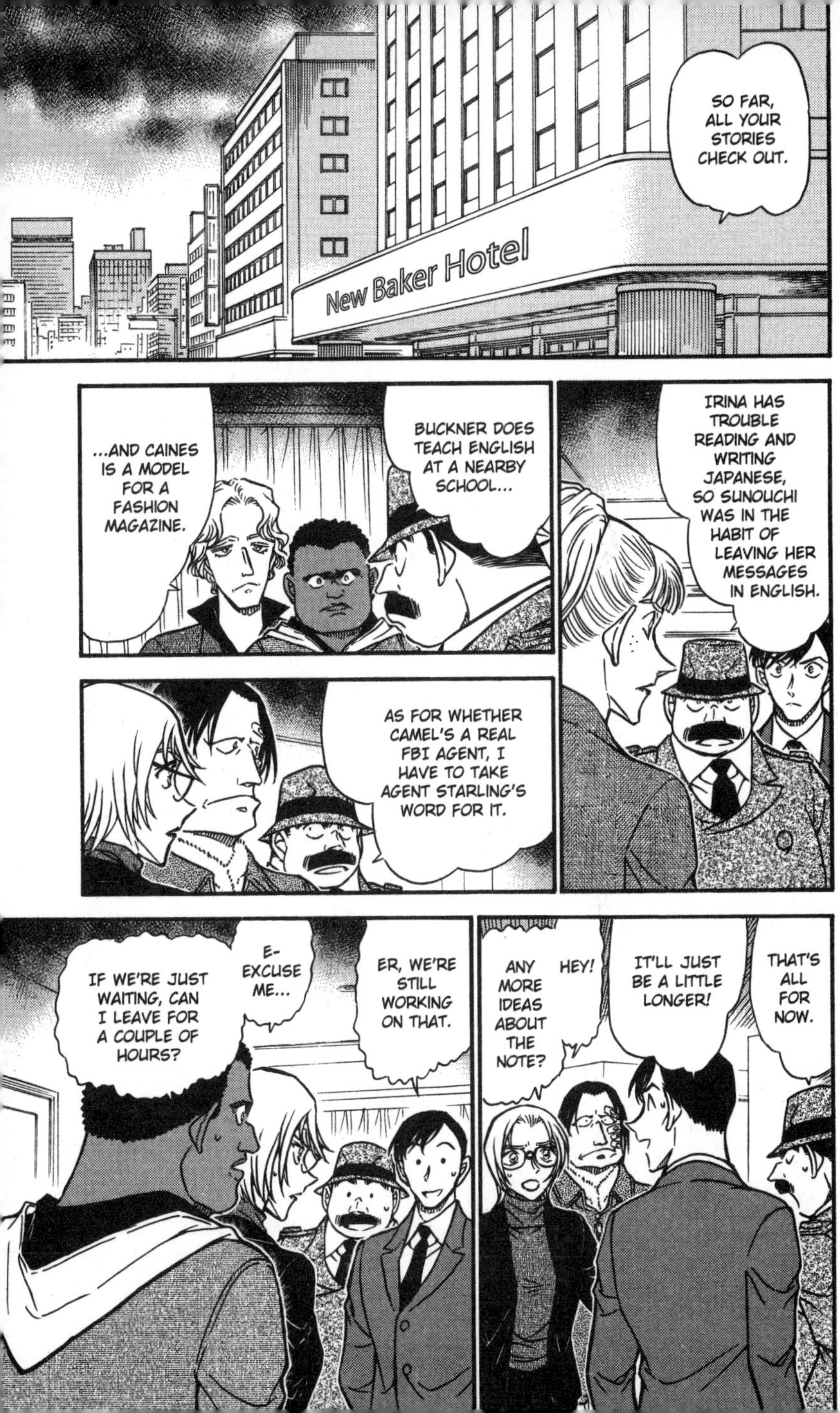
New Baker Hotel
SO FAR, ALL YOUR STORIES CHECK OUT.
IRINA HAS TROUBLE READING AND WRITING JAPANESE, SO SUNOUCHI WAS IN THE HABIT OF LEAVING HER MESSAGES IN ENGLISH.
BUCKNER DOES TEACH ENGLISH AT A NEARBY SCHOOL...
...AND CAINES IS A MODEL FOR A FASHION MAGAZINE.
AS FOR WHETHER CAMEL'S A REAL FBI AGENT, I HAVE TO TAKE AGENT STARLING'S WORD FOR IT.
THAT'S ALL FOR NOW.
IT'LL JUST BE A LITTLE LONGER!
HEY!
ANY MORE IDEAS ABOUT THE NOTE?
ER, WE'RE STILL WORKING ON THAT.
E-EXCUSE ME...
IF WE'RE JUST WAITING, CAN I LEAVE FOR A COUPLE OF HOURS?

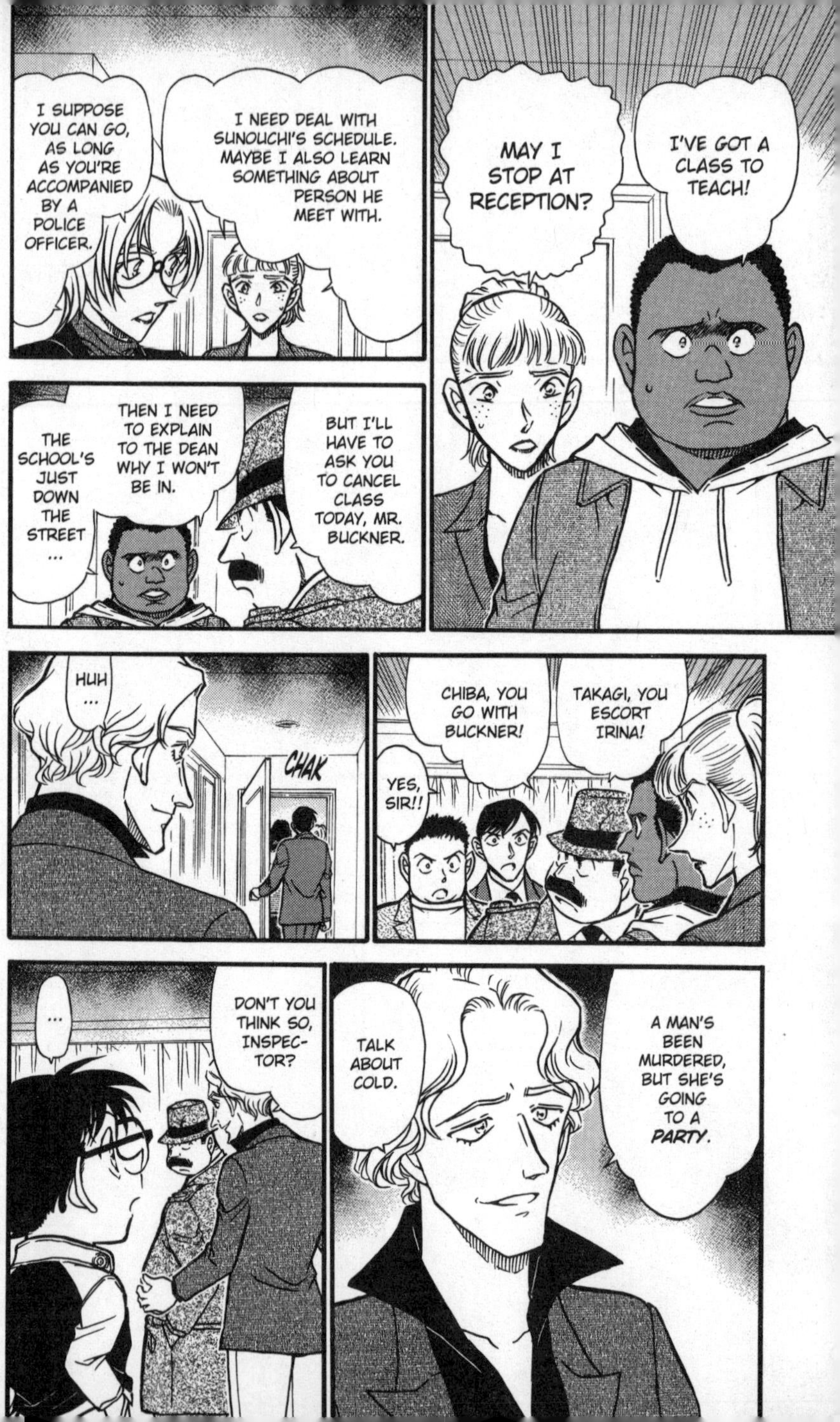
I'VE GOT A CLASS TO TEACH!
MAY I STOP AT RECEPTION?
I NEED DEAL WITH SUNOUCHI'S SCHEDULE. MAYBE I ALSO LEARN SOMETHING ABOUT PERSON HE MEET WITH.
I SUPPOSE YOU CAN GO, AS LONG AS YOU'RE ACCOMPANIED BY A POLICE OFFICER.
BUT I'LL HAVE TO ASK YOU TO CANCEL CLASS TODAY, MR. BUCKNER.
THEN I NEED TO EXPLAIN TO THE DEAN WHY I WON'T BE IN.
THE SCHOOL'S JUST DOWN THE STREET ...
TAKAGI, YOU ESCORT IRINA!
CHIBA, YOU GO WITH BUCKNER!
YES, SIR!!
CHAK
HUH ...
A MAN'S BEEN MURDERED, BUT SHE'S GOING TO A *PARTY*.
TALK ABOUT COLD.
DON'T YOU THINK SO, INSPECTOR?
...

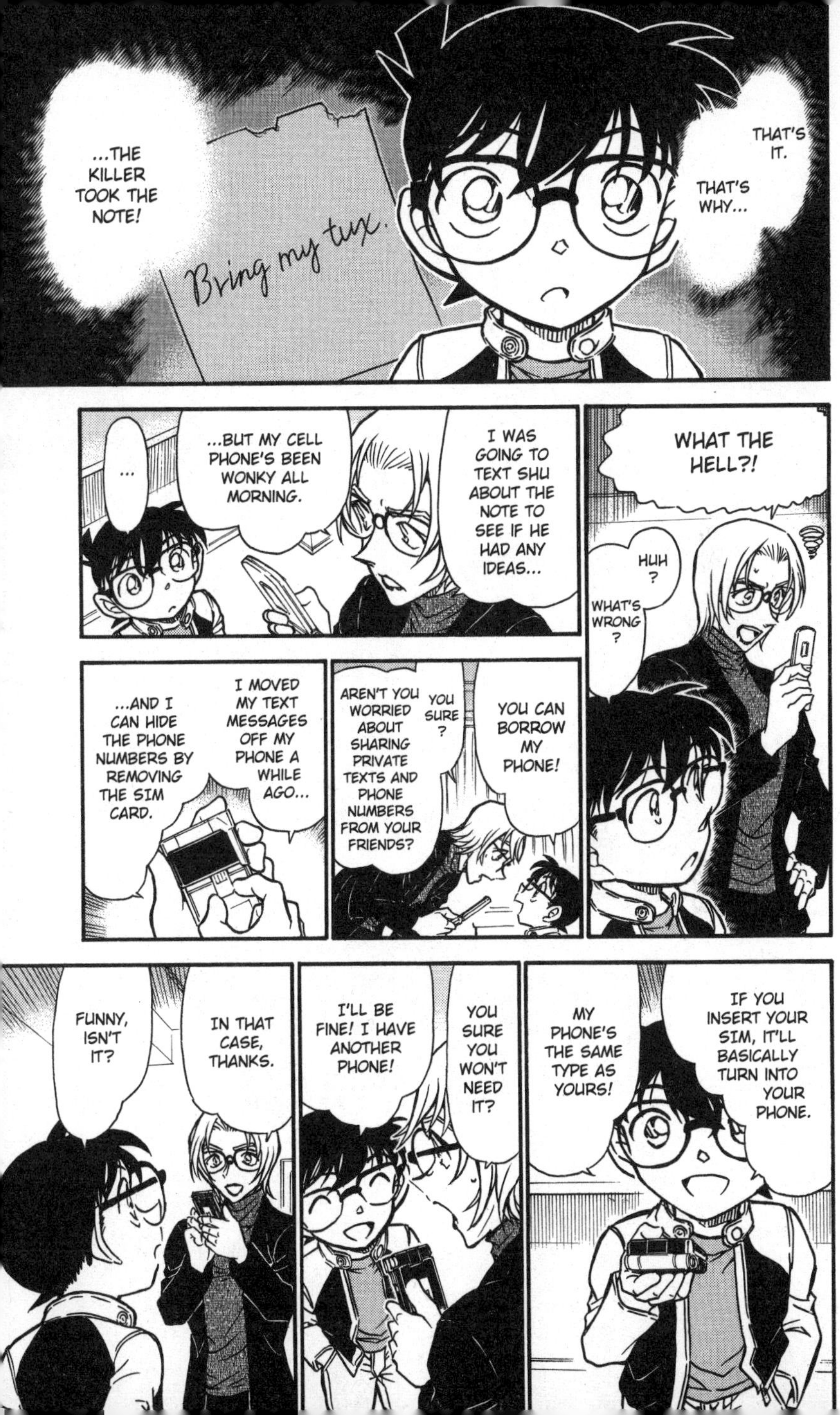
THAT'S IT.
THAT'S WHY...
...THE KILLER TOOK THE NOTE!
Bring my tux.
WHAT THE HELL?!
HUH?
WHAT'S WRONG?
I WAS GOING TO TEXT SHU ABOUT THE NOTE TO SEE IF HE HAD ANY IDEAS...
...BUT MY CELL PHONE'S BEEN WONKY ALL MORNING.
...
YOU CAN BORROW MY PHONE!
YOU SURE?
AREN'T YOU WORRIED ABOUT SHARING PRIVATE TEXTS AND PHONE NUMBERS FROM YOUR FRIENDS?
I MOVED MY TEXT MESSAGES OFF MY PHONE A WHILE AGO...
...AND I CAN HIDE THE PHONE NUMBERS BY REMOVING THE SIM CARD.
IF YOU INSERT YOUR SIM, IT'LL BASICALLY TURN INTO YOUR PHONE.
MY PHONE'S THE SAME TYPE AS YOURS!
YOU SURE YOU WON'T NEED IT?
I'LL BE FINE! I HAVE ANOTHER PHONE!
IN THAT CASE, THANKS.
FUNNY, ISN'T IT?

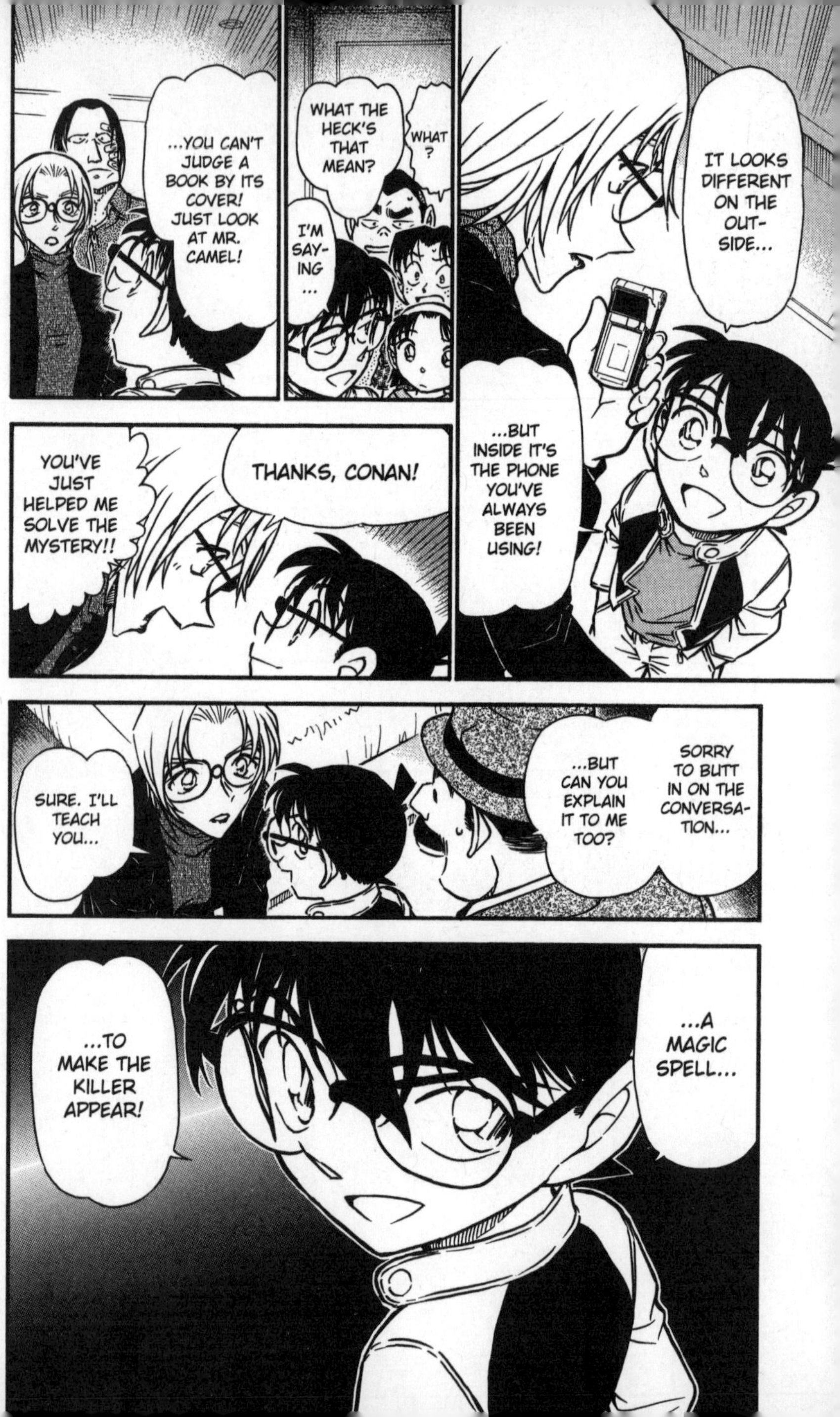
IT LOOKS DIFFERENT ON THE OUT-SIDE...
...BUT INSIDE IT'S THE PHONE YOU'VE ALWAYS BEEN USING!
WHAT?
WHAT THE HECK'S THAT MEAN?
I'M SAY-ING...
...YOU CAN'T JUDGE A BOOK BY ITS COVER! JUST LOOK AT MR. CAMEL!
THANKS, CONAN!
YOU'VE JUST HELPED ME SOLVE THE MYSTERY!!
SORRY TO BUTT IN ON THE CONVERSA-TION...
...BUT CAN YOU EXPLAIN IT TO ME TOO?
SURE. I'LL TEACH YOU...
...A MAGIC SPELL...
...TO MAKE THE KILLER APPEAR!

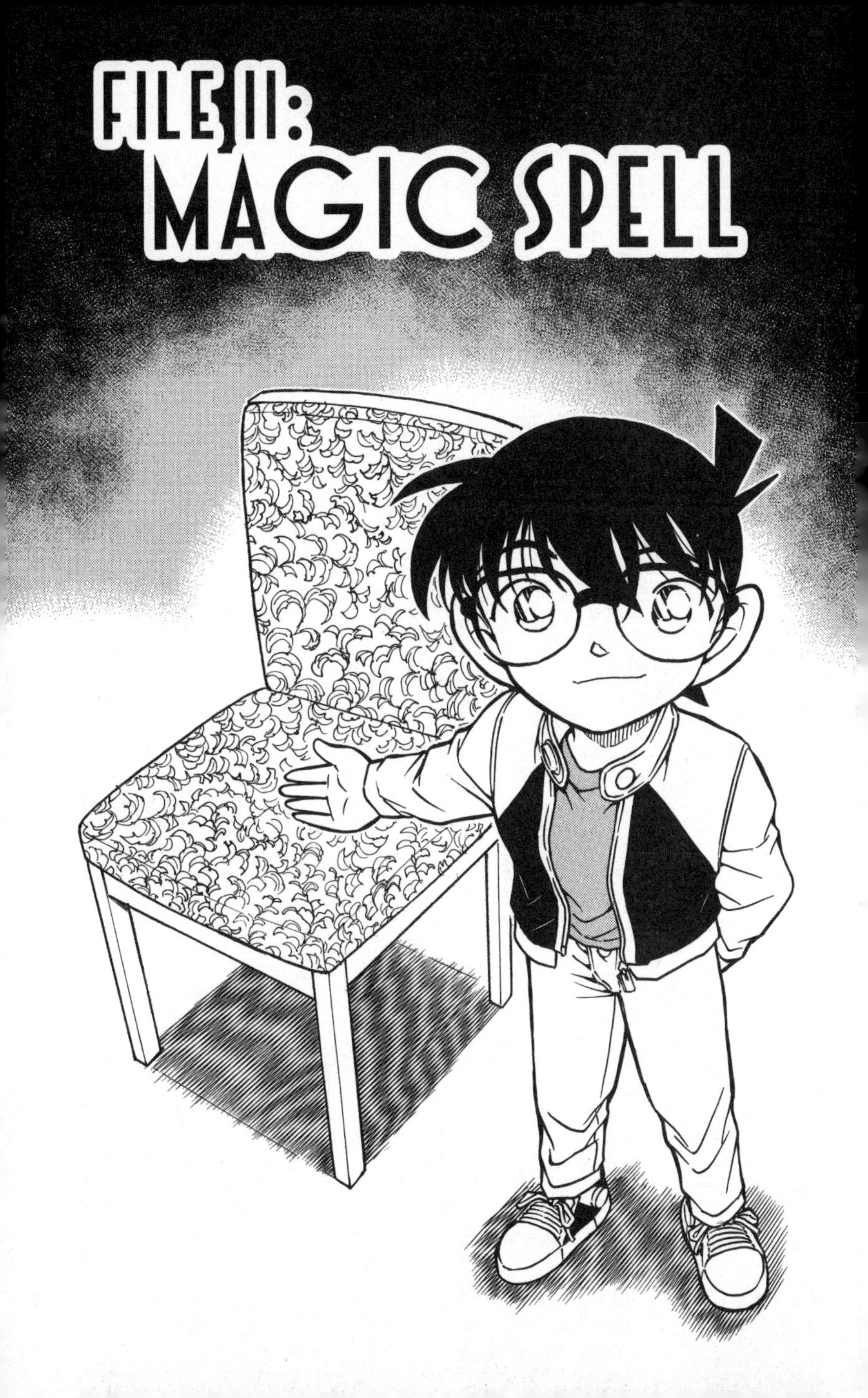
FILE 11:
MAGIC SPELL

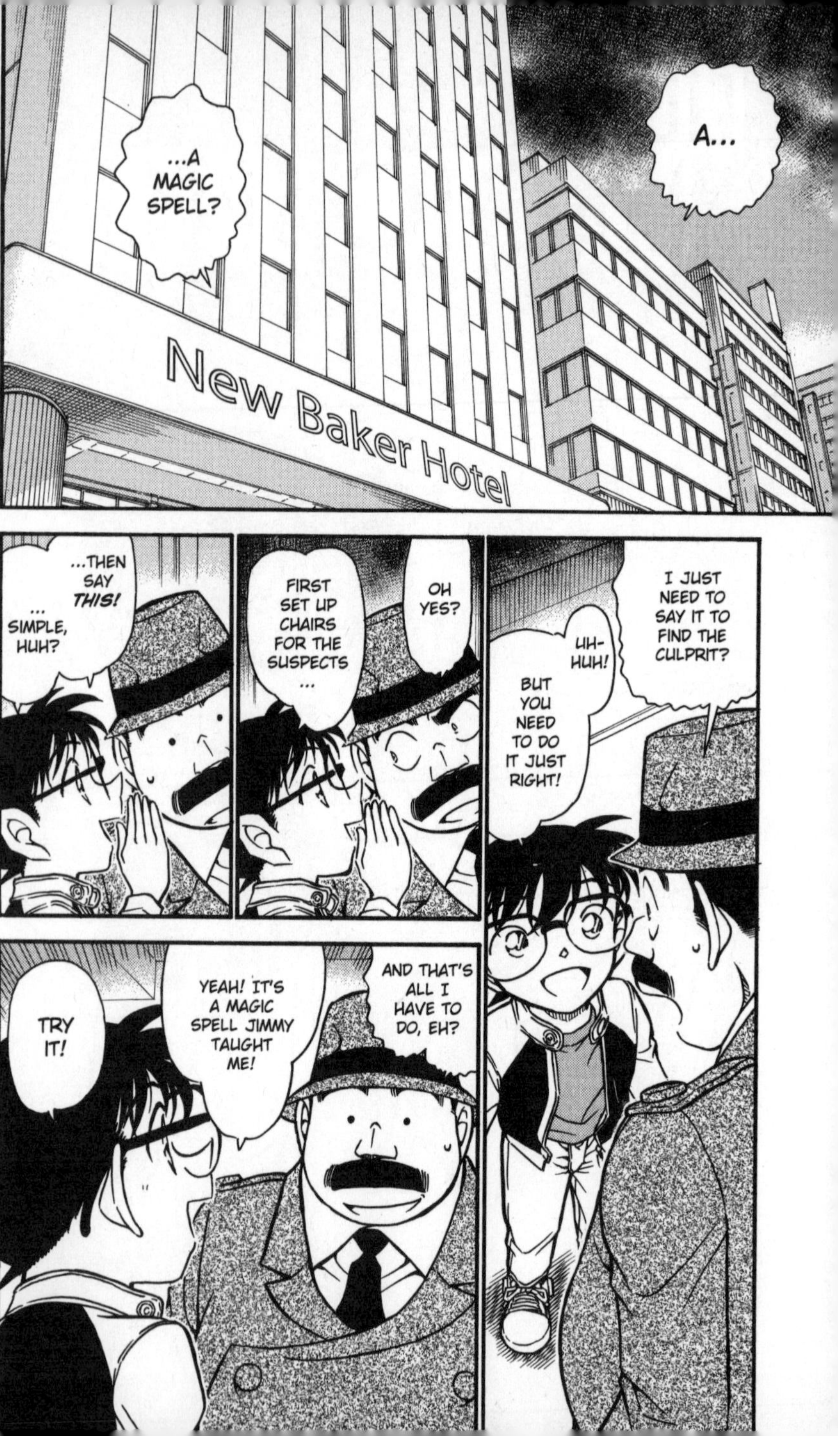
A...
...A MAGIC SPELL?
New Baker Hotel
I JUST NEED TO SAY IT TO FIND THE CULPRIT?
UH-HUH!
BUT YOU NEED TO DO IT JUST RIGHT!
OH YES?
FIRST SET UP CHAIRS FOR THE SUSPECTS ...
...THEN SAY *THIS!*
... SIMPLE, HUH?
AND THAT'S ALL I HAVE TO DO, EH?
YEAH! IT'S A MAGIC SPELL JIMMY TAUGHT ME!
TRY IT!

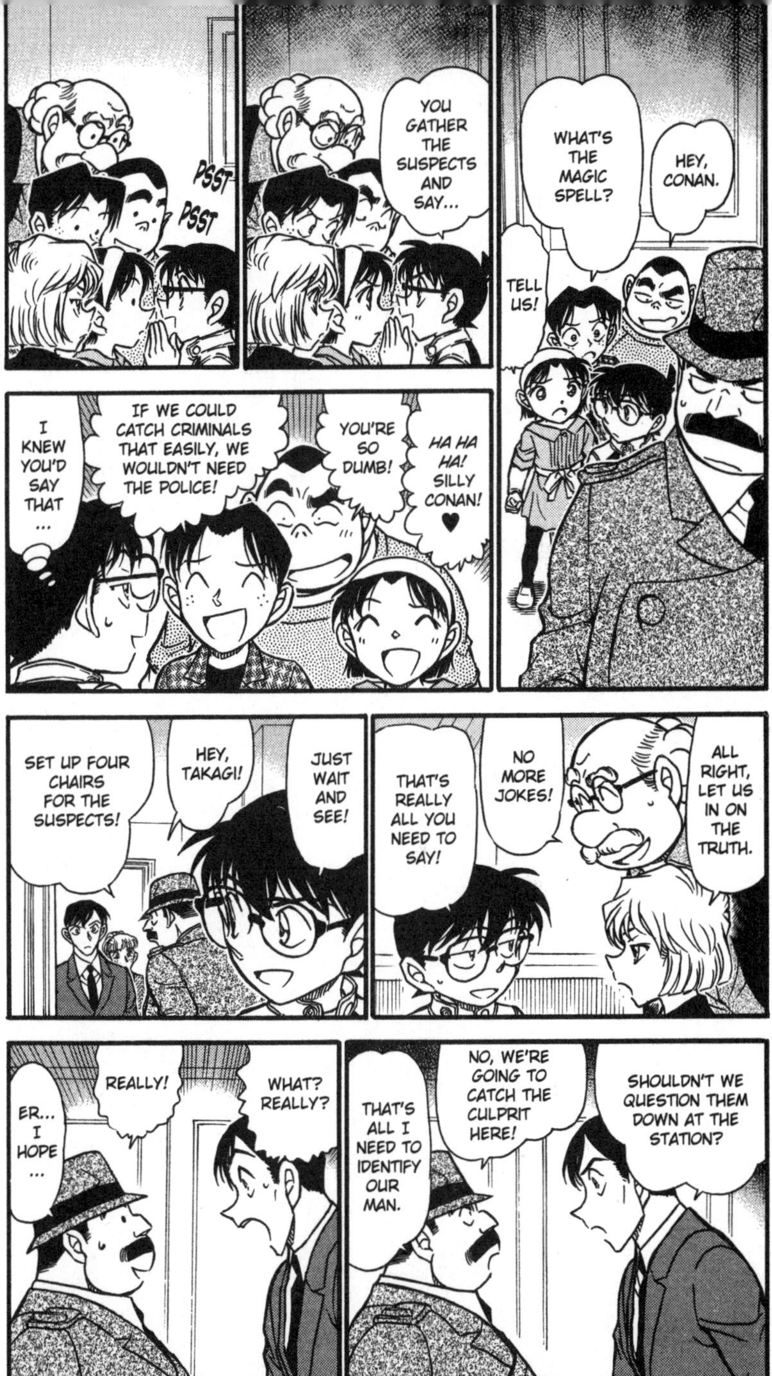
HEY, CONAN.
WHAT'S THE MAGIC SPELL?
TELL US!
YOU GATHER THE SUSPECTS AND SAY...
PSST
PSST
HA HA HA! SILLY CONAN! ♥
YOU'RE SO DUMB!
IF WE COULD CATCH CRIMINALS THAT EASILY, WE WOULDN'T NEED THE POLICE!
I KNEW YOU'D SAY THAT ...
ALL RIGHT, LET US IN ON THE TRUTH.
NO MORE JOKES!
THAT'S REALLY ALL YOU NEED TO SAY!
JUST WAIT AND SEE!
HEY, TAKAGI!
SET UP FOUR CHAIRS FOR THE SUSPECTS!
SHOULDN'T WE QUESTION THEM DOWN AT THE STATION?
NO, WE'RE GOING TO CATCH THE CULPRIT HERE!
THAT'S ALL I NEED TO IDENTIFY OUR MAN.
WHAT? REALLY?
REALLY!
ER... I HOPE ...

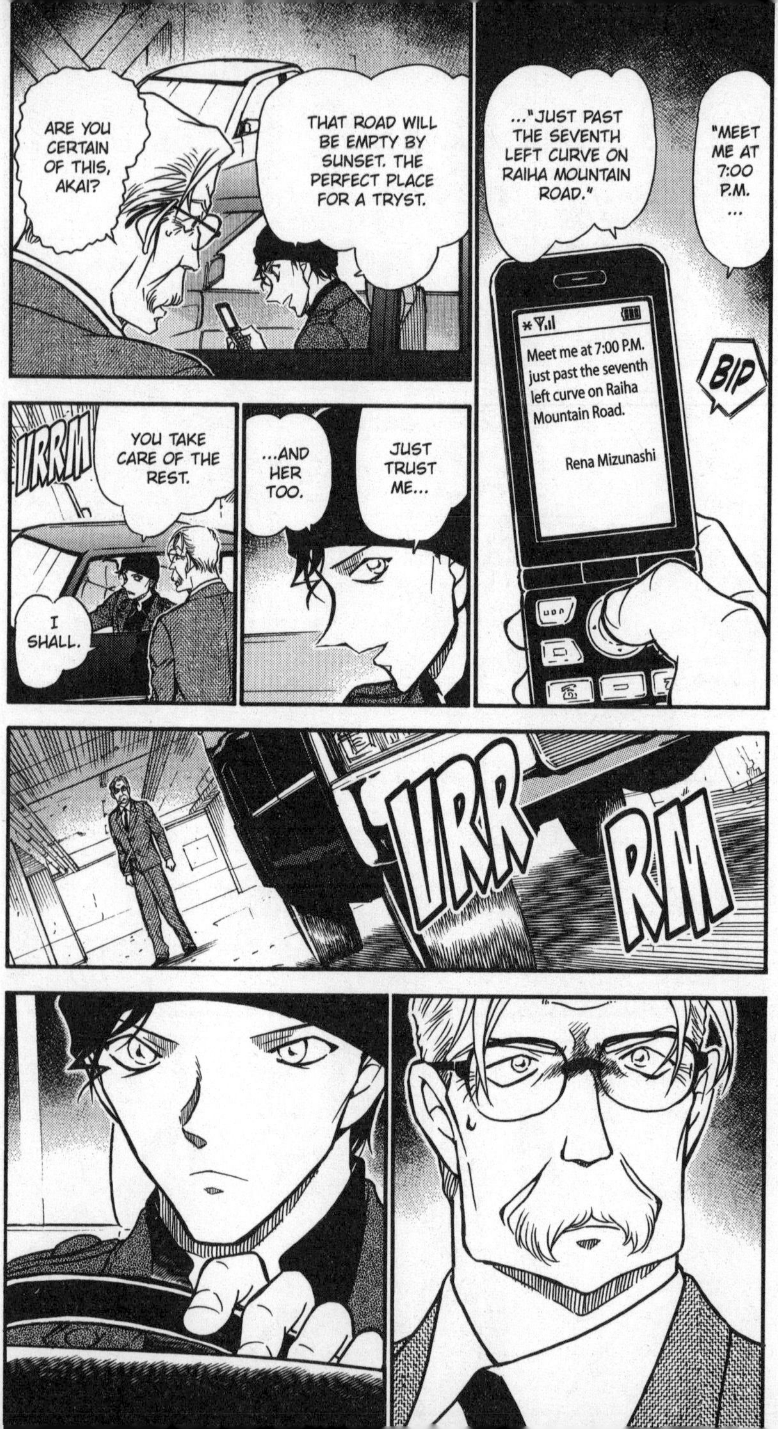
"MEET ME AT 7:00 P.M. ...
..."JUST PAST THE SEVENTH LEFT CURVE ON RAIHA MOUNTAIN ROAD."
BIP
Meet me at 7:00 P.M. just past the seventh left curve on Raiha Mountain Road.
Rena Mizunashi
THAT ROAD WILL BE EMPTY BY SUNSET. THE PERFECT PLACE FOR A TRYST.
ARE YOU CERTAIN OF THIS, AKAI?
JUST TRUST ME...
...AND HER TOO.
YOU TAKE CARE OF THE REST.
VRRM
I SHALL.
VRR RM

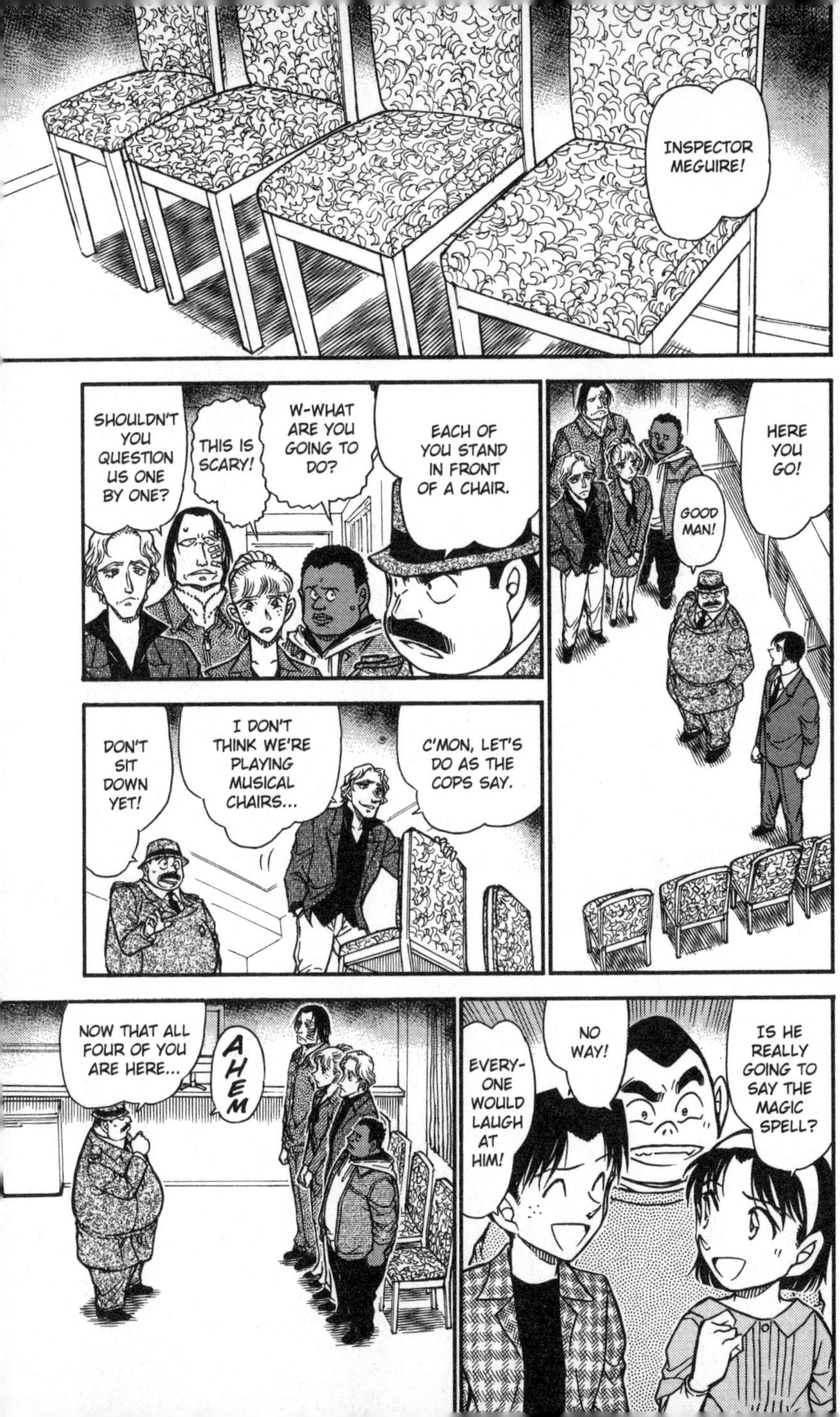
INSPECTOR MEGUIRE!
HERE YOU GO!
GOOD MAN!
EACH OF YOU STAND IN FRONT OF A CHAIR.
W-WHAT ARE YOU GOING TO DO?
THIS IS SCARY!
SHOULDN'T YOU QUESTION US ONE BY ONE?
C'MON, LET'S DO AS THE COPS SAY.
I DON'T THINK WE'RE PLAYING MUSICAL CHAIRS...
DON'T SIT DOWN YET!
IS HE REALLY GOING TO SAY THE MAGIC SPELL?
NO WAY!
EVERY-ONE WOULD LAUGH AT HIM!
AHEM
NOW THAT ALL FOUR OF YOU ARE HERE...

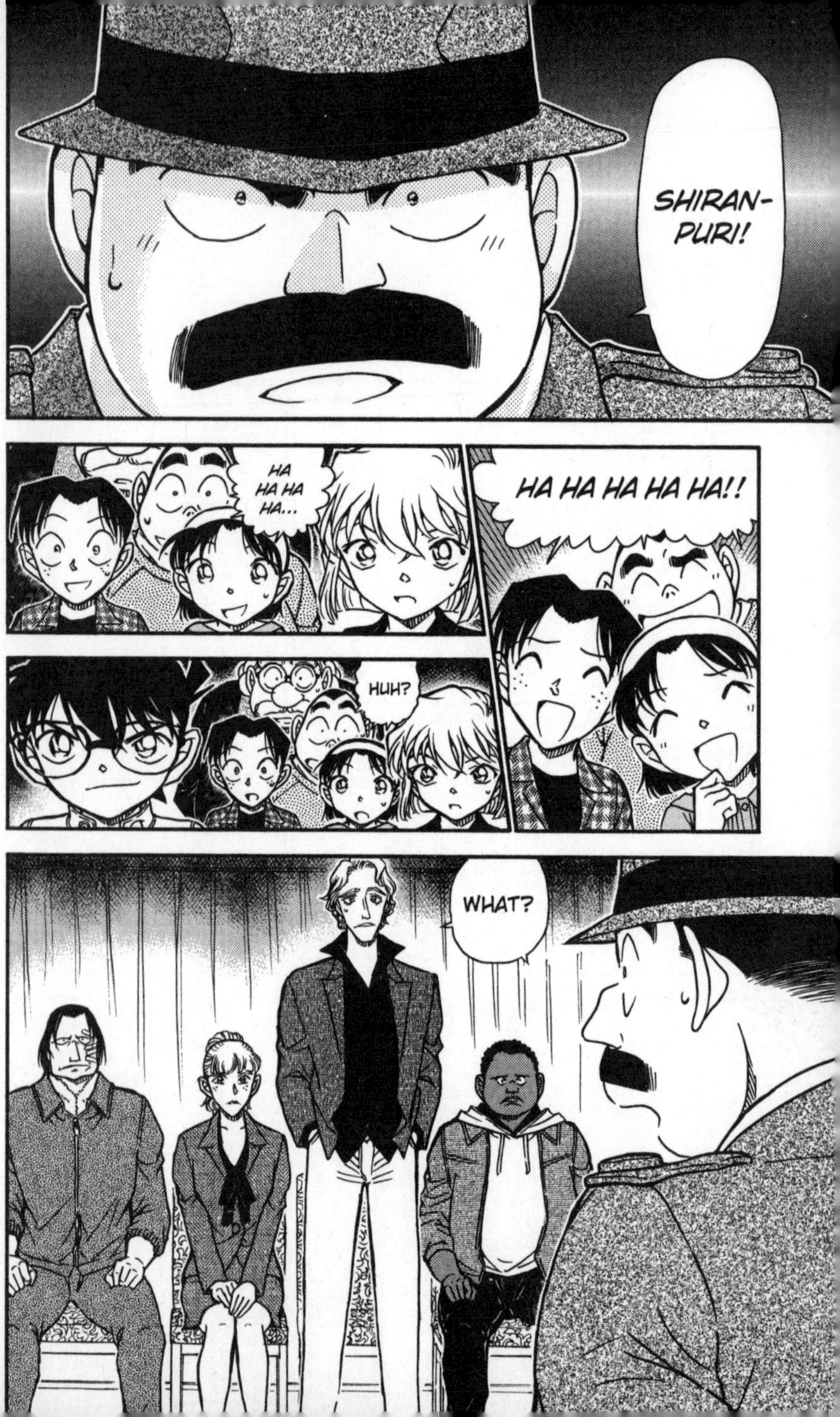
SHIRAN-
PURI!
HA HA HA HA HA!!
HA HA HA HA...
HUH?
WHAT?

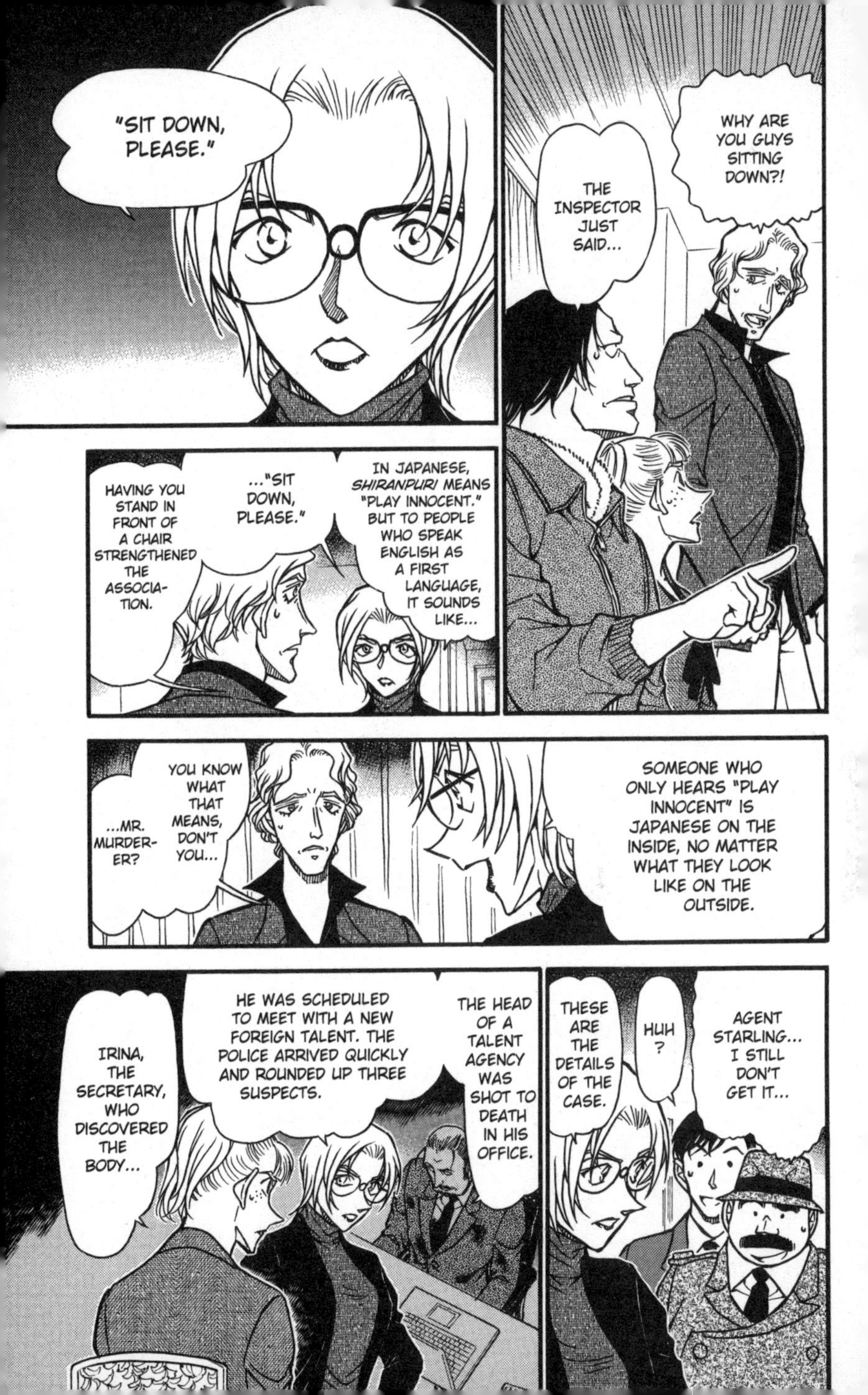
WHY ARE YOU GUYS SITTING DOWN?!
THE INSPECTOR JUST SAID...
"SIT DOWN, PLEASE."
IN JAPANESE, *SHIRANPURI* MEANS "PLAY INNOCENT." BUT TO PEOPLE WHO SPEAK ENGLISH AS A FIRST LANGUAGE, IT SOUNDS LIKE...
..."SIT DOWN, PLEASE."
HAVING YOU STAND IN FRONT OF A CHAIR STRENGTHENED THE ASSOCIATION.
SOMEONE WHO ONLY HEARS "PLAY INNOCENT" IS JAPANESE ON THE INSIDE, NO MATTER WHAT THEY LOOK LIKE ON THE OUTSIDE.
YOU KNOW WHAT THAT MEANS, DON'T YOU...
...MR. MURDERER?
AGENT STARLING... I STILL DON'T GET IT...
HUH?
THESE ARE THE DETAILS OF THE CASE.
THE HEAD OF A TALENT AGENCY WAS SHOT TO DEATH IN HIS OFFICE.
HE WAS SCHEDULED TO MEET WITH A NEW FOREIGN TALENT. THE POLICE ARRIVED QUICKLY AND ROUNDED UP THREE SUSPECTS.
IRINA, THE SECRETARY, WHO DISCOVERED THE BODY...

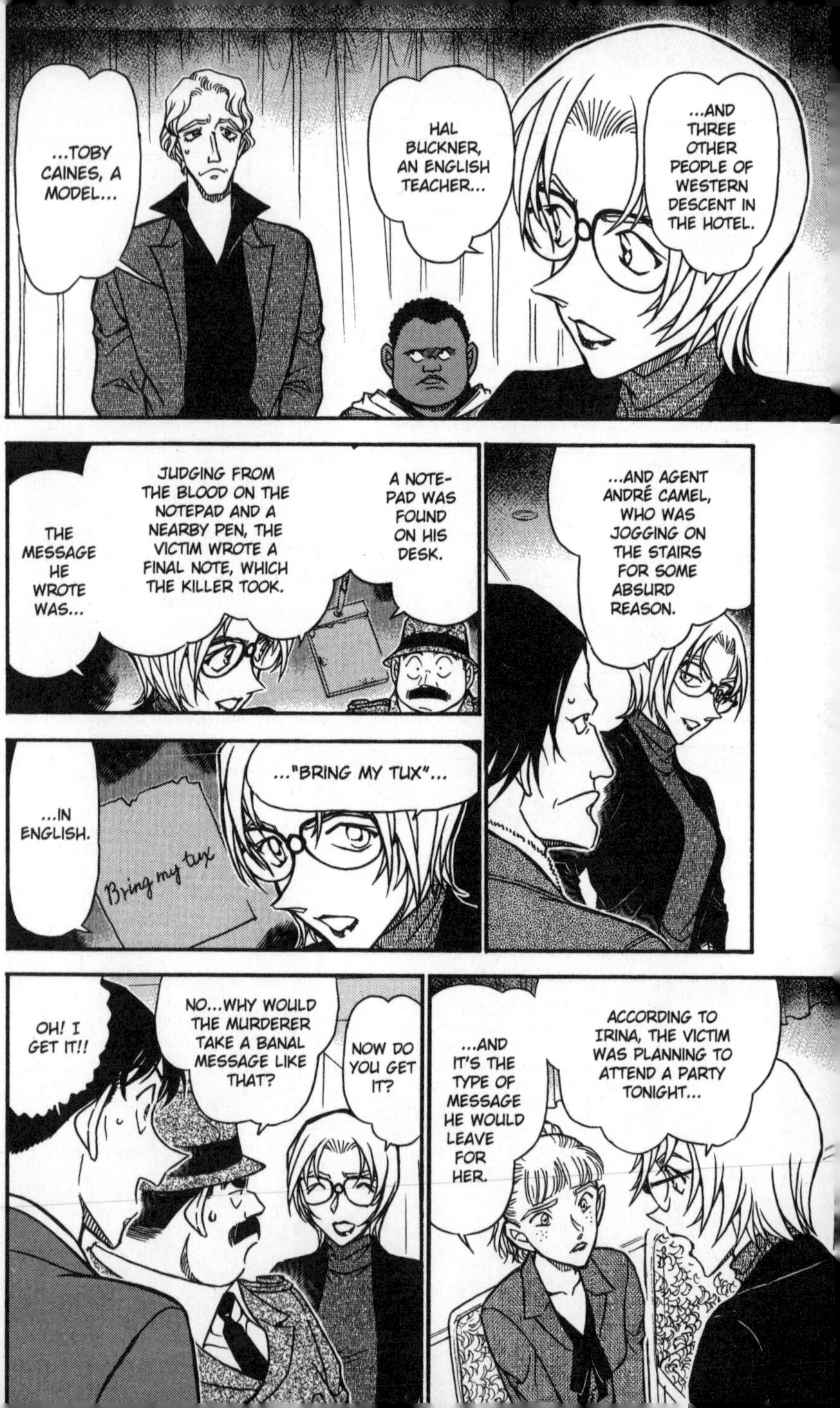
...AND THREE OTHER PEOPLE OF WESTERN DESCENT IN THE HOTEL.
HAL BUCKNER, AN ENGLISH TEACHER...
...TOBY CAINES, A MODEL...
...AND AGENT ANDRÉ CAMEL, WHO WAS JOGGING ON THE STAIRS FOR SOME ABSURD REASON.
A NOTE-PAD WAS FOUND ON HIS DESK.
JUDGING FROM THE BLOOD ON THE NOTEPAD AND A NEARBY PEN, THE VICTIM WROTE A FINAL NOTE, WHICH THE KILLER TOOK.
THE MESSAGE HE WROTE WAS...
..."BRING MY TUX"...
Bring my tux
...IN ENGLISH.
ACCORDING TO IRINA, THE VICTIM WAS PLANNING TO ATTEND A PARTY TONIGHT...
...AND IT'S THE TYPE OF MESSAGE HE WOULD LEAVE FOR HER.
NOW DO YOU GET IT?
NO...WHY WOULD THE MURDERER TAKE A BANAL MESSAGE LIKE THAT?
OH! I GET IT!!

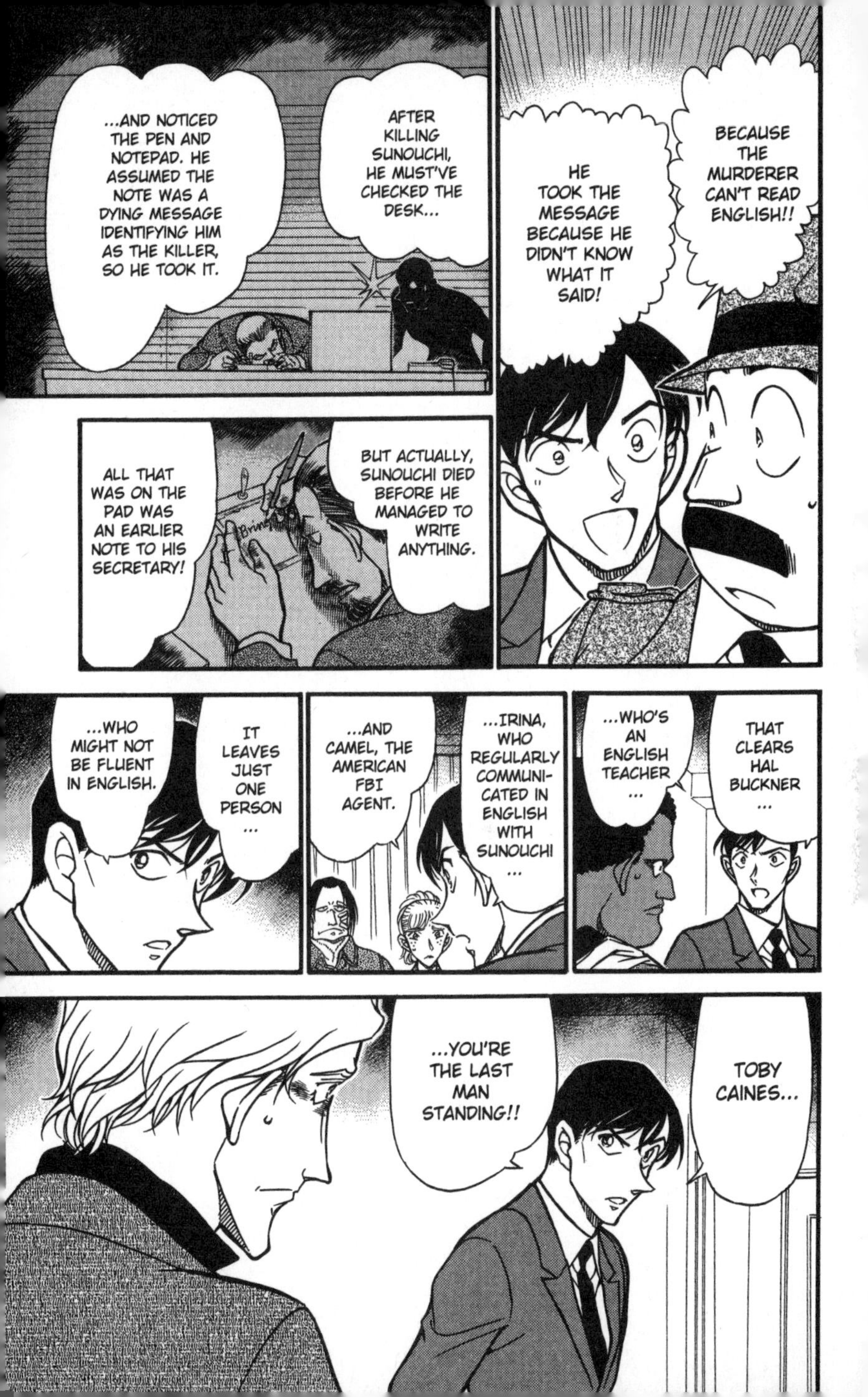
BECAUSE THE MURDERER CAN'T READ ENGLISH!!
HE TOOK THE MESSAGE BECAUSE HE DIDN'T KNOW WHAT IT SAID!
AFTER KILLING SUNOUCHI, HE MUST'VE CHECKED THE DESK...
...AND NOTICED THE PEN AND NOTEPAD. HE ASSUMED THE NOTE WAS A DYING MESSAGE IDENTIFYING HIM AS THE KILLER, SO HE TOOK IT.
BUT ACTUALLY, SUNOUCHI DIED BEFORE HE MANAGED TO WRITE ANYTHING.
ALL THAT WAS ON THE PAD WAS AN EARLIER NOTE TO HIS SECRETARY!
THAT CLEARS HAL BUCKNER...
...WHO'S AN ENGLISH TEACHER...
...IRINA, WHO REGULARLY COMMUNICATED IN ENGLISH WITH SUNOUCHI...
...AND CAMEL, THE AMERICAN FBI AGENT.
IT LEAVES JUST ONE PERSON...
...WHO MIGHT NOT BE FLUENT IN ENGLISH.
TOBY CAINES...
...YOU'RE THE LAST MAN STANDING!!

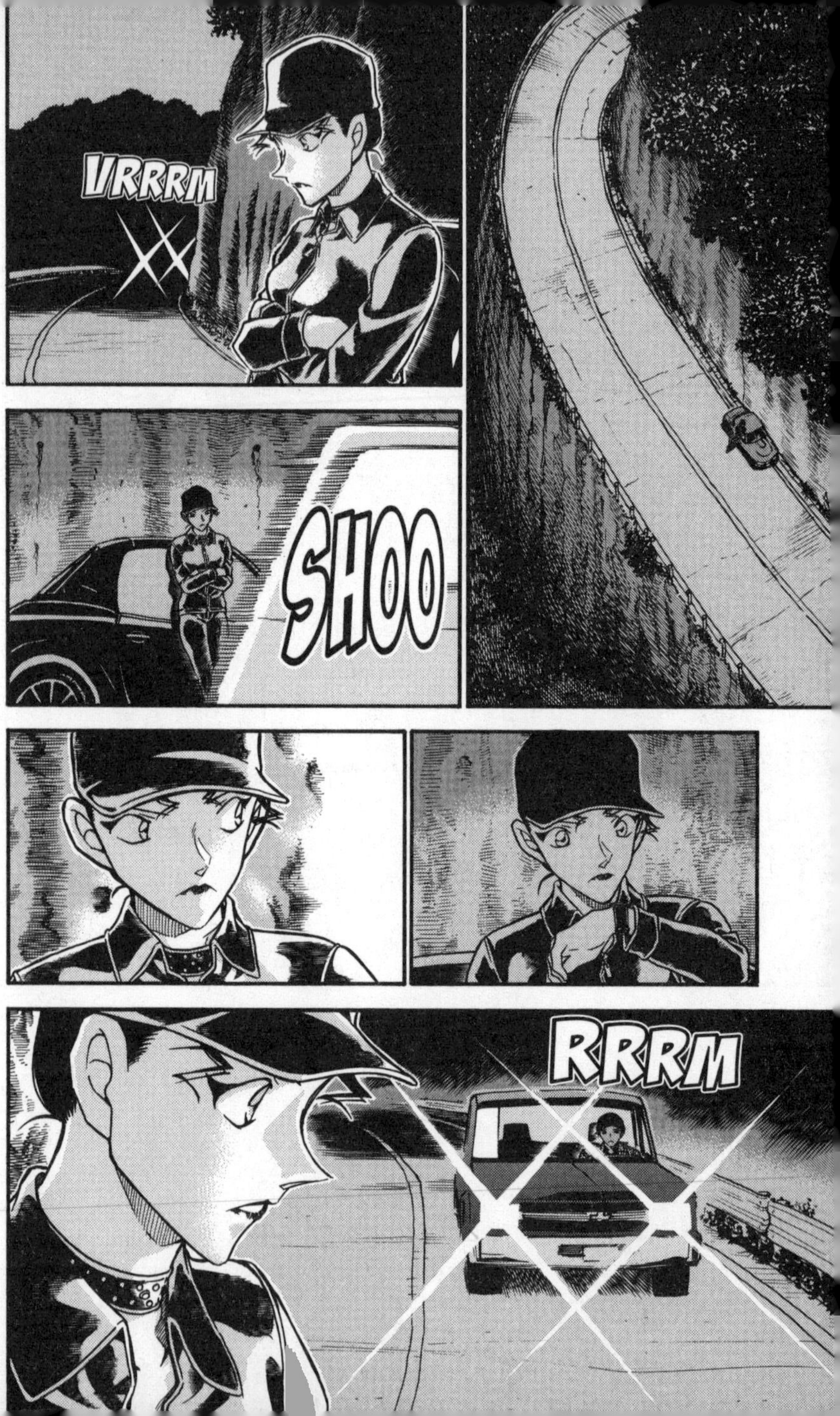
VRRRM
SHOO
RRRM

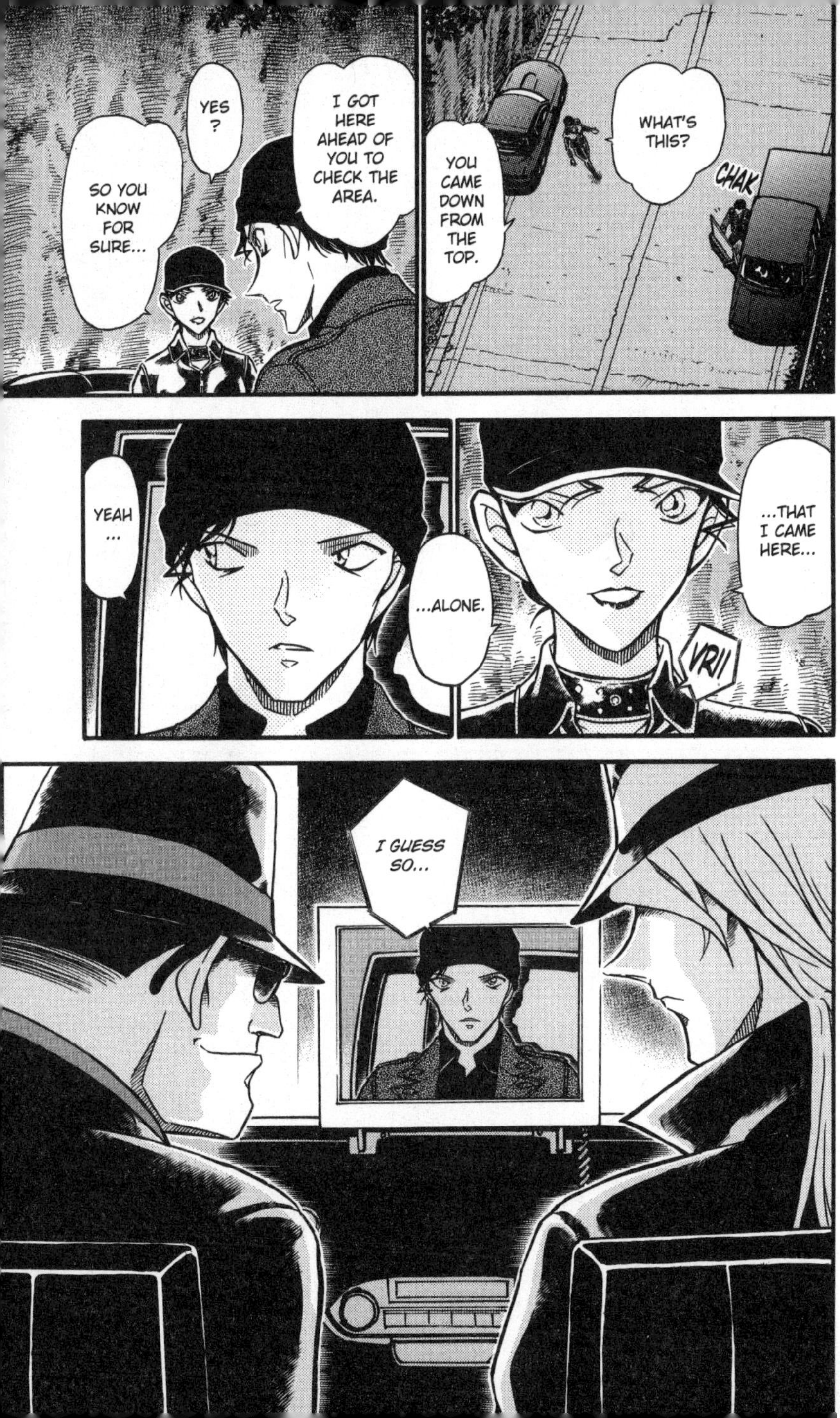
WHAT'S THIS?
CHAK
YOU CAME DOWN FROM THE TOP.
I GOT HERE AHEAD OF YOU TO CHECK THE AREA.
YES?
SO YOU KNOW FOR SURE...
...THAT I CAME HERE...
VRII
...ALONE.
YEAH...
I GUESS SO...

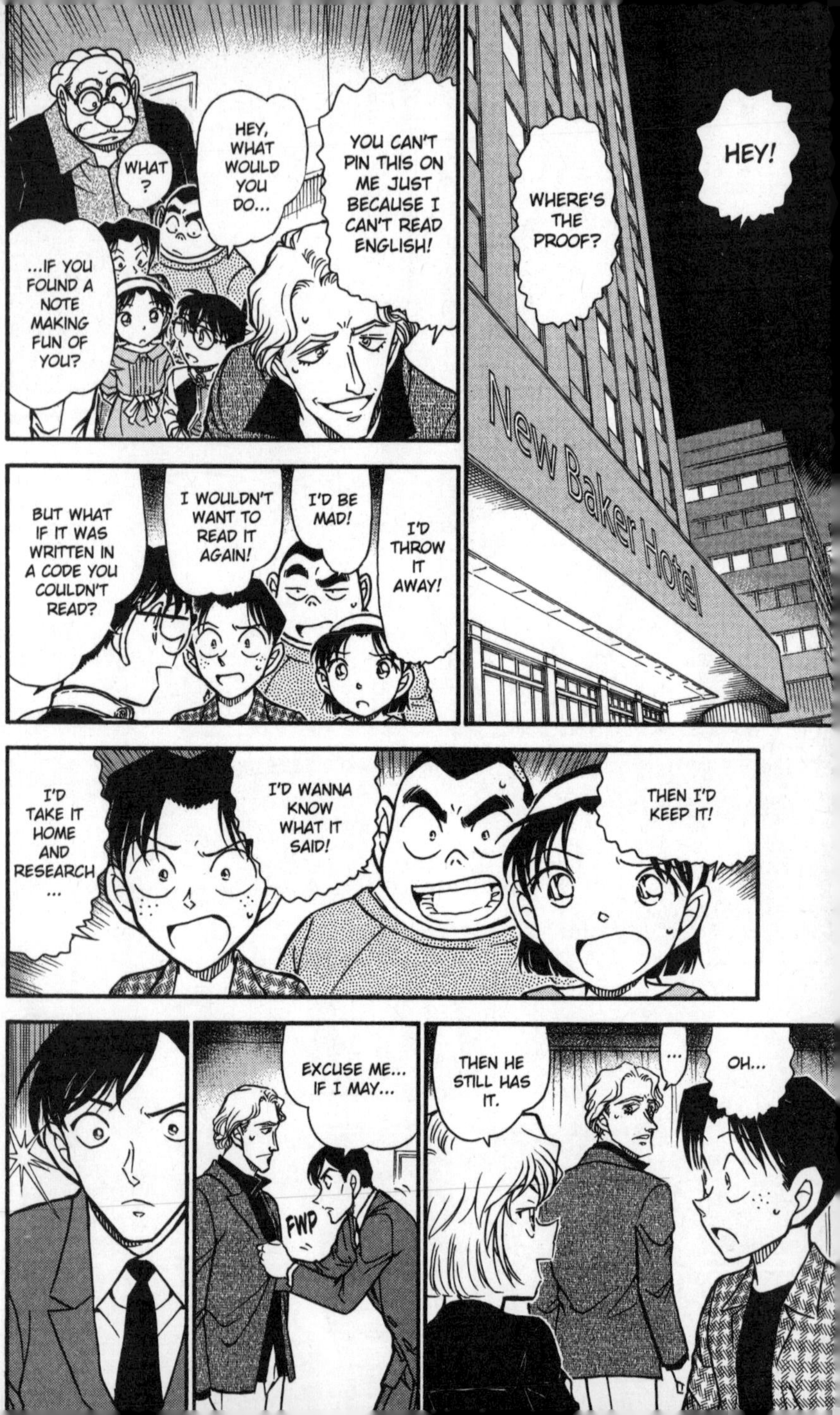
HEY!
WHERE'S THE PROOF?
New Baker Hotel
YOU CAN'T PIN THIS ON ME JUST BECAUSE I CAN'T READ ENGLISH!
HEY, WHAT WOULD YOU DO...
WHAT?
...IF YOU FOUND A NOTE MAKING FUN OF YOU?
I'D THROW IT AWAY!
I'D BE MAD!
I WOULDN'T WANT TO READ IT AGAIN!
BUT WHAT IF IT WAS WRITTEN IN A CODE YOU COULDN'T READ?
THEN I'D KEEP IT!
I'D WANNA KNOW WHAT IT SAID!
I'D TAKE IT HOME AND RESEARCH...
OH...
...
THEN HE STILL HAS IT.
EXCUSE ME... IF I MAY...
FWP

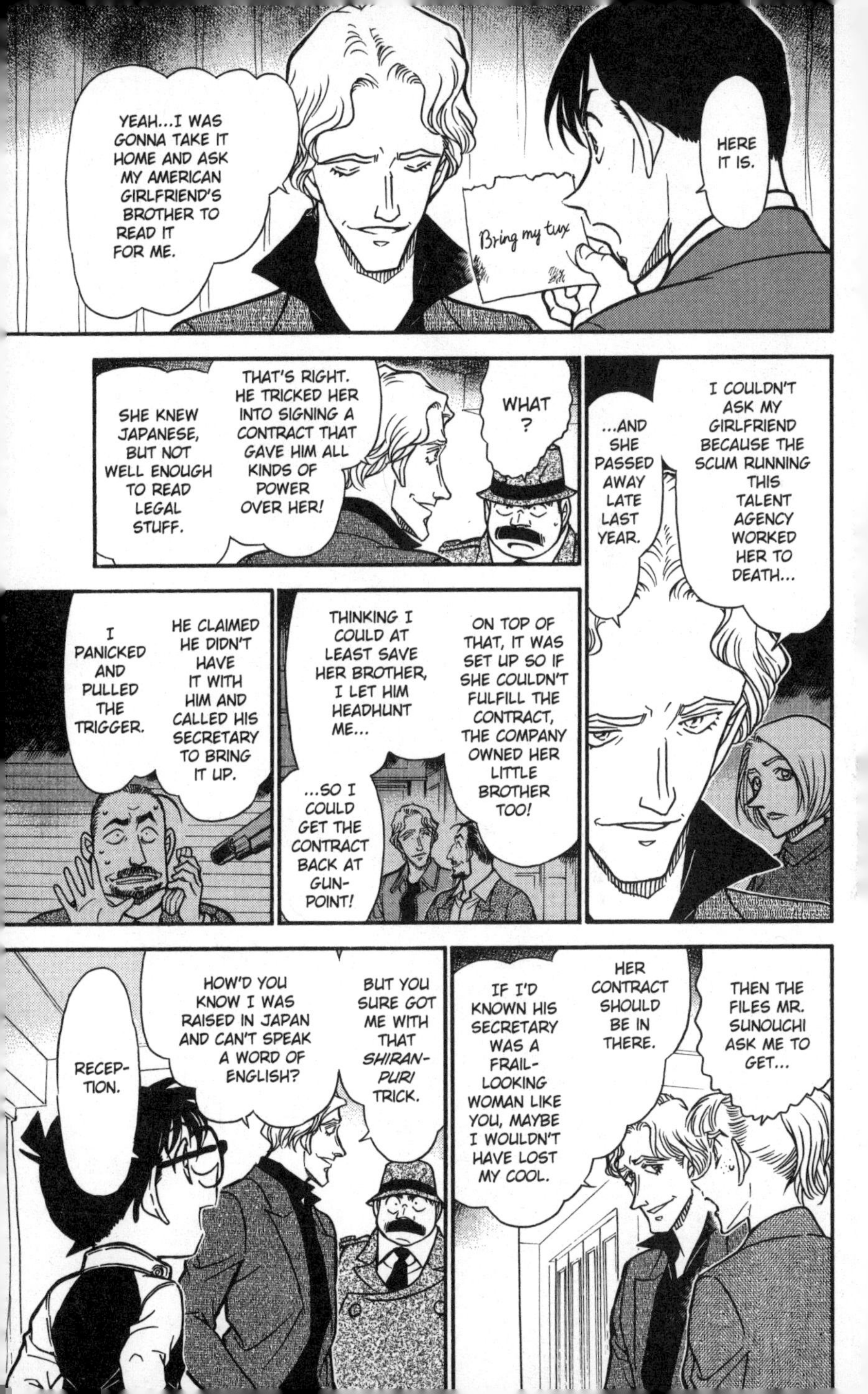
HERE IT IS.
Bring my tux
YEAH...I WAS GONNA TAKE IT HOME AND ASK MY AMERICAN GIRLFRIEND'S BROTHER TO READ IT FOR ME.
I COULDN'T ASK MY GIRLFRIEND BECAUSE THE SCUM RUNNING THIS TALENT AGENCY WORKED HER TO DEATH...
...AND SHE PASSED AWAY LATE LAST YEAR.
WHAT?
THAT'S RIGHT. HE TRICKED HER INTO SIGNING A CONTRACT THAT GAVE HIM ALL KINDS OF POWER OVER HER!
SHE KNEW JAPANESE, BUT NOT WELL ENOUGH TO READ LEGAL STUFF.
ON TOP OF THAT, IT WAS SET UP SO IF SHE COULDN'T FULFILL THE CONTRACT, THE COMPANY OWNED HER LITTLE BROTHER TOO!
THINKING I COULD AT LEAST SAVE HER BROTHER, I LET HIM HEADHUNT ME...
...SO I COULD GET THE CONTRACT BACK AT GUN-POINT!
HE CLAIMED HE DIDN'T HAVE IT WITH HIM AND CALLED HIS SECRETARY TO BRING IT UP.
I PANICKED AND PULLED THE TRIGGER.
THEN THE FILES MR. SUNOUCHI ASK ME TO GET...
HER CONTRACT SHOULD BE IN THERE.
IF I'D KNOWN HIS SECRETARY WAS A FRAIL-LOOKING WOMAN LIKE YOU, MAYBE I WOULDN'T HAVE LOST MY COOL.
BUT YOU SURE GOT ME WITH THAT *SHIRAN-PURI* TRICK.
HOW'D YOU KNOW I WAS RAISED IN JAPAN AND CAN'T SPEAK A WORD OF ENGLISH?
RECEP-TION.

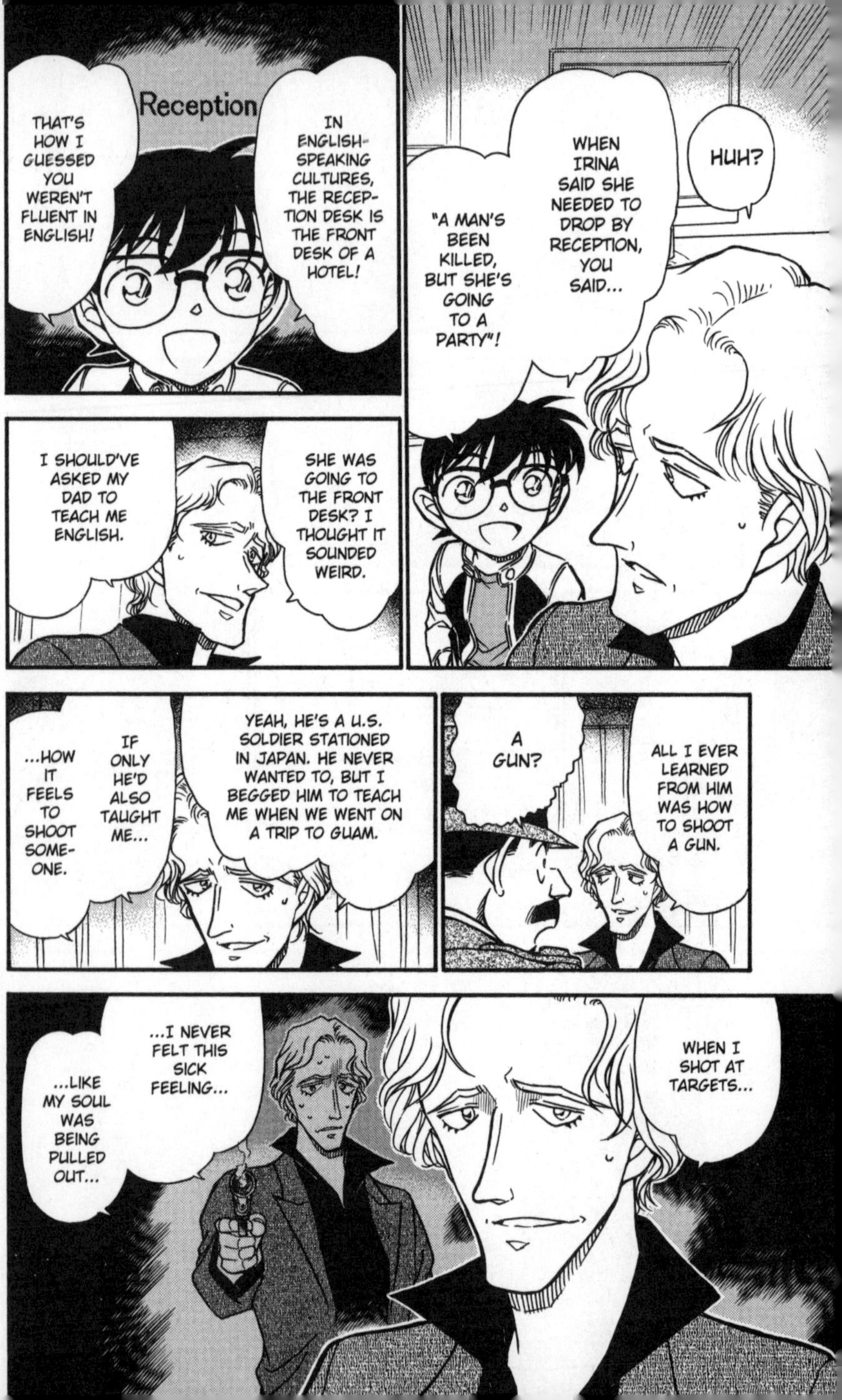
HUH?
WHEN IRINA SAID SHE NEEDED TO DROP BY RECEPTION, YOU SAID...
"A MAN'S BEEN KILLED, BUT SHE'S GOING TO A PARTY"!
Reception
IN ENGLISH-SPEAKING CULTURES, THE RECEPTION DESK IS THE FRONT DESK OF A HOTEL!
THAT'S HOW I GUESSED YOU WEREN'T FLUENT IN ENGLISH!
SHE WAS GOING TO THE FRONT DESK? I THOUGHT IT SOUNDED WEIRD.
I SHOULD'VE ASKED MY DAD TO TEACH ME ENGLISH.
ALL I EVER LEARNED FROM HIM WAS HOW TO SHOOT A GUN.
A GUN?
YEAH, HE'S A U.S. SOLDIER STATIONED IN JAPAN. HE NEVER WANTED TO, BUT I BEGGED HIM TO TEACH ME WHEN WE WENT ON A TRIP TO GUAM.
IF ONLY HE'D ALSO TAUGHT ME...
...HOW IT FEELS TO SHOOT SOME-ONE.
WHEN I SHOT AT TARGETS...
...I NEVER FELT THIS SICK FEELING...
...LIKE MY SOUL WAS BEING PULLED OUT...

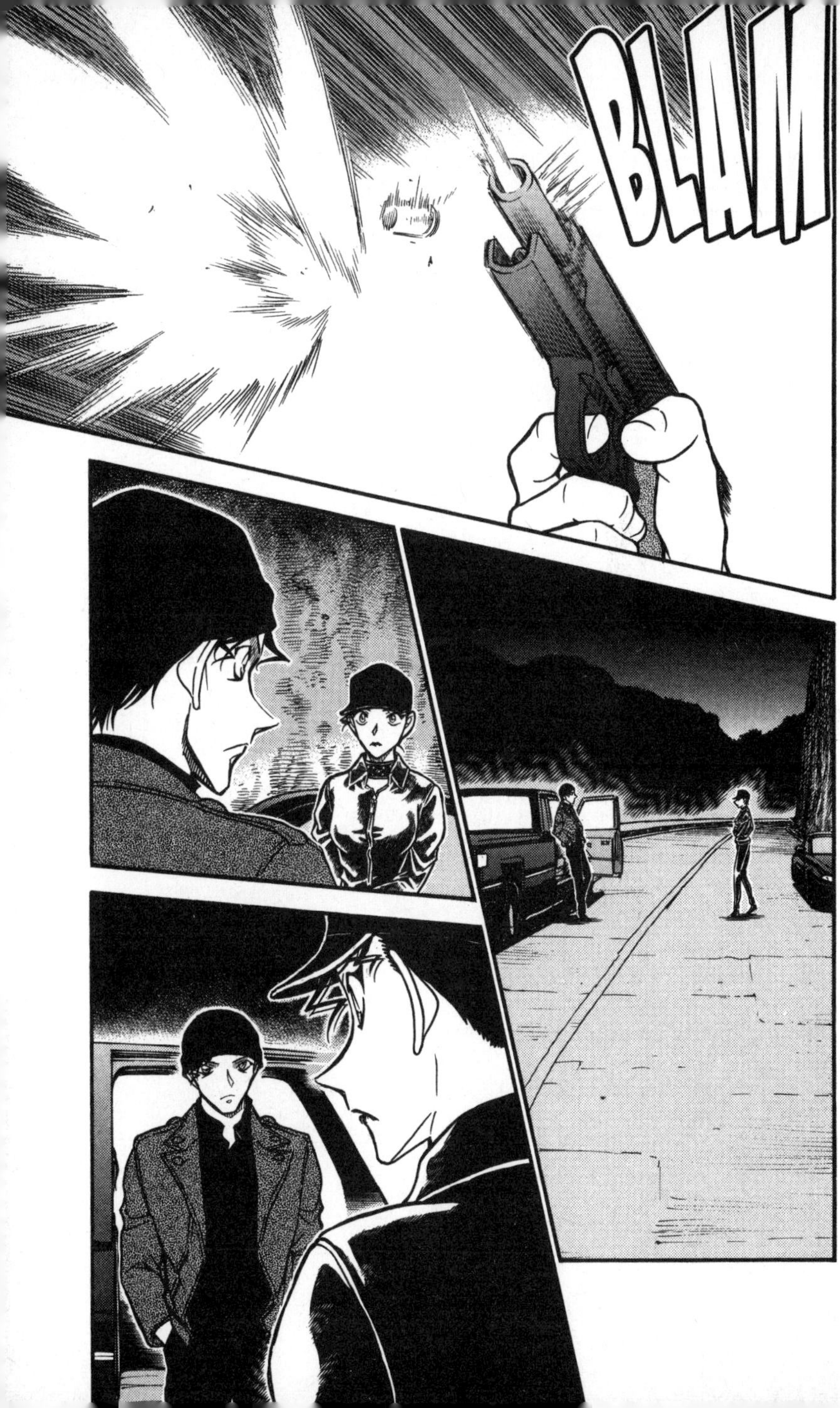
BLAM

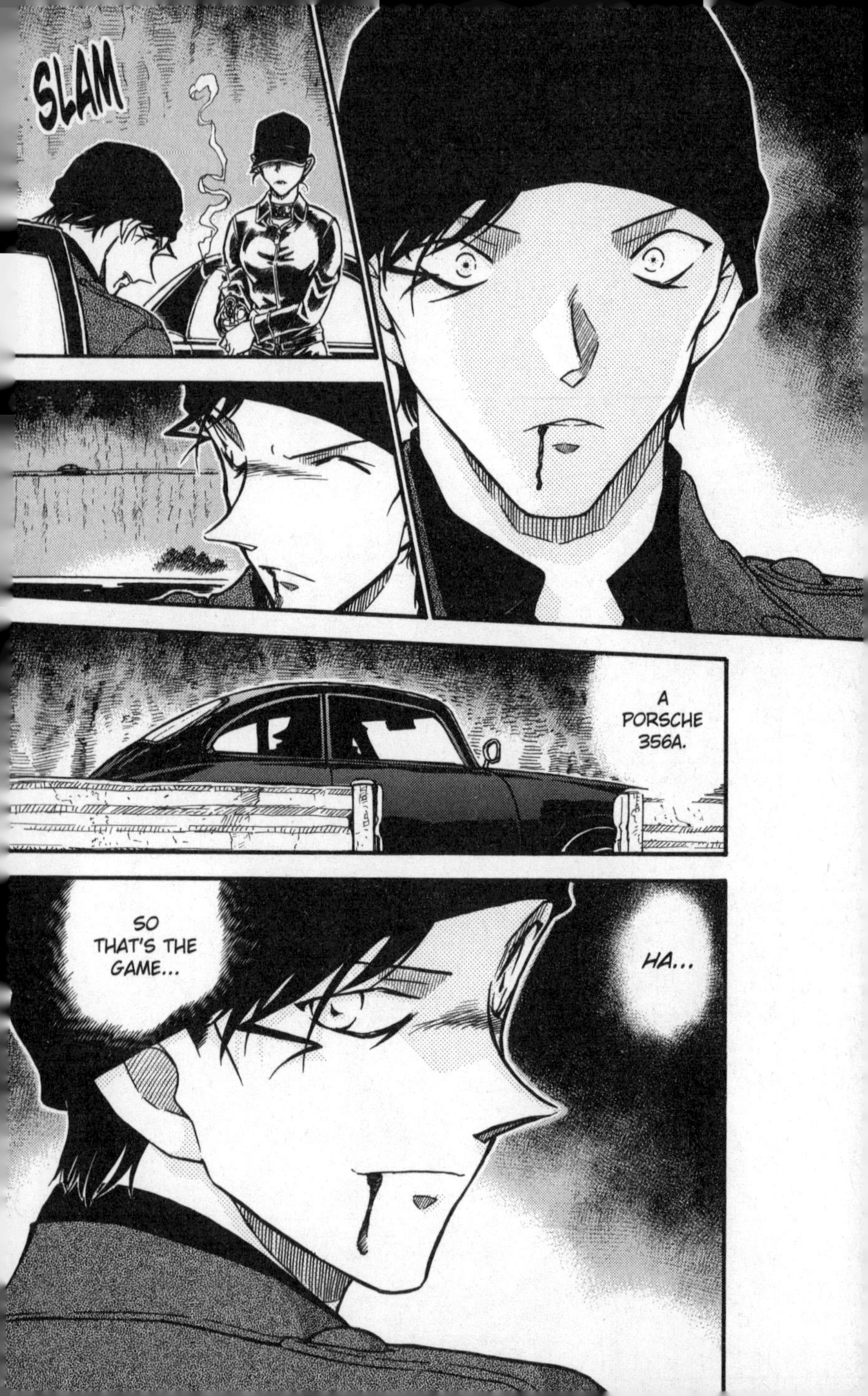
SLAM
A PORSCHE 356A.
HA...
SO THAT'S THE GAME...

Hello, Aoyama here.

A new agent, André Camel, appears in this volume! He's named after a character from *Mobile Suit Gundam*: Lieutenant Dren, the second-in-command of Camel Squadron under Char Aznable, the Red Comet. What? Why'd I name him that? Read for yourself and find out...

Gosho Aoyama's
Mystery Library

58

YOSHIFUMI TAKAGI

Today I'd like to introduce the most hardboiled detective in the Metropolitan Police, Inspector Yoshifumi Takagi! Small and slender, he's forty but his white hair and deeply lined face make him look ten years older. His favorite cigarettes are Gauloises, which he lights with an old-fashioned gasoline lighter. He has a habit of humming the tune to Stephen Foster's "Old Dog Tray," which gave him the nickname "Old Dog."

Even though he's a police officer, Takagi is a lone wolf who follows his own instincts and investigates cases solo. He'll stop at nothing to solve a case, even deceiving those who are on his side. His only weapon when facing a deadly criminal is the set of handcuffs he carries in his right hand!

Inspector Takagi first appeared in numerous works by Kenzo Kitakata as a minor character, but he had such a strong presence that he ended up getting his own series. My Detective Takagi started out as a minor character too, but he's more soft-boiled than hardboiled...heh.

I recommend *Sleepless Night.*